Windows NT: Inside & Out

Windows NT: Inside & Out

Tom Sheldon

Osborne McGraw-Hill

Berkeley New York St. Louis San Francisco
Auckland Bogotá Hamburg London Madrid
Mexico City Milan Montreal New Delhi Panama City
Paris São Paulo Singapore Sydney
Tokyo Toronto

Osborne **McGraw-Hill**
2600 Tenth Street
Berkeley, California 94710
U.S.A.

For information on translations or book distributors outside of the U.S.A., please write to Osborne **McGraw-Hill** at the above address.

Windows NT: Inside & Out

1234567890 DOC 99876543

ISBN 0-07-881826-5

Acquisitions Editor Jeff Pepper	**Project Editor** Wendy Rinaldi	**Indexer** Tom Sheldon
Associate Editor Bob Myren	**Copy Editors** Ann Krueger Spivack Joseph Ferrie	**Illustrator** Marla Shelasky
Technical Editors John Heilborn John Mueller	**Proofreaders** Jeff Barash Hannah Raiden	**Computer Designer** Fred Lass
		Cover Designer Mason Fong

Contents at a Glance

Part III
Customizing, Configuring, and Managing Windows NT

Contents

Part I
Features and Planning for Windows NT

1 Introducing Windows NT

Part II
Using Windows NT

Part III
Customizing, Configuring, and Managing Windows NT

Part IV
Network Applications

Part V
Appendixes

Acknowledgments

Special thanks to John Mueller for all his help in getting this project together and thanks also to John Heilborn for his technical edit and review.

Thanks also to everyone at Osborne McGraw-Hill, in particular project editor Wendy Rinaldi and associate editor Bob Myren.

Introduction

Welcome to *Windows NT: Inside & Out*. Microsoft Windows NT represents a new generation in operating systems. While similar in look and operation to Windows 3.1, Windows NT is radically different in the way it uses hardware and runs applications. It does not use DOS like Windows 3.1. This means you don't need to start DOS before starting Windows NT. However, you can still run DOS applications under Windows NT, as well as Windows 3.1 applications, and even applications written for other operating system environments like UNIX.

Windows NT takes advantage of high-performance processors like those available from Intel, MIPS, and Digital Equipment Corporation. It also takes advantage of systems that use multiple processors. Windows NT provides a computing environment for the future that is compatible with current applications.

This book is written for a diverse audience, including people who are familiar with DOS, Windows, and other operating systems like UNIX. Of course, you don't need to be familiar with any other operating system to read this book, but make sure you *are* familiar with the basic operating techniques of your computer.

The chapters are written in an order that helps you better comprehend the material if you are just starting out. However, you can still open to any chapter and get important information about a topic of interest. Most chapters bring together diverse information. For example, Chapter 17 covers all the features, commands, and options for maintaining and configuring network connections.

The first few chapters that make up Part I introduce the Windows NT operating system and talk about its features, including the security system. You might want to skip these chapters and start with Chapter 4 if you are anxious to begin using the operating system and run programs. Later chapters, however, do assume that you are familiar with some of the material in Part I.

Part II covers basic concepts for using the Windows NT interface, without getting into customization and configuration details that can easily overwhelm beginners. You learn about customization and configuration in Part III.

Part III also covers topics for system and network administrators. Some of the information is technical in nature, but plenty of explanations are provided to help get you through. Part IV covers two important network applications: Microsoft Mail, and Microsoft Schedule+.

Refer to Appendix A if you need to set up your Windows NT system, install the software, and/or troubleshoot problems with the installation.

The following is a description of each chapter.

Part I: Features and Planning for Windows NT

- Chapter 1, "Introducing Windows NT," provides an overview of Windows NT features.

- Chapter 2, "Hardware for Windows NT," describes the computer systems and hardware components you need in order to run Windows NT and how the operating system takes advantage of the hardware.

- Chapter 3, "NT Hierarchy and Security," provides a description of the user and security features available on Windows NT computers.

Part II: Using Windows NT

- Chapter 4, "Starting and Using Windows NT," provides a basic overview of the Windows NT graphical user interface.

- Chapter 5, "Starting and Using Applications," provides methods for starting applications so you can get to work right away.

- Chapter 6, "Global Techniques," describes how to use common Windows NT user interface options.

- Chapter 7, "Working with Files," describes the use of files in Windows NT, including the new file system called NTFS.

- Chapter 8, "Using Local and Remote Printers," provides the basics for accessing and using printers.

- Chapter 9, "Utilities and Accessories," gives an overview of the utilities and accessories supplied with Windows NT.

▧ Chapter 10, "Creating Compound Documents," describes methods for sharing information between documents you own and documents owned by other network users.

▧ Chapter 11, "The Command Prompt," describes how to access a DOS-like command prompt and execute DOS, OS/2, and other operating system commands.

Part III: Customizing, Configuring, and Managing Windows NT

▧ Chapter 12, "Customizing the Program Manager and Organizing Applications and Documents," describes methods for customizing Program Manager, which is the window used to start and organize programs.

▧ Chapter 13, "Customizing the File Manager," describes how to use the File Manager, which is Windows NT's utility for viewing and managing files stored on hard drives and CD-ROMs.

▧ Chapter 14, "Customizing the Interface," offers a discussion of utilities and techniques for changing the Windows NT graphical user interface for your own use.

▧ Chapter 15, "Configuring System Settings," describes methods for changing the settings of the operating system itself.

▧ Chapter 16, "Managing User Accounts," describes user management techniques, such as creating user and group accounts, and managing security rights and permissions.

▧ Chapter 17, "Server and Network Management," provides a discussion of network management techniques and commands.

▧ Chapter 18, "Managing Printers and Fonts," describes the Windows NT printing system and configuration commands.

▧ Chapter 19, "Disk Management," describes disk partitioning and management under Windows NT.

▧ Chapter 20, "Protecting the System," describes methods for protecting your system against data loss, power failures, and other problems.

▧ Chapter 21, "Monitoring the System," provides an overview of Windows NT monitoring and management utilities you can use to track system usage and evaluate problems.

Part IV: Network Applications

▧   Chapter 22, "Microsoft Mail," describes the Microsoft Mail electronic mail system provided with Windows NT.

▧   Chapter 23, "Microsoft Schedule+," describes the Schedule+ utility provided with Windows NT that lets you schedule appointments and activities with other users on the network.

Part V: Appendixes

▧   Appendix A, "Network Hardware Settings," outlines the steps for setting up hardware, installing Windows NT, and troubleshooting problems.

▧   Appendix B, "Command Cross Reference," provides a unique cross reference to Windows NT commands that you can access at the Command Prompt.

▧   Appendix C, "Internetwork Connections with TCP/IP," gives an overview of TCP/IP methods for interconnecting computers that use different operating systems or are connected on different networks.

PART ONE

Features and Planning for Windows NT

Inside

- Windows NT: An Inside Look

- Windows NT on the Outside

- Other Windows NT Features

& Out

CHAPTER 1

Introducing Windows NT

Microsoft Windows NT is a completely new operating system designed to take advantage—and to allow software vendors to design applications that take advantage—of powerful new desktop systems, such as Intel 486-based systems, MIPS R4000-based systems, and DEC Alpha systems. Windows NT expands on the features of Windows 3.1 and offers many features that make it unique among operating systems, as you'll see in this chapter. Windows NT has a wide target audience:

- End users who need performance and the ability to switch among multiple applications

- Workgroup users who need to share their system with other users, connect with other shared computers, exchange electronic mail, and schedule group meetings and appointments

- Software developers who want to create applications to run on the systems supported by Windows NT

- Network administrators who need a secure (government-certified) network environment that takes advantage of new multiprocessor computer systems

The last point is especially important. Windows NT is not restricted to Intel systems as are DOS and Windows. It runs on any of the following systems:

- Intel 80386, 80486, and Pentium processor systems

- MIPS R4000 64-bit reduced instruction set computer (RISC) systems

- Digital Equipment Corporation Alpha-based 64-bit reduced instruction set computer (RISC) systems

- "Super server" systems that use a combination of processors and special proprietary bus designs

Windows NT is not restricted to running applications designed specifically for it; it also runs DOS, POSIX, and OS/2 character-based programs as well as Windows 3.1 graphical programs.

WINDOWS NT: AN INSIDE LOOK

Windows NT is a 32-bit operating system with preemptive multitasking and memory protection, as well as support for symmetric multiprocessing and networking, all with a graphical user front-end. What does that mean? Let's take a look.

First of all, Windows NT is an operating system designed for *32-bit operation.* It takes advantage of advanced processors such as the Intel 80386 and 80486, as well as reduced instruction set computers (RISC) such as the MIPS R4000 and the DEC Alpha. Older processors use 16-bit or even 8-bit instruction sets. Imagine writing a number with 32 digits on a narrow piece of paper. If there is not enough room, you write 16 digits on one line and 16 digits on another. Similarly, 32-bit processors work with large numbers, memory addresses, or instructions without the need to split operations to fit within the smaller register sizes of older processors. Overall *throughput,* which is the combination of processor performance, data transfer, and memory access, improves.

Multitasking means that the operating system can do several things at once. *Preemptive* means that the user or another task can interrupt a task if necessary, rather than wait for it to completely finish. As processing speeds get faster, hardware-related activities such as accessing a disk can seem incredibly slow. When a non-preemptive operating system accesses the disk, the processor waits while the mechanical disk is accessed, thus wasting processing cycles. In Windows NT, multiple tasks can occur simultaneously so if one task gets hung up when accessing a slow device such as a disk, the processor can turn its attention to other tasks. Basically, there are no wasted processing cycles. Think of each task as a runner in a race. If one slows down, the others don't stop. The benefit is that users can do other tasks while disks are accessed in the background or a print job is prepared.

Memory protection ensures that multiple programs run in their own memory area and don't corrupt the memory used by other applications. If one application crashes, the other applications and the operating system remain alive so users can close their work and exit properly.

Symmetric multiprocessing is a unique feature of Windows NT that lets it take advantage of multiple processors. While multiprocessor systems have existed for a while, NT is one of the first major operating systems to properly and efficiently use multiple processors. Previous operating systems assigned dedicated tasks to each processor, such as network input/output. This *asymmetric multiprocessing*—having one processor dedicated to one task—meant that each processor sat idle when finished with its specific job. Symmetric multiprocessing, on the other hand, allocates tasks to any processor; if one processor finishes before another, the operating system can assign it other tasks. Symmetric multiprocessing is harder to implement, but provides superior performance.

Networking features in Windows NT let you share files on your system with other network users and connect with shared directories on other systems. Computers running Windows for Workgroups can participate in the network. In addition, Windows NT comes with software and drivers to support connections to other types of operating systems, such as UNIX and IBM mainframes.

The Windows NT Advanced Server product is an enhanced version of Windows NT that provides sophisticated file server features for large network environments. It includes additional features for data protection, such as automatic duplication of data to secondary disks.

WINDOWS NT ON THE OUTSIDE

Windows NT looks and operates like Microsoft Windows 3.1. In fact, the version number for Windows NT is 3.1, the same as the current Windows version number. Windows NT uses the same familiar graphical user interface that provides a consistent look and operation across applications. It also run thousands of Windows 3.1 and MS-DOS applications.

How Windows NT Presents Itself

After you first boot Windows NT and log on, you see the Program Manager window shown in Figure 1-1. Your computer name and logon name appear at the top in the title bar of the window.

You start programs from the Program Manager by double-clicking the icon of the program you want. You can see that the window currently open is the Main window. "Group" icons such as Main, Accessories, Administrative Tools, and the other icons at the bottom of the screen in Figure 1-1, help organize the program icons. You start the Command Prompt to execute DOS commands or run applications not specifically designed for Windows NT, such as POSIX compliant programs.

Mail, Schedule+, and ClipBook Viewer are network-compatible programs that let you communicate with and share files or graphic objects with other network users.

Use the File Manager, shown in Figure 1-2, to view and manage files, share directories on your system with other network users, or connect with shared drives on other computers. Network administrators can apply security measures to protect directories and files from unauthorized use in Windows NT.

If you open the Administrative Tools group in the Program Manager, the utilities listed below appear, each of which is described in later chapters of this book.

User Manager   Use to create accounts that other users log onto and groups that provide system security.

Disk Administrator   Use to prepare and manage the disks on the system.

Performance Monitor   Use to track system usage, monitor performance, perform troubleshooting, and plan for system expansion.

Backup   Use to back up directories and files on the system.

Event Viewer   Use to view logs that display system, security, and application events for troubleshooting and auditing purposes.

FIGURE 1-1

Windows NT Program
Manager

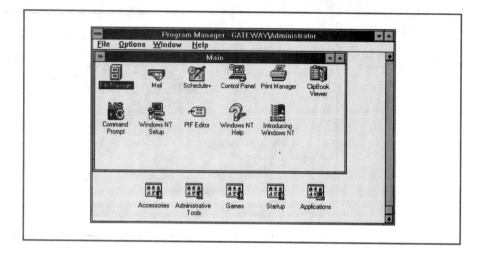

The Control Panel

Double-clicking the Control Panel opens the following window:

It contains a set of utilities you run to customize the settings of the Windows NT interface or the system hardware. Utilities like Mouse, Keyboard, and Server are used to set the features of these components. Others such as Desktop are used to customize the interface. All of these utilities are covered in later chapters.

OTHER WINDOWS NT FEATURES

Windows NT is truly designed with the future in mind. It is a *portable* operating system, which means it is easily altered to run on many different hardware platforms. Its symmetric multiprocessing capabilities give it a wide margin in potential performance over other operating systems. Other important features are described in the following sections.

FIGURE 1-2

Windows NT File Manager

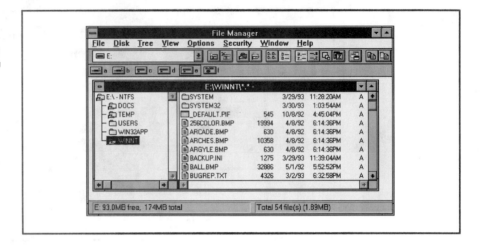

Support for Other Environments

Built into Windows NT is the Win32 environment that supports 32-bit NT applications. In addition, NT includes several other *environmental subsystems*. These subsystems allow applications designed for other operating systems to run under Windows NT. You access environmental subsystems by starting the Command Prompt in the Program Manager Main group. The following subsystems are provided:

▧   The *Virtual DOS Machine (VDM)* subsystem emulates the MS-DOS environment so you can run DOS applications.

▧   The *Win16 Virtual DOS Machine* subsystem emulates the Windows (16-bit) environment so you can run Windows 3.1 applications. Applications run in an 80286 emulation mode.

▧   The *OS/2 subsystem* lets you run character-based MS OS/2 1.*x* applications. This subsystem is not supported on MIPS or DEC Alpha computers.

▧   The *POSIX subsystem* runs applications that meet the Portable Operating System Interface for Computing Environment (POSIX) as defined by the Institute of Electrical and Electronic Engineers (IEEE).

Virtual Memory

Virtual memory provides a way to allocate more memory to the operating system and applications than is physically available on your computer. When memory starts to run low, parts of it are swapped to disk storage to make memory available for other processes.

For example, if a process has information in memory that it is not currently using, the information is moved to disk and the memory space is made available to another process.

The Windows NT installation program installs the Virtual Memory Manager. An initial size is recommended based on the amount of free disk space, but you can change the size of the virtual memory disk space at any time by accessing the System utility in the Control Panel. As an example, a system with 16 megabytes of physical memory and 8 megabytes of virtual memory has an effective memory size of 24 megabytes. Virtual memory is not always necessary, but if you need to manipulate large graphics files, it is indispensable.

File System Support in NT

You must partition and format all hard disks before you can store files on them. Formatting divides a disk into tracks and sectors and defines the methods used to store and retrieve files and directories. The primary file system for Windows NT is the new NT File System (NTFS), but Windows NT also supports the older file systems, described here:

FAT (File Allocation Table file system)   This is the file system for DOS. It uses a filenaming format with an eight-character filename and a three-character extension. Windows NT can access FAT drives, but if you boot the system with DOS, you cannot access NTFS drives.

HPFS (High Performance File System)   This is the file system designed for OS/2 that provides long filenames. It also has performance enhancing features that FAT does not have. Windows NT can access HPFS drives.

NTFS   This is the new NT file system. It provides long filenames, data protection and recovery, and security through directory and file permissions, which you'll read about in the next section.

| Note | You can install Windows NT on disks partitioned for FAT but if you do, file security and long filenames are not available. Only NTFS supports these features. |

The Benefits of NTFS

NTFS is designed to give users maximum speed when networking in the corporate environment. It supports large hard disks and the storage of files over multiple hard disks (called *spanning volumes*). For example, a large company database might be so large that it needs to span several drives.

NTFS provides built-in security features that control file ownership and access. Files on an NTFS volume are not accessible from DOS or other operating systems. That is part of the Windows NT security system, but only when you use NTFS.

NTFS allows filenames of up to 256 characters in length. While DOS users can't access the NTFS volume, NTFS files can be copied to DOS volumes. Each NTFS file includes a DOS-readable filename that conforms to the DOS filename format. This filename is generated by NTFS from the beginning characters of the long filename. Here are the filenaming rules for NTFS:

- You can have a maximum of 256 characters in file and directory names.

- You can use multiple period-separated extensions, if necessary, to create filenames such as REPORTS.SALES.SMITH.JUNE93.

- Names cannot include these symbols: ? \ " < > | :.

- NT preserves the uppercase/lowercase format of the name specified but does not use case to distinguish between filenames. For example, Reports.Sales.Smith.June93 is a mixed case filename with multiple extensions.

- You can use wildcard characters (? and *) when searching for and listing filenames.

Installation Options

If installing Windows NT on a new system, you will most likely format the entire disk as NTFS. On existing systems, you might want to keep part of the existing file system. You have several installation options:

- You can keep an existing partition for another operating system and install NTFS in a separate partition. When you boot the system, a screen appears that lets you select the operating system you want to start.

- You can convert the existing boot partition to an NTFS volume.

- You can reformat existing partitions to NTFS. This deletes existing files in the partition.

File and System Protection

Windows NT has several features that protect data stored on its file system from unauthorized users and from damage to files. To protect the file system from unauthorized access, all users must log on by typing an account name and password. The system administrator can apply various logon restrictions to accounts that, for example, disable the account after a period of time or force users to change their password. These options are covered in Chapter 3.

NT also provides file system protection mechanisms that detect and disable bad disk sectors and restore transactions that were written incompletely due to a power failure. Important file system information is also duplicated on the disk to guard against sector failures. The installation program also creates a repair disk that you can use to bring NT back up in case the boot information is corrupted.

Windows NT also supports *Uninterruptable Power Supplies* (UPS). These are devices that provide backup battery power to the system when AC power is lost. The system will operate for a designated period of time, which allows users to properly shut down the system and write all information in memory to disk. Support is provided in the form of signals provided by the UPS to warn the operating system that it is operating on backup power. The operating system begins an automatic shutdown after a specified period of time based on the battery's ability to supply power.

Networking

The networking services in Windows NT comprise one of its most important features. It is also an important feature of Microsoft Windows for Workgroups, Microsoft LAN Manager, and of course, Windows NT Advanced Server. Computers running any of these operating systems can share directories, files, and resources. They also can connect with other systems and access shared directories, files, and resources on those systems.

Network Communication

The transmission of information on networks is handled by specific types of communications protocols. A *protocol* is a set of rules that define how two or more computer systems talk to one another over a network. Basically, protocols define when a computer can talk and when it should listen, how to send data on the network cable, and how to operate with higher-level applications. Network communication on Microsoft Windows NT, LAN Manager, and Windows for Workgroups networks is handled by the protocols described here:

> *NetBIOS (Network Basic Input/Output System)* Windows NT applications use this interface standard to communicate with other NetBIOS-compatible applications. It sits on top of the NetBEUI communications protocol discussed next and performs high-level tasks, such as identifying network names, establishing sessions between two computers, and handling data transfers. (A *session* is a connection between two computers that is maintained until disconnected. Many tasks may occur during the session, such as the exchange of files and messages.)

NetBEUI (NetBIOS Extended User Interface)   This protocol was originally developed by IBM and operates under the Microsoft NetBIOS interface. It provides flow control and error detection when computers are communicating over a network cable.

TCP/IP (Transmission Control Protocol/Internet Protocol)   A protocol developed by the U.S. Department of Defense for networking over wide areas, TCP/IP provides a way to interconnect many local area networks into wide area networks. TCP/IP is commonly used in the UNIX environment. NT users can install TCP/IP and gain access to UNIX systems. As discussed in Appendix C, TCP/IP adds routing capabilities to NetBIOS.

Future versions of NT will support other industry-standard protocols such as Novell Corporation's IPX/SPX and Digital Equipment Corporation's DECnet protocols. By running other protocols, you can connect with and use the resources on networks and systems that support the protocol.

Network Interface Card Support

There are many different types of network communication methods. It would be unreasonable to expect manufacturers of network interface cards to write the software drivers that provide an interface for each method. To simplify the creation of drivers, Windows NT uses the Microsoft Network Device Interface Standard (NDIS) as the interface between network card drivers and higher-level communications processes. Network card vendors simply create drivers that are NDIS-compatible. End users then buy NDIS-compatible cards with the assurance that the cards will work with Windows NT.

NDIS supports multiple network interface cards in the same system, thus providing the system with a way to access several different types of networks. For example, an Ethernet card could access the LAN in the engineering department while a Token Ring card provides connections to the accounting department.

Security and User Hierarchy

Windows NT meets the Department of Defense C2 Controlled Access Protection security rating. The C2 rating requires that computers must implement a security policy and auditing of events, not only for access by network users, but for access by local users. Chapter 3 fully describes user hierarchy and the security it provides. The C2 level security in Windows NT provides the following:

▧   Users have special accounts that require logon with password identification. The account tracks various actions performed by a user for auditing purposes, such as logons, logoffs, and file accesses. Management tasks such as changing user accounts or server settings are also tracked.

- Administrators and users can control file, directory, and resource (printers) access on their own system.

- System administrators can track and view auditable events.

- Users are prevented from examining the contents of memory.

Because Windows NT provides file- and resource-sharing capabilities, security is a concern if the computer is accessed by multiple users. Administrators and users must be able to protect the files they share on their system against unauthorized use. However, security does require a certain amount of administration. Permissions must be applied to shared directories, and administrators must create user accounts that require logon passwords and provide logon restrictions.

Logon account information is stored in a master database (called a *security accounts manager* or SAM) on each NT system. When users log on, their user name and password are checked in the SAM of the system they log onto.

Trust Relationships

While the SAM database provides adequate security for the local NT system, it introduces some security and maintenance problems for other file- and resource-sharing computers on the network. For example, you can define access rights for groups of network users, but not for individual users who need to access your system from another computer on the network. That's where the Windows NT Advanced Server comes into play.

The Windows NT Advanced Server product can establish *trust relationships* with other computers on the network. That means that one computer can authenticate a user and provide access information about the user to other computers. Users can then log onto one computer and access other computers without logging onto each computer separately.

One interesting feature of the security system is that protection information assigned to files travels with the files. For example, if you grant a user the ability to open and read a file but not change it, the same rights will apply even if the storage device is moved to another system.

Printing

If your NT system is connected to a network, you can share its printers with other network users or access shared printers on the network. The Print Manager in Windows NT contains all the features and functions you need to install, configure, share, and otherwise manage printers. Those users who have Windows 3.1 probably installed printers using the Printer utility in the Control Panel. Selecting this option in Windows NT opens the Print Manager, which includes all printer management options.

Another printing feature that has changed is the location where printer drivers are stored for shared network printers. In Windows 3.1, you had to install a printer driver on your own system when accessing a printer of that type on a remote network computer. In Windows NT, printer drivers are stored on the computer where the printer is connected; that is, where printer drivers used to reside on the client, they now reside on the server. When you access the printer, your application uses the printer driver on that computer.

You can also set permissions that control the type of access users have to printers. For example, you can prevent or allow users to access a printer, and grant some users the ability to control documents in the Print Manager queue. Administrators have full control over printers.

Logon and Startup Options

The person that installs NT on a computer specifies the Administrator password and thus gains full control over the system. This administrative user can create accounts with password protections so other users can log onto the system. In addition, rights and permissions can be assigned to each user account to grant or restrict access to the system and its files. If you log onto an NT system and can't access certain files, it is because your logon account has these restrictions. User and group accounts are discussed further in Chapter 3, along with system access rights and file permissions.

Every user that logs on with their own account can customize the Program Manager to their own needs. For example, when John logs on, he can rearrange the Program Manager window and add some startup icons for the programs he uses. When Jane logs on to the same computer, she does not see John's changes and can create her own custom settings that John does not see. Administrators can create common settings that all users see, however.

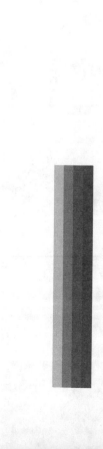

Inside

- Multiprocessing Systems and RISC-Based Systems

- NT's Storage Options

- Network Hardware

- Protecting Your System from Power Problems

& Out

CHAPTER 2

Hardware for Windows NT

This chapter covers hardware requirements for Windows NT and discusses hardware issues in general. Windows NT runs on computers that use the following processors:

- Systems using Intel-based 32-bit 80386 or 80486 processors
- MIPS R4000-based RISC (reduced instruction set computer) system
- Digital Equipment Corporation Alpha-based RISC systems

The system must meet the following memory, disk, and video requirements:

- 8MB of RAM (but 16MB or more is recommended)
- VGA or higher-resolution video display adapter and monitor
- Mouse or other pointing device
- 80MB of free disk space on the NT partition
- A high-density floppy drive for Intel-based systems
- An SCSI (Small Computer System Interface) CD-ROM for RISC-based systems
- Network interface cards if you plan to attach to a network

This chapter discusses computer systems, hardware configurations, and networks you can configure for Windows NT. In particular, it covers symmetric multiprocessing systems and fault-tolerant disk configurations.

MULTIPROCESSING SYSTEMS AND RISC-BASED SYSTEMS

The primary target machine for Windows NT is the standard off-the-shelf Intel 80386- and 80486-based system with ISA, EISA, or MCA bus. NT takes full advantage of the 32-bit processing available on these computers. But NT is capable of much more, and that is where special systems with multiple processors and proprietary designs come into play. This section discusses Intel-based multiprocessing systems and RISC-based systems.

The Benefits of Symmetric Multiprocessing

A *symmetric multiprocessing* (SMP) operating system optimizes throughput on multiprocessor systems. In a multitasking operating system such as Windows NT, work is divided into processes, and each process is allocated a certain part of memory and other system resources. A process also has at least one *thread* that executes the work of the process. Think of NT as a manager that hires an assistant manager (the process). The assistant manager then hires one or more workers (threads) to perform work.

Processes can create additional threads as necessary. For example, one thread might handle saving files, while another might monitor mouse activities. In this example, the user can save a file, then execute other commands with the mouse. There is no waiting while the file is saved as there is in operating systems like DOS. The processor doesn't need to complete one task before starting another. The operating system just issues another thread. The processor then allocates a little bit of its time, in turn to each thread. This happens very quickly, so the user doesn't notice too much of a slow down. However, if a system has multiple processors, Windows NT can allocate a thread to each processor, and this symmetric multiprocessing capability is where Windows NT truly surpasses other operating systems. Its performance is limited only by the number of processors you can install in a computer.

On systems with multiple processors, true multitasking is possible, since each processor can execute instructions simultaneously. In symmetric multiprocessing, threads are allocated to any available processor so that no processor ever sits idle, as shown in Figure 2-1. When the number of threads exceeds available processors, threads wait for the next available processor.

As you saw in Chapter 1, asymmetric multiprocessing operating systems dedicate each processor in a multiprocessor system to a specific task, and only that task. For example, the systems might dedicate one processor to network input/output, another to system processing, and another to interrupt handling. Bottlenecks occur when one processor is overloaded while other processors sit idle because the operating system cannot reallocate tasks from busy processors to idle processors. In Windows NT, which is a symmetric multiprocessing system, there are no wasted processing cycles because processes are divided into multiple threads that can execute on any available processor.

FIGURE 2-1

Symmetric multiprocessing

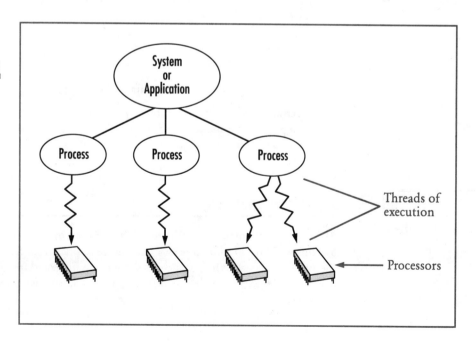

A symmetric multiprocessing system is able to do the following maneuvers:

☑   Quickly assign threads to any available processor

☑   Allow any thread, whether it belongs to the system or an application, to use any available processor

☑   Make thread assignment invisible to the application so the application can move from one machine to another and transparently take advantage of any number of processors available on that system

Note

UNIX does provide a form of symmetric multiprocessing, but only for processes; there are no thread divisions. This limits performance and often requires modifications to the operating system before it works properly.

There are many benefits to symmetric multiprocessing. The most important is increased throughput, especially in server environments where many users access the system. Desktop systems also can benefit from multiprocessor systems. As applications become more complex and vendors constantly add new features, performance on single-processor systems becomes limited. With NT's symmetric multiprocessing support, you can add more processors whenever you need better performance.

The top-end performance of symmetric multiprocessing systems is much higher than single-processing systems. Performance usually depends on the number of processors you can physically install in the system. Single-processor systems have a definite performance high end that you can't go beyond, even with Windows NT, because you can't add more processors.

Microsoft packages Windows NT as follows:

☑   A desktop version that takes advantage of one or two processor systems

☑   A server version that takes advantage of one to four processor systems

☑   Versions available from vendors of proprietary multiprocessor systems to support many processors and special bus designs. Microsoft relies on these vendors to support NT on their products

Intel-Based Systems that Support NT

Many system vendors support Windows NT on their symmetric multiprocessing systems. Systems with two or more processors can range in price from $8,000 to $1 million. At the low end are systems for advanced desktop computing, and at the high end are systems designed for enterprise-wide network computing. The following section describes available systems.

The AcerFrame 3000MP50 System   This system supports one to four Intel 486DX 50-MHz processors. A 64-bit Acer FrameBus is implemented, along with an EISA (extended industry standard architecture) bus. The system also supports up to 264MB of memory and 4GB of internal disk storage using the Acer Disk Array Subsystem that implements RAID level 5 protection.

Note

RAID (Redundant Arrays of Inexpensive Disks) systems are arrays of disks that provide speed and fault protection, as discussed later in this chapter.

Advanced Logic Research (ALR) Systems   ALR provides a variety of multi-processing platforms that support one or two Intel processors on an EISA-bus mother-board.

The AST Research System   The AST Manhattan SMP system supports up to six Intel 486DX 40-MHz processors, 256MB of memory, and a five-channel SCSI host bus adapter that provides RAID levels 0, 1, and 5. Drives can be hot-replaced, meaning you can swap out defective drives while the system is running. The system also has redundant power supply options and an EISA-bus design.

Compaq Systems   Compaq makes a range of symmetric multiprocessor systems that support from 2 to 16 processors. The Compaq SYSTEMPRO/XL provides SMP with two 486DX 50-MHz processors on a 64-bit processor bus. The system supports 512MB of memory and is preinstalled with a 32-bit NetFlex network controller than can be configured for Ethernet or Token Ring. RAID disk systems are available.

The NCR System 3000   The NCR System 3000 series is a fully scalable Intel processor-based platform with machines that range from desktop systems to mainframe class network computing systems. (*Scalable* means that it can accommodate products from palmtop systems to supercomputers.)

Olivetti LSX Systems   The Olivetti LSX series SMP systems support up to four Intel 486DX 33-MHz or 50-MHz processors. The systems support up to 256MB of system memory and up to 6.12GB of disk storage (30GB with a special expansion module). The systems implement an EISA-bus design. Olivetti is also designing MIPS R4000-based systems and Intel Pentium-based systems.

Sequent Symmetry 2000 Systems   The Sequent Symmetry 2000 series support up to 30 tightly coupled Intel 486DX processors that share common memory and a single copy of DYNIX/ptx, a multiprocessor-enhanced, POSIX and X/Open-compliant version of the UNIX System V operating system.

Tricord PowerFrame Systems   The Tricord PowerFrame series has independent, intelligent subsystems that support multiple Intel 486DX processors and
multiple Intel 386DX Intelligent I/O Processors (IIOPs) interfaced by a high-speed
proprietary system bus. The IIOPs are SCSI I/O processors that run independently of
the PowerFrame's EISA bus. This gives the system a mainframe-like design that avoids
bus bottlenecks. The PowerFrames are specially designed for the network computing
applications.

Digital Equipment Alpha AXP Systems

Digital Equipment Corporation has long been known for its PDP and VAX families of
computer systems. Its new Alpha AXP processor architecture is designed for a long support
life (25 years) and high performance at a low price

The first processor to use the Alpha AXP architecture is the DEC 21064-AA. It
has a clock speed of 150 MHz and is currently the world's fastest 64-bit microprocessor.
Over time, faster speeds will be available. The 21064 is a *dual-issue processor,* which means
it can launch two instructions at once. The processor can reach peak instruction execution
of 300 million operations per second (MIPS). In addition, the chips run at 3.3 volts
compared to the 5.0 volts common throughout the industry, so they use less power and
run cooler.

Digital plans to implement Alpha AXP in a variety of desktop and high-end
computing systems that start as low as $5,000. Systems include SCSI-2 disk interfaces,
Turbochannel slots, and support for up to 256MB of memory.

MIPS R4000 Systems

MIPS Computer System's R4000 microprocessor is a 64-bit processor based on earlier
32-bit R2000, R3000, and R6000 designs. An important vendor of MIPS systems is
Silicon Graphics, which recently purchased MIPS. The company's Indigo line includes
a graphics workstation with 16 megabytes of memory for $8,000.

NT'S STORAGE OPTIONS

Windows NT has several disk configuration options and provides protection from disk
disasters in several ways. Some forms of protection exist in software, while others are
provided by hardware. Tape backup is one obvious method of data protection. In
Windows NT Advanced Servers, another method is to duplicate data in real-time on
secondary disks, a process that can be done by either *mirroring* or *duplexing.* Additional

"fault-tolerance" features such as RAID level 5, which stores information on arrays of disks with parity protection are available. These and other features are covered in this section.

NT's Recoverable File System

Windows NT has a recoverable file system, which means that it can recover improperly written transactions. The system is quick and efficient, adding very little overhead to the file system.

All modifications to files on an NTFS volume are logged with *redo* and *undo* information. Redo provides information on how to repeat transactions while undo provides information on how to "roll back" transactions. With undo information, the disk can be restored to the state it was in before the transaction was ever started. The importance of undo becomes apparent when you consider what happens during a power outage. If the power goes out while a transaction is being written, the disk contains only half the correct information. Upon rebooting, NT scans the disk and determines whether it needs to redo transactions or back them out completely. If it must back out an incomplete transaction, it looks up the undo information and restores the records to their pre-transaction state.

The recovery options work on all drives formatted to the NTFS file system. You don't need special equipment to use these options.

Supported Disk Options

Windows NT supports the same disk devices that DOS systems support. These include drives that use ST506 controllers, ESDI (Enhanced Small Device Interface) drives and controllers, SCSI drives and bus adapters, and IDE (Intelligent Drive Electronics) drives and bus adapters. ST506 and ESDI controllers support the attachment of only two drives. You can install two such controllers in a typical Intel-based system.

The SCSI interface is more versatile. It allows up to seven devices—including hard drives, tape drives, and CD-ROM drives—to share the same SCSI host adapter. The host adapter is unique in that it provides a connection point for all the supported devices. Each device has its own built-in controller, rather than relying on controller circuitry in the adapter. Because of this, SCSI devices can read or write simultaneously because each handles those operations on its own. SCSI disk systems provide the highest performance of the standards discussed here. A new SCSI-2 standard boosts the performance of previous SCSI standards.

The IDE interface is a hybrid that combines features of the other interfaces with new features of its own. IDE devices were originally designed as low-cost alternatives to ESDI devices; however, their cost and performance have made IDE the disk of choice in most desktop systems. Like SCSI devices, each IDE device has its own control circuitry. The devices attach to an adapter that is typically mounted directly on the motherboard. Only two disks are supported per adapter and you cannot mirror the disks. You can, however, duplex the disks, as you'll see next. Note that SCSI still provides better performance than IDE.

Disk Mirroring and Duplexing

Disk mirroring and disk duplexing provide protection against disk failures when using Windows NT Advanced Server. Mirroring provides a way to back up one drive by continuously duplicating its contents to another drive. You must attach a secondary disk to back up (mirror) the primary disk as shown in Figure 2-2. Should the primary disk fail, you can put the secondary disk into service.

Note

You can only duplex IDE drives. The master/slave relationship of drives on a single IDE controller prevents mirroring.

One weak point in the mirroring scheme is the controller. Both disks are unavailable if it fails. Disk duplexing provides a higher level of data protection by duplicating the controller. As shown in Figure 2-3, you install two controllers and attach drives to each. Note that you can attach two drives to each controller on ST-506, ESDI, and IDE controllers, and multiple drives to each controller on SCSI systems.

FIGURE 2-2

Disk mirroring

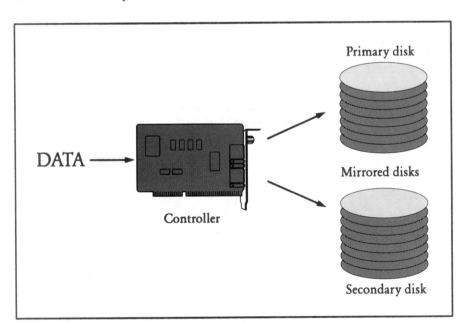

Primary disk

DATA

Controller

Mirrored disks

Secondary disk

FIGURE 2-3

Disk duplexing

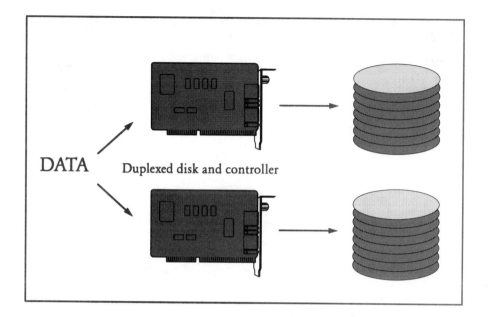

Disk Partitions and Formats

When you install a new disk, the entire disk space is free. You then partition the disk and format it to either FAT, HPFS, or NTFS drives. Under Windows NT, you can assign all the free space on a disk to one partition, or you can create up to four partitions. Each partition is assigned a drive letter when formatted, unless it is an extended partition or part of a volume. An *extended partition* can be further subdivided into multiple logical drives, but only one extended partition is allowed per disk. A *volume* is a partition or set of partitions, sometimes spanning several physical disks that are combined to provide a large amount of disk space.

Keep in mind that a drive letter is associated with a partition of a disk, not necessarily an entire physical disk. A *logical drive* is a subdivision of an extended partition. Figure 2-4 illustrates a single drive with a primary and extended partition. The extended partition is subdivided into logical drives D, E, and F.

Multiple partitions can make up a volume and are formatted together as a single drive. Figure 2-5 illustrates a volume that spans two drives. You span volumes to accommodate very large files, or a large number of files that you want to keep together.

Note

It is only recommended that you span volumes on Windows NT Advanced Servers, then mirror or duplex the volumes for protection in case one disk becomes faulty.

FIGURE 2-4

Primary and extended
partition scheme

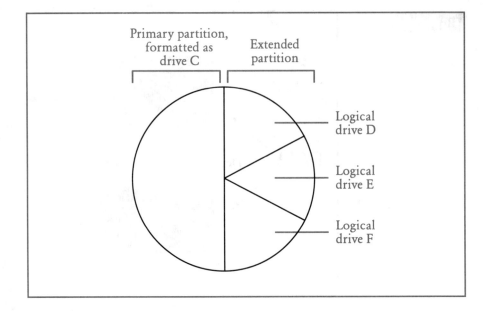

FIGURE 2-5

Spanning volumes

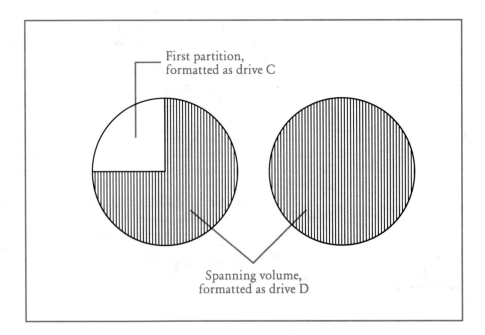

Disk Striping

Disk striping under Windows NT is a form of RAID level 0. It provides a way to increase disk performance by writing to several disks simultaneously. Disk striping is primarily done with SCSI disk systems due to the number of drives the standard supports, the speed of the drives, and a *disconnect* feature, which lets the drives perform their own tasks while the system moves on to other tasks.

As depicted in Figure 2-6, disk striping distributes data and writes it to multiple drives simultaneously. This can greatly improve the performance of disk reads and writes. However, be careful about implementing the RAID level 0 striping provided by Windows NT. If one of the disks in the set goes down, all the data on all drives is unrecoverable. Striping is best done in the Windows NT Advanced Server, which provides disk mirroring and duplexing to protect data.

RAID level 5 is a more secure form of disk striping implemented by the Windows NT Advanced Server. It provides disk striping with *parity*. Parity information is stored on a single drive and can be used to "rebuild" data on any single drive that fails. The parity information ensures that the striped set can be recovered if one of the disks goes down. Refer to the NT Advanced Server manual for more information.

Note	Some computer systems implement RAID in hardware so the operating system doesn't need to support it. The entire disk array appears as a single drive to Windows NT.

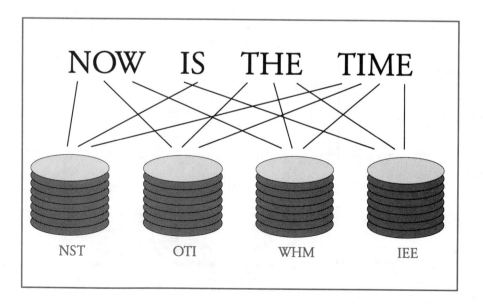

FIGURE 2-6

Striping distributes data over multiple drives

NETWORK HARDWARE

A computer *network* consists of two or more computers tied together into a communications system that lets users share files and resources among systems. Connections are made by installing network interface cards (NICs) in each machine and linking them with network cabling. Windows NT uses industry-standard networks as described in the following sections. The network cards you buy for every computer in the network must support the network type you choose, although computers can have multiple network cards to connect with multiple networks.

Network Types

If you are connecting your system into an existing LAN, your network administrator probably has already installed a network card in your system or has the card you need to make the connection. If you are planning a Windows NT installation, the information in this section will help you choose an appropriate network communications method and the interface cards to support it. Be sure to check with your local computer dealer or network installer for more information.

Thin Ethernet

Thin Ethernet, often referred to as *10Base2*, uses a thin coaxial cable (similar to television cable) that links computers, as shown in Figure 2-7. The coaxial cable is shielded and thus

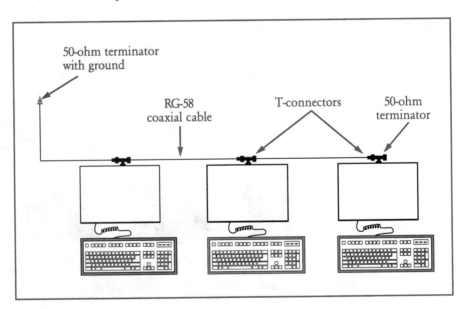

FIGURE 2-7

A 10Base2 Ethernet network

protected from outside electromagnetic interference. The entire length of the network cable cannot exceed 606 feet unless a special repeater device is used. This system cannot have more than 30 workstations. Ethernet has a data transfer rate of 10 megabits/sec. The transfer rate is meaningful when comparing network types.

Ethernet is relatively easy to configure and install. Its *topology*—its layout—is similar to a snake of wire. You start at one end of an office and connect machines in line until you reach the last machine. Both ends of the cable get terminated with a special cap, and one end (only one end!) gets grounded.

Ethernet is also relatively inexpensive. You can purchase an Ethernet NIC for as low as $80, and cable costs between 20 cents to 30 cents per foot in rolls of 1,000 feet. A T-connector is required to attach the cable segments at the back of each NIC (network interface card) and the terminators attach to the T-connectors at each end of the network.

Twisted-pair Ethernet

Twisted-pair Ethernet (often referred to as 10BaseT) has the same data transfer rate as 10Base2 Ethernet, but uses simple telephone wire (also called twisted-pair wiring) that costs approximately 15 cents per foot. The topology of 10BaseT is slightly different from 10Base2 Ethernet. The cable to each workstation branches from a central concentrator box into a star configuration, which makes wiring the network somewhat easier. In some cases, you can even use existing (unused) telephone wire that terminates in the telephone wiring closet of your building, as shown in Figure 2-8 (but have the cable checked by a

FIGURE 2-8

A Twisted-pair Ethernet network using existing telephone wiring

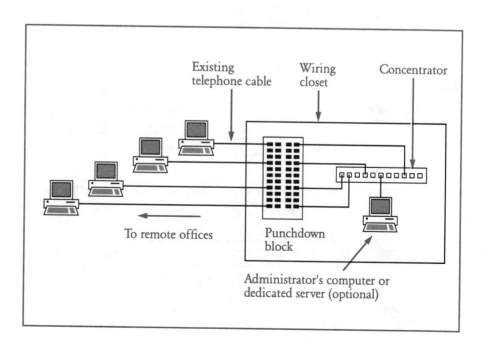

qualified electrician before doing so). The concentrator simply serves as a central connection point for all the computers in the network.

While twisted-pair wire is less expensive and easier to handle than the coaxial cable used in 10Base2 Ethernet, you must buy an additional concentrator box, which starts at about $500. The maximum length of the network cannot exceed 328 feet, about half that of 10Base2. Most 10BaseT network cabling systems use RJ-45 cable connectors. You can buy cable in set lengths, or make the cables yourself.

Token Ring

Token Ring is an IBM networking scheme that uses a special twisted-pair wire and star topology as shown in Figure 2-9. Each station branches from a central concentrator box known as the Multistation Access Unit (MAU). Token Ring provides data transfer rates of 4 megabits/sec or 16 megabits/sec, depending on the type of card purchased. The faster cards are more expensive. In fact, Token Ring tends to be more expensive than other network types, but unlike other networks, it does offer some protection from cable breaks and other problems. The MAU is actually a switching device that keeps the network up and running if one of the cable segments breaks or is disconnected.

The cable used to connect Token Ring is either shielded twisted-pair (STP) or unshielded twisted-pair (UTP). The type you choose depends on your budget, number of workstations, and distances you want to connect. Each computer can be up to 328 feet from the MAU device with STP cable, or 148 feet using UTP cable. You can connect multiple MAUs together to support up to 260 workstations with STP cable and up to 72 workstations with UTP cable. Token Ring MAUs can be placed in a phone closet and wired to workstations in the same way that Twisted-pair Ethernet can (see Figure 2-8).

FIGURE 2-9

A Token Ring network

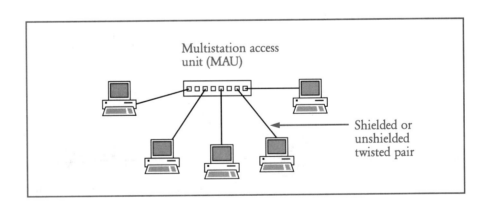

PROTECTING YOUR SYSTEM FROM POWER PROBLEMS

To protect your computer and network from power problems such as brownouts, blackouts, electrical noise, and grounding problems, you need equipment such as UPSs, surge protectors, and power conditioning equipment. Uninterruptable power supplies (UPS) can protect against brownouts and blackouts. Surge protectors and power conditioning equipment can protect against other problems. Failure to protect your equipment can cause corruption of data in memory from line noise, equipment failure from transient energy, and slow death of equipment that is repeatedly subjected to low-energy surges.

In recent years, failure of sensitive electronic equipment has been traced to inadequate grounding in commercial buildings and poorly designed surge-protection equipment. A surge protector that sends its surges to the earth ground, rather than absorbing the surges simply sends those surges to other equipment in the building. The very device you install to protect one network computer may be responsible for burning out another.

Chapter 20 gives several solutions to grounding problems along with other measures you can take to protect your equipment and its data.

Inside

- Accessing the NT System

- User Accounts

- Group Accounts

- Workgroups and Domains

- Rights and Permissions

& Out

CHAPTER 3

NT Hierarchy and Security

This chapter describes the NT local and network environment and the methods used to grant users access to directories, files, resources, and management functions. The topics discussed here are only applicable if other people log onto your system, or if you allow users at network workstations to access shared directories on your computer.

Note

If you are not sharing your system and want to move ahead with NT and running applications, skip to Chapter 4.

If you share your system and administer users and security, read through this chapter. It brings together diverse information about users, access rights, permissions, workgroups, and domains that will help you better understand the utilities and features for managing users and methods for organizing your system and network.

Chapter 16 gives further information about creating user and group accounts. Chapter 7 covers sharing directories and files on your computer with other users. Chapter 17 covers management topics for servers.

ACCESSING THE NT SYSTEM

The NT operating system provides several levels of user access. NT first assumes that more than one person might need to use the computer and so provides local user accounts that control the access each user has to the system and its resources (printers, CD-ROM drives, tape-backups, and so on). NT also has built-in networking that provides peer-to-peer sharing of directories, files, and resources with users at other workstations attached to the network. The two types of users are described next and depicted in Figure 3-1.

Local Users   The NT operating system allows multiple users to log on at the physical computer running NT. Obviously, users don't all log on at the same time, but NT maintains account information for each user and stores customized settings that are restored when a user next logs on. When a user logs on by typing an account name and

FIGURE 3-1

Local and network users

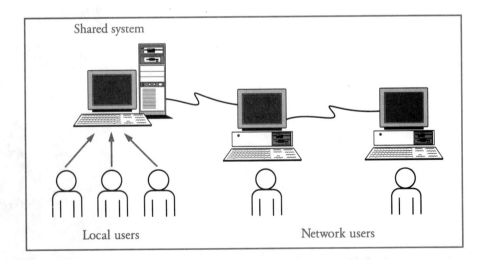

password, NT *authenticates* that user (that is, if the information matches an existing user account, NT logs you on). If the account is valid and has not expired, the user gains access to the system. Under Windows NT every user is given their own Program Manager. A user can customize the Program Manager interface to fit his or her needs. For example, Jill can change the arrangement of her group windows and add startup icons for the programs she runs. When Joe logs on, he does not see Jill's changes—he sees only the modifications he has made to his personal Program Manager settings. However, the Administrator can create settings that all users see.

Network Users   Network users access an NT system over a network from another computer. Once connected, they can access shared directories, files, and resources such as printers. Network connections under NT have a *client/server relationship.* An NT computer that shares its files and resources is the *server* and computers that access those resources are the *clients.* There is a special set of permissions that the Administrator of the server system can apply to shared directories that grants or restricts client activities in shared directories. These are discussed later in this chapter.

USER ACCOUNTS

Local user access to the NT operating system is controlled by user accounts. User accounts include the user's name, password, group membership, and access rights to system resources. An Administrator or Power User creates user accounts by starting the NT User Manager utility and filling out a form similar to the one shown in Figure 3-2. The Department of Defense C2 security requirements require that Windows NT use password-protected logon accounts to accommodate multiple users and protect data on the system.

| Note | Once a user account is created, you can add that user to a group. Groups, which you'll read about in the next section, simplify the task of assigning privileges and access to resources. |

Access to the system is determined by the properties of a user's account. To log on, the user types an account name and a password. If the information matches an existing user account, NT logs on that user. As you read earlier, this process is called authentication. It creates a special security access token that authenticates the user during any event that requires validation. The token is different every time the user logs on, thus providing an extra level of security.

The Administrator defines logon properties for users when creating or modifying their user accounts. These properties control or restrict logon, and set up a user environment if a logon is successful. The setup of logon properties and environment settings is covered in more detail in Chapter 16.

FIGURE 3-2

The form Administrators use
to create user accounts

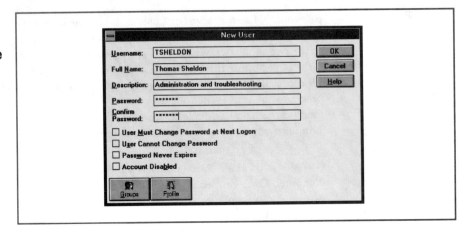

User Account Types

The Windows NT installation process creates three types of accounts:

☑ Administrator

☑ Guest

☑ Initial User

Whoever installs NT provides passwords for the Administrator account and for the Initial User account, which usually takes on the logon name of the person installing NT. If you plan for other people to use the system, you'll need to create additional user accounts for each person by logging on as the Administrator and using the User Manager utility to create those accounts.

The Administrator Account

The Administrator account is automatically created when NT is installed. You can rename the account but you cannot remove it. It is a member of the Administrator group and has all the access rights assigned to the group. You can add other user accounts to the Administrator group to give other users the same rights as the Administrator. The Administrator has the highest level of control on the NT system and is typically responsible for the following tasks:

☑ Changing system settings

☑ Configuring new hardware and software

☑ Managing user and group accounts

☑ Setting up directories and files to be shared for access by remote network users

☑ Creating connections to directories and files on remote NT servers

☑ Assigning directory and file access rights to users and groups

☑ Monitoring system usage and performance using tools provided with NT

If you are the Administrator, only log onto the Administrator account when absolutely necessary. Use the Initial User account or create a separate account through which you access the system for normal non-administrative tasks. You also can create an account that belongs to the Power User group (described shortly), which has some but not all of the rights available to the Administrator account. Don't be careless when using the Administrator account since you could cause data loss or unwarranted system changes. Always log off before walking away from the system. Never give out the Administrator password.

A fail-safe Administrator password is one in which two or more people type a portion of the password that only they know. Then, to gain Administrator access, all the people involved must retype their portion of the password.

The Guest Account

The Guest account, which is automatically created during NT installation, provides a way for users to log onto the system without a password. It is a member of the Guest group and has the rights of that group, which are extremely limited. Temporary users typically use the Guest account.

The Initial User Account

The Initial User is the person who installs NT and provides his or her own User name (for example, the Initial User account might have the name TSHELDON or IN-STALLER). The Initial User is the computer's primary user, and sometimes the only user if no one else needs to use the computer.

GROUP ACCOUNTS

All network operating systems provide group management features to simplify the task of assigning rights and permissions to large numbers of users. You create a user account, then make the user account a member of a group. Windows NT includes a set of predefined groups with predefined access rights that give its members the ability to perform various tasks and activities on the system.

There are two types of groups: local groups and global groups. *Local groups* only have rights at the workstation where the group is defined. A typical local group is the Power User group, which includes members with some but not all of the administrator rights for managing the local computer. *Global groups* include users outside the current workstation. A typical global group is NETWORK, which includes anyone accessing an NT server from another computer on the network.

Group Account Types

The following accounts are automatically created by NT. In most cases, one of these groups should provide an appropriate set of access rights for each specific user. If not, you can create your own groups and assign custom access rights by using the User Manager utility.

Note | The procedure is to create a user account, then add the user account to a predefined group that has the access rights appropriate for the user.

The Administrator Group

The Administrator group has the highest level of control and access on the NT workstation. The Administrator user account gets its access rights by being a member of the Administrator group. Initially, the group consists of the Administrator user account, the Initial User account, and, if the NT workstation is part of a Windows NT Advanced Server domain, the group called Domain Admins, which can be easily removed, if necessary.

The Administrator group has all the rights described in the "Rights" section later in this chapter. These capabilities allow the members of this group to perform these tasks:

- Create and manage user and group accounts on the local system
- Assign rights to users
- Lock and unlock the workstation
- Format and manage hard disks
- Create Program Manager common groups
- Make directories and printers shareable
- Maintain a local profile

The Power User Group

The Power User group is one step down from the Administrator group in its abilities to access the system. Members of the Power User group are accorded the right to do these things:

- ☑ Log on locally
- ☑ Access this computer from the network
- ☑ Change the system time
- ☑ Shut down the system

Members of the Power User group are like administrative assistants. One of the group's most important tasks is to create new user and group accounts and set up directory shares on the system. Power User group members can perform these tasks:

- ☑ Create and manage user and group accounts on the local system
- ☑ Lock but not override the lock on the workstation
- ☑ Create Program Manager common groups
- ☑ Make directories and printers shareable
- ☑ Maintain a local profile

The Users Group

All user accounts added after initial installation are added to the Users group. The Administrator, Guest, and Initial User accounts do not belong to the Users group. If the NT workstation is part of a Windows NT Advanced Server domain, the group called Domain Users is also part of the local Users group, but the Domain Users group can be removed for security reasons.

The Users group has the right to log on locally and shut down the system, and the ability to lock the workstation and keep a local profile. The group can be granted permissions to directories and files as needed.

The Guest Group

The Guest group, like the Guest account, provides limited access to the system for occasional or one-time users. Guest group members have the right to log on locally. You can grant the group directory and file permissions as needed. Think of guests as temporary employees.

Initially, anyone can sign in as Guest without a password; however, access to the system is extremely limited. For example, a guest user can start Write and save files to a floppy disk, but not to hard drives. You might want to upgrade the rights of the Guest account by creating a special document directory and granting guest users rights to store files in the directory.

The Everyone Group

The Everyone group includes all users who use the computer. When you need to grant rights and permissions to every user of the system, grant those rights and permissions to this group. The Everyone group also includes users who access the computer over the network, although these people are also included in the Users group. You can grant the group directory and file permissions as needed. Members of the group have the right to do these things:

☑   Log on locally

☑   Access this computer from the network

☑   Shut down the system

The Backup Operators Group

The Backup Operators group has the right to perform backup tasks, which requires the ability to read all files on the system, even files in which the owner has denied access to all users, including members of the Backup Operators group. The right to perform backup takes precedence over the file and directory rights applied by the directory or file owner. Backup operators have the right to do these things:

☑   Log on locally

☑   Shut down the system

☑   Back up files and directories

☑   Restore files and directories

Network and Interactive Groups

The Network group consists of all users who access the computer over a network connection and the Interactive group includes all local users of the computer. In other words, membership of these groups depends on who is currently accessing the system, either locally or over the network.

Creating Groups

Members of the Administrator and Power User groups can use the User Manager utility to create new groups and manage existing groups. The procedure for creating a new group is listed briefly here and covered in detail in Chapter 16:

1. Log on as an Administrator or Power User.

2. Start the User Manager, create a new group, then add members to the group from a list of user accounts.

3. Specify the rights the group has to the system. Rights are described shortly.

> **Note**
>
> In most cases, the default groups provided with Windows NT should have sufficient rights for most users.

WORKGROUPS AND DOMAINS

When an NT workstation needs to share its resources with other users or access shared resources on other computers, it participates in either a *workgroup* or *domain*. Workgroups are associated with NT's (and Windows for Workgroups) built-in peer-to-peer networking capabilities. Domains are associated with the NT Advanced Server product and provide enhanced security on large multi-server networks.

In a workgroup environment, the security accounts manager (SAM) database on each NT system holds information about how other users can access files and resources. In a domain, security information is stored on a central NT Advanced Server computer called the Primary Domain Controller (PDC). When users log on to a domain, they are authenticated by the PDC and can gain access to other servers based on the PDC information, rather than user account information at each server.

Workgroups

Every NT computer has a computer name and a workgroup name. The computer name identifies the computer to other users on the network. The primary purpose of the workgroup name is to organize computers into groups for browsing purposes. Assume you need to access files on a computer shared by another network user. You start the File Manager and choose the option that connects you with other computers. A list of those computers appears. If there are many computers attached to the network, it might take a while to search through the list, and the names might be ambiguous or misleading. By requiring workgroup names, NT (and Windows for Workgroups) provides a way to organize computers into groups such as departments, users, or tasks.

In small organizations, it's fine to include every computer in the same workgroup. In large companies, organizing computers into groups helps users easily locate specific computers. There are several possible organization methods. Figure 3-3 illustrates an organization with four departments. For clarity, only three users are discussed for each department and one of those users is a manager.

Figure 3-4 illustrates two possible ways you could organize workgroups. The left example organizes computers into a MANAGERS workgroup and a USERS workgroup. The right example organizes computers into departments. Note that these figures illustrate how the computers appear when browsing in the File Manager. The list is shown expanded but can be collapsed. For example, if you only wanted to see the computers listed under USERS on the left, you could collapse the list under MANAGERS. That's the point of workgroups. When browsing large lists, you can choose to view only selected groups of computers and ignore the rest.

Figure 3-5 shows one more example. This arrangement assumes that one computer in each department is a server and places those servers in their own workgroup called SERVERS. The USERS workgroup includes users' computers.

Domains

Windows NT Advanced Server domains are groups of networked computers most often associated with departments or workgroups in a company. Figure 3-6 shows three separate domains of a company.

FIGURE 3-3

An organization of workgroups

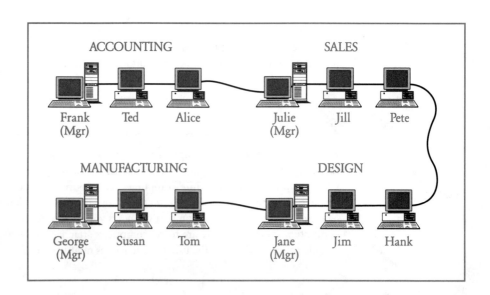

FIGURE 3-4

Two possible ways to
organize workgroups

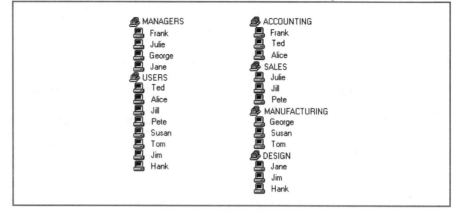

FIGURE 3-5

Workgroups can separate
server's from user's systems

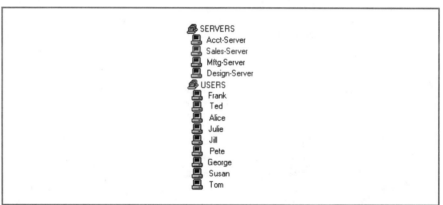

FIGURE 3-6

Domains

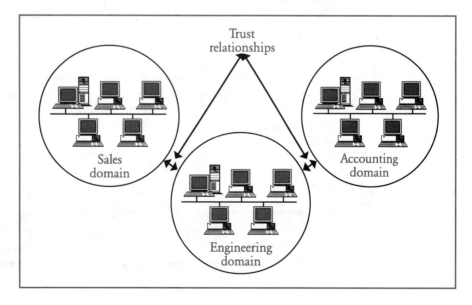

One server within a domain becomes a Primary Domain Controller (PDC) and a master user account database is placed on this server. Other servers in the domain are Backup Domain Controllers (BDCs), meaning they replicate the user account database on the PDC. Because there is a master database, users only need to log on once. Once authenticated, each user can access other servers on the network. If there are multiple domains, each has its own master user account database and users must have an account on each. However, Windows NT Advanced Server domains can trust each other. In other words, one domain trusts that another domain will properly authenticate users. The authenticated user can then access the trusting domain.

Administrators must specifically establish trust relationships. The separation of domains and the establishment of trust relationships is significant. For example, one company department can control which other departments can access its domain. In Figure 3-6, if the Sales domain can trust the Accounting domain, users in accounting can log onto servers in Sales.

More information on domains is provided in the Microsoft NT Advanced Server documentation, or you can contact your Microsoft representative.

RIGHTS AND PERMISSIONS

Rights and permissions control which actions users can perform on the system and the access they have to resources such as directories, files, and printers. There is a big difference between rights and permissions, however.

Rights control the actions a user can perform on the system, and usually come in sets. For example, the Backup Operator group has the *Backup* and *Restore* rights. Rights are attributed to groups, and users obtain the rights when made members of the groups.

Permissions give users access to directories, files, and resources such as printers. Permissions are assigned by Administrators, Power Users, or the owners of directories and files.

One important distinction between rights and permissions is that rights apply to the whole system, whereas permissions apply to specific directories and files. Another important difference is that rights are assigned or granted to users and groups through use of the User Manager utility. Permissions are granted to users in the File Manager or in the Print Manager.

Rights

Administrators assign rights to users and groups in the User Manager by opening the User Rights Policy dialog box, shown in Figure 3-7. You first choose one of the rights in the Right field, then select the user or group to which you want to grant that right by clicking

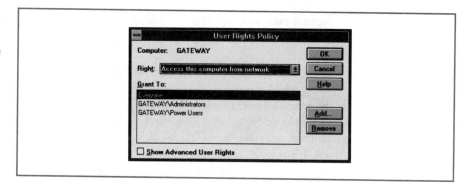

the Add button. A list of groups and users appears. When you select a group or user account, it appears in the Grant To field.

The following section explains each of the rights you can choose from in the Right field:

Log on locally   The right to log on locally allows the user to log on to the computer at the computer itself. All of the standard groups have this right.

Manager auditing and security log   Auditing provides a way to track and document major events on the system, such as disk saves, printing, or changes in security. An auditor can examine the auditing log when necessary. Users with this right specify the types of events to audit and can view and clear the auditing log. Chapter 16 describes auditing features. The Administrator group has this right by default.

Backup files and directories   Users with this right can back up files and directories, even if file and directory permissions normally prevent access to the files that need backing up. The Administrator and Backup Operator groups have this right by default.

Restore files and directories   Users with this right can restore files from backup sets. The Restore right supersedes file and directory permissions. The Administrator and Backup Operator groups have this right by default.

Change the system time   Users with this right can change the internal system time, which is not a trivial privilege. Changing the time affects event auditing, file date and time stamps, automatic backups, and other major events. The Administrator and Power User groups have this right by default.

Access this computer from network   This right allows network users to connect with the computer. The Administrator, Power User, and Everyone groups have this right by default. Since the Everyone group has the right, any user can connect with the system.

Shut down the system   This right allows users to shut down the NT operating system. All groups have this right except Guests.

Take ownership of files and other objects   This right allows a user to take ownership of a directory, file, printer, or other resource, thus overriding any permissions the previous owner may have applied. The Administrator group has this right. The Take Ownership event is auditable, which means it lets the auditor track the activities of administrators who might be looking at the private files of users.

Force shutdown from a remote system   This right is reserved for future versions of NT.

> **Note**
>
> There is an advanced set of rights typically used by programmers who write Windows NT applications. To see and administer these rights, enable the Show Advanced User Rights option on the User Rights Policy dialog box shown in Figure 3-7. Refer to the Microsoft NT manuals for more information.

Permissions

Permissions secure system resources such as directories, files, and printers. You grant permissions to users so they can access the resources. In other words, you select a directory, then select the users or groups that you want to access it, and finally select the specific type of access the user or group will have. For example, you could grant the Everyone group the Read (R) and Write (W) permission to a directory that holds documents. All users of the system, including network users, can then work with files in the directory since all users belong to the Everyone group.

> **Note**
>
> The following permissions apply only to local users, not to users accessing shared directories or files.

There are two types of permissions, *individual* and *standard.* Think of the individual permissions as the basic building blocks of standard permissions. Standard permissions are simply combinations of the individual permissions that users need to perform common tasks. They are grouped together to make permission administration easier. For example, Change is a standard permission that consists of the Read (R), Write (W), Execute (X), and Delete (D) individual permissions.

Permissions also come into play when you want to share a directory on your system with other network users. The permission you apply to the shared directory determines the type of access network users have to the directory.

Technically, only drives formatted to use the Windows NT file system (NTFS) support directory and file permissions. To secure drives formatted to use FAT and HPFS, use the File Manager directory sharing option to assign permissions. This is discussed later in this chapter in the "Granting Shared Directory Permissions" section.

Individual Permissions for Directories and Files

As mentioned, the individual permissions are the basic building blocks for the standard permission sets. The following describes each individual permission:

Read (R) If Read permission is given for directories, users can list files, display directory attributes, and display directory owners and their permissions. If given for a file or set of files, users can open the file and display its contents, its owner and permissions, and its attributes.

Write (W) If Write permission is given for directories, users can add files and subdirectories, change directory attributes, and display directory owners and permissions. If given for files, users can display the file's owner and permissions and change the file's attributes and contents.

Execute (X) If Execute permission is given for directories, users can display each directory's attributes, change to subdirectories, and display owners and permissions. If given for files, users can run the file as well as display the file's owner, permissions, and attributes.

Delete (D) The Delete permission allows users to delete directories or files, whichever they've been accorded permission to delete.

Change Permissions (P) The Change Permissions permission allows users to change permissions on directories or files, whichever they've been accorded permission to change.

Take Ownership (O) The Take Ownership permission allows users to assume ownership and control of a directory or file from another owner.

Standard Directory Permissions

The standard directory permissions control the access that local users and groups have to directories. Table 3-1 shows the individual permissions that each standard permission grants. Note that file permissions depend on the permissions set for each directory. The following paragraphs describe how permissions affect user access to directories.

TABLE 3-1

Standard Permissions and the Individual Permissions They Allow

Standard Permission	Individual Permissions in Directories	Individual Permissions for Files
No Access	None	None
All	All	All
List	R X	Not applicable
Read	R X	R X
Add	W X	W X
Add & Read	R W X	R X
Change	R W X D	R W X D
Full Control	R W X D P O	R W X D P O
Special	R W X D	Not specified

No Access   The No Access permission revokes all permissions users have to the directory or file.

List   For directories, the List permission allows users to switch to subdirectories, list files, and display directory attributes, owners, and permissions. It does not affect files.

Read   For directories, the Read permission allows users to switch to subdirectories, list files, and display directory attributes, owners, and permissions. For files, it allows users to run the file if it is a program, and display the file's data, owner, permissions, and attributes.

Add   For directories, the Add permission allows users to display each directory's attributes, owners, and permissions, as well as add and change subdirectories, files, and attributes. It does not affect files.

Add & Read   For directories, the Add & Read permission allows users to list files, display attributes, owners, and permissions, as well as create subdirectories, add files to them, and change their attributes. For files, it allows users to display each file's owner, permissions, contents, and attributes, as well as run the file if it is a program.

Change   For directories, the Change permission has all the features of Add & Read and also lets users delete directories and subdirectories. For files, it allows users to display each file's owner, permissions, and contents, as well as run the file if it is a program. Users also can view and change attributes and the file's contents, as well as delete the file.

Full Control   For both directories and files, the Full Control permission allows all the permissions of Change and adds the ability to change permissions and take ownership of the directory or file.

You assign permissions to directories and files with the Permissions option in the File Manager. You first select the directory or file, then open the Directory Permissions dialog box shown in Figure 3-8. The Name field lists current groups that have access to the directory or file. The Type of Access field shows the standard permission assignable to the selected user or group. In Figure 3-8, the list is open to show its available options.

Note that you can define your own set of individual permissions. The Type of Access drop-down list box contains two special options called "Special Directory Access" and "Special File Access." When you select one of these options, you see a dialog box like that pictured in Figure 3-9. You use this dialog box to essentially create a custom permission set that you can grant to a user or group.

Note how permissions appear in the Name field of the dialog box shown in Figure 3-8. The type of permission appears to the right of each user or group name. To the right of that are descriptions of the individual rights, first for directories, and then for files. The information listed in these fields is the same as that listed in Table 3-1.

The permissions that a user has to a directory or file may come from several sources. For example, a user might belong to two separate groups that grant different types of access to a directory. The user gets the highest level of access made possible by the two groups except that a No Access permission overrides all other permissions.

Files in directories inherit the permissions of the directory. If you create a subdirectory, it inherits the permissions of its parent directory, but you can change the permissions if necessary.

FIGURE 3-8

The Directory Permissions
dialog box

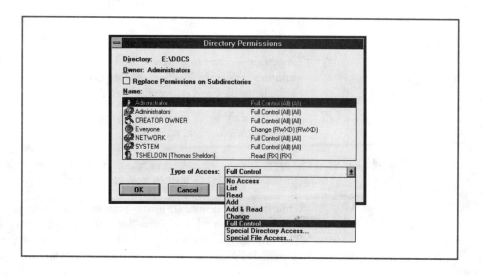

FIGURE 3-9

The Special Directory Access
dialog box

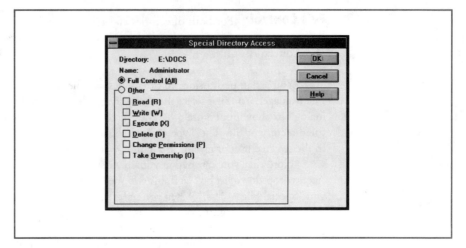

You also can create custom permissions from the individual permission set described earlier and apply the custom set to either a directory or file.

Granting Shared Directory Permissions

You use the File Manager to share directories on your system with other users on the network. There are four permissions that control what access network users have to the directory:

▧   *No Access* revokes all permissions users have to the shared directory and its files.

▧   *Read* allows users to switch to subdirectories, list files, and display directory attributes.

▧   *Change* allows users to switch to subdirectories, list files, and display directory attributes as does the Read permission. Users can also create subdirectories, add files, change files, and change file attributes.

▧   *Full Control* allows all the permissions of Change along with the ability to change permissions and take ownership of the directory or file.

Note

You can apply these permissions to FAT and HPFS drives—not just to NTFS drives. These permissions apply to all files and subdirectories of the shared directory.

While share permissions are usually granted to users who access the directories from another computer, they also apply to local users from whom you want to protect non-NTFS drives. Normally, only NTFS drives support access permissions. This information is included with the file itself. FAT and HPFS drives do not provide a place for permission information. However, you can use the sharing features to apply permission to FAT and HPFS drives for network users, although the permission sets are not as extensive as NTFS permissions.

PART TWO

Using Windows NT

Inside

& Out

CHAPTER

4

Starting and Using Windows NT

This chapter assumes that Windows NT is
already installed in your computer and you're
ready to start using it. Refer to Appendix A for
installation instructions. First, you'll learn about
starting Windows NT. Then you'll learn about
window elements, such as menus and scroll bars.
You'll also see how to rearrange windows to fit
your own needs.

STARTING WINDOWS NT

Windows NT is a secure operating system, which means you must always log on before you can do any work. There are several possible logon possibilities, as you'll see shortly.

   If the computer is off and you start it, you may see the OS Loader screen shown here:

```
OS Loader

Please select the operating system to start:

Windows NT
MS-DOS
```

   (This screen only appears if operating systems besides Windows NT are installed on your computer.) Choose Windows NT from the list. In a moment, you'll see a small dialog box that asks you to press CTRL-ALT-DEL to start Windows NT. Unlike DOS systems, the CTRL-ALT-DEL key sequence does not reboot the computer. Instead, it executes a new logon and clears any programs from memory that might attempt to capture your password. The Welcome dialog box shown in Figure 4-1 appears so you can enter your account name and password.

Never type your name and password in the Welcome dialog box unless you have pressed CTRL-ALT-DEL yourself to make it appear. Someone may have written a program that imitates the dialog box for the purpose of capturing your password. Always press CTRL-ALT-DEL to log on.

   In the Welcome dialog box, type your user account name in the Username field. The name of the last user to log on appears in the box by default. You might need to specify a workgroup name in the From field. Finally, type your password in the Password field and click the OK button with the mouse.

FIGURE 4-1

The Welcome dialog box

If you are logging onto a Windows NT Advanced Server domain, type the domain name in the From field or choose it from the list by clicking the down arrow button.

THE WINDOWS NT INTERFACE

When you first start Windows NT, you see the Program Manager window shown in Figure 4-2. The basic elements of this window are listed and discussed in the following sections. Note that this window may appear slightly different on your system.

The entire screen area is known as the *desktop*. The Program Manager window is placed on top of the desktop. Other application windows that you open also rest on the desktop. One window is always *active,* which means its title bar is highlighted and it reacts when you use certain keyboard keys. The active window usually overlaps other, nonactive windows. Use the mouse to click the nonactive windows and make them active. (Later you'll learn several keyboard methods of making nonactive windows active.)

A mouse is essential to using the Windows NT interface. With it, you click window elements such as buttons and scroll bars, or click and drag items on the desktop. Keyboard methods for accessing Windows NT are available, but using a mouse is much easier in most cases. There are three actions that you perform with the mouse in Windows NT:

- You click a button or option once to select it.

- You double-click an option to execute it.

FIGURE 4-2

The Windows NT Program Manager window

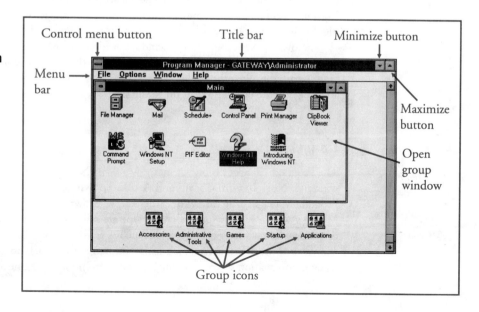

Group icons

☑   You click and drag. This action is the equivalent of grabbing an object such as a window or an icon and moving it to another location. You click, hold the button down while dragging, and then release the mouse to drop the object.

The Program Manager

Think of the Program Manager as the "main menu" for Windows NT. Its primary purpose is to provide a quick and easy method for starting applications. The Program Manager window holds icons that you double-click to start applications. Note that the title bar of the Program Manager window displays your computer name and logon account name.

Find the Control Panel icon in the Program Manager Main group and double-click it now. An hourglass appears as the application loads. In a moment, you see the Control Panel window overlapping the Program Manager window.

To move a window, position the mouse pointer over the Control Panel's title bar, and then click and hold the mouse button. Drag the window to another position on the desktop, and then release the mouse.

Click anywhere on the Program Manager window to make it active and bring it to the top of the stack.

The Program Manager contains groups of *program startup icons*, or icons that you double-click to start programs. The group called Main is open in Figure 4-2. Four other groups, Accessories, Administrative Tools, Games, and Startup are available, and if you installed Windows NT on an existing system, you may see an Applications group that contains icons of existing programs. These icons are *minimized groups*. Double-click these icons to open them as windows within the Program Manager window. Try double-clicking the Accessories group icon now to open its window and display the icons within it.

Now the Accessories group window overlaps the Main group window within the Program Manager window. Double-click one of the icons to start the associated program—for example, try double-clicking the Clock icon. When the Clock appears, click and drag its title bar to move it off to the side.

Document Windows

The Program Manager is one of many Windows NT applications that contains its own windows. Notice that the Main and Accessories windows are within the borders of the Program Manager. You cannot drag these subwindows outside the borders of the Program Manager window. Subwindows of this type are called *document windows*. They are most common when working in applications such as word processors or drawing programs that allow you to work on several documents simultaneously. Each document window holds its own information so you can quickly switch from one to the next.

Microsoft Word for Windows uses document windows. Figure 4-3 illustrates Microsoft Word for Windows with two open document windows. The title bar of each displays the loaded document name. The important thing to know about document windows is that each has its own window elements, but also shares the commands and menu options of the main application.

The Desktop

The desktop is the underlying background for Windows NT. It takes up the entire screen. As you open more applications, they'll begin to cover the desktop and overlap one another. If you opened Control Panel and Clock previously, you'll notice that they take up most of the desktop unless you have a high-resolution screen with a large desktop.

To make a different window active, click any visible portion of that window with the mouse. If you can't see the window, try one of the following techniques to make it active:

☑ Double-click any visible part of the desktop to display the Task List dialog box shown in Figure 4-4. Double-click the name of the application you want to work with to make it the active window.

☑ If windows completely cover the desktop, press CTRL-ESC to open the Task List dialog box.

☑ Minimize open windows (with the instructions given next).

FIGURE 4-3

Two open document windows
in an application

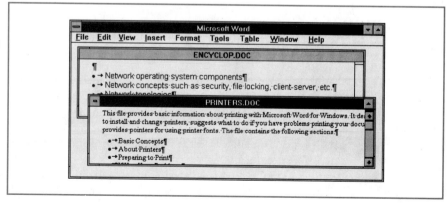

FIGURE 4-4

The Task List dialog box

Applications on the Desktop

When the desktop gets cluttered, you can *temporarily* shrink open windows by clicking the minimize button (the down arrow button in the upper-right corner of the window that you saw in Figure 4-2). When a running application is *minimized,* its icon appears at the bottom of the desktop. This icon looks like the icon in the Program Manager, but don't get the two mixed up. The one on the desktop is a running application; it's still in memory and may contain documents in its workspace.

Click the minimize button of the Clock and Control Panel. Note that Write's icon displays the name of the document in its workspace and that Clock still displays the time in its minimized state. To restore a minimized application, double-click its icon.

To *maximize* an application, or display the window of an application full-screen over the entire desktop, use the maximize button. This gives you the maximum amount of room to work with the documents in your applications, and improves performance since Windows NT doesn't need to update other windows on the screen.

Maximize the Clock now and notice that its maximize button converts to a Restore button with an up and down arrow. Click it to restore the window to its previous size, or click the minimize button to place Write as an icon on the desktop.

SIZING AND REARRANGING WINDOWS

You can resize windows by dragging their borders. If you drag a border inward, you shrink the window. Dragging a border toward the edge of the screen enlarges the window. There are several reasons you may want to resize windows. For instance, you may want to work with two applications side by side, or view the contents of one window while working in another. You also can resize windows to make underlying windows visible so you can easily select them.

The Clock is a good window to resize. It displays the time while you work in another window and doesn't need to be large. Try either of these methods to resize it:

☑   Change one side   Point to any side of an open window. When the double-headed arrow appears, click and drag inward or outward.

☑   Change two sides   Point to any corner of an open window. When the double-headed diagonal arrow appears, click and drag inward or outward.

As you drag the side or corner of a border, a shadow border follows the pointer to indicate the window's new size. Release the mouse button when the shadow border indicates the size you want the window to be.

After resizing a window, you'll probably want to move it or place it beside another window. Click the window's title bar, and then drag the window to its new location.

The Task List Dialog Box

The Task List dialog box provides a way to quickly rearrange the open windows on the desktop. Before you try using it, restore the windows of the applications you've opened so far (Control Panel, Clock, and Program Manager). Remember, a restored window is neither minimized nor maximized. When you use the restore button, the window reverts to its default size.

Cascading and Tiling Windows

Double-click a blank portion of the desktop, or press CTRL-ESC to open the Task List dialog box shown in Figure 4-4. The Task List dialog box has six buttons but for now you'll concentrate on just two: Cascade and Tile. Click each to see what happens to the open windows.

Cascade   Cascading arranges open windows so that they are staggered, one behind another. This arrangement is useful because it keeps windows large enough to work in, but makes them easy to select.

Tile   When you tile windows, they align edge to edge, like tiles on a countertop. Tiling is useful when you want to see the contents of each open window or place two open windows side by side.

Try this. Minimize the Clock, then open the Task List (CTRL-ESC) and click the Tile button again. Now only two open windows are tiled, assuming you still have the desktop arrangement discussed earlier. Notice how much easier two side-by-side windows are to work with.

Note	When windows are tiled or cascaded, click the maximize button of the window you want to use. When done, restore the window.

Other Task List Options

The Task List dialog box provides ways to switch to, close, and arrange windows or icons on the desktop. Here are several techniques:

- To close an application from the Task List dialog box, highlight its name and click the End Task button.

- To arrange icons on the desktop, click the Arrange Icons button.

- Start another application by typing its name in the New Task field and clicking the Run button.

Switching Among Applications

There are two keyboard methods of switching among applications:

- Press ALT-ESC to highlight each open application or application icon, one after the other, until the application you want is highlighted.

- Hold down the ALT key, then repeatedly press TAB to preview each open application or icon. A title box appears in the middle of the screen for each open application as you press TAB. Release the ALT key when the name of the window you want appears.

OTHER WINDOWS ELEMENTS

There are a few other windows elements to explore. This section explains menus, dialog boxes, and scroll bars.

Menus

The Program Manager has four *drop-down* menus: File, Options, Window, and Help. You can use one of the following methods to open a menu:

☑   Click the menu name with the mouse.

☑   Press ALT followed by the underlined letter of the menu name. For example, press ALT-F to open the File menu.

☑   If one drop-down menu is open, press the RIGHT ARROW or LEFT ARROW keys to scan across the menu bar and open other drop-down menus.

In some applications, you can actually click and drag drop-down menus to other places on the desktop for future use. These are called *tear-off menus.*
To choose an option on a drop-down menu, do one of the following:

☑   Click an option with the mouse.

☑   Type the underlined letter of the option.

☑   Press the DOWN ARROW key to move the highlight to the option, and then press ENTER.

Other items you'll encounter on menus are labeled in Figure 4-5 and described next.

Quick Keys   Some menu options have *quick keys* so you can execute the option when opening the menu. Click File on the Program Manager menu bar and notice that Move's quick key is F7, Copy's is F8, and so on.

Unavailable Options   An unavailable option is "grayed out," meaning that it's not currently available for selection. Usually, you must choose something before the menu option becomes available.

Ellipsis Options   The ellipsis (...) in a menu option indicates that a dialog box opens when the option is selected. You enter additional parameters and options in the dialog box when executing commands.

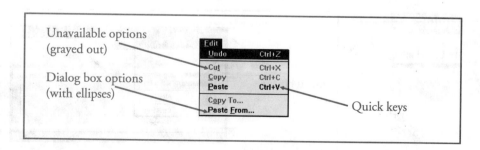

FIGURE 4-5

Items encountered on menus

Toggle Options   A toggle option has a check mark when enabled. If there's no check mark, it's disabled. Open the Program Manager Options menu and note the status of the Auto Arrange and Save Settings on Exit option. They are enabled by default. If you click the Auto Arrange option, you disable it and the menu closes. To reenable it, open the menu and click it again.

The Control Menu

The Control menu button is in the upper-left corner of every window. When you click the Control menu button, the so-called Control menu appears, as shown in Figure 4-6. You also can press ALT-SPACEBAR on the keyboard to display the menu (ALT-HYPHEN for document windows). The options on this menu are really designed for keyboard users. They provide keyboard methods for resizing, moving, minimizing, and maximizing a window.

To close a window, choose the Close option, or better yet, double-click the Control menu button. The Switch To option opens the Task List dialog box.

Dialog Boxes

A dialog box opens when you select a menu item that has an ellipsis. Click the About Program Manager option on the Help menu to display the About Program Manager dialog box shown in Figure 4-7. This dialog box indicates the version number of Windows NT, the serial number of your copy, and the owner's name. The amount of memory available to Windows NT is listed at the bottom of the dialog box.

> | **Note** | Most Windows and Windows NT applications have their own About dialog boxes that display the version number and other information.

Figure 4-8 shows a dialog box with a number of different controls. You use these controls to set options or make decisions about how a command should run. The advantage of dialog boxes is that they present you with options so you don't need to look

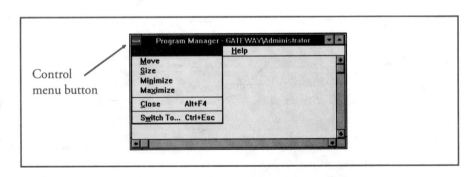

FIGURE 4-6

The Control menu

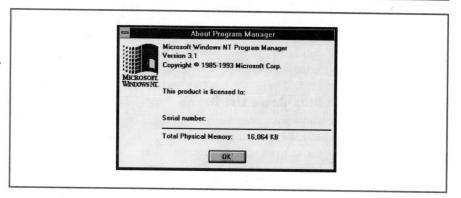

FIGURE 4-7

The About Program Manager
dialog box

them up in a book. Every dialog box is different, but you set options using the same
features, which are described next.

Command Buttons   Dialog boxes usually have an OK button to execute the
command or a Cancel button to abort. Most also have a Help button. Buttons with an
ellipsis display an additional dialog box when clicked.

Text Boxes   You simply type at the keyboard to input text in dialog boxes when you
need to supply additional information. You access a text box by clicking it, or by pressing
the TAB key until its contents are highlighted. When you type new text, the highlighted
text is overwritten.

FIGURE 4-8

Examples of fields and
options in dialog boxes

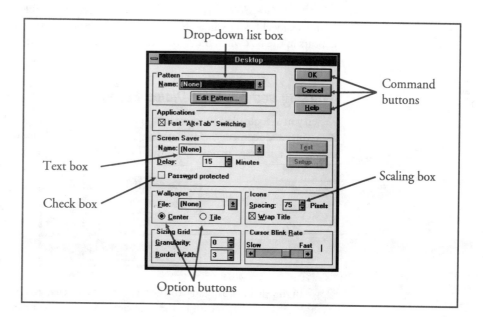

List Boxes   List boxes let you scroll to locate an option in a list of options. To select the option you want, simply click it when it appears. A list box has a scroll bar, as discussed in the next section.

Drop-Down List Boxes   A drop-down list box is a one-line text box with a down arrow button next to it. When you click the down arrow button, a drop-down list appears with a more complete list of options. When you click one of the options, it appears in the text box and the drop-down list disappears. Program designers use drop-down list boxes to save room in dialog boxes.

Scaling Boxes   Boxes with numeric values, dates, and the time have UP ARROW and DOWN ARROW keys you can click to increase or decrease the values in the boxes. You can also just type a new value in most cases.

Scroll Bars   You use the scroll bars in dialog boxes to change values. You can click and drag the scroll bar button, or click the arrow buttons at either end of the scroll bar. Note that scroll bars are also used on windows to move through the window's contents. You'll learn about scrolling in the next section.

Option Buttons   Option buttons are usually grouped in sets and surrounded by a box, as are the two option buttons in the Wallpaper field in Figure 4-8. If one is selected, the other is disabled. Only one option button can be on in each set.

Check Boxes   You click check boxes to enable or disable options. Unlike option buttons, any check box in a group can be set without affecting other check boxes. An X appears in the box when the item is enabled.

Warning and Message Dialog Boxes

When you execute illegal commands and options, or if you forget an important step (such as saving a document before closing an application), Windows NT warns you by displaying a message dialog box, similar to the one shown here:

In this dialog box, you can click Yes to save the changes, No to exit without saving changes, or Cancel to return to the application without saving or exiting.

Scroll Bars

There are two types of scroll bars: vertical and horizontal. A vertical scroll bar scrolls a window's contents up and down. A horizontal scroll bar scrolls a window's contents left and right when the contents are too wide to fit in the window. A scroll bar is shown here:

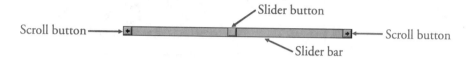

To experiment with scroll bars, double-click the Windows NT Help icon in the Main group window. If you don't see scroll bars, reduce the size of the window by clicking and dragging the lower-right corner up. Try the following experiments with the scroll bar:

- Click the scroll buttons to move through the text. The slider button also moves to indicate the new position in the text.

- Click and hold the scroll buttons for continuous scrolling.

- The slider bar is a measure of the document width or length. You can click it to scroll one page or screen at a time.

- Click and drag the slider button anywhere in the slider bar. The document view changes to display text relative to the position of the slider button in the slider bar. For example, if you move the slider button halfway down the slider bar, when you release it, the information onscreen will be about halfway into your document.

When finished working with Windows NT Help, click its minimize button to remove it from the desktop.

CUSTOMIZING WITH CONTROL PANEL OPTIONS

In this section, you'll get a chance to work with some Windows NT features by changing the colors of Windows NT, and by placing a picture on the desktop. To perform these tasks you'll use the options located in the Control Panel. Open the Control Panel now by double-clicking the Control Panel icon you have on your desktop, or if you closed it, double-click the Control Panel icon in the Main group window of the Program Manager. A window similar to Figure 4-9 appears.

You start utilities from the Control Panel that help you customize the Windows NT interface, install and configure hardware, change network settings, and change the settings of your system, such as its date, time, country settings, mouse settings, sounds, and more. Control Panel settings are discussed in appropriate sections throughout this book.

FIGURE 4-9

The Control Panel

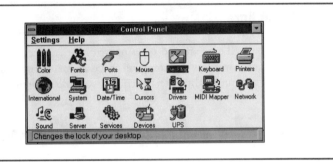

Changing Colors

To change the colors you see on your screen, double-click the Color icon. The Color dialog box opens. At the top is the Color Schemes drop-down list box. It is highlighted when you first open the dialog box, so simply press the DOWN ARROW key on your keyboard to scroll through the color scheme options. As you press the key, various color scheme samples appear in the middle of the dialog box. When you find one you like, click the OK button.

You can create custom color schemes by clicking the Color Palette button, which is explained in Chapter 14.

Pictures on the Desktop

Now try placing a picture on your desktop. Double-click the Desktop icon in the Control Panel. Figure 4-8 illustrates the Desktop dialog box, which has a wide range of options. Locate the Wallpaper field, then click the down arrow button on the File field. Scroll through the drop-down list until you can click the LEAVES.BMP file entry. Next, click the Tile button, then click the OK button to make the changes. A leaf pattern appears over the entire desktop. Take a few moments to try some of the other options. If you want to remove the wallpaper pattern, choose None in the field.

REARRANGING THE PROGRAM MANAGER

The Program Manager arrangement you see when Windows NT first starts is fine for new users, but you can resize its window and rearrange its group windows to fit your own needs. There are also a few options to enable, as discussed in the next sections.

Setting Options

The first thing to do is set the Program Manager options. Click the Options menu and note the status of the following options.

Auto Arrange   When Auto Arrange is enabled, icons within Program Manager groups automatically rearrange themselves to fit within a resized window. When Auto Arrange is disabled, you must manually rearrange icons or manually choose the Arrange Icons option from the Window menu. In most cases, you'll want this option enabled.

Minimize on Use   When Minimize on Use is enabled, the Program Manager shrinks to an icon when you start an application. When Minimize on Use is disabled, the Program Manager stays on the desktop. You can enable this option to minimize the number of windows on the desktop.

Save Settings on Exit   When Save Settings on Exit is enabled, any changes you make to the size and arrangement of windows are saved for the next session. For example, if you leave the Accessories window open on top of the Main group window when exiting, that's how it will appear the next time you start Windows NT. Disable this option if you've made an arrangement you don't want to keep.

Save Settings Now   After making changes to the arrangement of groups or the size of windows in the Program Manager, click this option. It saves your changes immediately. Use this option when the Save Settings on Exit option is disabled as a way to save any changes you've made.

Resizing and Rearranging Group Windows

You can resize and rearrange the group windows in the Program Manager the same way you resize and rearrange application windows on the desktop. Try the following examples to get an idea of the options available.

Tip

Before starting these examples, make sure Auto Arrange on the Options menu is enabled.

Tiling Group Windows

When you tile windows, they are placed side by side and made to fit within the current Program Manager window. Before choosing the Tile option from the Window menu, you might want to resize the Program Manager window. Try this now by tiling the group windows before and after resizing the Program Manager window. You also can try tiling after closing one group window or opening another.

Cascading Group Windows

Now cascade the group windows. Open the Games group, then choose Cascade from the Window menu. All the open group windows are stacked and staggered. Resize the Program Manager and choose Cascade again. Note that the last window selected is at the top of the cascade. Click any group window, then choose Cascade again to place that group window at the top of the stack.

Custom Group Arrangements

You don't need to rely on the Tile and Cascade options for your group window arrangements. You can resize each group window to a size that's appropriate for the number of icons they hold, then place them side by side in a custom tiled arrangement as shown in Figure 4-10.

Taking this a step further, you can even create your own groups, then copy the icons in the Main, Accessories, and Games groups into them. Thus, you might have a Daily group that contains the File Manager, Command Prompt, Write, Calendar, Calculator, and other programs you use on a daily basis. You can create your own icons to add to this group, as well. Chapter 12 explains how to create custom groups and icons.

FIGURE 4-10

A custom group arrangement

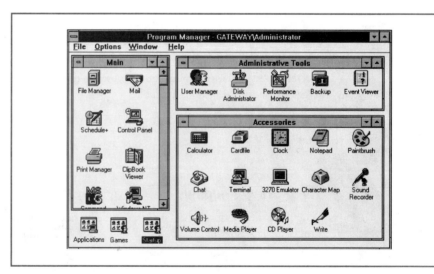

CLOSING APPLICATIONS AND LOGGING OFF

It is important to properly log off of Windows NT or shut the system down when you're ready to leave it. There are two methods for logging off:

 Choose Logoff from the File menu to close your user account. This option is preferable if another user needs to log on since some of Windows remains in memory and doesn't need to be reloaded. All of your private information is removed from memory, however.

 Choose Shutdown to completely close down Windows NT. When it's safe to shut off your computer, you'll see a dialog box with a Restart button.

Caution   Never turn off your computer without properly shutting down. Windows NT uses a disk-caching system that keeps information in memory until it can find a convenient time to write it to disk. This information may be lost if you turn off your computer without closing it first.

When you choose the Logoff option, the Logoff Windows NT dialog box appears, as shown here:

Click the OK button to execute the logoff procedure. In a moment, the Welcome menu appears that instructs a user to press CTRL-ALT-DEL to log on. You may turn off the computer at this point or turn access over to another user.

The Windows NT Security Dialog Box

Press CTRL-ALT-DEL at any time to lock your system, change your password, log off, or shut down Windows NT. The Windows NT Security dialog box shown in Figure 4-11 appears. This dialog box lets you perform all these tasks:

 Click the Lock Workstation button to prevent access to Windows NT. This is a convenient way to lock your system without closing the applications you have open if you need to go to lunch or briefly leave your computer. You must type your normal logon password to reaccess the system.

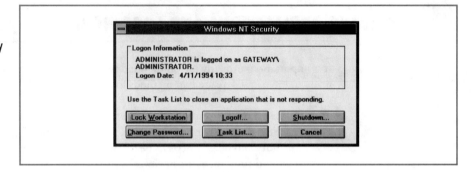

FIGURE 4-11

Press CTRL-ALT-DEL to display the Windows NT Security dialog box

☑ Click the Change Password button to change your logon password. You must type the current password, type a new password, and then retype the new password for confirmation.

☑ Click the Logoff or Shutdown buttons to properly exit your Windows NT user account. These are the same options found on the Program Manager File menu discussed earlier.

☑ Click the Task List button to display the Task List dialog box discussed earlier.

☑ Click the Cancel button to return to Windows NT.

Inside

- Starting Applications from the Program Manager

- Starting Applications from the File Manager

- Running Non-NT Applications

& Out

CHAPTER 5

Starting and Using Applications

Chapter 4 covered the basics of starting Windows NT. This chapter covers methods for starting applications for those who are anxious to get some work done with their programs.

STARTING APPLICATIONS FROM THE PROGRAM MANAGER

Once Windows NT loads and the Program Manager window is on the screen, you can start applications by double-clicking their icons. Program Manager groups have an interesting feature. The icon of the last program executed in a group is highlighted the next time you open that group. To start that program, just press ENTER. You can highlight any icon in a group by pressing the arrow keys, and then press ENTER to start it, but you can always use your mouse to double-click the icon of the program you want to start.

Another way to start a program is to press its quick-key combination. You also can place the icon for the program in the Startup group so it loads every time Windows NT starts.

Using Quick Keys

You can assign a quick-key sequence to icons in the Program Manager, making it possible to start any program from the keyboard. When starting a program with quick keys, you don't need to open the group window that contains the program. Quick keys reduce the number of steps it takes to start a program, and you don't have to search through group windows to find the startup icon. You do need to remember the quick keys, though.

To assign quick keys to an icon, first select the icon. For example, highlight the Command Prompt icon in the Main group by clicking it once. Now choose Properties from the File menu to display the Program Item Properties dialog box, as shown in Figure 5-1. Press TAB to get to the Shortcut Key field, then type a letter on the keyboard (such as C for Command). The quick-key sequence CTRL-ALT-C is automatically inserted in the field. Click OK to save your changes. After that, you need only press CTRL-ALT-C to start the Command Prompt. When you get to the DOS prompt, type **EXIT** and press ENTER to return to Windows NT.

FIGURE 5-1

Assigning quick keys to
start programs

Starting Minimized Applications

The Program Item Properties dialog box, as you've seen, is where you make changes to the startup properties of icons in the Program Manager. One interesting option is the Run Minimized check box. When enabled, the application starts, but immediately minimizes to an icon on the desktop. You don't need this setting if you normally use an application as soon as its starts.

Highlight the Command Prompt in the Main group again by clicking it once, then choose Properties from the File menu. The dialog box shown in Figure 5-1 appears again. Enable the Run Minimized check box and click the OK button to save your changes.

Note	Enable the Run Minimized option for programs you include in the Startup group, as discussed next.

The Startup Group

Any program icon added to the Startup group is automatically loaded when Windows NT starts. You can add multiple program startup icons to the Startup group.

To copy icons to the group, first open the group window that holds the icon you want to start. In the following example, you'll open the Main group and copy the File Manager icon to the Startup group. First make sure the Startup group icon is visible in the Program Manager window, and then follow these steps:

1. Hold the CTRL key, then click and drag the File Manager icon to the Startup group. This makes a copy of the icon.

2. Release the mouse button when the icon is over the Startup group.

3. Double-click the Startup group and click the File Manager icon. Choose Properties from the File menu, mark the Run Minimized check box, and click OK.

4. Close the Startup window since you don't need it open during normal operations.

The next time you start Windows NT, the File Manager will load automatically.

Holding the CTRL key makes a copy of the icon, but in cases in which you want to reorganize the Program Manager windows, you can "move" an icon from one window to another by simply clicking and dragging it.

Tip	Always copy icons (as opposed to moving them) into the Startup group. This leaves a copy of the icon in the group where you would most expect to find it later if you need to restart the application.

The Run Command

If an icon doesn't exist for an application that you want to run, choose the Run command from the Program Manager File menu. The Run dialog box appears, as shown here:

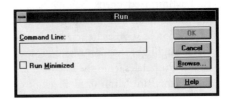

In the Command Line field, type the command that starts the program. If it is a DOS command, use the same syntax you would type at the DOS command prompt. Include parameters and options (such as document filenames) if necessary. Click the Run Minimized check box if you want the application to start as a minimized icon on the desktop. The following command starts Microsoft Word for DOS and loads the file REPORTS.DOC in its workspace:

```
C:\WORD5\WORD.EXE  C:\DOCS\REPORTS.DOC
```

The command includes the path to WORD.EXE and the path to the document files. If Word is on the DOS path, you can just type **WORD**. The path to the document file is necessary, however.

Click the Browse button if you can't remember the name of a program. The Browse dialog box appears so you can search through the file system for the program you want to start. This procedure is covered in Chapter 6.

Opening Associated Files

An *associated file* is linked by its filename extension to the program that created it. If you include a document filename in the Command Line field of the Run dialog box, the document will load into the workspace of the application, assuming the application is accessible on the system.

These are the most common filename extensions:

.BMP	Paintbrush
.CAL	Calendar
.CRD	Cardfile
.HLP	Help
.INI	Notepad
.TRM	Terminal
.TXT	Notepad
.WRI	Write

You can try this now. Open the Run dialog box and type **LEAVES.BMP** in the Command Line field. When you click OK, Paintbrush starts and loads the LEAVES.BMP file in its workspace.

Creating Your Own Startup Icons

Now you're ready to create your own startup icons. In this section, you'll create a startup icon for the Windows NT registration editor, which is an administrative tool used to inspect or modify configuration information contained in the Registry. As you become more proficient with Windows NT, you might need to use this utility to change the configuration. Follow these steps to create a startup icon for it:

1. In the Program Manager, open the Administrative Tools group.

Note

You must always select a group before creating an icon for it.

2. Choose New from the File menu.

3. The New Program Object dialog box appears with the Program Item option highlighted. Click OK to create a new program item.

4. The Program Item Properties dialog box appears, as shown here:

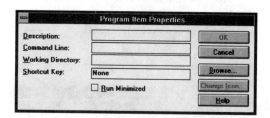

This is the Properties box you've already seen, but with blank fields.

5. In both the Description field and the Command Line field, type **REGEDT32**. Use the TAB key to move to the next field.

6. Don't worry about the remaining options for now. Click the OK button to create the icon.

The icon appears in the Main group. You'll use this same technique later to create icons for your own applications. You also can create icons for documents that you work with every day.

STARTING APPLICATIONS FROM THE FILE MANAGER

The File Manager is the Windows NT utility for viewing and working with files on your local system or remote server systems. You use it to copy, move, rename, delete, and execute documents or program files. If you are accustomed to managing files with DOS commands, you'll appreciate mouse techniques for selecting and copying files. You simply click a file icon and drag it to another folder to make a copy, or double-click a program file to execute it.

Note

This section concentrates on starting programs and opening documents with the File Manager. Using the File Manager for everyday tasks is covered in Chapter 7. Chapter 13 covers details about the File Manager interface and how to customize it.

Start the File Manager now by double-clicking its icon in the Main group. The File Manager window appears, as shown in Figure 5-2.

Note the document window in the File Manager workspace. Its title bar reads "E:\winnt*.*" which is the name of the directory listed in the window. The right half of the window lists files, and the left half lists the directory tree.

Note

The following discussions assume you have a directory window open to the \WINNT directory.

You start programs from the File Manager the same way you start them from the Program Manager, except you double-click the executable file that starts the program. For example, locate the icon called NOTEPAD.EXE in the file list, then double-click it. The Notepad accessory opens.

FIGURE 5-2

The File Manager window

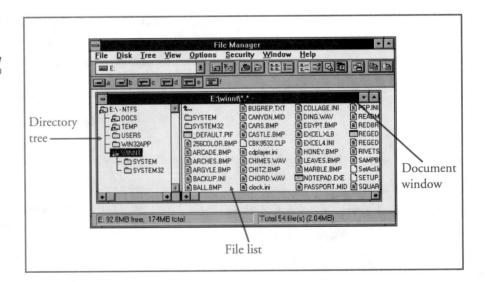

Directory tree

Document window

File list

The icons in the File Manager are described here:

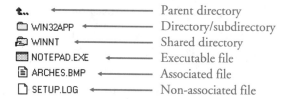

You can double-click any executable icon to start the program associated with it.
Now locate the icon for the file ARCHES.BMP in the file list and double-click it.
This file is associated with Paintbrush, so when you double-click it Paintbrush opens with
ARCHES.BMP in its workspace. Double-click the Control button of the Write window
to close it for now.

Locating Files

Instead of searching through the list of all files, you can list only executable files or only
associated document files. Try the following to see how this works. Choose By File Type
from the View menu to display the dialog box shown here:

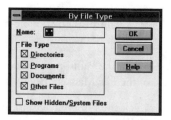

In the File Type field, disable all the options except Programs, then click the OK
button. The file list changes to show only program files.

Now open a new window and change the file listing so only associated document
files are listed. First, choose New Window from the Window menu (or double-click the
icon of the drive that holds your Windows NT files). A second directory window appears.
Choose By File Type from the View menu, then disable the Programs check box and
enable the Documents check box. Finally, click OK. The second directory window now
shows only associated document files in the directory. Choose Sort by Type from the
View menu to sort these files in order of their filename extensions. This groups associated
files.

You can do two other things to arrange the directory windows you've opened in
these exercises:

☑ Choose Directory Only from the View menu to remove the tree from the current directory window. Click the other directory window to make it active and remove the tree from it as well.

☑ Choose Cascade from the Window menu to fit both directory windows in the File Manager workspace.

With the cascade arrangement, you can easily start any program or open any document from the File Manager. Why use the File Manager instead of the Program Manager? The File Manager lists files in directories, and shows associated document files as well. While you can create associated document icons in the Program Manager, doing so takes time. It's often easier just to keep a directory window in the File Manager open to the documents you need to access often.

The Drag-and-Drop Method

When the File Manager is open, you can use the drag-and-drop method to open files for viewing or printing. You click an icon, then drag it over the application it is associated with, assuming that application is open on the desktop. Try this now using the following steps:

1. Start Paintbrush by double-clicking its icon in the Accessories group of the Program Manager.

2. When the Paintbrush window opens, rearrange the desktop so you can see part of the File Manager below.

3. Click the File Manager to make it active, and then locate the file CHITZ.BMP.

4. Click the icon and hold the mouse button, then drag the file icon over the Paintbrush window. The image opens in the Paintbrush workspace.

You can use this method to quickly view the contents of files. Rather than opening each file using the Open command of a program, simply drag the files from the File Manager into the workspace of the program.

You can also print documents by dragging and dropping a file's icon over a running copy of the Print Manager, as described in the last section of Chapter 8.

RUNNING NON-NT APPLICATIONS

Non-NT applications are DOS, Windows 3.1, OS/2, or POSIX applications that Windows NT runs in a separate environment. The advantage of running these applications from Windows NT is that you can easily switch among applications. You can also use cut and paste commands to move information from one application to another, no matter which operating system it is designed to run under. Further, if you installed Windows NT as the only operating system on your computer, you have no other way to run the applications except through Windows NT.

Running the Command Prompt

You start the Windows NT character-based interface by double-clicking the Command Prompt icon in the Program Manager Main group window. The command prompt is a separate environment that runs DOS, Windows 3.1, OS/2, or POSIX applications. Windows NT does not care that the applications were written for other operating systems, it simply emulates the environment so the application can run as normal. All you have to do is type the appropriate command to start the application. Windows NT recognizes the type of application it is.

Double-click the Command Prompt icon to open a window on the character-based interface. A window similar to the one shown in Figure 5-3 appears.

If you are familiar with DOS, you can try executing DOS commands that list files or execute programs. You also can issue Windows NT character-based commands. For a complete list of these commands, double-click the Windows NT Help icon in the Program Manager Main menu. The Windows NT Help dialog box shown in Figure 5-4 appears.

Click the icon labeled "Access the Command Reference Help." You then see the dialog box shown in Figure 5-5. On the left, you can click the button for any command for which you need help. To quickly jump to an alphabetical listing, click the letter of the alphabet in the upper-left box. On the right, you can read about several topics relatedto

FIGURE 5-3

The Command Prompt window

FIGURE 5-4

A Windows NT Help
dialog box

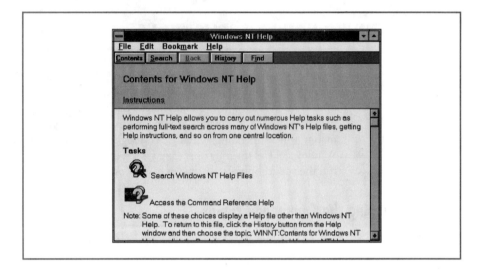

commands by clicking the buttons next to the topics. Appendix B provides a unique
cross-reference for these commands.

More About the Command Prompt Window

When you start the Command Prompt, it appears in a window on the desktop. You can
switch to a full-screen window by pressing ALT-ENTER. To switch back to windows, press
ALT-ENTER again, which restores the Command Prompt to a window. You also can press

FIGURE 5-5

Help information for
character-based
commands

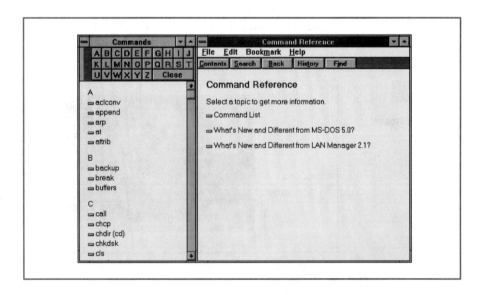

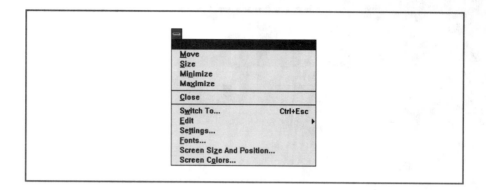

FIGURE 5-6

The Command Prompt
Control menu

CTRL-ESC in the Command Prompt to display the Task List, then choose another application that you want to switch to. Still another method is to press ALT-ESC to switch back to Windows NT. In this last method, the Command Prompt window remains in full-screen mode, but reduces to an icon when you switch back to Windows NT.

You can change some of the settings of the Command Prompt window by clicking the Control menu button in the upper-left corner. The drop-down Control menu appears on the Command Prompt window, as shown in Figure 5-6.

Most of the options on the Control menu are discussed in Chapter 11, but one option is of particular interest here. Choose the Fonts option from the Control menu to display the Font Selection dialog box, shown in Figure 5-7. You can change fonts for aesthetic reasons, or to better see listings. Use the UP ARROW and DOWN ARROW keys on the keyboard to scroll through the list in the Font field, watching the window size and font selection change in the other fields. When you find a size and font that you like, click OK. You also can change the color of the Command Prompt window by choosing Screen Colors on the Control menu.

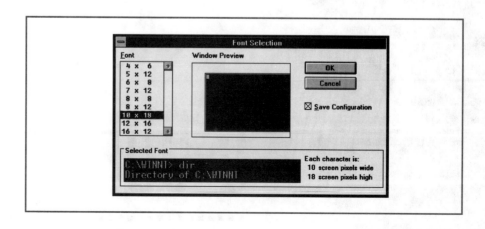

FIGURE 5-7

Changing the Command
Prompt's fonts

Inside

- Using the Help System

- Working with Files

- Editing Techniques

- Fonts and Special Characters

- Printing

& Out

CHAPTER

6

Global Techniques

One advantage of a graphical user interface like Windows is its consistent look and operation. Features used to access files, change fonts, and print documents are generally the same from one application to the next. For example, Figure 6-1 illustrates the File menus from three different Windows applications. Most applications have similar Edit and View menus as well.

This chapter introduces *global techniques*—actions that work the same way across Windows applications such as word processors, spreadsheets, and graphics programs. Keep in mind that every application has its own custom options, but the general options discussed here will help you get up and running with most applications.

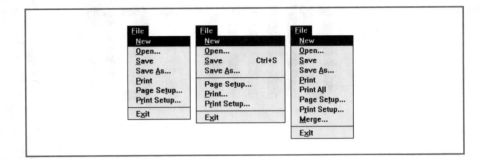

The File menus from Notepad, Paintbrush, and Cardfile have similar options

USING THE HELP SYSTEM

When you need some additional information before proceeding, you can access help by clicking the Help option on an application's menu bar, or by highlighting a specific command on a menu and pressing F1. Many dialog boxes also contain a Help button.

For example, choose Properties on the Program Manager File menu. You see the Program Item Properties dialog box for the selected icon. Click its Help button to display a complete set of help information on how to change properties. Notice that help information appears in its own window, so you can resize the window for viewing as you work with applications, or minimize it to an icon. Minimize the help window now; it appears on the desktop as a question mark with the title of the program it belongs to.

Each application has its own help file in the \WINNT\SYSTEM32 directory. These help files have names like CONTROL.HLP (Control Panel help), or NOTEPAD.HLP (Notepad help). When you press F1 to open help files, you'll see information about the task you are working on. For example, when you pressed F1 to get help for the Properties command, Windows opened PROGMAN.HLP and displayed the help information for the Properties dialog box. Once help is open, the entire PROGMAN.HLP file is available for browsing. Use the Help menu options and buttons to search for the specific area of help you need.

The other method for opening help files is to choose Help from the menu bar. You then see options for accessing any part of the help system. Click Help now to display this menu:

To see the table of contents of the help file, choose Contents. To search for specific topics, choose Search for Help on. To get assistance with using the Help system, choose How to Use Help.

Help Options

The typical help window is pictured in Figure 6-2. Note that topics are listed in outline form. Click the button next to a topic to open its subtopics or the help text itself.

Use the row of buttons directly under the menu bar to navigate through the help text. The buttons are described below. Help screens often have branching and related topics. You click a topic to view its text, then click the Back button to move back one topic, or click History to display a list of topics you've viewed. You can then return to any item in the history list.

Button	Action
Contents	Return to the table of contents
Search	Search for a topic
Back	Move back one step
History	Display a history list of topics viewed
Glossary	Display the complete glossary list

Underlined and colored text items embedded in the help text are "hot spots" that you can click to show glossary or additional help information.

Using Search

The Search button displays the Search dialog box shown in Figure 6-3. The dialog box is divided in half. Type search text in the field on the upper half of the dialog box. As you begin typing, a matching topic is highlighted in the list box. When the topic you want is

FIGURE 6-2

A typical help window

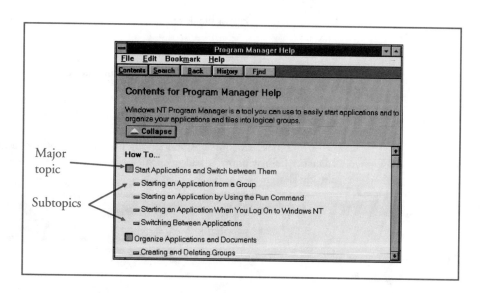

FIGURE 6-3

The Search dialog box

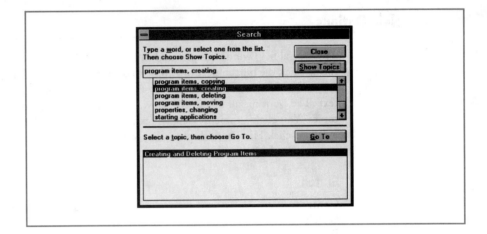

highlighted, either press ENTER, double-click the item, or click the Show Topics button. A set of topics then appears in the lower window. To view a topic, double-click it, or highlight it and click the Go To button. The help topic then appears on screen.

Using the Help Menu Options

The help window menus are described here:

File menu   Open other help files or print portions of the current help file.

Edit menu   Copy a block of help text to another application or annotate (add to) help text.

Bookmark menu   Insert place holders in help text so you can quickly refer back to the help text at any time.

Help menu   Get help on the Help system.

The next section steps you through the menu options. Make sure the Program Manager help window is still open. Choose Contents from the Help menu if it isn't already chosen.

Printing a Help Topic

You can print help topics if you like to keep help information posted next to your computer or in a binder. For example, you can print the entire set of keystrokes for the Calculator, or the procedure for creating new icons. Follow these steps to print a topic:

1. Start the Calculator and open its help window.

2. Click the button for any topic on the Help menu.

3. Choose Print Topic from the File menu to print the topic.

4. Repeat the above steps for other help topics.

Copying Topics

You can copy and paste the text of any help topic into another application. In this way, you can create your own manuals based on the information in the help files.

First display the topic to copy, then choose Copy from the Edit menu. The Copy dialog box appears with the text of the topic in its work space. To copy all the text, click the Copy button. To copy only part of the text, click and drag the mouse through the part of the text you want, then click Copy. Switch to the application where you want to paste the text, then choose the Paste command from its Edit menu. Copy and Paste procedures are covered later in this chapter.

The Annotate Option

The Annotate option lets you add notes and comments of your own to any help topic. When an annotation is added, a green (or colored) paper clip appears at the beginning of the help text for the topic. Try adding a comment to the current help window by following these steps:

1. Open a help topic that you want to annotate.

2. Choose Annotate from the Edit menu. The Annotate dialog box appears.

3. Type the text you want to add to the topic, then click the Save button.

Later, when you or another user is viewing the help topic, click the paper clip icon to view the annotations.

You can remove an annotation at any time by opening the annotation text and clicking the Delete button. The Copy and Paste buttons are used to copy existing annotated text from one annotation dialog box to another.

Defining Bookmarks

Use bookmarks to mark a place in the help text you want to return to later. You give titles to bookmarks that are added to the Bookmark drop-down menu. To move to a marked location in the text, simply choose the bookmark title from the Bookmark menu.

Try this now. First locate the help text you want to return to later, then click the Define option on the Bookmark menu. Type a short bookmark title, then click the OK button. The bookmark title is added to the Bookmark menu. Later, when you want to open the help text again, open the Bookmark menu and choose the title you added.

Create bookmarks for any topic you need to access quickly. Bookmarks are saved from one session to the next. When you don't need to reference a bookmark any longer, open the Bookmark Define dialog box, click the bookmark you want to delete, then click the Delete button.

WORKING WITH FILES

This section provides preliminary information about files and filenaming schemes you'll need to know when working with File Open and Save dialog boxes, or with the Command Prompt, as discussed later in the section.

Files Under DOS and Windows NT

A *file* is a collection of information, initially created in the memory of the computer, then saved to a disk storage device. All files must have unique names. While DOS filenames are somewhat restrictive, the NTFS file system allows up to 256 upper- or lowercase characters in a filename with multiple period separators. Files are stored in directories that are part of a directory tree. A *directory tree* has branching directories and subdirectories that separate and organize the hundreds of files stored in your system.

Files stored in the same location must have unique names. If you give a file the same name as an existing file, the new file will overwrite the old file. This is usually only a concern with the limited filenaming capabilities of DOS. The location of a file is important. You may need to specify its drive letter and directory name when accessing it. This is referred to as specifying the *search path* (or just *path*) to the file.

This book categorizes files into two broad categories: *program files* and *document files*. Applications such as Windows Write and Notepad are stored on disk as program files. The files you create with these applications are document files, and may contain text, graphic information, or other types of data.

Program File Types

Program files contain computer instructions or commands and have the extensions .EXE or .COM. In addition, some programs use auxiliary support files that also contain program code. *Support files* are program files with different filename extensions such as .OVL (overlay), .SYS (system), or .DRV (driver). You cannot "run" these files by typing their names on the command line. Generally, Windows NT retains the filenaming conventions used for program files that are used in DOS.

Document File Types

Document files may contain text, graphics, numbers, or other data. Document files are loaded into the work space or document windows of Windows applications. The naming conventions discussed here are typical for DOS file systems. NTFS provides more flexibility.

Text Files   *Text files* contain human-readable alphanumeric characters that follow the American Standard Code for Information Interchange (ASCII) format. These files are often referred to as ASCII files and can be opened by a wide range of programs on a wide range of computers, not just DOS or Windows NT systems. They are easily transferred over telephone modems to other systems and commonly have the extensions .TXT, .DOC, or one of several other possible extensions.

Graphics Files   Graphics files contain graphics information in several possible formats. The most common is the *bitmap* format, which saves the actual dot-by-dot representation of the image on the screen to a file. Another graphics file format, called *vector*, stores the series of commands required to rebuild the image on the screen. Graphics files have extensions such as .BMP, .TIF, .GIF, and .EPS.

Data Files   Data files contain information, usually created by a database program such as dBASE or a spreadsheet program such as Microsoft's Excel. These files are readable only by the applications that create them, or applications that can translate the information in the files to their own format. Information in data files is separated in various ways to form the fields of a database or cells of a spreadsheet. Common formats are comma-delimited files for databases and SYLK (SYmbolic LinK) or DIF (Data Interchange Format) files for spreadsheet data. Data files have many extensions such as .WK1, .WKS, and others. These files are discussed further in your application's manual.

Filenaming Conventions

The file systems supported by Windows NT have naming conventions. Files within the same directory cannot have the same name, but you can use names that have characters in common as part of a strategy to keep your files organized. Windows warns you if you try to create a file with a name that's already in use by another file.

Recall from Chapter 1 that you can name files on NTFS drives with up to 256 characters, including one or more extensions. NTFS filenames can have mixed case. NTFS preserves case, but does not distinguish it. Use mixed case for your own organizational purposes.

Remember that only drives formatted to the NTFS file system can store files with long filenames and security attributes. These filenames can be quite descriptive, as shown below. Notice how the mix of periods and upper- and lowercase letters helps differentiate parts of the filename.

AccountingReport.June92.PreparedByTomSheldon

However, keep in mind that long filenames are hard to retype. A file management utility like File Manager is essential when working with long filenames because you can quickly select the files.

Grouping files is another matter. You might want to create naming schemes so you can quickly locate files, or to ensure that they are grouped together in file listings. For example, you could set up a company-wide strategy that follows this pattern:

category.department.date.author.description

In the *category* field, type a standard file descriptor, like REPORTS, DATABASE, WORD-DOC, or other. In the *department* field, type the name of the department where the file was created. In the remaining fields, type further file descriptions. Note that the date is usually tagged to files automatically by the operating system, but you might want to come up with your own date coding scheme for sorting purposes.

Files that follow this naming scheme are listed first according to the type of file, then the department that created the file, and so on.

Note

Not all Windows NT applications let you save or open files that have long filenames.

The basic DOS filename consists of eight characters, followed by an optional three-character *extension*. The filename may be fewer than eight characters, but any characters beyond the maximum eight are truncated. Here is a typical filename:

YOURFILE.TXT

Another important part of a DOS filename is its location or path. When referring to a file not in the current directory, you need to include the drive and directory along with the actual filename. For example, the complete path of the file YOURFILE.TXT in the WINWORD directory on drive D is as follows:

D:\WINWORD\YOURFILE.TXT

Backslashes separate the drive, directory, and filename. If you need more information on filenaming conventions, refer to your DOS manual.

Note | All NTFS files are assigned a name that follows the DOS convention if copied to a DOS drive.

Filenaming Strategies

To keep your DOS files organized and track their contents, it's helpful to develop a naming strategy that uses descriptive filenames and extensions. Many programs automatically add filename extensions when a file is saved, as shown in Table 6-1. You can usually specify your own extension to override those added by the application.

Table 6-2 lists other common extensions you can use when creating files with the Windows accessories or with other programs. Recall that a filename extension is used to associate a document file with the program that created it. You can double-click an associated document file in the File Manager to open that file without first opening the application. You'll want to retain the extension used by Windows applications for this reason, or create other extension associations.

Use the filename itself to describe and categorize the contents of a file. Adopt a filenaming strategy for yourself or others in your company that makes a file's contents readily apparent and avoids duplication of names. When working with sets of data files,

TABLE 6-1

Filename Extensions for Windows Accessories

Program	Extension	Meaning
Paintbrush	.BMP	A Paintbrush bitmap image
Paintbrush	.MSP	An older Paintbrush bitmap image
Paintbrush	.PCX	A PC Paintbrush bitmap image
Calendar	.CAL	A Calendar file
ClipBook	.CLP	A saved Clipbook image
Cardfile	.CRD	An index card file
Program Manager	.GRP	A group information file
PIF Editor	.PIF	A Program Information File
Notepad	.TXT	A Notepad text file
Terminal	.TRM	A Terminal settings file
Write	.WRI	A Windows Write text file

TABLE 6-2

Common Filename
Extensions

Extension	Usage
.BAK	A generic extension given to backup of edited files
.BAT	A DOS batch file
.DAT	A generic extension for data files
.DTA	Another generic data file extension
.DOC	A generic extension for document files
.HLP	A commonly used extension for help files
.LOG	A log file that holds event tracking information
.MNU	A generic extension for menu files
.MSG	A generic extension for message files
.TMP	A generic extension for temporary files

a common strategy is to code the date and file type into the filename. Consider the following filenames used to store Microsoft Excel spreadsheet files:

RA930130.XLS
RB930130.XLS
RC930130.XLS
RA930228.XLS
RB930228.XLS
RC930228.XLS

Assume that these are files created every month. The R designates the files as reports (budget files might begin with B). The second letter is a code that indicates the type of report; here three separate reports are created at the end of each month (A, B, and C). Next comes the report date, followed by the .XLS extension added by Excel. Usually, for listing purposes, you'll want to put the year first, followed by the month, then the day; thus, the file RC920228 is a C-type of report entered on February 28, 1993.

Listing Files with Wildcard Characters

A *wildcard* character is a substitute for any letter or group of letters in a filename. The question mark (?) can represent a single letter, and the asterisk (*) can represent two or more letters. Veteran DOS users are familiar with wildcard characters and their usefulness in listing groups of files. Windows NT also accepts wildcard characters.

Using the previous list of files as an example, you can see how wildcard characters can be used to list or access specific files. The specification RA*.* includes the following files:

RA930130.XLS
RA930228.XLS

The specification R???1*.* includes these files:

RA930130.XLS
RB930130.XLS
RC930130.XLS

Finally, the specification RA??1*.* includes only this file:

RA930130.XLS

Notice how ? serves as a place marker; that is, any character may occupy its position. The *, on the other hand, designates a group of letters in the filename or extension. You'll use wildcard characters when opening files in applications, or listing files in the File Manager.

Directory Concepts

Directories provide a way to separate files on drives in much the same way that you would organize paper files in a filing cabinet. The following illustration shows the typical arrangement of the Windows NT NTFS drive.

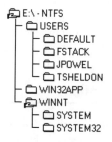

The top folder is the *root directory*. All disks have a root directory, and all other directories on the disk branch from it. The root directory is labeled NTFS, indicating that the drive is formatted as a Windows NT file system drive. Branching from the root are the USERS, WIN32APP, and WINNT subdirectories. Incidentally, personal directories for users branch from the USERS directory.

Part of every file's name includes the path of the directory where it is stored. You normally only need to specify the path when referring to files outside of your current working directory. For example, a file called JANBUDG.XLS in the JPOWEL subdirectory of the previous illustration has the complete filename shown below:

E:\USERS\JPOWEL\JANBUDG.XLS

Windows NT makes it easy to refer to such files. You can select other drives and directories from drop-down list boxes on Open and Save dialog boxes.

Organizing with Directories

Directories keep program files and data files separate. Always create a separate directory when installing a new program. This is often done automatically by the program's setup routine when you install the application. Keep data files in their own directory to prevent files from mixing with program files or other types of data files.

Backups are easier if your data files are separated from your program files. It is usually not necessary to back up an entire drive every time you do a backup. This saves time and tapes. Instead, you can back up just files that change often, such as your data files, but not your program files. Backing up data files is easy if they all branch from a single directory as shown here:

With this directory arrangement, you only need to back up the DATA directory, making sure that its subdirectories are included in the backup. Don't forget to perform an occasional "full system" backup.

Using File Menu Options

This section describes dialog boxes used to open, save, browse, and search through files. What you've learned about files and directories so far will help you access the common features of these dialog boxes.

For the exercises in this section, activate the Notepad accessory now by double-clicking its icon in the Accessories group of the Program Manager. When the Notepad window appears, click on the File menu option, or press ALT-F. The first four options are used to open and save files and are found in a wide range of Windows applications. What you learn about using them in Notepad applies to other applications as well.

The New Option

The New option clears the application's workspace or opens a new document window. If the existing work has not yet been saved, Windows asks if you want to save it before clearing the screen.

Some applications, such as Microsoft Word for Windows, let you open two or more documents at once. Consequently, the workspace is not cleared when you select New. Instead, another document window is opened for the new file. In this way, you can edit two or more documents at once, compare their contents, or cut and paste text or graphics among them.

| Note |

In some applications, you can press CTRL-N to select the New option.

The Open Option

The Open option is used to open an existing file. Select Open on the Notepad File menu to display the Open dialog box shown in Figure 6-4.

Select or type information in the following fields:

☑   In the File Name field, type the name of the file to open, or choose a file from the list. You can change the contents of the list by using wildcard characters in the File Name field.

☑   In the List Files of Type field, choose from a list of wildcard specifications. This is an optional step.

☑   In the Directories field, choose a new directory by clicking its icon.

☑   In the Drives field, choose the drive you want to use.

You can also click the Network button to access files on other computers connected to the network. The typical procedure for using the Open dialog box is given here:

FIGURE 6-4

The Open dialog box

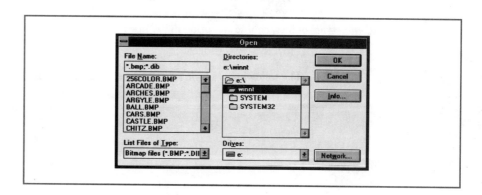

1. Select the drive by clicking the down arrow button on the Drives field, then click a drive in the list.

2. Select a directory in the Directories field. The current drive and directory are listed, but you can select other directories by clicking them with the mouse. Double-click a directory to open a list of its subdirectories. Once you've selected a directory, its files appear in the File Name list.

3. Specify the type of files you want to see listed by choosing an option in the List Files of Type field or by typing your own file specification in the File Name field. After you type your own specification, press ENTER to change the file list.

4. If you are opening a file, choose a file in the File Name field. Click the OK button to execute the Open or Save command.

Some of these steps are optional, of course. If a file is in the current drive and directory, you can simply type its filename or select it from the list and click the OK button. If you need to switch drives, the last directory you accessed on that drive in the current session is still selected in the Directories field.

If you're searching for a file because you can't remember the drive or directory where you saved it, first type a wildcard specification for the file in the File Name field, then click on different directories or drives. The file list will change to show files that match the wildcard specification each time you change the drive or directory.

Keyboard methods are useful when working with dialog boxes. You can easily jump from one field to another by pressing TAB. To access a specific field, press ALT and the underlined letter in the title of the field. For example, to jump to the Drives field, press ALT-V.

The following sections describe how to use the features in each field of the dialog box.

Changing the File Listing   When opening files, you can use wildcard characters to reduce the file list and show only specific types of files. While you could simply type the name of a file you want to open, you might not always know that name. The following techniques can help you quickly locate a file.

As an example, to see all executable files with the extension .EXE, type ***.EXE** and press ENTER. To see files with the text extension, type ***.TXT** in the field. To list other types of files, choose an option in the List Files of Type list box. Some wildcard examples are described below.

▨   The following example lists all files with the first four letters PROG:

▨ This example lists all files with the extension BMP:

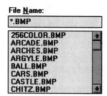

▨ This example list all files that start with A and have the BMP extension:

You can list all files by typing *.* in the filename field or choosing the *.* option in the List Files of Type field.

When the file list appears, use the scroll bar to scan through it if necessary. Click the file and its name appears in the File Name text box. Press ENTER or click OK to open it.

Working with NTFS Long Filenames   You can use wildcard characters when working with long filenames on NTFS drives. The concept is similar to DOS filenames. You can start the Command Prompt and create files with long filenames on NTFS volumes using the COPY CON command. For example, to create a test file, type the following:

COPY CON This.Is.A.Test

Type some text, then press F6 and ENTER to save the file. Now list the directory to see the filename. Type the following to make a copy of it:

COPY This.Is.A.Test *.*.*.Temporary.File

This creates a new file called This.Is.A.Temporary.File. If you typed COPY This.Is.A.Test *.Temporary, a file called This.Temporary would be created because the operating system would assume the single asterisk indicates you only want to copy the first word in the filename.

The text following the last period is considered the filename extension in the DOS sense. For example, in the following filename

    Reports.Sales.June.EastDiv

the word EastDiv is considered the extension, so if you issue the following command in the Command Prompt window:

    DIR *.*.*.EastDiv

you see a listing of all files that end in EastDiv, preceded by three period separators.

Assume a directory had the above file with another file called MAY-AR-CHIVES.EastDiv. Typing the following command would list both files:

    DIR *.EASTDIV

In this case, the asterisk represents all characters and period separators preceding the extension.

Note also that you can specify upper- or lowercase when listing files. Also, if the file Reports.Sales.June.EastDiv is copied to a DOS volume, the file is converted to a DOS name as follows:

    REPORT~1.EAS

A numbering scheme is used to differentiate the filename, and the first three characters of the last word are used for an extension.

The Save Option

Choose the Save option on menus to save a file that has previously been saved and has a filename. If you choose Save, and the document doesn't yet have a filename, the File Save As dialog box appears. Keep in mind that the Save option saves changes without asking for verification. In most cases, this will be fine, but there may be times when you want to load a file, make changes to it, then save it under a different name, so that you can retain the original file. Use the Save As option in this case.

Some applications have a Read Only check box that you enable for precautionary reasons. When this property is enabled, you can't save the file using its current name and overwrite the existing file. The application forces you to rename the file and opens the

Save As dialog box discussed next. You use this option when working with template files, which are files with default settings and text you use as a start when creating other files.

The Save As Option

Use the Save As option on the File menu to save a file for the first time, specifying its new filename. It also lets you save an existing file under a new name. The Save As dialog box has the same features as the Open dialog box. You type the new name for the file in the File Name box and specify the drive or directory location.

The Save As dialog box lists the names of files on the current drive and directory. The list lets you see what filenames have already been used when deciding on the new file's name.

Accessing Network Files

The Open dialog box shown in Figure 6-4 includes a Network button. You click this button to search for and select files on other network computers. When you click the button, the dialog box in Figure 6-5 appears.

Use this dialog box first to connect with another computer on the network. The lower box illustrates the workgroups and computers on your network. Select a network computer from this list. Note that workgroups are listed with an icon that looks like three computers. Indented under workgroups are computers on the network that belong to the workgroup. You might need to double-click a workgroup name to expand its list of

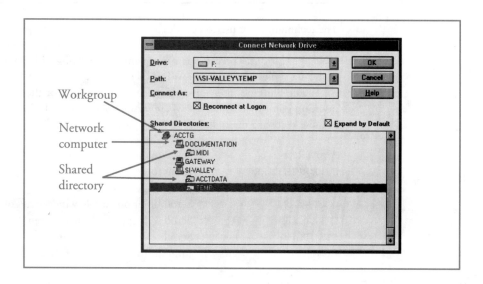

computers. If the list is large, you can collapse a workgroup list you don't need to see by double-clicking the workgroup icon. The whole purpose of workgroups is to make this browsing operation easier because the workgroup categorizes computers in lists you can expand or collapse.

When you see the computer you want to connect with, click it. A list of shared directories on that computer then appears under it. Click the directory you want to use. The complete computer name and directory name then appear in the Path field.

If you've previously connected with a directory on another computer, the path name might still be listed in the Path drop-down list box. You can choose it there rather than following the procedure above.

At this point, you can accept the default settings in the other fields and press OK to make the connection, or you can make these other changes:

- The first available drive letter appears in the Drive field. You can click the down-arrow button on the field to list other possible letters to choose.

- Specify your username in the Connect As field. This is optional.

- Clear the Reconnect At Logon if you don't want to make this connection the next time you log on.

- Disable Expand By Default if you don't want the directory tree in the Shared Directories field expanded automatically when you open the dialog box.

EDITING TECHNIQUES

The techniques you use to edit documents are similar among a wide variety of applications. In this section, you learn editing techniques used in Notepad, Write, and many other applications. You can open Write and follow along with this discussion. Open one of the TXT files located in the WINNT directory.

The blinking insertion point is at the beginning of the text. You reposition the insertion point by clicking elsewhere in the document with the mouse, or by using one of these keyboard methods:

Arrow keys	Scroll in any direction, one character or line at a time
CTRL-RIGHT ARROW	Jump to next word
CTRL-LEFT ARROW	Jump to previous word
PGUP/PGDN	Scroll up or down one window full of text
CTRL-PGUP	Scroll to beginning of text screen
CTRL-PGDN	Scroll to end of text screen
HOME	Jump to the beginning of a line

END	Jump to the end of a line
CTRL-HOME	Jump to the beginning of a document
CTRL-END	Jump to the end of a document

Once you've positioned the insertion point, you can press the DEL key to remove the character to the right or the BACKSPACE key to remove the character to the left. To insert new text, just type the text. It is automatically inserted. Some applications have an overtype mode that is toggled on or off with the INS key. When this option is on, any text you type overtypes existing text.

Selecting Text

In Windows NT, you highlight text before you format it, delete it, or move it to another location. For example, to delete a block of characters, first highlight the block, then press the DEL key. The simplest method of highlighting text is to click and drag over it with the mouse. Try this now in the Write document. Click anywhere in the text, hold the mouse button, and drag to another location. All text in between is highlighted.

The Selection Bar

In Write and many other Windows applications, a *selection bar* is situated between the left edge of text and the window border. You click in this bar to select either a line or a paragraph. Try this now by clicking once in the selection bar just to the left of text. Note that the mouse pointer converts to a right-pointing arrow in the selection bar. Now click once and drag the mouse pointer down to select multiple lines.

To select an entire paragraph, double-click to the left of the paragraph in the selection bar.

Selecting Text with the Keyboard

There are also keyboard methods for selecting text. When you use these methods, text selection starts at an "anchor" point and extends outward from there, depending on which keys you use. Selecting with the mouse is awkward if all the text is not on one screen. You might overshoot the text or lose track of how far you've scrolled. Try both the mouse and the keyboard methods to decide which you prefer.

SHIFT-DOWN ARROW	Extend the selection to the next line
SHIFT-UP ARROW	Extend the selection to the previous line
SHIFT-END	Extend the selection to the end of a line
SHIFT-HOME	Extend the selection to the beginning of the line
SHIFT-PGDN	Extend the selection down one window

SHIFT-PGUP	Extend the selection up one window
CTRL-SHIFT-RIGHT ARROW	Extend the selection to the next word
CTRL-SHIFT-LEFT ARROW	Extend the selection to the previous word
CTRL-SHIFT-END	Extend the selection to the end of the document
CTRL-SHIFT-HOME	Extend the selection to the beginning of the document

Using the Edit Menu and the Clipboard

The Edit menu has options for undoing mistakes, as well as copying, cutting, and pasting text within a document or in other documents. Most edit menus have the following options:

The Undo Option

The Undo option cancels the last editing change you made. If you deleted text or part of a graphic, or if you changed the format of a block of text, the change is undone. For example, if you delete a character by accident, press CTRL-Z to undo the deletion. You can press CTRL-Z again to cancel the undo.

The Clipboard Options

The Cut, Copy, and Paste options are called the Clipboard options. The *Clipboard* is a temporary holding area used to hold text until you paste it elsewhere. The options for working with the Clipboard are part of every application's Edit menu. Cut removes the selected text or graphics from the document and places it on the Clipboard. You can also press CTRL-X to cut (think of "X"ing out a portion of text from your document). Copy places a copy of the selected text on the Clipboard. You can also press CTRL-C. Paste copies the contents of the Clipboard to the position of the insertion point. You can also press CTRL-V (think of V as a caret or insertion mark to remember this keyboard method).

Some Edit menus have a Select All item. Select All selects all the text or graphics objects in a document or workspace. You then choose Cut or Copy to place them on the Clipboard.

Typically, you cut or copy an object or text from one window, press ALT-TAB to switch to another window, then paste.

Note | Transferring information to and from non-Windows NT applications requires special procedures covered in Chapter 11.

The Clipboard

You can open the Clipboard itself by starting the ClipBook utility in the Main group of the Program Manager. Within the ClipBook is the Clipboard icon. If you double-click it, you'll see the information you've cut or copied. Some of the options for the Clipboard are described below.

Choosing the Save option on the File menu is a convenient way to save graphics or text that you use all the time. Choose Open on the File menu to open a previously saved Clipboard image. Use the Delete option on the Edit menu to clear the Clipboard. The image on the Clipboard can use quite a bit of memory, so it's a good idea to clear it if you don't need it anymore. A quick way to clear a large image without opening the ClipBook is to highlight something small like a single character and choose Copy.

Refer to Chapter 9 for more detailed information on the ClipBook utility.

Note | The ClipBook stores often used images in a window so you can quickly access them later. You can also share those images with other users on the network, or use the ClipBook to connect with ClipBooks on other computers and access shared images on them. Refer to Chapter 9 for details.

FONTS AND SPECIAL CHARACTERS

Applications like Write and advanced word processors like Word for Windows provide character-formatting capabilities so that you can change the fonts and styles of text. The procedure for formatting text is consistent among Windows NT applications. You first select a block of text, then choose the character-formatting option from the application's menu.

Start Write and click the Character menu option. You'll see the following menu:

You can choose any of these options to format the selected text, or choose the Fonts option to display the dialog box pictured in Figure 6-6. The Font dialog box gives you more control over the fonts and styles.

Use the Font dialog box to choose a TrueType or regular font, to change its style, and to change its size. Highlight text you want to change before opening the box. However, if you make a font change, all text you type from the cursor position is affected.

There are two font types listed in the dialog box: TrueType fonts and printer fonts. TrueType fonts are designated with the TT symbol. They are scalable fonts that print at high resolution on dot matrix and laser printers. Use TrueType fonts whenever possible. You can send documents formatted with TrueType fonts to other Windows and Windows NT users who can print them on their printers without making special changes. The fonts automatically use the highest resolution possible on the printer. Printer fonts are designated by an icon that looks like a printer. These are the built-in fonts for the currently selected printer, so the contents of the list depends on the printer installed.

When you choose a different font, a sample appears in the Sample window. To choose a different style or size, select it in the Font Style or Size list box. Note that you can also type an unlisted font size in the Size dialog box. The TrueType fonts display even numbers in this box, but because they are scalable, you can enter any value from 4 points to 127 points. Sizes outside this range may not print properly. Once you've selected a font, click the OK button. The text in the document then changes to the new font.

In Write, superscript and subscript formatting are applied from the Character menu only. These options are not available on the Font dialog box. The Reduce Fonts and Enlarge Fonts options are useful for quickly resizing a fonts, but the increments are in multiples of two. To specify an exact size use the Font dialog box.

FIGURE 6-6

The common Fonts dialog box

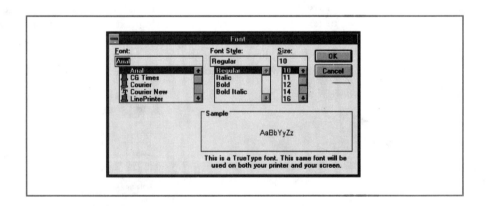

The Character Map

The Character Map utility helps you locate and insert special foreign language characters and symbols into your documents. You can keep the utility open on the desktop while you write documents in Write, Word for Windows, or other applications.

Double-click the Character Map icon in the Accessories window to display the utility, as shown in Figure 6-7.

The first thing to do is choose a font. Click the down arrow button in the Font field to display and choose from a list of fonts. The Symbol or WingDing fonts are useful because they contain characters not available on the keyboard or in other fonts. As you choose different fonts, note that the table of characters changes in style and content. Compare the Symbol font map to a text font such as Courier.

Note

Click a character to enlarge it, or click and drag to scan through the characters. Each character is displayed as the mouse pointer touches it.

Use one of two methods to insert a character into your document. The first method is to click a character in the table, then view its keystroke requirement at the bottom-right of the Character Map. In Figure 6-7, the heart is selected in the table, and its keystroke is listed on the bottom right as ALT-0169. Switch back to your application and type this keystroke. (Hold down the ALT key and type the four digits in sequence.)

The second method involves the Clipboard. Double-click the character or characters you want (or click the Select button). This places the characters in the Characters to Copy field at the top of the window. Click Copy to place the selected characters on the Clipboard, then switch back to your application and paste (CTRL-V).

The second method is useful when you need more than one character, for example, when building complex strings or mathematical expressions using the Symbol font. When you switch back to your application, be sure to position the cursor before pasting the characters.

FIGURE 6-7

The Character Map utility

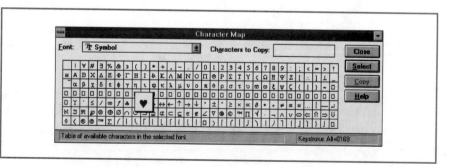

FIGURE 6-8

A typical Print dialog box

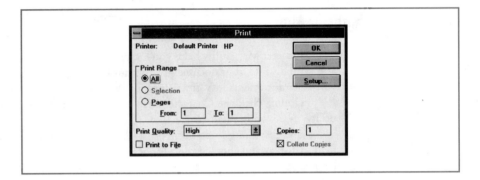

PRINTING

The Print and Print Setup options are common features on most Windows NT applications. Choose Print Setup to select a printer, print orientation (either portrait or landscape), and a paper size and tray. You then choose Print to send the document to the selected printer. A typical Print dialog box is pictured in Figure 6-8. In the Print Range field, you can choose to print the entire document, the currently selected text, or a range of pages. In the lower fields, you can choose the print quality and specify the number of copies to print. For more information on printing, refer to Chapter 8.

Inside

- The File Manager Window
- Working with Directory Windows
- Making Network Connections
- Climbing the Directory Tree
- Working with the File List
- Selecting Files for Operations
- Copying and Moving Files with the Mouse
- Using the File Menu Commands
- Working with Directories
- Using Disk Commands

& Out

CHAPTER 7

Working with Files

The file Manager displays files and directories that reside on your local hard disks or the disks of computers you are connected to over the network. If you are familiar with DOS, you'll find most of the commands you normally use to copy, rename, delete, and manipulate files, but presented now in a graphical interface that is much more intuitive than the DOS command line. You can list and sort files in several different ways, then manage those files in one of several ways: you can copy and move single files or groups of files by clicking and dragging their icons to other drives or directories; you can delete or rename files or groups of files; you can start executable program files by double-clicking their icons, or open documents by double-clicking their icons.

Of course, the the File Manager has many more features that you'll learn about as you read through this chapter and Chapter 13, which covers how to customize the File Manager. This chapter assumes that you understand file concepts and dialog boxes as discussed in the previous chapter.

THE FILE MANAGER WINDOW

The first time you start the File Manager, it looks similar to the window pictured in Figure 7-1. Like the Program Manager, the File Manager holds document windows within its borders, but in the File Manager these windows hold lists of files for different directories on your system, and so are more appropriately called *directory windows*. Directory windows have the following features:

- The *menu bar* has menu options for working with files and changing the features of the File Manager.

- The *drive icon bar* depicts each of the floppy drives, hard drives, RAM memory drives, and network drives available to the File Manager.

- The *Toolbar* gives you push-button access to the most popular menu options, and you can customize it to fit your own needs.

- The *directory tree* depicts the directories on the drive that is currently selected in the drive icon bar.

- The *contents list* shows the files for the directory selected in the directory tree.

FIGURE 7-1

The File Manager window

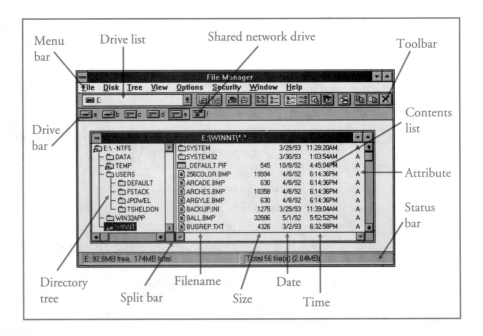

☑ A *split bar* separates the directory tree and contents list. You can click and drag the split bar left or right to enlarge either side of the directory window, or you can remove the split altogether and display only directories or only files.

☑ The *status bar* displays important information about the selected drive, such as the number of files and their total disk space.

WORKING WITH DIRECTORY WINDOWS

The first time you start the File Manager, one directory window is open with a list of files in the default directory. You can open additional directory windows and change the view of files in those windows.

Opening Another Directory Window

To set up a new directory window, first choose New Window from the Window menu. A new window opens with the same settings as the previously selected window. Next, choose Tile or Cascade from the Window menu to arrange the two windows. Notice that the title bar in each window indicates the current directory, but the original window is labeled 1 and the new window is labeled 2. Finally, click another directory in the directory tree to view its contents.

A quick way to open a new directory window is to double-click the drive icon for another directory window. A new window for that drive appears.

The Split Bar

Within the directory window, the split bar divides the directory tree and the contents list. When the mouse pointer is over the split bar, it changes to a double-headed arrow. Drag the bar to the left to provide more space for file listings in the contents list, or to the right to get a wider view of the directory tree when necessary. You can also remove the split altogether, and display only the directory tree or only the file listing. To remove the window split, choose the Tree Only or Directory Only options from the View menu. A directory-only window is visible in Figure 7-2.

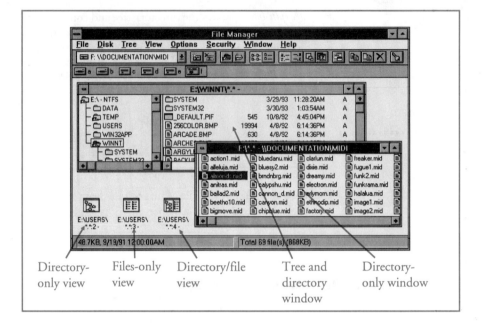

The File Manager with a directory-only window showing

Directory-only view   Files-only view   Directory/file view   Tree and directory window   Directory-only window

Arranging Windows

When more than one directory window is open, you can rearrange them by using the Cascade and Tile options on the Window menu, or by dragging them with the mouse.

You can also minimize directory windows, as shown at the bottom in Figure 7-2. Minimized directory window icons take on the name of the directory they list, as well as the type of files listed. The icon itself indicates the listing method. In Figure 7-2, the left icon indicates a directory-tree-only listing, the middle icon indicates a files-only listing, and the right icon indicates a directory tree and files listing.

Windows Refreshment Time

The Refresh option on the Window menu updates the list of files in a directory window to reflect a change in a directory or drive. You can use this option to update the list of files for a floppy disk drive after changing the floppy disk in the drive. It will show changes when you've performed a file operation outside the File Manager that affects the file list. You can also use this option when you restore a minimized directory window and you want to make sure its file list is current, or when you want to update network drive file lists.

MAKING NETWORK CONNECTIONS

So far, you've seen how to work with directory windows that display directories and files on your local system. This section explains how to open directory windows on other systems, and how to share directories on your system with other network users.

To establish network connections and shares, click the button on the File Manager Toolbar shown in Figure 7-3. Alternatively, you can choose similar options on the File Manager Disk menu. The List of Drives box on the Toolbar displays a list of the most recent network connections you've made. You can quickly reestablish a connection and open a directory window on the shared directory by choosing from this list.

Sharing directories involves some responsibilities. You must specify the permissions outlined in Chapter 3 to control how network users access a shared directory. Likewise, shared directories you connect to may have limited access.

Network directories you've connected to appear as normal directory windows. You can work with the files and start programs located in the directories as if they were local. Files copied from a network directory to a local directory are transferred over the network. Note that you can make these same connections from many Windows NT applications when the Open or Save As dialog boxes are open. However, connections made in applications do not appear in the File Manager.

> **Note** | You can share CD-ROM drives on your system with other users.

Connecting with Shared Directories

To access a shared directory on another system, follow the steps described here. On the File Manager Toolbar, click the down arrow button in the List of Drives box as shown in Figure 7-3. If you were recently connected to the directory, its name appears on the list. Click the name of the directory you want to connect with and a new directory window will open, displaying the contents of the directory.

FIGURE 7-3

Toolbar options for making network connections

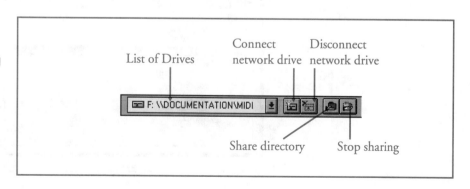

To create a new network connection, choose the Connect Network Drive button on the Toolbar, or choose Connect Network Drive from the Disk menu. A dialog box similar to Figure 7-4 appears.

Note

This dialog box also has a list of recent connections. To view the list, click the down arrow button in the Path field.

The Connect Network Drive dialog box that appears is the same box that you see when you click the Network button on Open and Save As dialog boxes. Follow these steps to make a network drive connection.

1. In the Shared Directories field, double-click a workgroup icon to see its list of shared computers.

2. Double-click a shared computer to see its lists of shared directories.

3. Click a directory to connect with. Its name appears in the Path field.

4. To override the drive letter of an existing network connection with the new connection, specify its drive letter in the Drive field.

5. Make sure the Reconnect at Logon box is enabled if you want this connection the next time you start the File Manager. Alternatively, if this is a temporary connection, make sure it is disabled.

FIGURE 7-4

Connecting with other network drives

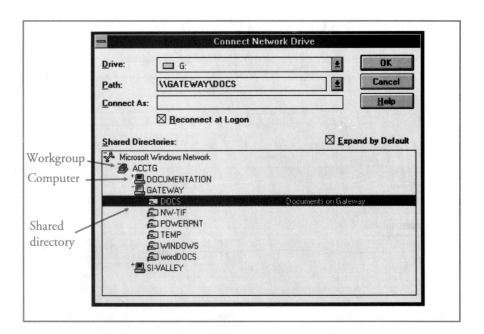

6. When everything is set the way you want, click the OK button to create the new shared directory connection.

Note that if the Open New Window on Connect option on the Options menu is enabled, Windows immediately creates a directory window for the new directory connection. If you disable this option, you can still access the directory by double-clicking its drive icon in the icon bar. Note also that the owner of a shared directory can hide it to prevent it from appearing in the browse list. If the owner has given you the shared directory name, type it in the Path field in the form shown below. Make sure to type a dollar sign after the directory name.

*computername**directoryname*$

If you know a shared directory won't always be available, disable the Reconnect at Logon check box. This prevents error messages from appearing if the File Manager can't find the directory.

Establishing a Shared Directory

To establish a shared directory on your system, you must be logged on as a member of the Administrator or Power Users group. Click the directory to share, then click the Share Directory button or choose the Share As option from the Disk menu. The New Share dialog box appears as shown in Figure 7-5.

The following sections discuss the fields and how you might fill them out.

Share Name The selected directory name appears in this field. It doesn't need to be the name of the directory; you can change to any name you like.

Dialog box for sharing directories

Note

To prevent the shared directory from appearing in browse lists, type a dollar sign at the end of the name, then give the directory name to only those users you want to access it. They must also type a dollar sign at the end of the name to access it.

Path   The Path field lists the path of the currently selected directory. You can type a new path to specify a different directory.

Comment   Any text you type in the Comment field appears in the browse list when other users connect to drives. Type informational text in this field.

User Limit   If Unlimited is selected, any number of users can connect with and use the shared directory. To prevent performance degradation, click Allow and specify the maximum number of users.

Note

If you are logged on as a member of the Administrators group, you can share a directory on another system, not just the system where you're working. Connect with the root directory of the drive you want to share. Root directories are listed as C$ or D$. Once connected to the root directory, select a branching subdirectory that you want to share.

Setting Permissions

Click the Permissions button to define which users and groups can access the shared directory. The dialog box in Figure 7-6 appears.

Note

To set permissions for local users on NTFS drives, as opposed to setting permissions for network users, select a directory or file, then choose Permissions from the Security menu, or click the "key" button on the Toolbar.

FIGURE 7-6

Defining who can access the shared directory

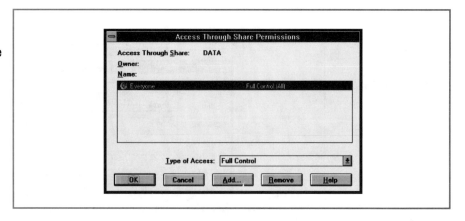

The primary tasks when defining permissions are to add or remove a user or group from the Name field, and define the type of permission for a user or group. You will recall from Chapter 3 that the Everyone group includes all users, both local and network users. The Network group includes any user accessing the shared directory over the network. The User group includes any user currently accessing the computer, including network users. Permissions for shared directories are as follows:

☑ *No Access* Prevents access by the selected user or group.

☑ *Read* Allows the user or group to view the contents of files but not change them.

☑ *Change* Allows the user or group to view, change, rename, and delete files.

☑ *Full Control* Grants the user or group full control over the directory.

To give any network user access to the directory, make sure one of the groups above appears in the Name field. Then choose an access option in the Type of Access field.

To add a user or group, click the Add button on the Access Through Share Permissions dialog box shown in Figure 7-6. The Add Users and Groups dialog box appears as shown in Figure 7-7.

The procedure for using this dialog box is as follows. First, choose a different domain in the List Names From field if you are connected to a Windows NT Advanced Server network. Next, choose a user or group in the Names field. To see users as well as groups, click the Show Users button. To see the members of a group, click the group, then click the Members button. Now click the Search button to locate a user or group in the current domain or another domain on a Windows NT Advanced Server network. When you've found the user or group you want, click it, then click the Add button. It

FIGURE 7-7

Assigning permissions to a
new user or group

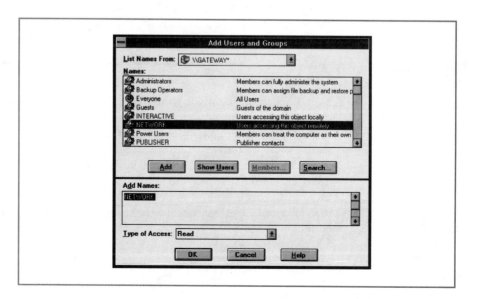

appears in the lower Add Names box. Repeat this step for as many users or groups as necessary. Choose a permission type for the selected users and groups in the Type of Access box. Once you've selected users and groups, and set all the options, click the OK button. The dialog box closes and you see the users or groups listed in the Name field of the Access Through Share Permissions dialog box.

To redefine permissions for any user or group, click the user or group, then choose a permission in the Type of Access box.

How to Stop Sharing Directories

You must stop sharing a directory if you want to ensure that other users don't access it. Alternatively, you could assign the No Access permission to all users or groups that access it.

It is also a good idea to disable any connections you've made to directories on other systems. This prevents error messages from appearing when the File Manager can't make a connection because the directories are no longer shared.

Stop Sharing a Directory on Your System

To stop sharing a directory on your system, click the Stop Sharing icon on the Toolbar, or choose Stop Sharing on the Disk menu. The Stop Sharing Directory dialog box appears:

Click the directory you want to stop sharing, then click the OK button. Note that directories listed with a dollar sign are hidden directories. You don't need to disable the root directory shares unless you want to prevent administrators on other systems from sharing your directories.

Don't stop sharing a directory if other users are still connected to it. Use the Chat utility discussed in Chapter 9 to warn users that you are disconnecting the directory so they can save their work. If you need to force a disconnection, open the Server utility in the Control Panel and click the User button. Refer to Chapter 17 for details on this option.

Disable a Connection to a Shared Directory

To disconnect from a directory on another system, click the Disconnect Directory button
on the Toolbar, or choose Disconnect Network Drive on the Disk menu. You'll see a
dialog box similar to the following:

Click the drive you want to disconnect, then click the OK button.

CLIMBING THE DIRECTORY TREE

Directory windows typically have a directory tree on the left and a file list on the right,
unless you've selected Directory Only from the View menu. The directory tree displays
the directories and subdirectories of the currently selected drive.

To select a different drive, click a drive icon. Some of these icons may represent
shared network drives. To display the list of files in another directory, click that directory
icon in the directory tree. You can use the arrow keys to move through the directory tree
list. As you do, files for each directory are listed on the right. Double-click any directory
to display its subdirectories, if any. This is called expanding the tree. Double click the
directory again to collapse the list.

If you double-click the root directory, the entire tree collapses. If you double-click
it again, only first level subdirectories expand. You can expand the entire directory tree
by pressing CTRL-*.

To see some other options, open the Tree menu. Choose Indicate Expandable
Branches. Collapsed folders will show a plus sign to indicate that they have branching
subdirectories.

WORKING WITH THE FILE LIST

To copy, move, rename, delete, or otherwise manipulate files, you must first select a file
or files. This section shows you how to change the directory listings to simplify file
manipulation and make file information easier to view.

Changing the File View

The File Manager View menu lets you change the way files are listed in the contents list. Here is the View menu:

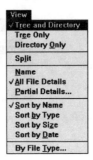

The first four options were discussed previously. This section is concerned with the remaining options on the View menu. These same options are also accessible by clicking the buttons on the Toolbar shown here:

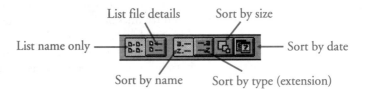

The Name, All File Details, and Partial Details options on the View menu or Toolbar let you change the amount of information displayed about each file. Displaying just the filename lets you see more in the window. Choosing the All File Details option displays the following file information:

Showing File Details

☑   The size of the file in bytes

☑   The date the file was created or last modified

☑   The time the file was created or last modified

☑   The *attributes,* or "status flags," of a file, which indicate if it can be changed and erased, or if it has been backed up

Custom Listings

To show only specific file detail information, choose the Partial Details option on the View menu. The following dialog box appears:

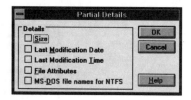

If you previously selected All File Details, all of the options in the Partial Details box will be marked. Enable or disable any options. When the MS-DOS filenames for NTFS option is enabled, the directory window shows the full NTFS filename, up to 256 characters and the DOS eight character filename and three character extension convention. To keep your directory windows small, choose only those options you need to see.

Sorting the File List

The four Sort By options on the View menu or Toolbar change the order in which files are listed. This makes it easier to see and select groups of related files. The Sort By options are discussed in the following sections.

Sort By Name   The default option. Files are sorted by the first eight characters of the filename.

Sort By Type   Arranges files by their filename extension. For example, all executable (.EXE) files are listed together so you can quickly locate a program to start.

Sort By Size   Arranges files in the order of their size. Choose this option to view large, unnecessary files you might want to move or delete.

Sort By Date   Arranges files in the order of their creation or last modification date. The most recent files are listed first. Use this option to find and delete old, unnecessary files.

Listing Specific Files

You can use the By File Type option to specify exactly which files you want to list, using wildcard characters or special check-box options. Choose the By File Type option on the View menu to display the following dialog box:

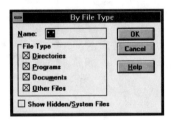

In the name field, type a wildcard specification for the types of files you want listed in the directory window (wildcard characters were discussed in Chapter 6). You can also mark the following check boxes to display various predefined groups of files.

Directories Check this box to include the names of any subdirectories that branch from the current directory in the file listing.

Programs Check this box to include executable files with the extensions .EXE, .COM, .BAT, or .PIF in the file listing. Choose this option to create a directory window where you can start executable programs.

Documents Check this box to include associated document files.

Other Files Check this option to list files that are not programs or associated files.

Show Hidden/System Files Enable this option to display files with the Hidden or System attribute on DOS drives. DOS creates these files and typically hides them in directory listings at the DOS level to prevent accidental deletion. There is little reason to display these files.

SELECTING FILES FOR OPERATIONS

Before executing commands on the File menu, you must select the files to work with. Several techniques for selecting files are discussed below.

Selecting Contiguous Files

Contiguous (adjacent) files are easy to select. Simply click the first file you want to select, hold down the SHIFT key, and click the last file. If the last file you want to select is not visible in the window, you can scroll the list to place the file in view.

To quickly jump to a file in a list, type the first letter of the file's name.

Selecting Noncontiguous Groups of Files

When the files you want to select as a group are not listed together, but scattered throughout the file list, they are *noncontiguous* files. If you can't group these noncontiguous files using the Sort By options or wildcard characters, hold down the CTRL key and click on each file. If you come across a group of files while using this method, you can select through them by holding SHIFT and clicking the last file in the group.

You can combine both contiguous and noncontiguous file selection techniques. Just keep holding the CTRL key while you make contiguous and noncontiguous selections.

Deselecting Files

If you change your mind about selecting a file, press the CTRL key and click the file again to deselect it. Similarly, you can deselect a whole group of selected files by holding down the SHIFT key and clicking the files' icons. These techniques are handy because it is often easier to select a large group of files and then deselect one or two that you don't want.

Using the Select Files Option

The Select Files option on the File menu provides another way to select files. Choose Select Files to display the Select Files dialog box:

To select files using the Select Files dialog box, type a file specification in the File(s) text box, using wildcard characters. Initially, the specification *.* is suggested in this field, but you can type over it. Note that if files are currently selected in the contents list, you can deselect them by clicking the Deselect button in the Select Files dialog box. To select files, type a wildcard specifier such as *.EXE in the File(s) field and press the Select button. You can continue to add more selections: just type a new specifier and click the Select button. The Set Selection dialog box can be closed and reopened without losing your current selection of files in the contents list.

Use the Select Files option whenever you know the filenames or extensions of the files you want to select. Use the mouse selection methods when you don't know the filenames, or if you simply prefer to scroll through the file list and manually select files. You can also combine both selection methods.

COPYING AND MOVING FILES WITH THE MOUSE

You can move and copy files in the File Manager using either mouse techniques or menu commands. Mouse techniques are the easiest to use, assuming that both the source file icons and the icon for the destination directory are visible on the screen. If the icons are not visible, you'll need to open and arrange windows to make them visible, or use the Copy or Move menu commands.

Note	Copying a file makes a duplicate of that file in the destination. Moving a file removes the file from its original location and places it in the destination.

Use the selection techniques to highlight one or more files, then use one of the following techniques to copy and move the files.

- ☑ *Copying files from one directory to another* Hold down the CTRL key, then click and drag the file or selected files from the source to the destination. The files are duplicated in the destination directory.

- ☑ *Copying files from one drive to another* Do not hold down the CTRL key. Simply click and drag the file or selected files to the drive icon in the icon bar, or to a directory window for the destination drive. The source or destination drive can be a shared directory on a network computer.

- ☑ *Moving files from one directory to another* Windows assumes you want to move files when clicking and dragging, so you don't need to hold down a key. Simply click and drag the file or selected files to the destination.

- ☑ *Moving files from one drive to another* Hold down the ALT key and click and drag the files to the destination. The source or destination can be a shared directory on a network computer.

....
USING THE FILE MENU COMMANDS

The File menu holds a set of commands that you use to manipulate the files and directories you've selected in directory windows. Examine each command as you work through the following sections. Note the following buttons on the Toolbar:

Copy   Delete

Move

Keep in mind that commands act on the currently selected directory or files. Read all warning boxes when they appear so you don't accidentally delete or alter directories or files.

Opening Selected Directories and Files

The File menu Open option performs the same operation as double-clicking a directory or file icon. In the directory tree, it expands or collapses the selected directory. In the file list, it starts executable files or opens associated files.

Moving and Copying Files

Use the File menu Move and Copy commands to move or copy files and directories instead of using mouse techniques. The commands are useful when you can't conveniently use mouse techniques. For example, it might be inconvenient to open a directory window on the files, or to position one directory window next to another so you can use mouse click and drag techniques.

In addition, Move and Copy have certain advantages over mouse techniques. If you know the filenames and locations of the files you want to copy or move, you don't need to select them first. Conversely, you can select files in a source window before opening the Move or Copy dialog box, then simply specify the destination once you open the dialog box. When using Copy or Move, you can use wildcard characters to specify the exact files to copy or move. This method may be easier than clicking each file or using the Set Selection dialog box. Copy and Move are available even if your mouse is disabled. You can specify a shared network directory as the source or destination, even if you are not connected to the directory. You specify the source or destination in the following format:

\\servername\sharename \filename

Here's the Move dialog box. A list of files appears in the From box because these were selected before choosing the command. You can type a destination drive and directory in the To box. The files are moved to the destination and removed from the source. The Copy dialog box has the same fields, but it causes duplicates of the files to be copied to the destination drive or directory.

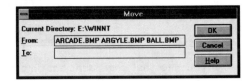

Deleting Files

One of the easiest ways to delete a file or directory is to click its icon with the mouse and then press the DEL key on the keyboard. A warning message appears asking you to confirm your deletion request. If you select multiple files, a confirmation box appears for each. You can use this as a selective method for deleting files.

Use the Delete command on the File menu to type in the names of the files you want to delete. If any files or directories are selected when you open the dialog box, the names appear in the Delete field, so use caution with this command. For example, the following dialog box appears when the root directory of drive E is highlighted:

Choosing OK would delete all the files on the drive. Fortunately, warning messages appear before the operation actually takes place, but be aware.

Renaming Files

The Rename command on the File menu lets you change the names of your directories and files. Choose a file to rename before opening the dialog box. You can rename groups of files, but there must be a common element in the names of all the files. For example, the following illustrates how you would rename two files with the extension .TXT to files with the extension .DOC:

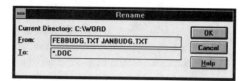

Viewing and Changing File Properties

Choose Properties from the File menu to display the attributes, or *properties*, of files and directories. These properties protect files from unauthorized changes or accidental deletion, or tag the files as having been backed up. When you select a file and choose Properties, a dialog box similar to Figure 7-8 appears.

The top portion of the dialog box lists file information such as the creation date and version number. If the file is an executable program, you'll see version information in the lower windows. The four properties are described in the following sections.

Read Only Files marked R, or Read Only, cannot be changed or deleted unless the Read Only attribute is removed. This option is useful on shared network drives as a way to prevent users from changing or accidentally deleting files. However, it is not fully secure. If, for example, another user has full security rights in the directory, he or she could simply remove the protecting attribute.

FIGURE 7-8

A Properties dialog box displaying information for a specific file

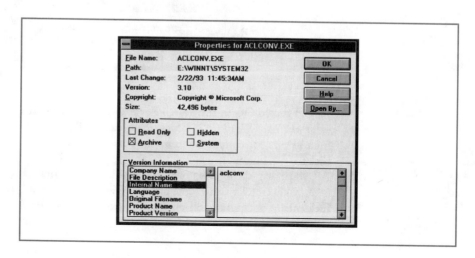

Archive   When a file is first created, or when it is altered, its Archive flag (A) is set on. Backup utilities look at the Archive flag to determine if a file should be included in an incremental backup. During the incremental backup, the Archive flag is set off so the file is not included in the next backup. If the file changes in the meantime, its Archive flag is once again set on and it will be included in the next backup.

In most cases, you won't need to worry about the Archive bit (flag). However, there may be times when you want to manually set it to include or exclude a file from a backup. For example, to create a second set of backup disks, it may be necessary to set the archive bit on for files in directories you want to back up.

Hidden   Files marked Hidden (H) will not appear in a DOS file listing, and will only appear in directory windows if the Show Hidden/System Files check box is marked in the By File Type dialog box.

System   Files marked System (S) are DOS files that are hidden in DOS file listings, and only appear in directory windows if the Show Hidden/System Files check box is marked in the By File Type dialog box.

Searching for Files and Directories

The File Search option is used to locate files and directories within your disk filing system or within shared directories. You can search for a file by specifying its full filename, or by specifying a partial name and using wildcard characters. In the following exercise, look for files with the filename extension .LOG on the current drive.

Begin by choosing the Search option on the File menu: you'll see this dialog box:

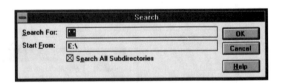

Type *.**LOG** in the Search For text box. In the Start From field, type the drive letter where the Windows NT files are stored. You'll see the WINNT directory branching from its root directory. Make sure the Search All Subdirectories box is highlighted and click the OK button. In a moment, you'll see a Search Results dialog box, shown in Figure 7-9, which lists the location of all the log files on the drive.

You can follow this same procedure to locate executable files and document files. Incidentally, you can double-click any executable or associated file in a search dialog box to start or open the file.

FIGURE 7-9

The Search Results
dialog box

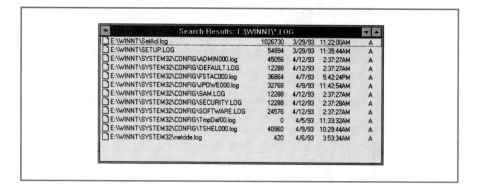

E:\WINNT\SetAcl.log	1026730	3/29/93	11:22:00AM	A
E:\WINNT\SETUP.LOG	54894	3/29/93	11:35:44AM	A
E:\WINNT\SYSTEM32\CONFIG\ADMIN000.log	45056	4/12/93	2:37:27AM	A
E:\WINNT\SYSTEM32\CONFIG\DEFAULT.LOG	12288	4/12/93	2:37:27AM	A
E:\WINNT\SYSTEM32\CONFIG\FSTAC000.log	36864	4/7/93	5:42:24PM	A
E:\WINNT\SYSTEM32\CONFIG\JPOWE000.log	32768	4/9/93	11:42:54AM	A
E:\WINNT\SYSTEM32\CONFIG\SAM.LOG	12288	4/12/93	2:37:27AM	A
E:\WINNT\SYSTEM32\CONFIG\SECURITY.LOG	12288	4/12/93	2:37:28AM	A
E:\WINNT\SYSTEM32\CONFIG\SOFTWARE.LOG	24576	4/12/93	2:37:27AM	A
E:\WINNT\SYSTEM32\CONFIG\TmpDef00.log	0	4/5/93	11:33:32AM	A
E:\WINNT\SYSTEM32\CONFIG\TSHEL000.log	40960	4/9/93	10:29:44AM	A
E:\WINNT\SYSTEM32\netdde.log	420	4/6/93	3:53:34AM	A

WORKING WITH DIRECTORIES

You can create, copy, and move directories in the File Manager. When copying or moving directories, the File Manager can copy an entire directory tree or branches of it to a new directory or disk. It's easy to delete directories as well, but you'll want to use caution when you do, because the File Manager will also delete a directory's branching subdirectories unless you specify otherwise.

Creating Directories

Choose the Create Directory option on the File menu to create new directories, but first select the directory you want the new directory to branch from. Alternatively, you can type the full path for the new directory in the Create Directory dialog box.

Try the following exercise to create a new directory called TEMP. You'll delete the directory later.

First, click a directory in which to add the new directory. Next, choose Create Directory on the File menu. A dialog box similar to the following appears:

In the Name text box, type **TEST** as the name of the new directory, then click OK to create the directory. If you didn't select a parent directory ahead of time, you can type the full path for the new directory in the Name field.

Copying and Moving Directories

When you copy a directory, Windows makes a duplicate at the new location. When you move a directory, Windows deletes the original directory after it is moved to the new location. You copy and move directories to reorganize your system. Remember that any branching subdirectories of a directory are copied or moved along with it, unless you specify otherwise.

You can copy an entire directory and its subdirectories from one network computer to another. This is useful for making backups, or for duplicating the file structure of one computer on another system.

Try the following exercise to move the TEST directory from one parent directory to another. Don't worry about where you move it. You'll delete the directory later.

First, locate the TEST directory and click it. Next, click and drag the TEST directory's icon over the icon of another directory. A confirmation message will ask if you are sure you want to move the directory: choose Yes. In a moment, you'll see the new structure of the directory tree with the TEST directory in its new location.

Typically, you'll move rather than copy directories from one location to another—copying creates duplicates of every file, which wastes disk space.

When you want to copy an entire directory, hold down the CTRL key and drag the directory icon to the new location. To copy directories between different drives, just click and drag. To move directories between drives (rather than copy, which is the default), hold down the ALT key while clicking and dragging.

You can also use the File Copy and File Move commands to copy directories. The advantage of this method is that you can type the exact source and destination path.

Deleting Directories

In this section, you delete the TEST directory. You have learned in previous exercises how to copy and move files to it, and how to move the directory to another location. Now it's time to delete this practice directory so that it doesn't take up space on your hard drive. To delete a directory, highlight its icon in the directory tree and press the DEL key. Alternatively, select File and choose the Delete option, then type the path and directory name.

When deleting directories, you are asked to confirm the deletion of every file in the directory. If there are subdirectories, you are then asked to confirm deletion of those files. You're also asked to confirm the deletion of the directories themselves. Make sure you read the dialog boxes and know what you are deleting. On the other hand, if you are sure you want to delete the entire directory and its subtree, you can bypass the confirmation messages when they first appear.

USING DISK COMMANDS

Besides the network options discussed earlier, the Disk menu has options to copy files between floppy disks, change a disk's electronic label, and format floppy disks. Refer to Chapter 19 for hard disk management options.

Note | Disks are formatted with the DOS FAT, not the NTFS file system.

Copying Disks

Choose the Copy Disk option on the File Manager Disk menu to copy the contents of one disk to another. A dialog box similar to the one shown here appears:

The copy operation is similar to the DOS DISKCOPY command. You cannot copy to different disk types (for example, from 5 1/4-inch disks to 3 1/2-inch disks). If your drives are different sizes, you'll need to swap disks. The disk to copy is the *source* and the disk to copy to is the *destination*.

Choose the location of the source disk in the Source In field and the location of the destination in the Destination In field. If the second drive is a different format, you can't use it. Instead, specify the same drive letter in both the Source In and Destination In fields. The File Manager asks you to change disks. If the first and the second disk drives are the same type, you can specify the letter of each drive in each of the fields.

Labeling a Disk

The Label Disk option on the Disk menu is used to change the electronic label on disks. You see this label at the top of directory windows, or when you list a directory of a disk with the DOS DIR command. The electronic label is used by programs to identify which disk is in a drive. In some cases you may need to change this label if you are using an old disk for a new purpose. Or you can change it for aesthetic reasons, if you prefer to display a different name in directory windows. A disk label cannot exceed 11 characters.

To change a hard disk label, click the drive icon of the disk you want to change, then choose the Label Disk option on the Disk menu. Type the new disk label and click the OK button.

To change a floppy drive label, place the disk in a floppy drive, then click the icon for that drive. Choose the Label Disk option from the Disk menu, type the new label, and click the OK button.

Note

You cannot change the label of a shared disk that you are attached to.

Formatting Disks

Use the Format Disk command on the Disk menu to format floppy disks. When you choose the command, the following dialog box appears:

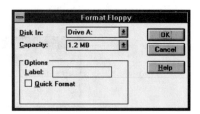

Follow these steps to format a floppy disk:

1. Place a disk to format in the floppy drive you want to use for formatting.

2. Choose the Format Disk command.

3. Choose the disk drive where you place the floppy disk in the Disk In field.

4. Choose the capacity for the disk in the Capacity field.

5. Type an electronic name for the disk up to 11 characters long in the Label field.

6. Enable the Make System Disk field to make the disk bootable. Enabling this option adds the DOS system files to the disk. If the disk will only be used for data storage, don't enable this option, since the system files take up room on the disk.

7. Enable the Quick Format field to erase a disk that was previously formatted.

8. Click the OK button to begin disk formatting. A dialog box displays the progress, and you can continue with other tasks while the disk is being formatted.

Note

When a disk is quick formatted, its file allocation table (FAT) and root directory are deleted. It is not scanned for bad sectors, but all space on the disk is made available for new files. Because this option removes all directories and subdirectories, it is a quick way to prepare old disks for new uses. However, if you suspect a disk has bad sectors, do not enable this option.

When the format is complete, you are asked if you want to format another disk. If you choose Yes, the Format Disk dialog box stays open with some of the parameters you previously set. If you choose No, the dialog box closes.

Inside

& Out

CHAPTER 8

Using Local and Remote Printers

This chapter explains how to print from your applications and how to control print jobs sent to local or remote printers using the Print Manager utility. You'll see how to connect with a printer that is shared on another system.

Printer drivers are files that define the features and functions of a printer. A driver must be loaded before print jobs can be sent to a printer. However, if you are connecting with a network printer, you won't need a printer driver on your local system since Windows NT uses the driver located on the network computer that shares its printer. Printer installation involves copying printer drivers from the Windows NT disk set or from disks supplied by the printer manufacturer to the computer where the printer is attached, then configuring the driver to fit your needs.

This chapter assumes that a printer driver was installed on your system during installation, or that you intend to connect with a network printer. If you need to install a new printer or change the properties of an existing printer, refer to Chapter 18, which covers printer management topics. This chapter covers only the basics of printing.

PRINTING FROM APPLICATIONS

Most applications have a Print option and a Print Setup option on their File menu, as shown here:

The Print Option   Choose the Print option to send the document to the printer (which is selected with the Print Setup option). You can usually specify the number of copies, resolution, and other printer options.

The Print Setup Option   Choose the Print Setup option to select the printer you want to print to, including printers attached to the network. You can also specify various printer configurations and features.

Printing a document is as simple as choosing Print on the File menu and clicking the OK button. However, you might need to set up the printer first, so the Print Setup option is discussed in the next section. You'll work through some examples using the Print Setup dialog box in Write, so start the accessory now by double-clicking its icon.

Printer Setup

When you choose the Print Setup option from an application's File menu, you see dialog boxes like the ones shown in Figures 8-1 and 8-2. The dialog box lists your current printer connection, the orientation for printing, and in some cases, the form in use. The actual layout of the dialog box may differ among applications, but the features are usually similar.

| Note | If you are printing to PostScript printers, or sending documents to service bureaus that use PostScript files, refer to Chapter 18. |

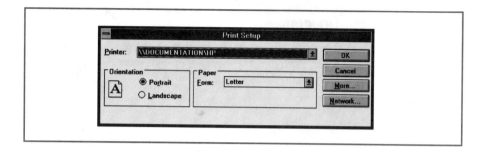

FIGURE 8-1

One form of the Print
Setup dialog box

Printer

In Figure 8-1, you can view and select a different printer in the Printer field by clicking
the down arrow button. In Figure 8-2, a default printer is specified, but you can choose
another printer by clicking the Specific Printer button and selecting the printer you want
from the drop-down list box. Note the following:

- Local printers are listed with the name assigned to them during setup.

- Network printers include the computer name and where the printer is located.
  In Figure 8-1, the printer field lists a network printer located on a computer
  called "DOCUMENTATION." The format used to give the computer name
  and printer location is shown below. The dual backslashes indicate a computer
  name. You only need to type this information if the printer you want is not in
  the list.

  computername on *printername*

- To connect with a network printer not listed in the Printer drop-down list box,
  click the Network button. For further directions, refer to the "Connecting with
  Network Printers" section later in this chapter.

Once you select a printer, you can change some of the other options in the dialog
box, as described next.

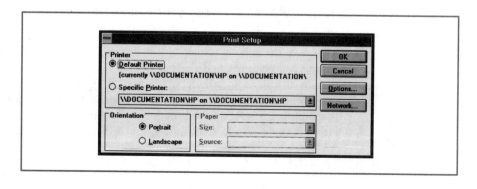

FIGURE 8-2

Another form of the Print
Setup dialog box

Orientation

The orientation specifies whether a document is printed horizontally or vertically on the paper. Portrait is the standard, upright vertical printing mode; landscape is the sideways, horizontal printing mode.

Paper

In the Paper field, choose the form you want to use. Forms define paper sizes and margins. Forms are usually assigned to the trays of laser printers and other multi-tray printers. A number of forms are already defined in the printer driver that comes with Windows NT:

Paper Type	Paper Size
Legal	8.50in width, 14.00in height
Letter	8.50in width, 11.00in height
Statement	5.50in width, 8.50in height
6 3/4 Envelope	3.62in width, 6.50in height
Envelope #10	4.12in width, 9.50in height

You choose a form in the Form drop-down list box. You occasionally might need to create your own forms—to print on company letterhead, for example. In a multi-tray printer, you would place the letterhead in one of the trays, then create a special form with appropriate margins and assign it to the letterhead tray. To define your own forms, choose the Forms option in the Print Manager as described in Chapter 18.

Forms play a role that is more important than just defining the paper and margin size. They let Windows NT know what type of form is actually loaded in the printer. If a network user connects with the printer and sends a print job with a form definition that is different than the form currently assigned to the printer, the print job waits until the form is loaded. An "owner" or "operator" of the shared printer must load the requested paper and specify in the Print Manager Properties dialog box that the form has changed. The print job then continues.

Setting Advanced Document Properties

Click the More button or the Options button on the Print Setup dialog box to set special features of the selected printer. A dialog box like the one in Figure 8-3 appears. (The options and fields of this dialog box depend on the type of printer selected. You might need to click an additional Options button to see this particular style of dialog box.)

Most dialog boxes will have the Graphics Resolution field. Choose a resolution that is appropriate for the type of print job and the quality of printing you want. Click the Help button to see additional information on the options that appear for your printer.

FIGURE 8-3

Setting special printer
options

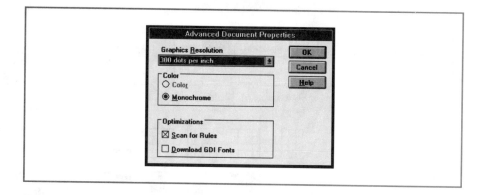

Halftone

Some Print Setup dialog boxes will have a Halftone button that you click to specify how, among other things, color graphics should be printed on black-and-white printers. *Halftoning* is a process of converting colors into patterns of dots that simulate variations in gray, or "gray scales." The following image is a halftone:

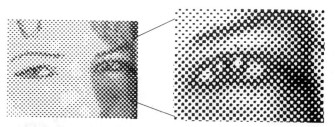

In the exploded view, notice that each "dot" is actually a matrix that is either fully or partially filled in with black. Each dot is associated with the dots-per-inch resolution of the printer.

The matrix, or *halftone cell*, is a grid size you specify such as 2x2, 4x4, 6x6, and so on, depending on the quality of color-to-black-and-white conversion you want. As the cell size (matrix of dots) increases, so do the number of gray scales, but the image resolution decreases. This is because each matrix forms a black (or white) dot in the printed image and the larger the matrix, the larger the dots in the image. Typically, this is not a problem on high-resolution printers that print in the range of 1200 to 3000 dots per inch since each matrix of dots will still be so small that a magnifying glass will be needed to see it. However, on low-resolution laser printers (300 dots per inch), large halftone cells pose a problem.

When converting color images to black and white, the more grays available, the better. However, that requires increasing the dot matrix and thus reducing the image resolution. In Figure 8-4, the upper image illustrates how a 2x2 grid produces black, white, and three shades of gray. The lower image illustrates how a 4x4 grid produces black, white, and 15 shades of gray.

FIGURE 8-4

Increasing the halftone cell size produces more grays

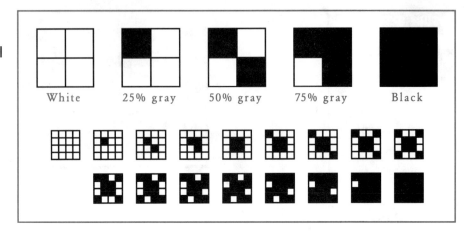

White   25% gray   50% gray   75% gray   Black

Note

Keep in mind that the matrix is the dot that forms the image. The larger the matrix, the larger each individual dot and the less the resolution.

You use the Halftone options on the Print Setup dialog box to specify the type of resolution and grayscale quality you want. The dialog box that appears depends on the printer selected, so refer to the help options for each printer.

Printing

Choose Print from the File menu to display a dialog box like the one shown in Figure 8-5. Note that this box may not look identical from application to application, but its features are similar.

In the Print Range box, choose All to print the entire document, choose Selection to print only a highlighted part of the document, or choose Pages to specify a range of

FIGURE 8-5

A typical Print dialog box

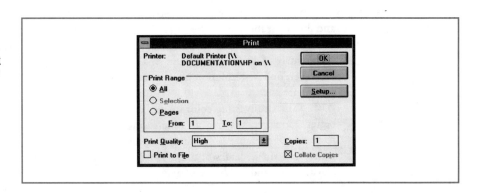

pages. If you choose Pages, type the starting page number in the From text box and the ending page number in the To text box. Set the other fields as follows.

- ☑ You can choose a Print Quality on some printers. Printing at higher resolutions takes more time (and toner), but gives better results when printing pictures.

- ☑ In the Copies field, type the number of copies you want. If Collate Copies is enabled, each copy prints separately. If disabled, Windows prints all copies specified of the first page, then all copies of the second page, and so on.

- ☑ Enable the Print to File option to send the print information to a file on disk. You can then print this document whenever you like, on this system or on another system, without loading the applications used in creating the document. When you print to a file, Windows opens a dialog box in which you specify the filename.

THE PRINT MANAGER

The Print Manager is the main utility for installing and managing local and network printers. Start it by double-clicking the Print Manager icon in the Main group of the Program Manager or in the Control Panel. A Print Manager window like the one shown in Figure 8-6 appears.

Most of the options on this dialog box are for installing and managing printers, but you can monitor your print jobs and change their order if you have the right permissions.

The window in Figure 8-6 shows several printer names. Some are local and some are shared network printers. You double-click a printer icon at the bottom of the window to view and change its contents. The icons represent local and network printers you are connected with. You might want to view the list of jobs in a printer window when deciding which printer to use, then use the one that is least busy.

Note the Toolbar under the menu bar. You can click these buttons to quickly access items found on the menus. These buttons are described next.

Resume   If a printer has stopped, click the Resume button after adding paper, changing toner, or otherwise servicing the printer.

Pause   Click the Pause button to stop printing on the selected printer.

Connect   Click the Connect button to connect with a shared network printer.

Disconnect   Click the Disconnect button to disconnect from a shared printer.

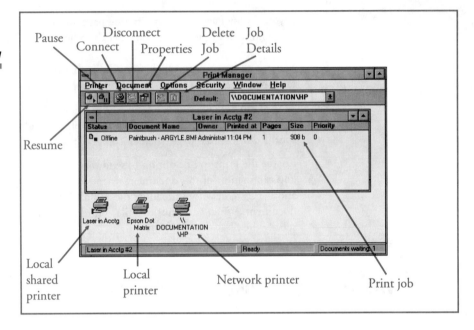

FIGURE 8-6

The Print Manager window

Properties   Click the Properties button to view or change the properties of the selected printer.

Delete Job   Click the Delete Job button to remove the selected print job.

Job Details   Click the Job Details button to view information about the selected print job.

Connecting with Network Printers

You can connect with printers on your network by choosing the Connect To Printer option on the Printer menu, or by clicking the Connect button on the Toolbar. A dialog box similar to Figure 8-7 appears.

A list of computers with shared printers appears in the Shared Printers field. Note the description of each printer. Use the list to browse for available printers. Click each printer, then view the Printer Information field at the bottom of the dialog box. It tells you how many print jobs this printer has waiting. You might want to continue browsing for a printer that is not busy.

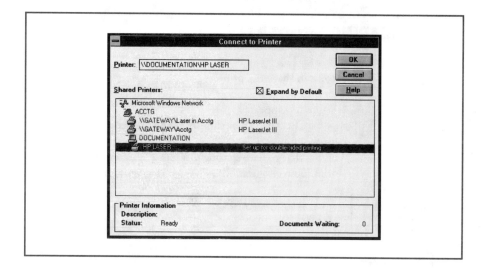

FIGURE 8-7

Connecting with network printers

Once you find the printer you want to use, click its name in the Shared Printers field. The name then appears in the Printer field. Click OK to connect with the printer. A document window appears for the printer with a list of print jobs, if any.

Permissions set by the owner of the printer may control your access. These permissions are as follows:

- **No Access** You cannot access a printer with these permissions unless you are an administrative user.

- **Print** This right lets you send print jobs to the printer. If you have permission to print, you can also control printing of the document since you are the "creator/owner" of the document.

- **Manage Documents** With this permission, you can control the settings of documents and pause, resume, restart, and delete documents.

- **Full Control** With this permission, you have full control over the printer and can even change permissions on this printer.

Disconnect from a Printer

When you're done with a shared network printer, you can remove it. First select the printer's window or its icon, then choose Remove Printer from the Printer menu, or click the Disconnect button.

SHARING PRINTERS

You can share the printers on your system with other users on the network. First select the printer, then choose the Properties dialog box. A dialog box similar to the one in Figure 8-8 appears.

Click the "Share this printer on the network" box, then type a name and description for the printer. Click OK to share the printer. There are certain management responsibilities that go with sharing printers. For example, you can set permissions, priorities, and print job configurations. Chapter 18 gives more details on printer management.

Note	When you're ready to stop sharing a printer, open the Properties dialog box again and disable the "Share this printer on the network" box.

BASIC PRINT MANAGER TASKS

This section describes how to manage the print jobs you send to local or network printers. You can pause a print job, change its order in the queue, and remove it from the queue. Usually, you can control only your own print jobs unless you are a member of the Administrator or Power User group, or you have the Manage Documents permission.

The window for each printer lists the print jobs that are waiting to print. Figure 8-6 shows one print job waiting because the printer is offline. Keep in mind that some print jobs in the window may belong to other users if the printer is a shared network printer.

FIGURE 8-8

Sharing a printer

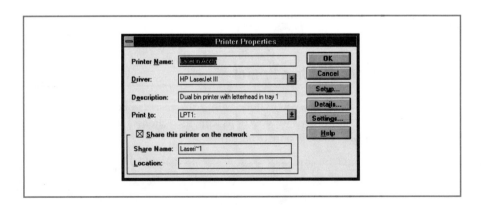

Viewing Document Details

You can view the details about a specific print job by first highlighting the print job, then choosing Details from the Document menu. You also can click the Details button on the Toolbar. A dialog box similar to Figure 8-9 appears.

The following tells you what each piece of information displayed in the Document Details dialog box means (follow along in Figure 8-9):

Document Title   Gives you the name of the document and the applications that created it.

Status   Tells you whether the job is printing or paused.

Pages   Tells you the number of pages to print.

Size   Gives the size of the file waiting to print.

Owner   Tells the user account name of the person who sent the print job.

Printed On   Tells which printer is printing the job.

Notify   When a print job completes, the owner is notified. To notify another user, change the name in the Notify field.

Printed At   Gives you the time the print job was sent.

FIGURE 8-9

Displaying details about
a print job

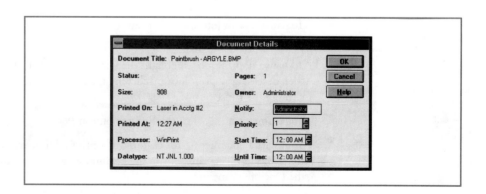

Priority   Tells you the priority of this job. Jobs with higher priorities print before those with lower priorities. You can change the priority of a print job so it prints before other print jobs. The priority range is from 1 to 99.

Processor   Tells you the Windows NT printing utility used to print the job. Some special applications use their own print processor.

Start Time   Lets you specify the time a print job starts. Use Until Time to specify a specific time that you want printing to halt.

Datatype   Applications that use their own print processors may also supply a special datatype as listed in this column.

Until Time   Lets you specify how long a print job is allowed to print.

Setting the Default Printer

If the Printer Manager has several local and network printer configurations, you can select one of them as the default. Then when you print from some applications, print jobs are sent to the default printer unless you specify otherwise.

Choose a default printer by clicking its name in the Default drop-down list box on the Toolbar.

Managing Your Print Jobs

You can pause, resume, and rearrange your print jobs in a printer's window as described here:

- To pause a print job, click the print job you want to pause, then choose Pause from the Printer menu or click the Pause button.

- To pause all print jobs, highlight the window of the printer you want to pause, then deselect any print jobs by clicking them with the right mouse button or by clicking the Pause button.

- To resume printing, click the Resume button.

- To restart a document—for example, if a print job is unsuccessful because the toner was low—reprint it from the beginning by choosing the Restart option on the Document menu.

▧   To rearrange print jobs, click a print job and drag it to a new position in the list of print jobs.

▧   To delete a print job, click the job you want to delete, then click the Delete Job button on the Toolbar.

PRINTING FROM THE FILE MANAGER

In the File Manager, you can print a document by *dragging and dropping* its icon onto one of the printer windows in the Print Manager. In addition, only associated files can be printed with the drag-and-drop method.

Another way to print in the File Manager is with the Print option on the File menu. Click the file you want to print, select File, and choose Print. When the Print dialog box appears, the file you selected will be listed in the Text field. Click the OK button to print the file. Alternatively, you can just type the name of the file you want to print in the field.

Inside

- The ClipBook Viewer

- Chatting with Other Users

- Notepad

- Windows Write

- The Bitmap Editor: Paintbrush

- Multimedia Accessories

& Out

CHAPTER 9

Utilities and Accessories

This chapter provides detailed coverage of the ClipBook and gives an overview of other Windows accessories. Refer to the extensive help procedures for detailed information on options, features, and procedures not covered in this chapter.

THE CLIPBOOK VIEWER

The ClipBook Viewer stores text, graphics, and other information and lets you share that information with other users. Its icon appears in the Program Manager Main group. ClipBook lets you cut and paste information among applications (much like the Clipboard) but it also provides a cataloging feature that lets you permanently store Clipboard images and other information for later use in an area called the Local ClipBook.

Figure 9-1 shows what you see when you double-click the ClipBook Viewer icon.

ClipBook Viewer Features

The ClipBook Viewer has these features:

☑ The regular Clipboard appears as an icon on the lower left of the screen. It holds the most recent image you cut or copied using commands on the Edit menu of an application.

☑ The Local ClipBook window displays images in a reduced view called a *thumbnail.*

☑ Each image exists on a *page.*

☑ You can paste text, graphics, spreadsheet data, and just about any type of information on a page of the Local Clipboard. The information is referred to as an *object* once it's on the page.

FIGURE 9-1

The ClipBook Viewer

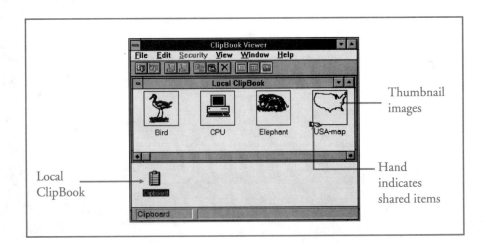

◪ To display ClipBook images full size, or simply list them by name, you can choose a view method on the View menu.

◪ Each image in the Local ClipBook has a name. This is how you refer to the image when sharing it with other users on the network, or how other network users refer to it.

◪ The ClipBook Viewer can hold as many as 127 pages of information.

Objects on the Clipboard are temporary and overwritten every time you execute another Copy or Cut command within an application. However, you can paste Clipboard objects to the Local ClipBook, which retains them for later use, even if you close the ClipBook and shut your system down. You don't need to execute any Save commands once you've pasted an object. ClipBook Viewer automatically saves your updates so you see them the next time you start ClipBook.

The best feature of the ClipBook Viewer is that you can share Local ClipBook objects with others. Network users who connect with your ClipBook see the objects you've shared and can copy them for use in their own documents. They cannot see objects in your ClipBook that you have not shared.

Figure 9-2 shows how a ClipBook window from another computer appears when you connect with it over the network. In this example, the ClipBook on the network computer called SI-VALLEY is visible. You can use ClipBook images from other computers in the same way you use your Local ClipBook. Typically, you copy objects from your ClipBook and paste them to your own ClipBooks. However, with special permissions you can paste objects into other users' ClipBooks.

The ClipBook Viewer can enhance one-on-one work projects. For example, suppose you are discussing a project with a coworker at a distant location. Your coworker wants to see the art you've developed so far, so you place it on your Local ClipBook and

FIGURE 9-2

Connecting with another ClipBook over the network

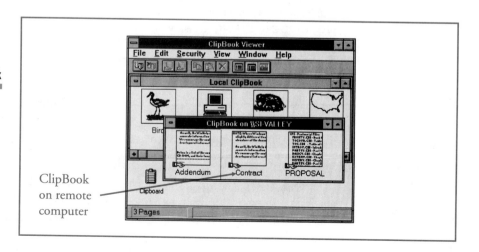

ClipBook on remote computer

share it over the network. Your coworker can connect with your ClipBook and look at the art during the course of your conversation.

Now consider how the ClipBook can facilitate company-wide projects. With it workers can integrate information for a report, including spreadsheet data from the accounting department, text from the marketing department, and art from the graphics department. Each department places its information on its ClipBooks and shares it. The project manager then integrates the shared information into the final document.

In Chapter 10, you'll see how to create even more sophisticated compound documents by combining linked information that is automatically updated when the original source information is changed.

The ClipBook Toolbar

Table 9-1 describes the buttons on the Toolbar. Each Toolbar button is also represented by a menu option on the ClipBook menu, as discussed later in the "Setting ClipBook Features" section.

When you first start ClipBook, the Clipboard is minimized. Before you read further in this chapter, you might want to restore the Clipboard and rearrange the ClipBook Viewer so you can see both the Clipboard and Local ClipBook.

The Clipboard

In Chapter 6, you learned how to use the Copy, Cut, and Paste commands on the Edit menu of Windows applications. You still use these same commands when working with the ClipBook. To place information on the Clipboard, you first outline or highlight the information (as described next), and then choose Copy or Cut from the Edit menu, or press CTRL-C or CTRL-X, respectively.

- To select text in a word processing program, you typically drag through the text with the mouse pointer.

- In drawing applications, you usually click the graphic object you want to copy, or drag a box around it.

- In a spreadsheet program such as Excel, you click and drag the mouse pointer through the cells you want to copy.

Once the information is on the Clipboard, you can paste it elsewhere. Open the application in which you want to paste the information, and then position the mouse pointer or insertion point and choose the Paste command, or press CTRL-V.

TABLE 9-1

The ClipBook Toolbar
Buttons

Click		To
	Connect button	Connect to a ClipBook on another computer
	Disconnect button	Disconnect from a ClipBook on another computer
	Share button	Share a ClipBook page
	Stop Sharing button	Stop sharing a ClipBook page
	Copy button	Copy the selected ClipBook page onto the Clipboard
	Paste button	Paste the contents of the Clipboard onto the ClipBook
	Delete button	Delete the contents of the Clipboard or selected ClipBook page
	Table of Contents button	Display the titles of the pages saved on the ClipBook
	Thumbnails button	Display small pictures (thumbnails) of each page on the ClipBook
	Full Page button	Display the contents of the selected ClipBook page

Capturing the Screen and Windows to the Clipboard

You can capture the entire screen or the active window to the Clipboard using the following methods. The objects are captured as bitmaps that you can paste into Paint-brush or other bitmap editors. You can then change the images as necessary.

Capturing the Entire Screen   Press the PRINT SCREEN key to capture the entire screen. On older keyboards, you may need to press ALT-PRINT SCREEN or SHIFT-PRINT SCREEN.

Capturing the Active Window   Press ALT-PRINT SCREEN to capture only the active window.

Saving Clipboard Objects to Files

While ClipBook provides a method for saving Clipboard objects to the Local ClipBook for later use, you also can save a Clipboard object to a separate file. For example, you might need to save a Clipboard object on disk and mail the disk to another user. Or, you might have an object that you want to save, but you don't want it on the Local ClipBook. Follow these steps to save the object:

1. Capture the graphic, text, or other information you want to save using Clipboard commands.

2. Open the ClipBook and click the Clipboard icon or document window to make it active.

3. Choose Save As from the File menu. Type a name for the file and click the OK button. Clipboard files are automatically assigned the .CLP extension.

   Remember that Clipboard objects are overwritten when you capture a new object. Use the Save As option as an alternative method of saving an object you don't place on the Local ClipBook. To retrieve a previously saved object, choose the Open command on the ClipBook File menu and specify the name of the previously saved file.

Setting ClipBook Features

The View menu shown in Figure 9-3 has options for customizing the ClipBook window and choosing the type of view you want to see in the Clipboard and Local ClipBook. The following sections describe these options.

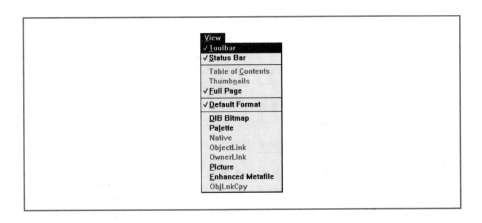

The Toolbar Option   Enable this option to display the Toolbar. Disable it to remove the Toolbar so you can reduce the size of the ClipBook Viewer window. When the Toolbar is disabled, you can still access related options from menus.

The Status Bar Option   The status bar displays messages related to your activities. You can disable the option to reduce the size of the ClipBook window if necessary.

The Table of Contents Option   This option is only available when the Local ClipBook (or a ClipBook shared from another network computer) is active. If you enable it, the Local ClipBook (or shared ClipBook) window appears as shown here:

Each object is listed by name. If the object is shared, a hand appears in the left corner under its icon.

The Thumbnails Option   When this option is enabled, you see a reduced view of the objects on the Local ClipBook with enough detail to discern the image. The Local ClipBook in Figure 9-1 shows how thumbnails appear.

The Full Page Option   Click this option to display images in the Local ClipBook (or shared ClipBook) at their full size. When you click this option, an extra set of buttons appears in the scroll bar of the window; these let you jump between object pages.

Format Options

The remaining options on the View menu depend on the type of image on the Clipboard or object selected in the ClipBook. The Clipboard accepts a number of text or graphics formats so you can transfer information between different applications. For example, when you copy an image in Paintbrush, the object is placed on the Clipboard in a default format, a bitmap format, and a picture format. When you paste the object into another application, the application uses the format that it understands the best. In other words, the application doesn't need to convert the image because the source application (in this case, Paintbrush) has already supplied several different possible formats.

You can see how the image or text appears in the different formats by clicking any of the available options, such as DIB, Bitmap, Palette, or Picture. Doing so has no permanent affect on the image or text, however.

Text is stored in three formats:

✓   *Owner Display* is the way text looks in the document, based on the character formatting you applied to it.

✓   *Text* displays the characters as plain text.

✓   *OEM Text* is the MS-DOS-based text format.

Graphic image formats vary widely. You'll see a list of different formats, but some are usually grayed, which means they are not available for the current image.

Working with Your Local ClipBook

When you have information on the Clipboard that you want to save for later use or share with other users on the network, you can paste it to the Local ClipBook. Remember, however, that you can paste objects to other users' ClipBooks if you have special permissions, as discussed later. To paste an object, follow these steps:

1.   Capture the graphics, text, or other information on the Clipboard using the Copy or Cut option on the Edit menu of the application that holds the information.

2.   Open the ClipBook. You'll see the captured information in the Clipboard window.

3.   Click the Local ClipBook window to make it active.

4.   Choose the Paste option on the Edit menu, or press CTRL-V. The following dialog box appears when you paste the object to the Local ClipBook:

5.   Type a name for the object in the Page Name field.

6.   Enable the Share Item Now option if you want to make the item shareable. If not, disable the check box. If you're not sure whether you'll need to share this

object, don't make it shareable now—you can always choose to share it at a later date by choosing the Share As option on the File menu.

7.   Click the OK button to paste the object onto the Local ClipBook window.

Sharing a Local ClipBook Object

This section describes how to share ClipBook pages. When you share a ClipBook page, other users at remote network computers can copy the object on the page to their Clipboard and paste it into applications. If you decided to share the object as described in step 6 above, the Share ClipBook Page dialog box appears as shown here:

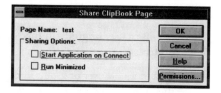

| Note |

If you want to share a page that's already pasted on the Local ClipBook, you can share that page by clicking it and choosing Share from the ClipBook File menu.

The Share ClipBook Page dialog box options are discussed below.

▰   Enabling the Start Application on Connect option allows remote users to establish a link to the application you used to create the shared object.

▰   Enabling the Run Minimized option reduces the application to an icon when it starts.

▰   Clicking the Permissions button lets you define the type of access users have to the shared object, as discussed next.

ClipBook Permissions

You can control who can access shared ClipBook pages by setting permissions. Do this when pasting the object by clicking the Permissions button on the Share ClipBook Page dialog box, or later by first clicking the shared object, then choosing Permissions from the Security menu. Either way, the ClipBook Page Permissions dialog box shown in Figure 9-4 appears.

The procedure for using this dialog box is the same as the procedure for sharing directories or printers:

FIGURE 9-4

The ClipBook Page
Permissions screen

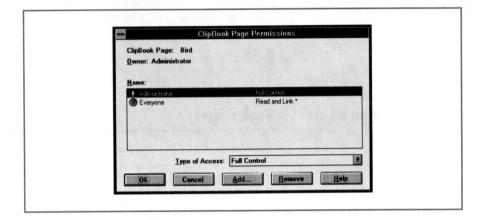

✓   Choose a user or group in the Name field, then select a permission in the Type
    of Access field.

✓   To add a new user or group in the Name field, click the Add button and follow
    the procedures discussed in other chapters for selecting another user or group.
    When the Add Users and Groups dialog box appears, click a new user or group,
    then click Add and the OK button.

✓   To delete a user or group from the permissions list, click the Remove button.

After selecting a user or group, you select permissions in the Type of Access dialog
box. The available permissions are described here.

No Access   No users in the selected group have access to the object.

Read   Users with this permission can access pages of your ClipBook that you've made
shareable and copy shared object from them.

Read and Link   Users with this permission can access pages of your ClipBook that
you've made shareable, copy objects from them, and establish links for creating compound documents, as discussed later in this chapter and in Chapter 10.

Change   Users with this permission can change (re-paste) shared images on your
ClipBook.

Full Control   Users with this right have all the permissions listed above, and can
control the permission levels of shared objects.

Connecting with Other ClipBooks

You connect with other users' ClipBooks to use the shared items on those ClipBooks. When you make a connection, a window appears in your ClipBook with the computer name of the remote ClipBook. Follow these steps to make the connection:

1. Open the ClipBook Viewer if it is not already started.

2. Choose Connect from the File menu.

3. The Select Computer dialog box appears; it will look similar to the screen shown in Figure 9-5. Choose a computer from the list in the Select Computer field and click OK.

    In a moment, the ClipBook of the remote computer appears in your ClipBook Viewer window. You can now copy the ClipBook objects to the Clipboard and paste them in documents, as reviewed in the next section.

Using ClipBook Objects in Your Documents

When you need to use an object on your Local ClipBook or the ClipBook of a remote user, simply locate the object and copy it to the Clipboard as described in the following steps:

1. Open the ClipBook.

2. If the object you need is on a remote computer's ClipBook, follow the procedures in the previous section to connect with that ClipBook.

3. Make the Local ClipBook or remote ClipBook window active by clicking it with the mouse.

FIGURE 9-5

Connecting with another computer

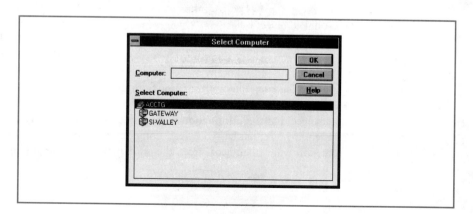

4. Change the view by choosing Table of Contents (name listing), Thumbnails (small pictures), or Full Page (full-size image) from the View menu.

5. Click the page you want to use.

6. Click the Copy button on the Toolbar, or press CTRL-C to copy the object to the Clipboard.

7. Switch to the window where you want to paste the object and position the insertion point.

8. Choose Paste from the Edit menu or press CTRL-V. The object appears in the document.

Object Linking and Embedding

Most Windows applications now provide support for object linking and embedding (OLE). Chapter 10 fully covers OLE, but for now you should know that objects pasted from other applications can be much more than static items in your documents. Objects can be *embedded* in documents, or *linked* to the original file from which they were copied, as discussed next.

Embedded Objects   Most objects you paste are embedded. If you double-click an embedded object, the application used to create that object automatically starts and comes up on screen with the object in its workspace ready to be edited. For example, if you create a company logo in Paintbrush, and then copy and paste the logo into a Write document, you can double-click the pasted object in the Write document at any time to quickly start Paintbrush and make editing changes to the object. An embedded object "remembers" the application that created it. Note, however, that the application must be available on the local system.

Linked Objects   A linked object is an embedded object with a few extra properties. A linked object reflects any changes made to the original object. For example, you could paste-link a column of numbers from an Excel spreadsheet called BUDGET.XLS into a Write document. Later, if anyone makes changes to BUDGET.XLS from Excel, those changes are automatically made to the pasted information in the Write document. If you copied the spreadsheet information from another network user's ClipBook, and that other user made changes to the spreadsheet on their system, the ClipBook information is changed and the information in your document also changes! Linking is an extremely useful feature that lets you create compound documents over the network. If you paste art into your documents from the art department's shared ClipBook, any changes the artists make to the art in your document are automatically updated the next time you open the document.

Creating Document Links

Creating compound documents with network links enables workgroups to collaborate on projects without a lot of running around and organizational management. OLE keeps the information updated as it changes. Here are the steps for linking ClipBook informa- tion into your document:

1. Start your ClipBook and click the Connect button.

2. Connect to the ClipBook of the remote computer that has the object you want to integrate into your document.

3. Select an object on the remote ClipBook and click the Copy button.

4. Switch to your application and position the insertion point where you want the object pasted.

5. Choose Paste Special from the Edit menu. A dialog box similar to the following appears:

6. In the Data Type field, click the format you want to use for the pasted data. The highlighted default format is usually sufficient.

7. Click the Paste Link button.

This pastes the information into your document and establishes a link to the source document file that contains the information the remote user pasted to his or her ClipBook. Note that the information must exist in a file, as well as on a shared ClipBook page. Any changes made to the source file are automatically updated in your document. Chapter 10 goes into much greater depth about embedding and linking.

CHATTING WITH OTHER USERS

The Chat accessory provides a convenient way to converse with another user over the network. While a phone call might initially seem more convenient, with Chat you can copy and save messages, which often prove helpful later. You also can insert blocks of text written with other applications into the Chat window. Thus, CHAT provides an easy way to contact users and send them some text they need for a document. The standard Cut, Copy, and Paste commands are available on the Chat Edit menu for doing this. Figure 9-6 shows the Chat window.

Click one of the three buttons in the Toolbar to either dial, answer, or hang up a connection, respectively. You can also choose these options on the Conversation menu. To dial, follow these steps:

1. Click the dial button to display the Select Computer dialog box. (Refer back to Figure 9-5.)

2. Click the name of the computer you want to connect with. A "Dialing" message appears in the message bar. The other system beeps, and the Chat icon appears on its desktop with the handset "rattling" in the holder.

3. The person being called double-clicks the icon to answer the call, or if the Chat window is open, clicks the Answer button.

4. To end the conversation, click the Hang-up button, or choose the Hang Up option from the Conversation menu.

Messages you type appear in the upper window; messages received from other users appear in the lower window. You can change this arrangement by choosing Preferences

---

FIGURE 9-6

The Chat window

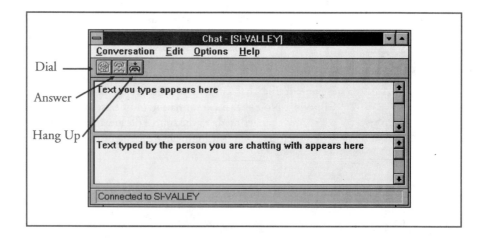

from the Options menu. The following dialog box appears:

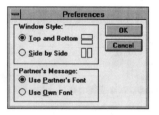

In the Window Style field, choose one of the window arrangements. You also can choose which font to use by clicking an option in the Partner's Message field. If your partner is sending formatted messages, be sure that Use Partner's Font is selected. If you want to change the default font used by Chat, choose the Font option on the Options menu. To change the background color, choose the Background Color option on the Options menu.

NOTEPAD

Notepad is an ASCII text editor used to view, create, and edit small text files such as batch files, notes, and log files. The Notepad window shown here consists of a title bar and workspace:

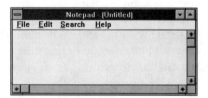

The following menu options are available.

The File Menu   The Notepad File menu has all the standard Open, Save, and Print options discussed in Chapter 6.

The Edit Menu   The Edit menu has the standard Clipboard Cut, Copy, and Paste options. You also can click the Undo option to restore any editing changes you made. These are the other options:

☑   *Select All*   Choose the Select All option to select all the text in the Notepad workspace so you can copy it to the Clipboard.

☑   *Use Time/Date*   Choose the Time/Date option to insert the current time and date at the location of the insertion point.

☑   *Word Wrap*   Choose the Word Wrap option to wrap the text at the current window border. You can resize the window to change the current word wrap. The text fits into the new window size and prints using that width.

The Search Menu   This menu has these Find and Find Next options:

☑   *Find*   Choose Find, then type the text you want to search for. Click Match Case to search for text that matches the case of the word or phrase for which you're searching.

☑   *Find Next*   Choose Find Next (or press F3) to find the next instance of the text you searched for in the previous search.

WINDOWS WRITE

Write is an advanced version of Notepad that includes character and paragraph formatting capabilities. In addition, you can control page layout by adjusting the margins, indents, and page numbers, as well as the headers and footers of a document. Write does not have editing tools such as spelling and grammar checkers, or a thesaurus like more advanced word processors do, but it is an extremely useful word processor, and it's included with Windows NT.

Use Write to exchange documents with other Windows NT users if you're not sure what word processors they use, since every version of Windows NT comes with Write. You can format text with TrueType fonts and know that your document will look the same when opened on another user's system. In addition, since TrueType prints on all graphics printers, the printed document will resemble what you created when other users print it out on their systems. The Write window is shown in Figure 9-7.

Choose the Ruler On option from the Document menu to display a ruler and buttons for aligning text and formatting paragraphs.

The Write Window and Workspace

The Write workspace is where you enter the text of your documents or insert pictures from Paintbrush or other graphics programs. It consists of an insertion point (the I-beam) and an end-of-document marker, which moves down as you type.

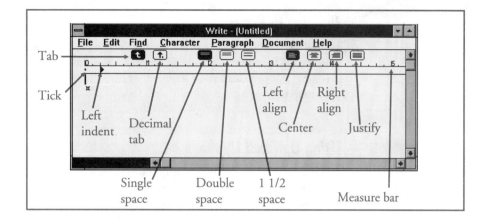

FIGURE 9-7

The Write window

Each paragraph in Write is defined by a paragraph end marker, and each paragraph can have its own indents and paragraph formatting. For example, you can center one paragraph, left align another, and double-space still another. The text within a paragraph automatically wordwraps at the right margin, so press ENTER only when you want to start a new paragraph. To start a new line, but keep it as part of the existing paragraph, press SHIFT-ENTER. This is useful when creating tables or putting together lists of names and addresses.

You must select text before applying character or paragraph formats to it. The *selection bar* is the space between the left edge of text and the left window border. In the selection bar, the mouse pointer changes to a right-pointing arrow. To select a line of text, point to the line in the selection bar and click once. To highlight and select an entire paragraph, double-click in the selection bar to the immediate left of the paragraph. To select any block of text in a paragraph, simply click and drag through it. You double-click a word to select it. To select additional words, hold the mouse button and drag through them.

Page Breaks and Repagination

Page breaks determine where a new page starts when a document is printed. Choose the Repaginate option on the File menu to set up page breaks after a document is written. When you run this option, Write recommends a page break, but you can move the page break up to avoid breaking a page on a section header, title, or table. If you don't use the Repaginate option, Write inserts page breaks automatically when you print a document.

To insert custom page breaks at any time while writing a document, press CTRL-SHIFT-ENTER. A dotted line appears in the text to indicate a page break.

Jumping to Pages

To quickly position the insertion point on a specific page, choose Go To Page from the Find menu. Type the number of the page you want to jump to and click the OK button. If you haven't paginated the document, or if you insert new text after paginating, you'll need to repaginate before you can accurately use Go To Page again.

Using Optional Hyphens

You use hyphens to specify where a multisyllabic word should break at the end of a line. Press CTRL-SHIFT-HYPHEN to place an *optional hyphen* in a word. The hyphen is only used if the word falls at the end of the line.

Find and Replace Techniques

Use the Find option on the Find menu to quickly locate text within a document. Use the Replace option to replace occurrences of text with new text that you've specified.

Using Find

Choose Find from the Find menu to quickly locate text within a document. The following dialog box appears:

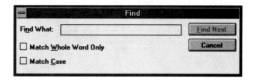

To search for text, follow these steps:

1. Type the text you want to find in the Find What field.

2. Click the Match Case check box to find only occurrences of text that match the case of the text you've specified (for example, if you want to search for *Windows* and not have the system return *windows*).

3. Click Match Whole Word Only to find occurrences that are not part of another word (for example, if you want to search for *ham* and not have the search turn up the word *hamstring*).

4. Close the Find dialog box, and then press F3 to find the next occurrence of the text. Find starts its search from the current position of the insertion point.

Place markers such as "&&&" or "$$$" in your document, then use Find to quickly jump to those markers.

Using Replace

The Replace option locates a specified block of text and replaces it at your discretion or automatically. Choose Replace on the Find menu to display the following dialog box:

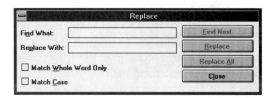

You can use Replace to update a document or replace coded words with long strings of text. For example, when typing a document, you could type simply **NASA**, then later replace all occurrences of NASA with "National Aeronautics and Space Administration." You use Replace basically the same way you used the Find dialog box in the previous section:

1. Type the text you want to replace in the Find What field.

2. Type the replacement text in the Replace With field.

3. To selectively replace in the document, click the Find Next and Replace buttons.

4. To replace all occurrences, click the Replace All button.

Before using Replace All, find and replace a few occurrences manually to make sure you've specified the correct text.

To search for text that includes tabs, paragraph markers, manual page breaks, or spaces, use the following characters in the Find What box:

Type	To Search For
^d	A page break inserted with CTRL-ENTER
^p	A paragraph mark
^t	A tab character
^w	A space character
?	Any character or string of characters in a file

You can use these codes in a number of ways. For example, if the search text is *hea?*, Write finds every occurrence of *hea* followed by at least one character, such as *theater*, *figurehead*, or *heat*.

To limit your search to a specific area, place the cursor just above the text you want to search. As soon as that particular area has been searched click the Close button. With some Windows applications (not Write), you can highlight an area and limit the search to that area.

Designing the Page Layout

This section describes the options and settings you use to define how and where the document is printed on the page, the location of headers, and how to set tabs. This section gives the key options used to define the page layout. For more information on each of these topics, refer to the Help menu.

Setting the Printer

Choose Print Setup from the File menu to select a printer, the print orientation (landscape or portrait), a form, and other options.

Setting the Page Layout

Choose Page Layout from the Document menu to set document margins and the starting page number. The left and right margin settings determine the default width of all paragraphs in the text. Use paragraph indenting to change individual paragraphs.

Setting Tabs

Tab settings in Write affect the entire document, not individual paragraphs. Default tabs are set every half-inch. To set custom tabs, either choose Tabs on the Document menu to open the Tabs dialog box, or click one of the tab buttons on the ruler and drag it down to the appropriate position on the measure bar. Use a decimal tab for number alignment.

Setting Headers and Footers

Headers and footers are text that prints at the top or bottom, respectively, of every page. Typically, you include a chapter or section title in a header and the date and/or a page number in the footer. Choose the Header or Footer option on the Document menu.

Type the header or footer you want in the text window that appears and specify header or footer options on the dialog box that appears.

Formatting Characters

You can apply character formatting such as bold, italics, and special fonts and styles to text that you've highlighted. Open the Character menu and make a formatting selection, or choose Fonts to select a new font. If using the keyboard, press CTRL-B to boldface text, CTRL-I for italics, and CTRL-U for underlining. Press F5 to revert to normal text. Use the Reduce Font and Enlarge Font options to decrease or increase the size of a font. Chapter 6 gives more information on applying fonts and inserting special symbols and foreign characters.

Formatting Paragraphs

The three paragraph formatting methods are indents, line spacing, and paragraph alignment (center, right, left, and justify). You can control the first two from the ruler bar by first selecting a paragraph, then clicking one of the ruler buttons shown in Figure 9-7.

To control indenting, you adjust the indent symbols in the measure bar. Note that the tick initially overlaps the left indent marker. You need to click and drag it off before you can adjust the left indent, and then you can readjust the tick by clicking and dragging it.

- The *left indent marker* is a triangle that points right. Move it to adjust the left edge of text away from or closer to the left margin.

- The *first-line indent marker* (referred to as the *tick*) is a tiny square that you click and drag to adjust the indent of the first line of text. To create bulleted or numbered lists, adjust the tick to the left of the left indent marker.

- The *right indent marker* is the triangle that points left and is used to adjust the right edge of text away from or closer to the right margin.

THE BITMAP EDITOR: PAINTBRUSH

Windows Paintbrush is a bitmap painting program that offers a full set of painting tools and a wide range of colors for creating business graphics, company logos, illustrations, maps, and many other types of artwork. The Paintbrush window, shown in Figure 9-8, is described here.

- ◪ *Canvas* The space where you paint the picture.
- ◪ *Color palette* Where you select foreground (left mouse button) colors and background (right mouse button) colors.
- ◪ *Tools* You select a tool, then drag the cursor to the canvas to work with it.
- ◪ *Linesize box* Where you select the width used to paint lines and other shapes.

You select colors with either the left or right mouse button in the palette. The current colors appear on the left of the palette. Most tools paint with the foreground color; however, when painting filled boxes, circles, and polygons, borders paint with the background color and fill paint with the foreground color. When using the Color Eraser, the foreground color is replaced by the background color.

In the Linesize box, choose a width for lines, borders, brush tips, and eraser points.

The Toolbox

The Toolbox holds the tools you use to paint on the canvas. You select a tool, then click and drag it onto the canvas to use it in most cases. Be sure to select a color and linesize first. Hold SHIFT to drag the tool along a straight line.

FIGURE 9-8

The Paintbrush window

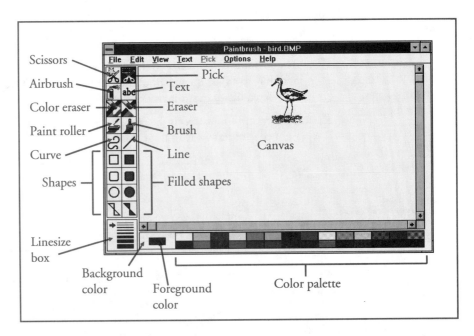

☑   *Scissors*   Use to select irregularly shaped cutouts. Use the options on the Pick menu to manipulate the cutout.

Note   A cutout is a part of the painting you outline, then move, copy, resize, delete, and manipulate in other ways.

☑   *Pick*   Use to select rectangular cutouts. Use the options on the Pick menu to manipulate the cutout.

☑   *Airbrush*   Sprays a dot pattern of the foreground color.

☑   *Text*   Lets you type captions and titles. Open the Text menu to change fonts.

☑   *Color Eraser*   Erases the foreground color and changes it to the background color.

☑   *Eraser*   Erases/converts all colors to the canvas or background color.

☑   *Paint Roller*   Fills enclosed areas with the foreground color.

☑   *Brush*   Paints the current color as you drag the mouse. You can choose the width of your painting tip by selecting the size you want in the Linesize box. Double-click the tool to choose a shape.

☑   *Curve*   A freehand painting tool for creating curved shapes. Click and drag out a line from one point to another, then click elsewhere to stretch the curved line.

☑   *Line*   Paints lines of the width selected in the Linesize box.

The remaining Paintbrush tools are grouped in pairs. The tool on the left creates hollow shapes (boxes, circles, polygons) while the tools on the right create filled shapes. The fill is the foreground color and the border is the background color. To create a filled object without a border, select the same foreground and background color.

Painting Techniques

Here are some tips for painting with Paintbrush. Experiment with these techniques to get a feel for how they work.

☑   To erase part of what you've just painted, press the BACKSPACE key. A box with an X appears. Drag over the object you just created to erase it.

☑   Choosing the Undo command on the Edit menu also gets rid of the work you just did, but Undo deletes all of the work you've done with the current tool. Click the tool occasionally to "lock down" what you've done. Then, if you need to redo, only the work you've done since the last click is reverted.

- ☑ Choose the Cursor Position option on the View menu to create objects of an exact size, to align objects such as boxes or circles, or to move objects precisely.

- ☑ After defining a cutout, click and drag it elsewhere. For small adjustments, click and hold the mouse button on the cutout, then press the arrow keys. To make a copy of a cutout, hold the CTRL key. To create multiple copies of a cutout as you drag, hold the SHIFT key while dragging. Click and drag with the right mouse button to drag the cutout "opaquely," which copies the background with the cutout, overlapping any art underneath it.

- ☑ Other cutout options, such as Tilt, Shrink + Grow, Inverse, and some flipping options are found on the Cutout menu. When using Tilt and Shrink + Grow, you first define the cutout, then outline a new size elsewhere on the canvas. Pick Clear to remove the original cutout after defining a new one.

- ☑ Choose Zoom In to magnify part of the picture and edit its individual picture elements. Click an element with the right or left mouse button to change its color to the foreground or background color, respectively. Choose Zoom Out to return to regular mode.

- ☑ Choose Zoom Out to get an overall picture of your painting.

The Paintbrush Canvas

The canvas is your painting area. You can change its color, change its size, and zoom out to see the entire canvas.

Choose Image Attributes from the Options menu to change canvas settings. Initially, the canvas is the same size as your screen. Change the width and height to reduce the memory requirements of a saved image, or to create images you can tile on the desktop with the Desktop utility in Control Panel.

To clear the canvas, choose New on the file menu or double-click the Eraser. When you choose New, the canvas becomes the color of the currently selected background color. To see more of the canvas, disable the Palette option and disable the Tools and Linesize options on the View menu.

Saving Your Work

Choose the Save and Save As commands on the File menu to save paintings. To save cutouts, choose the Copy To option on the Edit menu. When saving a file, Paintbrush automatically saves files in the .BMP (bitmap) format. Choose a different file type option in the Save File as Type drop-down list box.

You can install images saved in the .BMP format as desktop backgrounds. Open the Desktop utility in the Control Panel and select the file in the Wallpaper field. Choose Tile if you create an image with a smaller-than-screen-size width and height.

Printing Art

Choose the Print option on the File menu to print your paintings. The following explains the features of the Print dialog box:

- Click Partial to print only a selected portion of the picture. Drag over the portion you want to print.

- Choose draft mode to print at lower quality but higher speeds.

- Enlarge or shrink the picture for printing by entering a value in the Scaling field.

- Select the Use Printer Resolution box if you want your painting to print at the resolution of your printer rather than at screen resolution. This sets up a one-to-one relationship between the pixels on the screen and the dot resolution of your printer.

- Define headers and footers for printouts by choosing the Page Setup option on the File menu.

MULTIMEDIA ACCESSORIES

If you have sound boards and CD-ROM players installed in your system, you can use the multimedia accessories discussed next.

The Sound Recorder

The Sound Recorder is a digital recording and playback utility that is useful for creating small voice and sound effects files to include in e-mail messages and documents, or to assign to system events such as logon, logoff, message display, and others. You can have some fun with the Sound Recorder by shrinking, stretching, overlapping (mixing), reversing, echoing, and generally editing sounds you've recorded or sound files obtained from other sources.

The Sound Recorder dialog box appears in Figure 9-9. Choose Open on the File menu to open an existing sound, then use the buttons as follows:

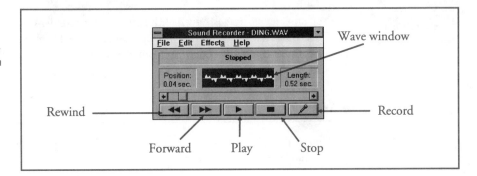

FIGURE 9-9

The Sound Recorder utility

✓ Click the Play button to play the sound. If your sound board and sound system are connected properly, you'll hear the sound through the speakers.

✓ Click the Pause button to temporarily stop the sound playback.

✓ Click the Rewind button to go back to the beginning of the sound.

✓ Click the Forward button to go to the end of the sound.

✓ Click the Record button to start recording a new sound.

✓ Move the slider button to any part of the sound, then click the Play button to hear the sound from that point onward. You also use the slider button to position the sound for editing or mixing.

✓ Click the left or right slider button to move through the sound .1 second per click or click the scroll bar itself to move exactly 1 second forward or backward.

Recording Sounds

You'll need a microphone to record a new sound, or a direct connection from a sound source such as a stereo. Choose New to create a new sound, then click the Record button. To stop recording, click the Stop button.

Watch your recording time. One minute of recording time can require from 1MB to 5MB of disk space, depending on the recording quality (voice or high quality). Stereo recording requires double the disk space.

Editing Sounds

You can mix sounds into an existing sound file by first opening the sound file, then appending another sound file to it. Several mixing techniques are described below.

Position the cursor at the end of a sound to append new sounds to it, or anywhere in the sound to insert or mix in new sound elements.

- Try opening two Sound Recorder windows—one for working with a master sound, and another for opening sound files or recording new sounds that you then mix into the master.

- Choose Insert File on the Edit menu to insert an existing sound file at the cursor location. Any sound past the insertion point is moved further out. Paste Insert on the Edit menu to insert a sound stored on the Clipboard.

- Choose the Mix With File option from the Edit menu to mix a sound file from disk with the existing sound. The sounds are combined. Using the Paste Mix option from the Edit menu mixes a sound that you have stored on the Clipboard.

- Remove unwanted sounds or silence by positioning the cursor, and then choosing the Delete Before Current Position option or the Delete After Current Position option.

- Choose one of the Effects options to change sounds. The effect affects the entire sound.

The Sound Recorder is an interesting and entertaining utility. You can spend hours recording and mixing new sounds. If you like working with sounds, you might want to investigate more advanced sound editors that provide "zoom-in" capabilities and better cut and paste options. Here are a few more tricks to help you get more out of the Sound Recorder:

- Create eerie, low-frequency sounds by slowing down a small portion of a sound five or six times. Choose Decrease Speed on the Effects menu, but keep in mind that this changes the pitch of the sound. Speed up sounds to create electronic effects such as beeps and chirps.

- Create a repeating sound by positioning the cursor at the end of a sound, then inserting the same sound file several times. Try increasing the speed when you're finished inserting the sounds.

- When you insert a sound at the end of another sound, there is often an audible gap of silence. To smooth the gap, use the Mix File option instead of the Insert File option when appending a sound. Position the scroll bar at the end of the current sound, then click the left scroll button several times to "backtrack" over the trailing end of the existing sound. Mix in the new sound. During playback, as the first sound fades out, the appended sound starts.

◩   Before mixing in a new sound, compare its volume with the existing sound. Open two Sound Recorder windows and place a sound in each. If one sound is louder than another reduce it before mixing the two sounds.

The Media Player

The Media Player is a multipurpose interface for controlling multimedia devices such as audio compact discs and videodiscs. This is what the Media Player window looks like:

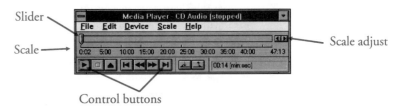

Slider — Scale — Scale adjust — Control buttons

You also can use the Media Player to play back prerecorded sound files and MIDI (Musical Instrument Digital Interface) files. MIDI files are sound *event* recordings such as the press of a key on a MIDI-compatible electric piano, as opposed to actual sound waveform recording as is possible with the Sound Recorder.

To play an audio CD or videodisc, choose the device type from the Device menu. To load a sound file or MIDI file, choose Open from the File menu, then search for .WAV or .MID files.

Once you have a file or device loaded, control it with the buttons on the Media Player as described in Table 9-2. Depending on the file or device being played, you can change the scale on the Media Player window to show time intervals, video sequence frames, or audio tracks by choosing an option on the Scale menu.

You can mark a selection that you want to play by dragging through it while holding the SHIFT key.

There are number of keyboard quick keys you can use to control the Media Player, as well as a number of other techniques for handling devices not covered here. The Media Player has an extensive help facility that you can refer to for more information.

The CD Player

The CD Player controls the playback of audio compact discs in your CD-ROM drive. This is the CD Player window:

TABLE 9-2

The Media Player Control Buttons

Click		To
▶	Play	Start playback of a device or file. The button changes to a Pause button during playback.
■	Stop	Stop playback
▲	Eject	Eject the media if a compact disc or videodisc is inserted.
◄|	Previous Mark	Jump to the previous marked area.
◄◄	Page Left	Go back through the media sequence in 10 percent increments.
►►	Page Right	Go forward through the media sequence in 10 percent increments.
►|	Next Mark	Jump to the next marked area.
⬇	Mark In	Mark the beginning of a selection you want to play. Position the slider, then click this button.
⬆	Mark Out	Mark the end of a selection you want to play. Position the slider, then click this button.

Its functions are almost identical to the functions of the Media Player, except that the CD Player lets you play tracks in random order, or create a "playlist" of audio tracks that play back the next time you insert the CD. Discs are recognized by the CD Player, and if you have not created a playlist, the CD is played back in sequential order.

The control buttons on the CD Player window shown here are similar to those found on any physical CD player:

	Play
▮	Pause
■	Stop
◄◄	Previous Track
◄◄	Reverse Scan
►►	Forward Scan
►►|	Next Track
▲	Eject Disk

You can show or remove the Toolbar, disc/track information, and status bar by choosing options in the View menu. The Toolbar buttons are described in Table 9-3. Note that you'll find similar options on the Options menu.

Editing the Play List

You use the Play List to create a name and title list for your CDs, and to specify the order in which you want tracks to play. Click the Edit Playlist button, or choose Edit Play List from the Disc menu to display the CD Player Disc Settings dialog box shown in Figure 9-10. You work with this dialog box as follows:

▨   In the Artist and Title fields, type the label information for the current CD.

▨   Initially, track numbers appear in the Available Tracks field. Click a track number, then type its title in the Track field at the bottom of the dialog box.

▨   After you've typed each track name, you can create a playlist. Highlight a track, then click the Add button. The name appears in the Play List field. You can remove tracks or clear all the tracks with the Remove and Clear all buttons.

Once you've added titles and created a play list, click the Close button. You can then click the Selected Order button to play the CD according to the playlist.

TABLE 9-3

The CD Player Toolbar Buttons

Click		To
►►►	Selected Order	Play tracks in the order specified in the play list.
🔀	Random Order	Play tracks randomly. If a multiple CD player is attached, tracks from each CD are played randomly.

TABLE 9-4

The CD Player Toolbar Buttons (continued)

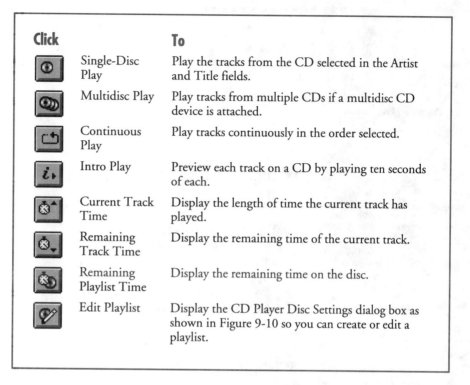

Click		To
	Single-Disc Play	Play the tracks from the CD selected in the Artist and Title fields.
	Multidisc Play	Play tracks from multiple CDs if a multidisc CD device is attached.
	Continuous Play	Play tracks continuously in the order selected.
	Intro Play	Preview each track on a CD by playing ten seconds of each.
	Current Track Time	Display the length of time the current track has played.
	Remaining Track Time	Display the remaining time of the current track.
	Remaining Playlist Time	Display the remaining time on the disc.
	Edit Playlist	Display the CD Player Disc Settings dialog box as shown in Figure 9-10 so you can create or edit a playlist.

FIGURE 9-10

The CD Player Disc Settings window

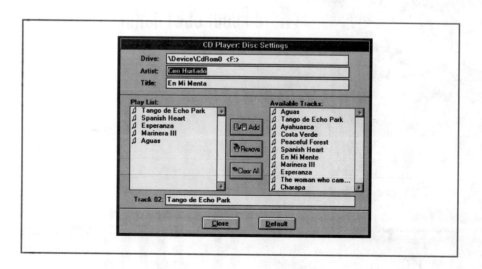

Inside

& Out

CHAPTER 10

Creating Compound Documents

Don't let the title of this chapter scare you. It's about traditional Clipboard cut-and-paste techniques. It's also about *object linking and embedding* (OLE), a Windows 3.1 and Windows NT feature that can provide automatic linking and updating of information from many sources into a single document, called a compound document. Figure 10-1 illustrates a compound document. This particular compound document is composed of the following:

- Spreadsheet information from Microsoft Excel

- Graphics from Paintbrush

- An icon that displays a video clip when selected

- An icon that plays a voice annotation when selected

- An icon that plays music from an audio CD when selected

- An icon that opens the Cardfile utility so users can browse through a database

Think of each of these separate document components as packages of information. They are usually called "objects." Each object contains information about the application that created it, and in some cases the location of the file that contains the original information.

When you double-click an object in a compound document, the application that created the object appears on the desktop, as shown in Figure 10-2. You can then change the object and place it back in the document. With OLE, objects in documents (called *embedded* objects) have the same application startup capabilities as icons in the Program Manager. This greatly simplifies compound document editing: it eliminates the need to

FIGURE 10-1

A compound document contains information from many sources

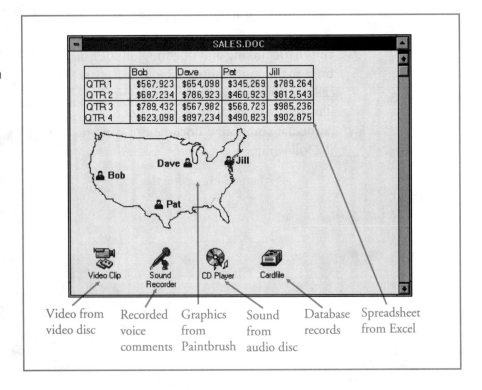

FIGURE 10-2

Applications open when objects in compound documents are double-clicked

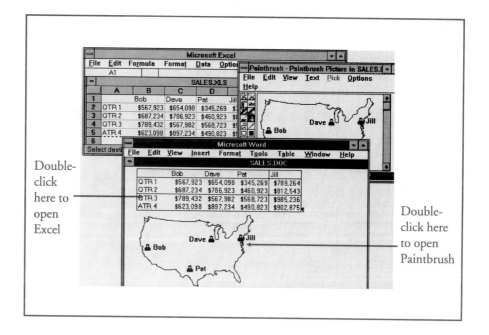

Double-click here to open Excel

Double-click here to open Paintbrush

open the Program Manager, start the application, open the original graphic or spreadsheet file, then copy and repaste the object back into the document. With OLE, you copy and paste only once.

But OLE goes further. It provides *linking*, which is a form of *dynamic data exchange* (DDE). *Dynamic* is the key word here, as opposed to *static*. Pictures, text, charts, and other information that you've pasted into compound documents maintain a link to the file where the original information exists. If the original file is updated or changed, the pasted information in compound documents is also updated. Most important, links work between separate computers on a network, as shown in Figure 10-3. An artist in the graphics department is responsible for creating and updating the map. The sales department has a compound document that includes the map object and spreadsheet information from the accounting department. When the artist changes the map, the changes are sent across the OLE network link to the compound document where the "linked" map object is updated with the new changes—without any work or knowledge required by the sales staff.

Note

You can only establish links to information that is saved in a disk file by the application that created it.

You create compound documents using the Clipboard to copy and paste information between applications—you paint a picture in Paintbrush, for instance, then copy the picture to the Clipboard, and finally paste it into a compound document.

FIGURE 10-3

Object links can extend to other network computers

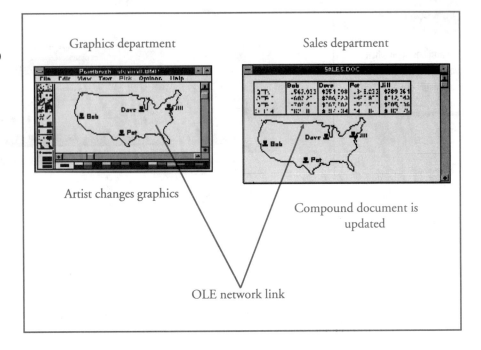

Graphics department

Sales department

Artist changes graphics

Compound document is updated

OLE network link

Applications that support OLE appear to have features they don't normally have. For example, you can copy sound files from the Sound Recorder into a Write document and then double-click the pasted sound objects to play them back. Write thus appears to have this sound capability; in reality, however, the objects call the playback functions from the application used to originally create the sounds. Both Write and the Sound Recorder have built-in OLE functions, as do Cardfile and Paintbrush. Check your applications to see if they are OLE compatible.

While a compound document normally displays all information, compound documents also can include packaged objects represented by icons (as shown at the bottom of Figure 10-1). Compound documents with icons are typically read on screen, rather than printed. That is because the reader might want to click the icon (called a *package*) to see what it contains. Documents that contain OLE packages are usually passed around a network using an electronic mail package, the ClipBook Viewer, or directory sharing methods. Users view OLE packages placed on the compound document by other users, and add packages of their own. Here are some examples of packages you might find on a compound document. The icons pictured in Table 10-1 are arbitrary. You can use any icon that best represents the information in the package.

Note

Packages can display information, start applications, or execute an audio, video, or other multimedia sequence.

TABLE 10-1

Examples of Possible
Packages on a Compound
Document (the icons
pictured are arbitrary)

Click		To
	Text	Display text the reader can optionally view.
	Pictures	Display blueprints, cover art, or other graphics.
	Charts	Display charts for a set of numbers in the document.
	Messages	Play back a recorded voice message, or start an electronic mail package that executes a routine to retrieve the reader's mail.
	Audio	Play back an important quote, the minutes of a meeting, or other audio clips.
	Photos	Display photographs. For example, a real estate office might embed this icon in a home information database.
	Video	Play video clips. For example, you might embed such a package in a document that reviews the latest movie rentals.
	Secure Information	Display security procedures, but only to readers who are authorized to open and view them.
	Audio	Play audio segments. For example, this icon might play selected segments of a CD in a document that reviews the CD.
	Help	Display help information.
	Warnings	Display warning information.

It's important to note that packages only contain links to other information. The actual pictures, graphics, sound, or video in a package are not added to the compound document. Thus, the file size of compound documents can remain relatively small. You store the information referenced by OLE packages in one place, which means one or more OLE packages can use the information without duplicating it, thus reducing disk requirements. In addition, the owner of the information can update it in one location, rather than worrying about all the possible places the information might be located.

UNDERSTANDING OLE CONCEPTS

As the name implies, OLE provides linking and embedding of objects into one or more compound documents. Those links can remain on the local computer, or extend out over a network. This section provides more detailed information on OLE concepts.

An Example of Linking and Embedding

Let's compare OLE with the cut-and-paste methods you already know. Imagine you're putting together a conference and trade show. You've created documents related to the conference using several different Windows applications—you used Windows Write to prepare press releases and other in-house documents, Microsoft Excel to create schedules, Paintbrush to draw a map of the conference rooms, and Cardfile to keep track of exhibitor and speaker information.

Let's say you need to piece all this information together into several compound documents:

- ☑ A general press release
- ☑ A brochure for attendees
- ☑ An in-house document to inform the rest of your company of the conference schedule and events
- ☑ A handout for the exhibitors and speakers

Each document will, of course, be designed for its intended audience, but all will contain some of the information described earlier, such as the map and the schedule of events.

Initially, you need to create, copy, and paste various objects into your four documents, so the amount of work is the same whether you're using OLE or not. The real advantage of OLE comes when you need to make changes to your schedules, floor plans, and the other information you've pasted into the compound documents. In non-OLE applications, you would need to repaste edited information into each of the four documents. With OLE, however, linked objects in the documents are automatically updated. Altering the floor plan in Paintbrush changes the floor plan in all four linked compound documents.

Using OLE Over the Network

Now let's look at how you might use OLE over your network. If you have a multimedia sound board in your system, you can record voice messages and embed them in Microsoft Mail messages that you send to other people on the network. Of course, the recipient must have the proper equipment to play them back, but more and more Windows systems now include audio components or drivers that play sounds on built-in speakers.

Assume you are a department or group manager creating a business report that includes charts, tables of numbers, and text. You'll let the other people in your department create these individual compound document objects, but you will combine all elements in the final compound document. You start by creating an outline that describes the elements you want in the report—such as graphics, text, and spreadsheet information—and who in the department or workgroup is responsible for creating and editing that information, then you send this outline via Microsoft Mail to the appropriate people.

Part of this process needs to include a procedure for combining the information. There are two methods of doing this:

- *Common directory method* In this method, all users in the workgroup connect with a common shared directory and copy the elements they create into the directory. The workgroup manager then assembles the compound document from all the files in the directory.

- *ClipBook method* In this method, workgroup users place objects they have created on their ClipBook and share them. The workgroup manager then accesses the shared ClipBook and pastes objects from it into the compound document.

Of course, information is pasted as linked objects into the compound document. That way, members of the workgroup can change information in the files they created, rather than the compound document. OLE links ensure that these changes are automatically made in the compound document.

OLE COMPONENTS

Many Windows and Windows NT applications provide OLE support. Commands for copying and pasting information as OLE objects are usually found on Edit menus. In some cases, OLE is a natural extension of the application. For example, in the File Manager, you can click and drag a file to a document in an OLE-compatible application. An OLE packaged object icon then appears for the file in the document. Readers of the compound document can double-click the icon to display, edit, or play back (in the case of a sound or video file) the information.

Note

The *server* is the application or document that is the source of the embedded or linked information. The *client* is the destination of the embedded or linked information.

If an application supports OLE and you can copy information from it, it is a server application. If an application supports OLE, but you can only paste information to it, it is an OLE client application. Some applications are both clients and servers, as described in Table 10-2.

There are, of course, many other OLE-compatible client and server applications. Check the specifications of your applications or look at the Edit menu to see if it holds OLE commands such as Copy Object, Paste Special, Paste Link, Links, and Insert Object.

Verbs

A verb is the action an object takes when double-clicked; the type of action that results depends on the type of object double-clicked. The most common verb is *play*. An object such as a sound file or an animation routine in a multimedia document plays. Packaged objects that start programs more appropriately *run* instead of play.

The other important verb is *edit*. When double-clicked, an edit object opens for editing in the workspace of the application that created it. The type of object dictates whether objects are played or edited. If a graphic object is double-clicked, it opens for editing, whereas a sound or video package plays (although there are ways to open them for editing).

Creating Linked and Embedded Objects

This section describes how to create embedded and linked objects. The commands found on the Edit menu of OLE-compatible applications are discussed.

TABLE 10-2

Some OLE Applications. OLE Applications Can Be Either Clients or Servers or Both

Icon	Application	Description
Paintbrush	Paintbrush	Paintbrush is a server application that only provides OLE bitmap graphic objects to client applications. Objects can appear as full embedded or linked images in the client applications, or as packaged objects.
Write	Write	Write is solely a client application. It accepts embedded, linked, and packaged objects.
Cardfile	Cardfile	The Cardfile accessory is solely a client application that accepts embedded, linked, and packaged objects.
Sound Recorder	Sound Recorder	Sound Recorder is a server application. Use Sound Recorder to create sounds and embed them in your documents. For obvious reasons, sounds only appears as packaged icons in documents where they are pasted.
Media Player	Media Player	Media Player is a server application. You use it to designate part or all of a sound or video clip as an OLE object that you can paste in client applications.
Microsoft EXCEL	Microsoft Excel	Excel is both a server and a client. You can paste Excel spreadsheet data into most client applications. You can also paste sound files, graphics, and other information into an Excel spreadsheet.
Microsoft WINWORD	Microsoft Word for Windows	Word is primarily a client application (that is, you paste objects into it); however, you can paste Word document icons into other applications. The readers of those documents can double-click the icons to view the Word documents.

Clipboard Methods of Linking and Embedding

The most common method of linking and embedding objects is to use the Clipboard commands on the Edit menu of most applications. Follow these steps:

1. In the source application, highlight or select the information or image you want to copy, and then choose the Copy command on its Edit menu, or press CTRL-C.

2. Switch to the destination application and choose one of the paste commands (described shortly).

You can see OLE copy and paste commands on the Edit menu of OLE-compatible applications such as Write, Cardfile, Word for Windows, Excel, and others. The Paste commands for the Write Edit menu are described in the following list. Note that Paste Link is only available if the source information is saved as part of a file. This is the Write Edit menu:

The Paste Option   Choose Paste to embed the information on the Clipboard as an object in an OLE-compatible destination. The information becomes an embedded object, not a linked object.

The Paste Special Option   Use the Paste Special option only if the object can't be pasted in the normal way. The Paste Special option is similar to Paste, except that a dialog box similar to this one opens so you can choose a format for the pasted object:

If you want to embed the object, you usually choose the top item in the list that is called "Object." If embedding is not supported, you won't see this option. The other items paste the object as a normal object. If the object is from a source that is also saved as a file, the Paste Link button is available and you can create a link if necessary.

The Paste Link Option   If the object on the Clipboard is from a source that is saved as a file and linking is supported, the Paste Link option appears on the Edit menu. Choose it to create a paste-linked object.

The Links Option   Use the Links option to change the links of an object. You might do this when a link has been lost because the original file was moved or when one machine on a network can't find the original file located on another network machine.

The Object Option   The name of this option changes, depending on the current OLE object you have selected in the document. You choose it to edit the object, and get the same results that you would if you double-clicked the object. For example, if a Paintbrush embedded object is highlighted, you see Edit Paintbrush Picture Object in the Edit menu.

The Insert Object Option   The other options described above assume you already have information on the Clipboard. This option assumes you need to get the information, so it displays a dialog box similar to the following so you can pick a source application. The application opens so you can capture information to the Clipboard in the normal way.

Changing Embedded or Linked Objects

When you double-click an editable object in a client document, the server application opens with the object in its workspace for editing. After making changes, you open the file menu and choose one of the following options. These options only appear in OLE server applications when you are editing an OLE object.

The Update Option   Choose Update to add the changes you have made to the object into the client document. You remain in the source application for further editing.

The Exit and Return To Option   Choose the Exit and Return To option to return to the destination application. If you've made changes, you'll be asked if you want to update the destination with those changes.

Creating Object Packages

As mentioned previously, OLE packages contain links to files located elsewhere on the computer, or on another network computer. With a package, you only need to store the information in one location, rather than in each document that needs the information. This cuts down on disk space.

Figure 10-4 shows one way to use object packages. The Cardfile accessory, which is included with Windows NT, is a mini-database that imitates an index file. You can type text on each card and paste graphics or OLE objects. In this example, each card in the deck contains an OLE package along with a description of the package. Note that each card has a header for sorting and indexing purposes. The top card in Figure 10-4 actually opens another Cardfile database, so in this example, the main database is used as a table of contents for other database files, which you can quickly open by double-clicking the packaged icons.

In Figure 10-5, a Write document contains two embedded icons. One opens an English-text document and the other opens the same document translated into Spanish. You could enhance this by including Sound Recorder voice annotations that "speak" the translations.

Using Security Features

In a multiuser environment, it is necessary to restrict access to directories and files. When using packaged objects, you can restrict which users can open the linked files by applying file access permissions to those files.

FIGURE 10-4

Cardfile can serve as an index for files

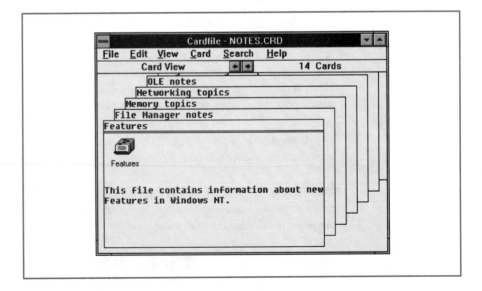

FIGURE 10-5

Packages for English or
Spanish text

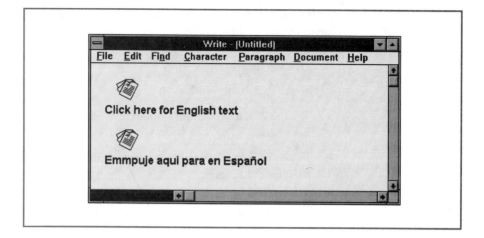

For example, in Figure 10-6, you can control access to the file linked with the
packaged icon by granting only certain users and groups permission to open and read the
file. In this case, you would apply permissions to the file SECURITY.TXT.

EXAMPLES OF EMBEDDING OBJECTS

To embed an object from a source application to a destination document, use the
copy-and-paste procedures with which you are already familiar. However, you'll choose

FIGURE 10-6

You can embed text files
that require special
permissions to view

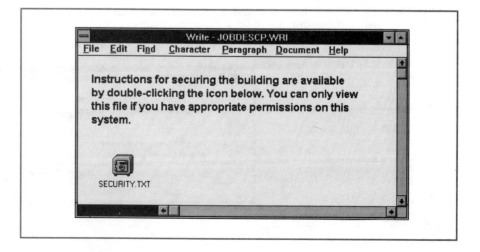

the OLE options from the menus as you'll see in the following procedure. Follow these steps to embed a Paintbrush image into a Write document:

1. Open Write and Paintbrush.

2. In the Paintbrush window, paint a picture or open an existing picture file.

3. Use the Pick tool to create a cutout of the image, then choose Copy from the Edit menu.

4. Switch to the Write window, position the insertion point, and choose Paste from the Edit menu.

    Because both Paintbrush and Write support OLE, the selection is embedded in the Write document. Now try editing the image.

5. Double-click the pasted image. Paintbrush opens with the image in its workspace.

6. Change the image in any way.

7. Open the File menu. It appears like this:

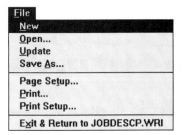

8. Choose Update to add the changes back to the embedded object and stay in Paintbrush or choose Exit & Return to update the embedded image and return to Write. If you choose to exit, you see a warning message similar to the following:

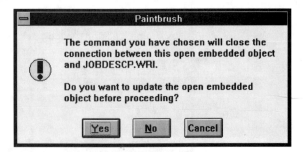

Choose Yes to update the image before exiting.

Use similar procedures to embed objects on Cardfile cards, Mail messages, and most other Windows applications.

Now try embedding a sound from Sound Recorder into the Write document. (The following exercise assumes that you have a sound board or speaker driver installed.) Follow these steps:

1. Start Sound Recorder.

2. Open any sound, or record a new sound.

3. Choose Copy from the Sound Recorder Edit menu.

4. Switch to the Write document.

5. Choose Paste from the Edit menu.

The sound is pasted into the document as a microphone icon. Double-click the icon to hear the pasted sound.

LINKING OBJECTS

The procedure for linking objects is similar to the procedure for embedding objects, except that you choose Paste Link on the destination application's Edit menu.

The source object must be from a saved file to create links.

Try the following exercise with Paintbrush and Cardfile. Keep in mind that you can use this procedure to create a catalog of graphics images or sounds in Cardfile.

1. Open Cardfile and Paintbrush.

2. In Paintbrush, create an image or open an existing file.

3. If you created a new image, save it as a file.

4. Use the Pick tool to create a cutout. Choose Copy from the Edit menu.

5. Switch to Cardfile, and choose Picture from the Cardfile Edit menu so you can paste the graphics image.

6. Choose the Paste Link option from the Edit menu to paste the object in the card.

    The Paintbrush image and the Cardfile object are now linked. You can edit the Paintbrush file at any time. Changes are dynamic and occur in real time. You can see this by placing the Paintbrush and Cardfile images side by side, then making changes in Paintbrush, as described next.

7. Double-click the linked and embedded image in Cardfile to open Paintbrush for editing.

8. Arrange the Cardfile and Paintbrush windows side by side.

9. Make changes in Paintbrush and watch the changes in Cardfile.

You can continue this example by opening Write and paste-linking the image from Paintbrush into the Write window. Then change the image in Paintbrush and watch the linked objects change in both Cardfile and Write.

Using Linked Documents Over Networks

Because linked objects hold information about the location of files they are linked to, moving the files breaks the link. It's best to keep compound documents and their related link documents in the same directory. You can then share the directory with network users who need to access the compound document.

Use the ClipBook to create cross-network links when compound documents and their associated link documents must reside in different locations (if, for example, the owners of the linked documents wish to maintain security permissions of their own).

Remember

The computer sharing the images is called the server and the computer accessing the images is called the client.

To create network links with the ClipBook, follow these steps:

1. At the server machine, copy an image to the Clipboard, then open ClipBook and paste it to the Local ClipBook.

2. When the Share dialog box appears, type a name in the Page Name field and enable the Share Item Now option.

3. Fill out the Share ClipBook Page dialog box as discussed in Chapter 9 and click the OK button. The object appears on the ClipBook as a shared item.

4. The user at the client computer can now open ClipBook and connect with the server computer. Its ClipBook appears in the ClipBook Viewer window.

5.   Click an object and choose Copy from the Edit menu.

6.   Start the client application where you want to paste the object.

7.   Choose Paste Link. The object is pasted with a link to the ClipBook on the remote network computer.

You can save and close the compound document. The next time it is opened, a dialog box appears to inform you that the document contains a linked object that may need updating, and you are given the option to update it. If you choose to update the linked object (by selecting Yes), OLE gets the latest information from the linked file on the remote computer.

Viewing and Updating Link Information

You can view and update the *link information* for a linked object by first selecting the object, then choosing Links from the Edit menu. You'll see a dialog box similar to this one:

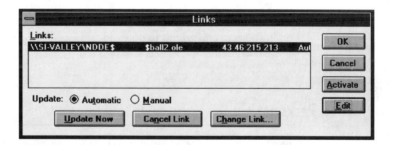

The type, name, and size information for the linked object appear in the Links display box.

The two Update options, Automatic and Manual, determine the current update method for the linked object; you can switch to Manual if you prefer to manually update links. To update a link manually, choose the Update Now button after you've made your edits.

Another way of editing the linked object is by clicking the Edit button and making your changes; this is the same as double-clicking the linked object.

For linked objects that play back a script or sounds, click the Activate button to play the objects.

To cancel a link, choose the Cancel Link button, or choose Change Link if you want to define a new file for the link.

MORE ABOUT OLE PACKAGES

OLE packages can execute commands, open other documents, or start other applications. The package contains a set of instructions for accomplishing the assigned task. To create packages, you can click and drag icons from the File Manager to your documents, or you can use the Packager accessory in the Program Manager Accessories group.

In the following example, you use the click-and-drag method to place an icon for a file on a card in Cardfile. Follow these steps:

1. Open both the File Manager and Cardfile, and arrange the windows side by side.

2. Locate a file—say any Paintbrush .BMP file—in the WINNT directory.

3. Click the filename and drag it over the top card in Cardfile, then release the mouse.

This automatically embeds a package on the card. You can now double-click the icon in Cardfile to open the file you just pasted.

Try the same procedure with a Sound Recorder .WAV file, or even another Cardfile. Double-clicking the embedded icon will play the sound or start the application. Remember that you can use these techniques in Write or other OLE-compatible applications to create links to other documents. Try copying an icon for a text file into a Write document.

Using Packager

The Object Packager is a utility you can use to create object packages. It provides an alternative to the click-and-drag method just described for embedding a package.

The Object Packager gives you a way to specify the parameters of a package, such as its filename, location, and icon type. For example, you could use an envelope icon for a recording of your voice. The Object Packager appears when you choose Package from the Edit menu of an OLE-compatible application.

The following exercise demonstrates the Object Packager:

1. Open Write.

2. Choose Insert Object from the Edit menu. A dialog box appears, listing all the currently available applications that can supply OLE objects.

3. In the Object Type list box, double-click Package to display the following dialog box:

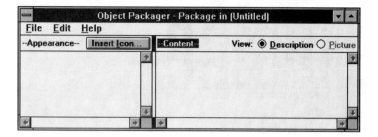

Packager contains all the tools you need to create your own embedded icons. In this case, Packager will insert the icon in the Write document when you're done. Create a link to a document as described in the remaining steps.

4. Select an icon for the new object. Click the Insert Icon button, and choose an icon from the list.

5. Choose Label from the Edit menu to create a label for the icon you have selected.

6. Define the command to execute when this package is double-clicked by choosing Command Line from the Edit menu, then typing the command. To open an associated document, type its filename.

7. Choose Exit from the File menu. The Object Packager asks if you want to update the object; choose Yes.

Your Write document now contains the embedded icon, and you can double-click the icon to open the document or execute the command you specified.

Inside

- Getting Command Help

- Command Execution

- Features of the Command Prompt Window

- Command Environments

& Out

CHAPTER 11

The Command Prompt

The Command Prompt provides a way to
execute text-based Windows NT commands
and commands for other operating systems,
such as DOS, Windows 3.1, Microsoft OS/2
1.*x*, or POSIX. When you double-click the
Command Prompt, the window in Figure 11-1
appears.

FIGURE·11-1

The Command Prompt
window

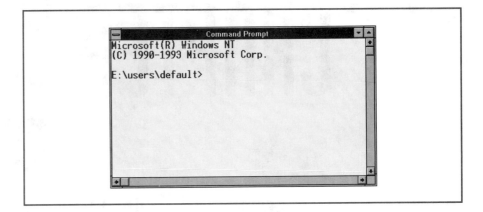

This window has a prompt similar to the DOS command prompt, and while you can issue most MS-DOS 5.0 commands, you can also execute a variety of other commands. Here's the complete list of commands available to you:

■ 32-bit Windows NT operating system commands, many of which are similar to MS-DOS 5 commands.

■ Subsystem commands (16-bit non-native commands), which are typically comprised of older MS-DOS commands. Some are no longer required in the 32-bit Windows NT interface but are included for compatibility.

■ Configuration commands (similar to the commands you would place in an MS-DOS CONFIG.SYS file), that you place in a new file called CONFIG.NT that executes whenever you start a Command Prompt session. The CONFIG.NT file sets up an environment for running MS-DOS commands and programs.

■ TCP/IP utilities for connecting and working with UNIX-based systems and/or Internet networks.

GETTING COMMAND HELP

The Windows NT Help system provides a complete description of every Windows NT Command Prompt command. Double-click the Windows NT Help icon in the Program Manager to see the window shown in Figure 11-2. Click the embedded icon labeled Access the Command Reference Help to display the Command Reference help system shown in Figure 11-3.

FIGURE 11-2

Using the Windows NT
Help system

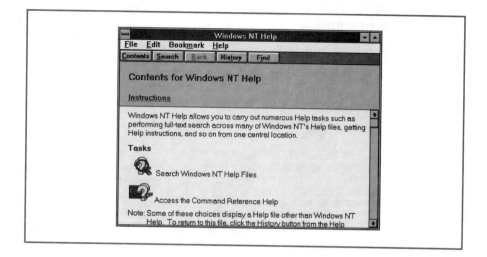

Your primary focus when using the command reference system is the set of command buttons on the left. You click the button panel at the top to quickly jump through the alphabetical listing. Click the button next to a command to display information about the command in the right window. The right window may contain a button of its own, which, when pressed, usually displays additional notes or command examples. If the description is long, scroll to the bottom to see these buttons.

Note

Appendix B provides a unique command cross reference for the Command Prompt command list.

FIGURE 11-3

Getting Command
Reference help

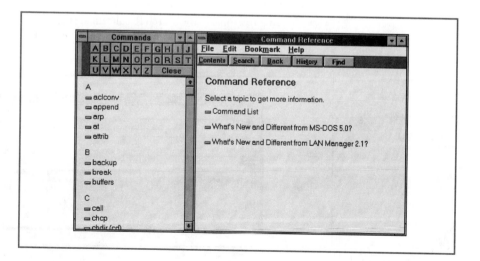

The Find Button

When you can't remember the name of a command but you know the task you want to perform, click the Find button on the Command Reference window. The window in Figure 11-4 appears. You use the Search window to search for topics and phrases about commands. For example, if you wanted to run a disk check, but couldn't remember the command to do this, you could search for *disk*. The resulting list would display the titles of topics you might want to read.

Type the text you want to search for in the Search For text box. If you've previously searched for the same topic, click the down arrow button to reuse the search criteria.

Specify one of the options in the Look At field. To search just through the titles of topics, choose Topic Titles Only. To search through the complete text description of a command, choose All Text.

When the search is complete, a list of topics appears in a window similar to this one, which shows the search results for the word *disk*:

Note that this particular search resulted in 86 topics. You can narrow this list by using AND, OR, and other constructs when typing the search criteria. Click the Hints button for more information. For example, to narrow the disk topic down to seven items, type **disk AND check** in the Search For field.

To jump to a topic in the Search Results dialog box, double-click it. The Command Reference then shows the topic with each word you search for highlighted.

FIGURE 11-4

The Command Reference Search window

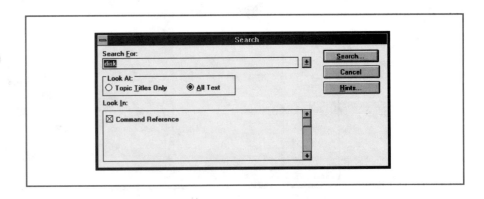

COMMAND EXECUTION

Those familiar with DOS already know how to issue and execute commands in the Command Prompt. The command syntax is the same as the command syntax for DOS, as shown here:

command parameters /switches

Parameters are usually the names of files you want the command to affect. If you need to specify two files (as in a Copy command), separate them with a space. The first file is the source and the second file is the destination. The destination might be a directory or a drive letter.

Switches provide custom information and execution settings for a command. For example, the DIR switch /W displays a wide listing of files. You can specify multiple switches, but must type a slash character for each.

> **Note**
>
> To pause a command so you can view its output, press CTRL-S or the PAUSE key. To stop a running command, press CTRL-BREAK or CTRL-C. If a command has completely locked up, open the Control menu by clicking the upper-left button in the window, then choose Settings and click the Terminate button.

When loading programs from the command line, you can usually specify filenames that load into the workspace of the program. For example, to start Microsoft Word and load the file REPORTS.DOC, you would type this:

WORD REPORTS

It's not necessary to specify the extension since it is associated with Word.

Starting Programs from the Command Prompt

You can start any Windows NT program or accessory from the Command Prompt. Type the executable filename of the program you want to load when the Command Prompt window appears. You can use this method to start Windows NT programs such as the File Manager, ClipBook, and others. However, when you start such programs, the Command Prompt window becomes unavailable even though it remains on the desktop. You need to exit the program to regain use of the Command Prompt, or start a new Command Prompt.

To retain the ability to execute other commands in the Command Prompt window, precede program commands with the START command. For example, to start the File

Manager from the Command Prompt, so that you could return to the Command Prompt and execute other commands, you would type the following:

START WINFILE

Reusing Commands

You can use the Command Prompt copy and paste feature to execute a previous command. Use this method if DOSKEY is not loaded. (DOSKEY, a utility that lets you reissue commands you've previously typed, is discussed in the next section.) In the following steps you use the mouse to copy and paste commands that are still visible in the window:

1. Click the Control button in the upper-left portion of the Command Prompt and choose Settings.

2. When the Settings dialog box appears, mark the QuickEdit Mode option, then click OK.

3. Hold the left mouse button and drag through the command you want to re-execute.

4. Click the right mouse button to copy the command to the Clipboard.

5. Click the right mouse button again to reexecute the command.

The screen buffer size determines the amount of screen information that is still available. If you increase the buffer size, you'll be able to scroll back through more of the commands and screen displays. You increase the buffer size by changing options on the Settings menu (discussed later in this chapter).

Using DOSKEY

The steps just given are only useful if you can see the command on the screen, or if you've increased the buffer size sufficiently so that you can scroll back through the commands you've executed. The DOSKEY utility provides a way to keep a list of commands in a buffer that you can scroll through when you want to select and reexecute a previous command. Type **DOSKEY** to load the basic DOSKEY service.

Once loaded, press the UP ARROW or DOWN ARROW keys to scroll through the lists of commands you've previously executed. You can also press F7 to display a menu of previous commands. Refer to the Command Reference for additional DOSKEY instructions. There are a number of switches you might want to use to customize how DOSKEY works. For example, you can create a macro by assigning a series of commands to keys on the keyboard.

Copying and Pasting Information

You can copy information from one window to another using any of the following techniques. These techniques copy text or graphics information to the Clipboard. You can then switch to another window and paste the information.

- ☑ To copy a selected block of text, open the Control menu by clicking the upper-left button, then choose Edit and Mark. Drag through the text you want to copy with the mouse and press the right mouse button.

- ☑ To copy all the text in the current window, press the PRINT SCREEN key. You might want to first press ALT-ENTER to switch to full-screen mode before pressing PRINT SCREEN.

- ☑ To copy the window itself (as a graphic image), press ALT-PRINT SCREEN. This method is useful if you need to capture screens for training material. When you paste the image in another document, the entire window and its contents appears.

Once the screen information is on the Clipboard, switch to the destination window. Position the insertion point and choose Paste on the Control menu's Edit subwindow (if you switched to another Command Prompt window) or press CTRL-V (if you switched to a normal window).

NTFS Filenames

Recall that Windows NT supports three file systems: DOS FAT, HPFS (High Performance File System), and NTFS (NT File System). If your system contains a mixture of these drives, you need to be aware of the differences when working with files on the drives or copying files between them.

As mentioned in Chapter 6, NTFS drives allow filenames of up to 256 characters in length. You can experiment with this by typing a command similar to the following on an NTFS drive. COPY CON provides a way to create a file from the console.

COPY CON ThisIsATestOfLongFileNames.TESTFILE.ByTomSheldon

When you press ENTER after typing this filename, the prompt moves down to the next blank line; you can type some text, then press the F6 key and ENTER to close and save the file.

The filename just given demonstrates the descriptive capabilities of NTFS filenames. You can use multiple period separators, (which you can't with DOS because DOS assumes that any characters following a period are the filename's extension). You can also use mixed case, which helps to set off individual words in the filename.

Note that users who start a computer and boot DOS can't access NTFS drives. However, if you start Windows NT on the same computer, you can access DOS, HPFS, and NTFS files. In addition, you can copy files on NTFS drives to DOS drives. If the long filename given earlier actually had a file, and you copied that file to a DOS drive, the filename would be truncated to the DOS filename standard (an eight-character filename and three-character extension), as follows:

THISIS~1.BYT

Note that the first six letters of the filename are used, followed by a number. The number distinguishes the file in case there are other files that start with "THISIS." The first three characters of the last extension in the NTFS filename are used for the DOS filename extension. In addition, all characters are converted to uppercase.

Here are the filenaming rules for NTFS:

- You can have a maximum of 256 characters in file and directory names

- You can use multiple period-separated extensions in names

- Names cannot include these symbols: ? \ * " < > | ? :

- NT preserves the uppercase/lowercase format of the name you specify but does not use case to distinguish between filenames

- You can use wildcard characters (? and *) to search for filenames

Batch Files

A *batch file* contains a series of commands that execute when you type the batch file's name. Batch files have the extension .BAT. For example, you could create a batch file that starts a set of Windows NT programs you like to use when working on a particular project, as described in the following example.

To create a batch file, start the DOS Edit utility or use the COPY CON command. COPY CON provides a way to create text files from the console (CON).

```
COPY CON NewsletterProject.BAT
START CLIPBRD
```

```
START WRITE
START PBRUSH
```

After typing the text of the file, press F6 and ENTER to save your changes. For this example, you would type the following to execute the batch file and start the three programs. Note that case is not important when executing commands. You can use case to help users later distinguish words within filenames.

NEWSLETTERPROJECT

FEATURES OF THE COMMAND PROMPT WINDOW

Before proceeding further, let's look at the features of the Command Prompt window itself. You can customize its size, color, and fonts. You also can switch between window and full-screen mode, and use copy and paste commands to transfer information between applications.

Click the Control button in the upper-left corner of the Command Prompt window to display the Control menu as shown in Figure 11-5. Note that the Edit submenu appears when you click the Edit option.

The following explains the pertinent options.

The Edit Option   Supplies commands for copying and pasting screen information.

The Settings Option   Supplies options for changing the window display setting, edit mode, and for terminating a locked command.

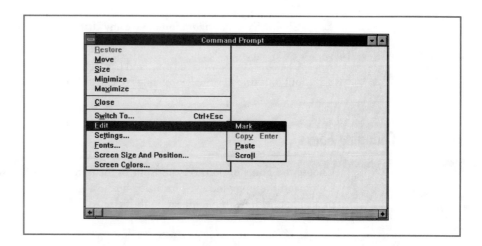

FIGURE 11-5

The Edit submenu on the Control menu

The Fonts Option   Lets you change the font size used in the window.

The Screen Size And Position Option   Lets you increase the buffer size so you can scroll through more of your previous commands and display output.

The Screen Colors Option   Supplies options for changing the background, text, and menu colors.

Customizing the Window Settings

Choose Settings on the Control menu to display the following dialog box:

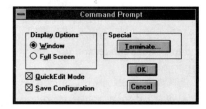

You use this dialog box to set window features and save them for the next session, as follows:

- In the Display Options field, choose whether the Command Prompt should open in full-screen mode, or as a window. You also can press ALT-ENTER when working in the window to switch between these modes at any time.

- Choose QuickEdit Mode to enable mouse copying and pasting, as discussed earlier.

- Choose Save Configuration to save any changes you've made to settings in this session for the next session.

- Click Terminate when a command has locked the system and you can't break out of it using normal commands (CTRL-BREAK or CTRL-C).

Changing Fonts

Choose the Fonts options on the Control menu to change the size of the text in the Command Prompt window. The dialog box in Figure 11-6 appears. Choose a font size in the Font field. A sample appears in the Selected Font box and a preview of the window

FIGURE 11-6

Changing the fonts

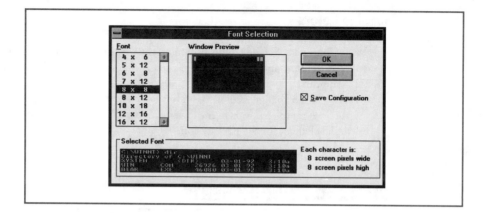

size appears in the Window Preview box. Click the Save Configuration option if you want to save your changes for the next Command Prompt session.

Changing the Screen Buffer Size

The screen buffer is a memory area that retains the information displayed in the Command Prompt window. As you execute new commands and output is displayed, text scrolls off the screen and drops out of the screen buffer memory. If you increase the size of the screen buffer memory, you'll be able to scroll back through the commands and command output for reference, or to copy commands and screens for pasting.

To increase the screen buffer size, choose Screen Size And Position on the Control menu. The following dialog box appears:

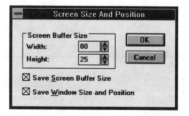

Change the Height setting to increase the number of lines you want to save. A scroll bar appears if the lines exceed the current window size.

Change the width setting if you can't see some of the characters at the end of a command. You might also want to decrease the font size as discussed previously.

Click the Save Screen Buffer Size option to save your changes for the next session, and click Save Window Size and Position to save the current window size and position on the desktop for your next session.

Changing Colors

Choose the Screen Colors option on the Control menu to change the background colors, text colors, and menu colors of the Command Prompt. The dialog box in Figure 11-7 appears.

To change a color for an option, click its button, then choose a color in the color bar. A sample appears in the lower windows. Mark the Save Configuration option to save the changes for the next session.

COMMAND ENVIRONMENTS

The Command Prompt provides access to the Windows NT subsystems. These subsystems, listed here, are complete operating environments where you can execute commands and run programs that are native (belong to, or are typically used with) to the environment.

☑ *Windows NT* Windows NT native commands and programs

☑ *Windows 3.1* A command environment for running 16-bit Windows 3.1 applications

☑ *MS-DOS* A command environment for running MS-DOS-based commands and programs

☑ *OS/2* A command environment for running MS OS/2 1.*x* text-based commands

☑ *POSIX* A command environment for running applications that were written to the IEEE 1003.1 POSIX standard

FIGURE 11-7

Changing window colors

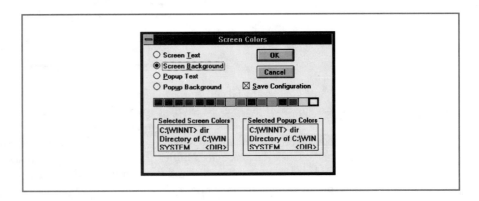

Windows NT sets up an environment for each program you run, and each program is protected from others. One program cannot write into the memory used by another. Typically, you start applications from the File Manager, or you can create startup icons for them in the Program Manager, as discussed in Chapter 12.

Each environment requires some configuration, as discussed in the following sections. Refer to the Windows NT manual if you need more information.

MS-DOS Environment

On systems that have a DOS partition and a Windows NT partition, the AUTO-EXEC.BAT file in the DOS partition is read by Windows NT when it starts. Any configuration information in the file—such as the path setting—is then added to the Windows NT environment.

Windows NT has its own version of the AUTOEXEC.BAT and CONFIG.SYS files called AUTOEXEC.NT and CONFIG.NT. The configuration information in these files is used whenever you start a DOS application. The files are located in the \WINNT\SYSTEM32 directory and can be edited using Notepad or the Edit utility at the Command Prompt.

You can create PIF (Program Information Files) to configure each individual DOS program to run under Windows NT. PIF files hold startup information for the programs, such as the directory to use for data files and the extended or expanded memory requirements. You use the PIF Editor to create PIF files. The utility contains an extensive help utility that explains each PIF option you might want to set. You also can specify an alternate AUTOEXEC.NT or CONFIG.NT file that the application should read when it starts.

For more information on running DOS applications or creating PIF files, refer to the Windows NT manual, or refer to *Windows 3.1: The Complete Reference*, also by the author of this book.

Windows 3.1 Environment

The Windows 3.1 environment provided by Windows NT is similar to the 386 enhanced mode of Windows 3.1. If Windows 3.1 is present when installing Windows NT, the setup program can check the Windows 3.1 directory and configure a similar environment for running Windows 3.1 programs under Windows NT. The configuration information in the Windows 3.1 WIN.INI and SYSTEM.INI files is added to the Windows NT registry.

The registry information is coordinated with the Windows 3.1 WIN.INI and SYSTEM.INI files on an ongoing basis. That means you can boot the computer with the DOS operating system and run Windows 3.1 at any time. The next time you start Windows NT, it checks the WIN.INI and SYSTEM.INI files to see if there are any updates. Also note that some 16-bit Windows applications that you run under Windows NT still need to add configuration information of their own to the WIN.INI and SYSTEM.INI files.

PART THREE

Customizing, Configuring, and Managing WindowsNT

Inside

& Out

CHAPTER 12

Customizing the Program Manager and Organizing Applications and Documents

This chapter shows you how to organize the applications, utilities, accessories, and other program items in the Program Manager. You'll see how to create new startup icons and group windows, and rearrange startup icons into new groups that best fit the way you work. You'll use some of the techniques you learned in previous chapters to resize windows and move them to other locations in order to create an arrangement that shows only the icons that you want to see and hides those you don't often use.

Because a computer running Windows NT might be used by several users, the Program Manager provides a way for each logged on user to create a personalized Program Manager window configuration. Every user can have a *personal group* configuration, but members of the Administrator or Power User group can create *common group* configurations that every user sees. When a user logs on, they see common groups, and their personal groups, but not the personal groups of other users.

CREATING A NEW GROUP

To have easy access to the applications and documents in your system, it's a good idea to arrange them according to your work habits. Windows lets you move a program icon into another existing group, or create new groups as you need them. For example, you can organize all of the applications and tools that you use for writing into a window called "Writing Tools," and all the applications and tools that you use to create pictures and art into a window called "Drawing Tools."

Figure 12-1 illustrates two groups that contain *document startup icons*. You create them to load specific documents. Double-clicking a document startup icon starts the program represented by the icon itself, and loads a document represented by the name under the icon. Creating group windows such as these improves your access to the files you work with regularly. The DAILY group has startup icons for business and personal use, and the COMPANY NEWSLETTER group includes startup icons used when creating a newsletter.

The initial organization of the icons in the Program Manager window may be helpful as you're learning to use Windows, but eventually you'll find it beneficial to reorganize these icons to fit your personal taste and the way you work. The following exercise demonstrates how to create a new group window and add program items to it.

Creating a New Group Window

This exercise shows you how to create a new personal group window using the New command on the Program Manager File menu. You'll keep your existing groups but copy

FIGURE 12-1

Use groups to organize your programs and documents

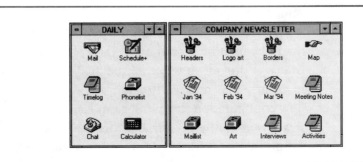

(not move) some of the icons from them to your new group. You'll call the new group "Everyday Tools."

1. Choose New from the Program Manager File menu. This opens the New Program Object dialog box, shown here:

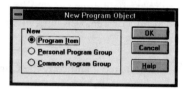

2. Click Personal Program Group if you want to create a group for your own use, or if you are logged on as a member of the Administrator or Power User group, click Common Program Group to create a group for all users.

3. Click OK to display the following dialog box:

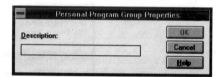

4. Type **Everyday Tools** in the Description field and click OK.

When the dialog box closes, the Everyday Tools group appears in the Program Manager as an empty group window. Now you're ready to add program startup icons to the new group.

Copying Program Items to a New Group

Now that the group window exists, you can add application and document icons to it. In this next exercise, you copy existing application icons from the Main and Accessories windows to the Everyday Tools window.

Start by considering which applications and accessories you'll use on a daily basis. For this example, let's copy the File Manager, ClipBook Viewer, Mail, Schedule+, Write, and the Command Prompt icons to the new group. Later you can add other icons to the group to fit your needs.

The easiest way to copy icons from one window to another is by dragging them with the mouse, as described in the following steps. (You also can use the Copy command on the File menu, as discussed shortly.)

1. Open the Main group window. Make sure you can still see at least part of the Everyday Tools window.

2. Press the CTRL key, and then click and drag the File Manager icon in the Main group to the Everyday Tools group.

If you fail to hold down the CTRL key while dragging, the icon will be moved, not copied. Moving an icon removes it from the source group and places it in the destination group.

3. Repeat step 2 and copy the ClipBook Viewer icon to the Everyday Tools group.

Now perform the same exercise using the keyboard. Copy the Mail icon from the Main group to the Everyday Tools group, by following these steps:

1. Click the Mail icon in the Main group, then choose Copy from the File menu. The following dialog box appears:

2. Click the down arrow button in the To Group field and select the Everyday Tools group.

3. Click OK to copy the icon to the selected group.

On your own, copy the remaining icons and any others you want using either the mouse or the keyboard. When the group is complete, you can resize and move its window to fit in the Program Manager.

Resizing and Arranging the New Window

Once you've finished copying the icons as described in the previous paragraphs, close the Main and Accessories windows, then follow these steps to resize and move the Everyday Tools window:

1. Click the Program Manager Options menu; if the Auto Arrange feature is not checked in the drop-down menu, enable it now.

2. Resize the Everyday Tools group window to fit around its icons. Point to a border or corner of the window, then click and drag. The icons rearrange as you change the window's size.

3. Move the resized window to the upper-left corner of the Program Manager screen.

Saving Arrangements

Once you've arranged the Program Manager to your satisfaction, you need to make sure the new arrangement is saved so you see it the next time you start Windows NT. To immediately update the changes, choose Save Settings Now.

Because there are times when you want to save your arrangements and times when you don't, disable Save Settings on Exit. If you leave this option enabled, you might inadvertently exit Windows NT when you have a window arrangement on the screen that you don't want to see the next time you start Windows NT. To save custom arrangements only when you're sure you want to save them, choose the Save Settings Now option.

CREATING NEW PROGRAM ITEM ICONS

In this section, you'll create icons for program items using the New command on the Program Manager File menu. In addition, you'll learn about using the Setup utility to automatically search your hard drives for applications and create startup icons for them.

The New Option

Use the New option on the Program Manager File menu to create new program item icons, as well as new groups. In this example, you create a new program startup icon in the Main group window for a program called WINVER. This program resides in the \WINNT\SYSTEM32 directory on the drive that holds your Windows NT system files. The utility is quite simple—it displays the version number of Windows NT—but will serve us well for this example. Follow these steps to add the new startup icon:

1. Click the Everyday Tools group, or any other group you want to add a startup icon to. You must make the group active before you can add an icon to it.

2. Choose New from the File menu to open the New Program Object dialog box.

3. This time you are creating a new program item icon, so click the Program Item button and the OK button. You'll next see the following Program Item Properties box, which is described in the following section:

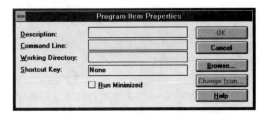

Program Item Properties

You define the name, program file, and other startup information for program icons in the Program Item Properties dialog box. Each field in this dialog box is explained here, but you won't always need to fill out every field.

Description   In the Description text box, type the name you want to appear under the icon or in the title bar of the window that runs the program. If you don't type a name, the Program Manager uses part of the name in the Command Line field for the icon name.

Command Line   In the Command Line text box, type the name of the executable (.EXE or .COM) file used to start the program, with a drive letter and path if necessary. You also can click the Browse button to search for the filename. The Command Line field can also contain the names of associated files.

Working Directory   In the Working Directory text box, type the name of the directory in which you want the application to open and save files. The program itself doesn't have to be in this directory, but it will access files in this directory while it runs.

Shortcut Key   In the Shortcut Key text box, specify a keystroke to start the application. All you have to do is type a letter; The Program Manager then inserts CTRL-ALT before the letter. So if you type **W** in the field, the keystroke becomes CTRL-ALT-W. The Program Manager does this to avoid keystroke conflicts with its own key assignments.

Run Minimized   Check the Run Minimized option if you want the application to reduce to an icon on the desktop whenever the program starts. This is useful if you have set up the application to start when you turn your system on, but you don't always use it right away.

Browse   If you don't know the name of the executable file for the program, click the Browse button to open a dialog box so you can search for the file. This is discussed in the next section.

Change Icon   Use the Change Icon button to select an icon to use for the program, as discussed later in this chapter.

Browsing for the Filename

The Browse button in the Program Item Properties dialog box provides a quick way to locate the full drive, path, and filename of the .EXE and .COM files on your system's drives. The Browse dialog box also lists .BAT and .PIF files. In the following steps, you use Browse to search for the WINVER.EXE file:

1.   From the Program Item Properties dialog box, click the Browse button. A Browse dialog box appears.

2.   In the Directories field, locate the \WINNT\SYSTEM32 directory as shown in Figure 12-2, and double-click it so its file list appears in the File Name field.

3.   Scan through the file list for the WINVER.EXE file. Double-click the file to select it and close the Browse window.

The complete drive, path, and filename of the file appear in the Command Line field. You can now select an icon for the utility. While WINVER.EXE and other Windows NT programs have built-in default icons, you can still specify a different icon by following the steps in the next section.

FIGURE 12-2

Browsing for program names

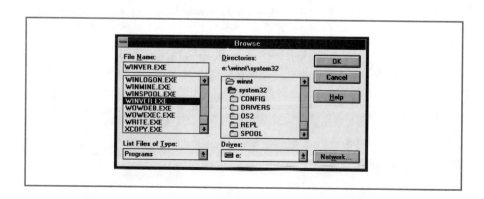

The Browse dialog box also has a Network button you click to locate executable files on other systems. Keep in mind, however, that network files might not always be available if the owner of the system stops sharing the directory or moves the files.

Selecting the Icon

You're almost done creating the startup icon. If you click OK on the Program Item Properties dialog box at this point, the Program Manager would use the default icon for the utility. The following exercise shows you how to select other icons:

1. In the Program Item Properties dialog box, click the Change Icon button. The Change Icon dialog box appears as shown here with the default WinVer icon:

    In the Change Icon dialog box, the File Name field contains the drive, path, and filename of the WinVer executable file. The default icon for this file appears in the Current Icon field. You can choose a different icon by following the remaining steps. Several Windows NT files contain icons, and you can open the files to view and use those icons. We'll first look at MORICONS.DLL:

2. Click the Browse button to open the Browse dialog box (shown in Figure 12-2).

3. Locate the file MORICONS.DLL in the \WINNT\SYSTEM32 directory and double-click it.

    The Current Icon list changes to display a large set of icons. Figure 12-3 shows the complete list.

4. Scroll through the list by dragging the slider button right, then left.

5. To see a more generic assortment of icons, click the Browse button again, then double-click the PROGMAN.EXE file. The assortment of icons in the Current Icon field now appears as shown in Figure 12-4.

6. Choose an icon from this list, or simply click Cancel to get back to the Program Item Properties dialog box and use the WinVer default icon.

FIGURE 12-3

Icons in MORICONS.DLL

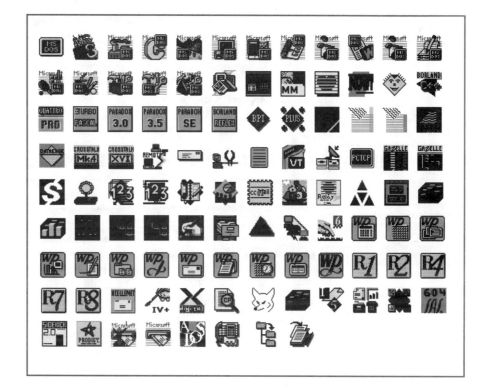

Completing the Task

In the Shortcut Key field, you can specify a quick-key sequence that executes the WinVer utility. You can press the Quick Keys if the icon's group is not open or visible. Tab to the Shortcut Key field in the Program Item Properties dialog box and type **W** to create the CTRL-ALT-W shortcut key.

FIGURE 12-4

Icons in the
PROGMAN.EXE file

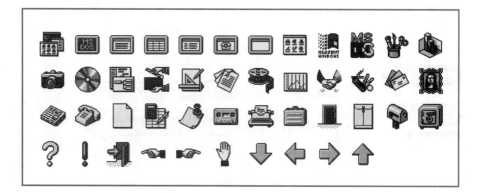

There are several other items in the Program Item Properties dialog box that you might need to designate for some programs, but not for WinVer. For example, there is no need to mark the Run Minimized box because WinVer simply displays a message box. Also, WinVer doesn't need a working directory.

Click OK on the Program Item Properties box to create the new WinVer startup icon. The icon appears in the group window you selected before starting this process.

USING THE SETUP UTILITY TO CREATE STARTUP ICONS

The Windows NT Setup utility offers yet another way to create startup icons for applications. Setup can search your hard drive for executable files and create startup icons for those it finds. You usually do this for DOS-based programs since most Windows-based programs install their own icons during setup. Also, when you install Windows NT, it locates any existing Windows 3.1 programs and creates icons for them.

Start the Windows NT Setup utility by double-clicking its icon in the Main group window of the Program Manager. In a moment, you'll see a dialog box similar to the one shown in Figure 12-5.

Follow these steps to create a new application startup icon using Setup:

1. Select Options, and choose Set Up Applications to display a dialog box similar to the one shown in Figure 12-6.

2. You can search specific drives or the current path. Choose one or more of the options in the field, then click the Search Now button.

   In a moment, the Set Up Applications dialog box appears as shown in Figure 12-7. On the left of the Set Up Applications dialog box is a list box containing filenames of applications that are not currently set up as program item icons. (Every system is different, of course, and your list will represent what's available on your computer.)

3. Click the applications you want to set up in the left box, then click the Add button to add them to the right box. Click Add All to add them all, or if you

FIGURE 12-5

The Windows NT
Setup window

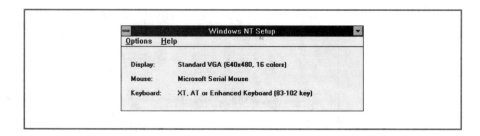

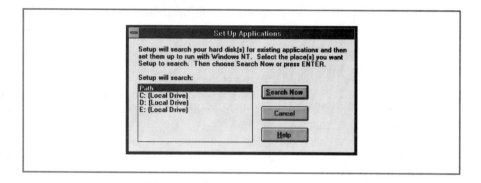

FIGURE 12-6

The Set Up Applications dialog box

make a mistake and don't want to add an application you've selected, click it on the right, then click the Remove button.

4.   When finished selecting applications, click OK.

Windows Setup will create icons for the applications you selected in a Program Manager group called Applications or a group called Non-Windows Applications. You can open these groups now to see where your new application icons appear.

USING THE FILE MANAGER TO CREATE STARTUP ICONS

You can use the File Manager to create startup icons for applications. First position the File Manager and the Program Manager side by side, then locate the executable file of the program you want to create a startup file for, and drag it over the appropriate Program Manager group. When you release the mouse, the Program Manager creates a new startup icon with all the appropriate settings.

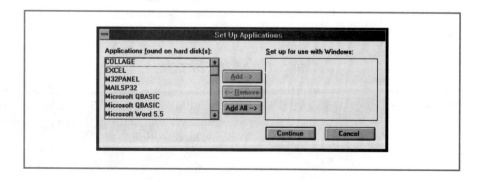

FIGURE 12-7

The list of filenames of applications that are not currently set up as program item icons

You might want to highlight the new icon and choose Properties on the File menu to check or edit its properties. You could add a working directory, quick keys, or specify a new icon.

Refer to Chapter 13 for more detailed information about creating startup icons with the File Manager.

You can use this same method to create startup icons for associated documents. Click and drag the document's icon from File Manager to an appropriate Program Manager group.

OTHER PROGRAM MANAGER OPTIONS

In the remaining sections of this chapter, you learn how to change the properties of existing groups and program items, how to delete program items, and how to make applications start every time you start Windows.

Changing the Properties of a Group or Icon

After selecting an icon in a Program Manager group, you can edit its startup options by choosing the Properties option on the File menu. You get the same Program Item Properties dialog box that you see when creating new startup icons. Program item properties that you can change include all those that were available when you created the item:

- ✓ You can change the name of the icon in the Description field.

- ✓ You can specify a different startup command, or add parameters and switches to the command.

- ✓ You can specify a working directory (discussed in the next section).

- ✓ You can add or change the shortcut key and specify whether the application should run minimized when selected.

Defining a Working Directory

Most of the applications and accessories that come with Windows NT automatically open and save files in the default directory specified by your logon account. You can specify another directory where an application stores its files by typing the drive and path of the directory in the Working Directory field.

As an example, try changing the startup directory of the Command Prompt, which usually opens to the default directory for the currently logged user. Follow these steps:

1.   Highlight the Command Prompt by clicking it once, and then choose Properties from the File menu.

2.   In the Working Directory field, type **C:** (or type the letter of your Windows NT drive).

3.   Click OK to save the changes.

4.   Double-click the Command Prompt icon to start it.

The Command Prompt now starts up in the root directory of your Windows NT drive. You can make similar changes to your other program items to ensure that files created with those programs are stored in specific directories. For example, create a directory called \DOCS, then change the Working Directory property of the Write icon to \DOCS. Any files you create with Write are then stored in this directory.

DELETING A PROGRAM ITEM OR GROUP

You use the Delete option on the Program Manager File menu to delete the currently selected group or program item. Deleting a group also deletes any program item icons within the group. If you want to save any of the items, move them to another group before deleting the first group.

To delete a program item or group, first reduce it to an icon, and highlight the icon. Press the DEL key or choose Delete from the File menu. Windows displays a message box asking if you really want to delete the icon. Answer Yes to go ahead with the deletion, or No if you change your mind.

INSTALLING APPLICATIONS

Installation of Windows NT applications is straightforward. First, always follow the instructions in your owner's manual. This normally involves executing the application's setup routine. Choose the Run command from the Program Manager or File Manager File menu, then type **A:SETUP** or **A:INSTALL**. The installation procedure asks you for the name of the destination directory and, once you give it, handles the rest.

Most installation procedures for Windows NT applications create a separate group window in the Program Manager and place startup icons in it. This is fine if the application contains several associated applications and you want to keep their startup icons together in the same group. As an alternative, you can copy the icons into a larger group, and then remove the group window. For example, instead of keeping separate groups for a drawing program, a paint program, and a scanning program, you could copy all the icons to a single group called Graphics.

If you already have applications on your system, and you don't see startup icons for those applications in the Program Manager, run the Setup utility as described earlier.

Organizing Application Directories

Most of the applications that are bundled with Windows NT are stored in the \WINNT\SYSTEM32 directory. By default, files you create with those applications are stored in your user account directory, which typically branches from the USERS directory on the Windows NT drive.

When installing new applications, install them in a directory that branches from the root or a program directory. For example, when installing Word for Windows, the directory \WINWORD is recommended. However, you can create a directory structure that's easy to back up by appending all application directories to a single directory called \PROGRAMS or \APPS. Then when you back up, you specify the \PROGRAMS or \APPS directory for the backup, making sure to include subdirectories. An example is shown here:

Startup icons created during the installation of a program specify the path to the program's directory. You need to specify working directories for the storage of data files on your own by selecting the icon and choosing Properties from the Program Manager File menu. Type the working directory path in the Working Directory field.

If you reorganize your directory structure and move program directories to other locations, you'll need to update the program startup icons so they can find programs in their new locations.

Installing Non-Windows Applications

To install non-Windows applications, start the Command Prompt and follow the procedures outlined in the application's documentation. After installation, start Windows and create a startup icon for it using the Windows NT Setup utility.

Note

Use the Setup utility because it knows how to create PIF files for most popular non-Windows NT applications.

If the Setup utility doesn't recognize the program, it will recommend that you use the New option on the Program Manager File menu to create a startup icon and PIF file on your own. If you don't create a PIF file for an application, Windows uses the settings in its default PIF (_DEFAULT.PIF) when you run the application. This may cause problems for some applications if the default settings are not the optimum ones. You can change the settings of the default PIF, but it's best just to create a PIF for each application using the PIF Editor. Before doing so, check to see if the application came with a PIF of its own. Manufacturer-supplied PIFs contain settings that optimize the application for Windows NT. Check the disks or program directory of the application.

Note

Once you've installed an application, protect its files from accidental deletion or modification by granting read-only permissions to users and groups.

ORGANIZING DOCUMENTS

There are many ways to organize the documents created in your applications. You could create one directory called \DOCS and store all documents created by all applications in it. However, you won't be able to use the same filenames, and similar filenames can be confusing. A better way to organize is to create directories that reflect the way you work or the projects that you're working on.

For backup reasons, it's a good idea to create directories that branch from a single directory, such as \DATA. Typical directory structures are shown in the following illustration:

The directory structure on the left is organized according to the documents created by each application. The structure on the right is organized by the types of files you create and their use. You also could create data directories like PROJECT1, GRAPHICS, or NEWSLET (newsletter). For example, the newsletter directory would contain all the files you use (graphics and text) to create a newsletter.

Once you've created the directory structure (including data directories), change the Working Directory field on the Program Item Properties dialog box for program startup icons to reflect the destination data directories. You might want to go through all your program startup icons now and change the working directories.

If you save personal files in one data directory and business files in another, just duplicate a program startup icon and modify the properties of each icon as follows:

☑   Change the icon name to BUSINESS or PERSONAL

☑   Change the working directory to the business or personal directory

For example, you might have a Write icon called BUSINESS that saves data files in a directory called \DATA\BUSINESS and another Write icon called PERSONAL that saves data files in a directory called \DATA\PERSONAL. The following shows an example of a Program Manager group with these types of startup icons:

Inside

- Options for Customizing

- Program and Document Associations

- Modifying the Toolbar

- Creating Program Manager Startup Icons with the File Manager

- Starting Applications from the File Manager

& Out

CHAPTER 13

Customizing the File Manager

Chapter 7 discussed the basic file management techniques you can perform in the File Manager. This chapter continues Chapter 12's discussion of customizing Windows NT by showing you the features and options in the File Manager that you can change to suit your own needs. At the end of this chapter, you'll see how to set up special File Manager directory windows for launching applications and opening documents that can replace the Program Manager in some cases.

This chapter shows you how to perform these, and other, tasks:

- ☑ Set confirmation messages for file operations on or off
- ☑ Change the features of the File Manager window
- ☑ Add custom buttons to the Toolbar
- ☑ Add new document associations
- ☑ Create special directory windows

OPTIONS FOR CUSTOMIZING

You can customize the File Manager in a number of ways. For example, you can change the fonts that display filenames, turn the status bar on or off, or change how the File Manager asks you to confirm your commands. The options discussed in this section are on the File Manager Options menu.

Save Settings on Exit

When the Save Settings on Exit option on the Options menu is enabled, the following settings are saved for your next File Manager session:

- ☑ Check-marked options on the Options menu
- ☑ Changes to directory windows and their contents
- ☑ The arrangement of directory windows
- ☑ Any open windows are automatically opened the next time you start the File Manager

If Save Settings on Exit is enabled, you can avoid screen clutter in your next session by closing any windows that you don't want reopened before exiting the File Manager in this session.

Note

To immediately save any changes you make to the arrangement or settings of the File Manager, hold the SHIFT key and choose Exit from the File menu. This saves the new arrangement but doesn't actually exit Windows.

Suppressing Confirmation Messages

When you delete or copy files in the File Manager, warning messages appear asking you to confirm your actions. If you feel these confirmation messages are unnecessary, you can use the Confirmation option on the Options menu to turn some or all of them off. Choose Confirmation now to display the following dialog box:

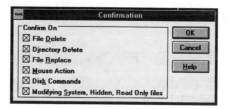

You can control the following confirmation messages:

File Delete   Clear this option if you don't want to see warning messages when deleting files.

Directory Delete   Clear this option to suppress warning messages when deleting directories and subdirectories. When cleared, you also don't see warning messages for files in the directories.

File Replace   Clear this option to suppress messages that warn of file overwrites, for instance, when you copy a file from one directory to another directory containing a file with the same name. Clear this option only when you are sure a copy operation is safe.

Mouse Action   Clear this option to suppress messages that appear when copying and moving files with mouse click-and-drag techniques, for example, when you copy a set of files by dragging them from one directory to another.

Disk Commands   Clear this option if you don't want to see warning messages when copying or formatting disks.

Modifying System, Hidden, Read Only Files   Clear this option if you don't want to see messages when moving, replacing, or deleting system, hidden, and read-only files.

If you are a new user, leave all these options checked until you become more familiar with File Manager operations. In addition, only turn confirmation off temporarily, for example, if moving or deleting large groups of files to reorganize your system, and only then when you are sure the operations are safe.

In some cases, it's advantageous to temporarily turn off a confirmation request. For example, you can disable the File Delete confirmation when deleting large groups of files that you're sure are safe to delete. Be sure to turn the option back on, however, so you'll see the warning messages for future file operations.

Controlling File Deletions

The confirmation warning boxes are useful, not just to warn you of file overwrites or deletes, but to help you selectively delete files. For example, assume that Confirm File Delete has not been cleared and that you select a block of files to delete. You'll see a warning message similar to the following when the File Manager attempts to delete the first file in the group:

If you click Yes, the file is deleted and a warning message appears for the next file. If you click No, the file is not deleted and you see a warning message for the next file. If you click Yes to All, all the files are deleted without further warning messages.

If you select a directory, you must be aware of the current confirmation settings in your Windows environment. You first see a message similar to the following that asks for confirmation to delete the directory:

You then see a confirmation box for each file in the directory. If you decide that any one file in the directory cannot be deleted, then the directory is not deleted.

If you delete a directory that has subdirectories, a confirmation message appears for the first file in every subdirectory. If you choose Yes to All, all the files in the subdirectory are deleted and you see a confirmation message for the first file in the next subdirectory. Read warning messages carefully and be aware of what you are deleting.

Changing Fonts

Choose the Font option on the Options menu to change the font used to display filenames in directory windows. The dialog box in Figure 13-1 appears.

Here's how to change the font:

1. In the Font list box, use the scroll bars or arrow keys to scroll through, and click a font. The font appears in the Sample field.

2. In the Font Style list box, choose a style for the font you want to use.

3. Choose a font size in the Size box. Keep in mind that large fonts reduce the total amount of information you can see in the window.

4. Set the lower check boxes depending on the case you want to use for listings.

Displaying the Status Bar

The status bar at the bottom of the File Manager window displays the following useful information about disk space and file sizes for the currently selected disk:

☑ When a directory is selected, you'll see information about the drive at the left of the status bar, and about the directory at the right of the status bar.

☑ When a file is selected, the status bar tells you the size of the file.

☑ When multiple files are selected, the status bar indicates the number of files and their total number of bytes.

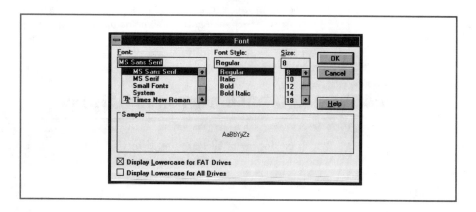

FIGURE 13-1

Changing fonts for file listings

Turn the status bar off and on by choosing Status Bar from the Options menu. Turning the status bar off is not usually necessary unless the desktop is so crowded that you need to make the File Manager window as small as possible.

Toolbar and Drive Icon Bar Status Options

If you need more room to work in the File Manager, turn off both the Toolbar and drive icon bar by disabling the Toolbar or Drivebar options in the Options menu. However, disabling these options is not recommended.

Minimizing the File Manager on Use

When the Minimize on Use option is set, the File Manager reduces to an icon whenever you start an application from the File Manager.

If you want the Program Manager to minimize in this way whenever you start applications, keep the Minimize on Use option marked; otherwise, disable it.

Indicating Expandable Branches

Expanding the entire directory tree is a convenient way to see all directories and branching subdirectories for the selected drive. However, if the list is long, you can't see the entire tree, and you'll need to scroll through it using the arrow keys or the scroll bar.

When the option Indicate Expandable Branches on the Tree menu is set, a plus sign appears in the icon of directories that have branching subdirectories. A minus sign appears if the directory is fully expanded. In this way, you can tell at a glance which directories have subdirectories.

The Indicate Expandable Branches option may cause a slight delay when opening the File Manager or expanding and collapsing branches. Try it for a while to see if you like it, and to see if it slows your system down.

PROGRAM AND DOCUMENT ASSOCIATIONS

Associated document files are linked to the application that was used to create them. Various filename extensions are reserved for applications, as listed here:

Application	Filename Extension
Paintbrush	.BMP
Paintbrush	.MSP
Paintbrush	.PCX
Calendar	.CAL
ClipBook	.CLP
Cardfile	.CRD
PIF Editor	.PIF
Notepad	.TXT
Notepad	.INI
Terminal	.TRM
Write	.WRI

If you double-click an associated document in the File Manager, the associated application starts and the document loads into its workspace. As you'll see later, you can create File Manager directory windows that list only associated documents. You can then quickly open any document in the window by double-clicking its icon.

The File Associate command lets you create your own file associations. For example, if you add a new program that creates files with the extension .ZAP, you can use the Associate command to link the .ZAP files with the program. Then you can double-click the .ZAP files to open them. Alternatively, you might want to associate .ZAP files with Notepad or another application.

Caution

If you associate a filename extension with more than one application, the last program that you associated with the document will start.

Documents created by Windows applications are already associated. The File Associate command is your tool for linking non-Windows applications with the documents they create, or to change associations. For example, you could remove the association that .TXT has with Notepad and assign it to the text editor of your choice.

Assume that you are creating a set of files that log your time with the Notepad utility. You save the files with the .LOG extension. To associate these files with Notepad, follow these steps:

1. Choose Associate from the File menu to display the following dialog box:

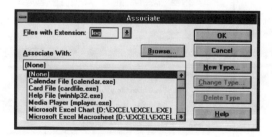

2. Type a filename extension in the Files with Extension field, or choose an extension from the drop-down list box. In this example, you would type **LOG**.

3. In the Associate With list box, locate the application you want to associate with the extension. In this example, choose "Text File (notepad.exe)".

4. Click the OK button to save the association.

To remove an association, open the Associate dialog box, type its extension in the text field, and choose None in the Associate With list box.

MODIFYING THE TOOLBAR

The Toolbar is a set of buttons you click to execute File Manager commands as an alternative to choosing those same commands from the menus. The File Manager has a set of default buttons that you can use to share and connect with network drives or change the way files are displayed in directory windows. If you don't like the button arrangement or you want to add your own, read through this discussion to customize your Toolbar.

To change the Toolbar, choose Customize Toolbar from the Options menu or double-click the Toolbar background. The dialog box in Figure 13-2 appears.

On the left in the Available Buttons field is a set of buttons you can add to the Toolbar. On the right in the Toolbar Buttons field are the current Toolbar buttons. To add buttons, select a button on the left, then click the Add button. To remove a button from the Toolbar, choose it from the Toolbar Buttons field on the right and click the Remove button.

The Toolbar has limited space, so you'll need to remove some buttons to add others. The networking buttons are good candidates for removal if you are not connected to a network, or you don't make connections or shares often. You also can remove the Move and Copy buttons if you use your mouse to move and copy files. The details of these operations are discussed in the following sections.

FIGURE 13-2

Customizing the Toolbar

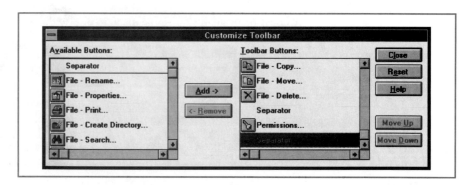

Adding a New Toolbar Button

In this exercise, you'll add a button that opens the Search dialog box so you can search for files on your local hard drive or on the network. Follow these steps:

1. Double-click the Toolbar background or choose Customize Toolbar from the Options menu.

2. Select the position in the Toolbar Buttons list where you want to place the new button. Remember that this list is displayed left to right on the Toolbar itself. If you want the new button all the way to the right on the Toolbar, scroll to the bottom of the list and click the last item, which is a separator.

3. Scroll through the Available Buttons list box until you see the File—Search button, which has a "binoculars" icon.

4. Double-click the File—Search button to add it to the Toolbar Buttons box on the right.

5. Click the Close button to add the File—Search button to the Toolbar.

The Search button now appears on the File Manager Toolbar. To add more buttons, you'll need to remove others, so follow the steps in the next section.

Removing Toolbar Buttons

If you run out of room on the Toolbar, use these steps to remove buttons. You can execute this first procedure directly on the Toolbar without opening the Customize Toolbar dialog box. Follow these steps:

1. Hold down the SHIFT key.

2. Click the button you want to remove and drag it off the Toolbar. When you release the mouse, the button is removed.

To remove buttons in the Customize Toolbar dialog box, follow these steps:

1. Double-click the Toolbar background to open the Customize Toolbar dialog box.

2. Scroll through the Toolbar Buttons list until you find the button you want to remove.

3. Double-click the button, or click it once and click the Remove button.

4.   Click the Close button. The button is removed from the Toolbar.

Rearranging the Toolbar Order

You have two ways of rearranging the order of the buttons on the Toolbar. The first is the best, and you can do it without opening the Customize Toolbar dialog box. Follow these steps:

1.   Hold down the SHIFT key.

2.   Click the button you want to move with the mouse and drag it to another position. When you release the mouse, the button moves to the new position.

If you also are adding or removing buttons to or from the Toolbar, use the following method of rearranging the Toolbar from the Customize Toolbar dialog box. Follow these steps:

1.   Double-click the Toolbar background to open the Customize Toolbar dialog box.

2.   In the Toolbar Buttons box, click the button you want to move.

3.   Click the Move Up or Move Down button until the button is placed where you want it to be.

4.   Click the Close button to save the new arrangement.

Resetting the Toolbar

To revert to the original Toolbar, open the Customize Toolbar dialog box by double-clicking the Toolbar background, and then click the Reset button. When you click the Close button, the list reverts to its default setting.

CREATING PROGRAM MANAGER STARTUP ICONS WITH THE FILE MANAGER

The File Manager provides an interesting way to create startup icons in Program Manager groups. When you add a new application and want to create a startup icon for it, simply locate its .EXE file in the File Manager and drag and drop the file icon on a group in the Program Manager. The file icon supplies the Program Manager with all the file property information it needs to create the startup icon, including the path and name of the executable file that starts the program. Keep in mind that most applications create startup icons during installation.

You can create document startup icons in the same way. In the following exercise, you'll create a text file with Notepad, and then create a startup icon for the text file in the Program Manager Accessories group. Follow these steps:

1. Start the Notepad utility in the Accessories group of the Program Manager.

2. When the Notepad window opens, type your name or any other text, then choose Save As from the File menu and save the file in your personal directory with a name such as DAILY.TXT.

3. In the File Manager, open a directory window on your personal directory.

4. Arrange the Program Manager and the File Manager windows so they are side by side, then make sure you can see the icon of the file you just created in the File Manager and the Accessories group in the Program Manager.

5. Click the file icon and drag it over the Accessories group in the Program Manager, and then release the mouse.

A Notepad icon appears in the Accessories group with the name of the file. You can repeat these steps for any documents that are associated with an application. You might want to create a Program Manager group for document startup icons.

STARTING APPLICATIONS FROM THE FILE MANAGER

While the Program Manager provides an excellent way to start programs, the File Manager might be a better choice. The File Manager gives you a view of all files on your drives and makes it easier to open specific documents. For example, you can create directory windows that list only associated documents, then double-click the documents to open them. In contrast, you have to specifically create document icons in the Program Manager.

The File Manager also has a Search command that can produce a list of program files or document files scattered throughout your drives. For example, you could search for all files with the .DOC extension in all directories on a drive. You can then open any file that appears on the list. Another advantage of the File Manager is that you can sort files in various arrangements, then quickly locate the files you want to start or open.

Establishing Launch Windows

In this section you'll see how to set up the File Manager for use as a program launcher to replace the Program Manager. The arrangement described here and shown in Figure 13-3 is only a suggestion, based on normal Windows NT directories and files. Consider organizing your own system so associated document files are in one or more special data directories. Here are some suggestions for organizing the File Manager to access the files on your system:

▨ Create a "normal" directory window (containing a directory tree and contents list) that shows all files (*.*) in the selected directory. This will be your "working window," which you can use to list the contents of other drives and directories when necessary.

▨ Create directory windows that list executable (.EXE) files so you can easily start programs. You won't need a directory tree in this window.

▨ Use a directory window that lists documents sorted by their filename extensions so you can easily find files associated with programs. You won't need a directory tree in this window.

FIGURE 13-3

One example of setting up the File Manager to function as a program launcher

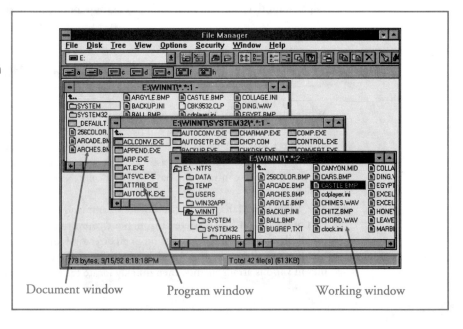

Creating the Working Window

The working window should contain the directory tree and contents list. You use this window for general use to display the contents of any directory. If you're still in the File Manager, you should already have a directory window open. Make sure it displays the directory tree and file list; if necessary, choose Tree and Directory from the View menu. Resize the window so that other windows are available on the desktop. Alternatively, you can use the Cascade or Tile option on the Window menu to reorganize all the windows into the desktop arrangement that works best for you.

Creating an Executable Files Window

Here are the steps to create a new directory window that lists the executable files in the \WINNT\SYSTEM32 directory:

1.   Choose New Window from the Window menu.

2.   In the directory tree, choose the \WINNT\SYSTEM32 directory.

3.   Choose Directory Only from the View menu.

4.   Choose By File Type from the View menu, then disable all the File Type options except Programs to list all the .EXE files in the directory. Click OK.

5.   If you don't need to see file details, click the Name button on the Toolbar.

6.   Click the Sort By Name button on the Toolbar to sort the list in filename order.

You now have an organized list of executable program files. You can resize the window now, if necessary, but later you'll "cascade" all three of your new windows.

Creating the Documents Window

With these steps, you create a window that lists only documents:

1.   Make sure the window you just created is active, then open the Window menu and choose New Window (you could also double-click the drive icon of the window). A new window appears that looks like the window you just created.

2.   To list documents only, choose By File Type from the View menu. Check the Documents option and make sure the other options aren't marked. Click OK.

3.   Choose Sort By Type button on the Toolbar to organize the listed files by their filename extensions.

4. Temporarily choose Tree and Directory from the View menu, then click the
\WINNT directory icon. Choose Directory Only to restore the list of files.

Organizing and Saving the Arrangement

Now you can organize the three windows in a cascade arrangement on the desktop. If
you have other windows open in addition to those created here, minimize them now.
Since the working window has a directory tree and is used to view other directories, place
it on top. Click it to make it active, and then choose Cascade from the Window menu.
Your arrangement will look similar to the one in Figure 13-3.

You now can launch applications by double-clicking their icons in the executable
files window, or open documents by double-clicking their icons in the document window.

Note

To save this arrangement for the next File Manager session, hold down the SHIFT key
and choose Exit from the File menu. Also, make sure the Save Settings on Exit option
is disabled.

Inside

& Out

CHAPTER 14

Customizing the Interface

This chapter covers ways you can customize
Windows NT using the Control Panel utilities.
Only the Windows NT user interface options
are covered here. Chapter 15 covers methods for
changing hardware settings. The Control Panel
is pictured in Figure 14-1, and its utilities are
described on the next page.

FIGURE 14-1

The Control Panel

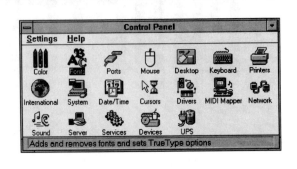

Color　Use the Color utility to alter the foreground, background, border, and other color schemes of Windows.

Desktop　Use the Desktop utility to change the colors and patterns of the background, install a screen saver, and to change blink rates, icon settings, and grid size.

Keyboard　Use the Keyboard utility to change keyboard settings such as the repeat rate of keys.

Mouse　Use the Mouse utility to control the operating characteristics of the mouse.

Cursor　Use the Cursor utility to change the mouse pointer to an animated pointer, or a pointer that clocks events.

Sound　Use the Sound utility to assign sounds to system events such as error messages or the sound you hear when starting or exiting Windows. You need a sound board to hear the sounds, or an optional driver to power your system's internal speaker. This topic is covered later in this chapter and in Chapter 15.

CHANGING THE COLOR SCHEME

Use the Color utility in the Control Panel to change the colors of window borders, title bars, backgrounds, text, menus, and other features. You can select a predefined color scheme or create your own. The background is the underlying desktop; you can do any of the following things to it:

☑ Change its color using the Color utility.

☑ Install a repeating pattern on the desktop as discussed in the "Desktop Patterns" section later in this chapter. The colors of the pattern are set using the Color utility.

☑ Overlay the desktop with a graphic image, as covered in the "Wallpaper" section later in this chapter.

Tip

Images and patterns on the desktop take up memory. If your system is low on memory, don't install them.

Double-click the Color icon in the Control Panel to display the basic Color dialog box shown in Figure 14-2. (There are two Color dialog boxes—a basic one and a full one.) Use the basic dialog box to select a predefined color scheme. Press the UP ARROW or DOWN ARROW key on the keyboard to scroll the list. Each color scheme is displayed as you scroll. You also can click the down arrow button on the Color Schemes list box to see a list of color schemes.

When you find a color scheme you like, click OK. The dialog box closes and the new color scheme is installed.

Creating Custom Color Schemes

Windows comes with the color schemes listed in the Color Schemes box as discussed previously. Each color scheme has its own name. If you can't find a combination you like

FIGURE 14-2

Changing color schemes

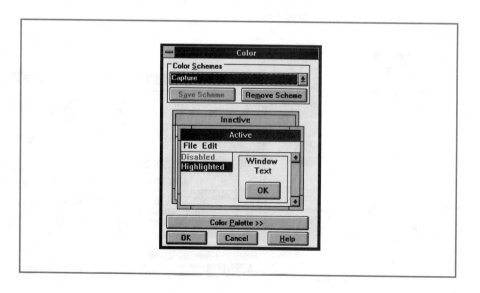

in this list, create your own by clicking the Color Palette button in the Color dialog box. Doing so displays the full Color dialog box shown in Figure 14-3.

Rather than creating a color scheme from scratch, it's easiest to choose an existing color scheme that is close to the scheme you want, then alter it and save it under a different name.

To create a custom color scheme, you click the window element you want to change (border, title bar, and so on), then click a new color for it from the Basic Colors palette. Once a color is created, save it by clicking the Save Schemes box and name it. Let's take it step by step.

Start by selecting a screen element. Click on that element in the sample window scheme on the left, or press the DOWN ARROW key on the keyboard to scan the list of elements in the Screen Element drop-down list box. If the box is not highlighted, click its down arrow button with the mouse. The Basic Colors palette indicates with a bold box the color currently assigned to the element you've selected.

With the element name in the Screen Element box, click a color in the Basic Colors palette. The sample window scheme changes to reflect your new color selection. After creating a new color scheme, click the Save Scheme button, then type the new color scheme name in the dialog box that appears and press ENTER.

Mixing Custom Colors

You can mix your own colors if those in the Basic Colors field don't suit your needs. Click the Define Custom Colors button to display the Custom Color Selector window shown in Figure 14-4.

FIGURE 14-3

Creating custom colors

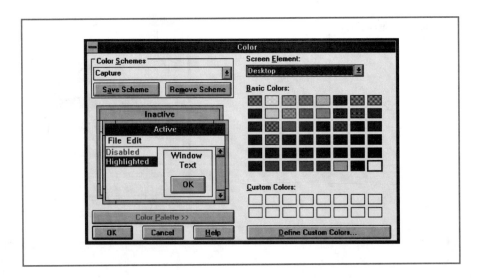

FIGURE 14-4

The Custom Color
Selector window

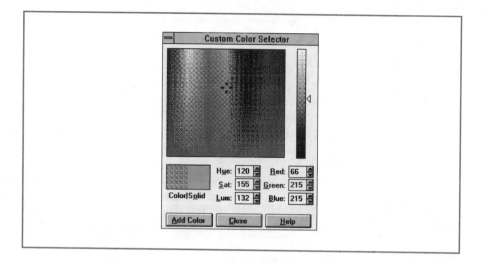

Use the slider bars and text boxes to adjust your color's mix of red, green, and blue (RGB color model), or hue, saturation, and luminosity (HSL color model). When you click the Add Color button, the custom color is added to one of the 16 Custom Color boxes in the lower-right corner of the Color dialog box. The Custom Color Selector screen consists of these elements:

☑ The color refiner box in the upper-left portion of the screen.

☑ The luminosity slider bar in the upper-right section of the screen.

☑ The Color|Solid box in the lower-left portion of the screen.

☑ The text boxes (Hue, Sat, Lum, Red, Green, Blue) in the lower-right portion of the screen.

Click the color refiner box and drag the pointer to select different colors. You also can slide the luminosity arrow up or down to adjust the color's brightness. As colors are adjusted, their color values are listed in either the Red/Green/Blue (RGB) text boxes or the Hue/Sat/Lum (HSL) text boxes.

The RGB color model defines colors with values from 0 to 255 with 0 indicating the minimum intensity and 255 the maximum intensity. The HSL color model defines colors with values in the range of 0 through 240. What HSL stands for is explained here:

☑ *Hue* relates to the intensity of red, blue, or green in the color and corresponds to a horizontal movement across the color refiner box.

☑ *Saturation* relates to the purity of a color (or its lack of gray) and to a vertical movement of the cursor in the color refiner box.

☑ *Luminosity* is the brightness of a color on a scale from black to white, with 0 being black and 240 being white.

The value of a color is known as its *RGB triplet* or *HSL triplet*. When all colors are set to 0, the color is black. When all colors are set to 255 (RGB) or 240 (HSL), they are at their maximum brightest and the color is white. Anything in between is a custom color. Table 14-1 lists the RGB and HSL triplets for the standard colors and their common mixes.

Because some monitors are incapable of displaying the full range of colors supported by Windows, a dot pattern is used to approximate the color as closely as possible using a process called *dithering*. As you select colors, the Color|Solid box displays the dithered color on the left and the closest non-dithered solid color on the right. Once you've found a color you like, click either the dithered or solid color. The color then replaces the selected color in one of the 16 Custom Color boxes.

> **Note**
>
> Some applications, such as Paintbrush, are incapable of displaying the full range of colors and revert to the 20 colors provided by Windows' default palette.

Use the text boxes to enter specific color values, make fine adjustments, or to simply note the value of a color for future reference. The values are important if you want to create a similar color later, or on another computer.

To create a color with the mouse, start by placing the luminosity pointer about halfway up the scale, then in the color refiner box point to the color that's closest to the color you want. Click and drag the mouse in the refiner box or slide the luminosity pointer to make adjustments to the color. The Color|Solid box displays the dithered or solid version of the color.

To add the new color to the Color window, select either the dithered or solid color in the Color|Solid box, then click the Add Color button. To add the color to a Custom Color box of your choice, or to overwrite an existing custom color, click the Custom Color box before clicking the Add Color button.

TABLE 14-1

Standard Colors and Their Common Mixes for RGB and HSL Triplets

Color	RGB Triplet	HSL Triplet
White	255,255,255	240,240,240
Red	255,0,0	0,120,240
Green	0,255,0	80,120,240
Blue	0,0,255	160,120,240
Yellow	255,255,0	40,120,240
Magenta	255,0,255	200,120,240
Cyan	0,255,255	120,120,240
Black	0,0,0	0,0,0

Be sure to click the Close button to leave the Custom Color dialog box, then click the OK button to leave the Color dialog box. Your changes are then saved.

DESKTOP PATTERNS

The desktop pattern is an 8x8 pattern of dots that is repeated over the desktop surface. To add a pattern to the desktop, and to create custom patterns, open the Desktop utility. You can change patterns by making a selection in the Pattern box of the Desktop utility, as shown here:

To install a pattern, choose one from the Name drop-down list box, then click the OK button in the Desktop dialog box. The pattern is repeated over your desktop. Before you decide to keep this pattern, look at the titles of icons on the desktop. If they are illegible due to the pattern, change or remove the pattern, or install wallpaper instead (you'll see how to use wallpaper shortly).

 You can have a pattern and wallpaper installed at the same time; however, wallpaper will always overlay the pattern and both together will use a lot of memory.

Editing a Pattern

You can view patterns before placing them on the desktop or create a new pattern by opening the Edit Pattern dialog box shown in Figure 14-5. Click the Edit Pattern button in the Pattern field of the Desktop dialog box.

Press the DOWN ARROW key on the keyboard to scroll through the list of existing patterns. As you scroll, a sample pattern appears in the Sample box on the left. The middle box displays an enlarged view of the pattern. To change the pattern, click in this box with the right mouse button. You'll see that white areas convert to black, and black areas convert to white. As you edit a pattern, the Sample box changes to show the new view.

After editing a pattern, use one of the options detailed in the following sections to save or remove it.

FIGURE 14-5

The Edit Pattern
dialog box

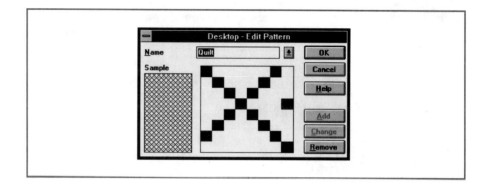

The Add Button Click the Add button to save an edited pattern under a new name. To do so, begin typing a new name in the Name box; the Add button then becomes available.

The Change Button Click the Change button to save an existing pattern that you've edited under its current name.

The Remove Button Highlight a pattern name in the Name box and press the Remove button to remove that pattern.

Changing the Color of a Pattern

If you have a white background, the pattern is black over white. To change the pattern colors, open the Color utility and change the settings to colors you find more pleasing. The Windows Text setting determines the color of the pattern, and the Desktop setting determines the color that shows through the pattern.

WALLPAPER

The Wallpaper box in the Desktop dialog box is shown here:

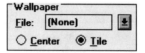

Use this to place a bitmapped image on the desktop. *Bitmapped* images are those created in programs such as Paintbrush. There are several images included in the \WINNT directory that you can try placing on the desktop. Click the File box's down arrow button to display a list of files.

Some of the wallpaper patterns are small tile shapes that are designed to repeat over the surface of the desktop much like tiles on a floor. Choose one of the patterns by selecting it in the File box, then click Tile. Click the Desktop OK button to install the pattern on the desktop. You can experiment with wallpaper by trying some of the other bitmapped images. If you want to view and edit the bitmaps, open them in Paintbrush (discussed next).

If you are short on memory, don't use wallpaper. It can take as much as 164K to display a bitmapped picture on the desktop.

Creating Your Own Wallpaper

The bitmapped images supplied with Windows NT were created in Paintbrush. That means you can load the wallpaper files in Paintbrush for editing. For example, you could change the colors of an existing wallpaper, or combine it with another wallpaper image. Try the following example, which combines CHITZ.BMP with MARBLE.BMP. (If you're not familiar with Paintbrush, refer to Chapter 9.) Follow these steps:

1.   Open CHITZ.BMP in Paintbrush.

2.   Use the Cutout tool to completely surround the image, then choose Copy from the Edit menu.

3.   Open MARBLE.BMP in Paintbrush.

4.   Choose Paste from the Edit menu in order to paste the chintz image over the marble image.

5.   Move the upper image until you're happy with the way the underlying marble pattern shows through.

6.   Use the Color eraser to convert the underlying blue in the marble to red, yellow, or any color you like.

7.   When done editing the image, use the Pick tool to surround the overlying chintz image. Try to be exact since the edges are matched when the image is repeated on the desktop.

8.   Save it to a new file by choosing Copy To from the Edit menu.

It's important to use the Copy To command when saving tiled images. Doing so saves only the selected portion so tiles "connect" correctly when placed on the desktop. Using the Save option would include the entire image, including the extraneous marble around the chintz pattern. After saving the image, load it on the desktop using the techniques described earlier.

You can use Paintbrush to create a large image that fits on the entire desktop. You also can obtain images from friends or bulletin boards, or scan them using hand or desktop scanning devices. Here are some suggestions for using wallpaper:

- Place your company logo on the desktop.

- Create a list of common keystrokes used in Windows or its applications.

- Scan pictures of your kids and create a collage that includes their birth dates.

- Create a list of important telephone numbers in Paintbrush and place it on the desktop.

- If you're working on a project, place the timetable of events on the desktop.

- Create a wallpaper with reference information, such as weights and measures, metric conversions, formulas, and tables.

- Create an "Out to Lunch" or "I'm out for the day" banner.

While these desktop references may not be as visually exciting as the graphic images supplied with Windows, they are definitely more functional.

ICON SPACING

You can control the amount of space between icons on the desktop and in the Program Manager. The current setting for your display is in the Icons box of the Desktop utility. To change the spacing, enter a new value in the Spacing text box shown here:

The icon spacing value sets the *horizontal icon spacing*, or the distance between icons in a row, between icons on the desktop, or icons in Program Manager groups. Note also the Wrap Title option. If disabled, long titles appear on one line and may overlap the titles of adjoining icons. Leave this option enabled in most cases.

Changing the Font, Size, and Style of Icon Titles

You can change the font, size, and style of the text used to display icon titles. Once you do, you may need to increase icon spacing as described in the previous section. To make font changes, add or alter the following options in the Registry Editor.

Start the Registry Editor by double-clicking its icon if you created one as outlined in Chapter 6. If not, choose Run from the Program Manager or File Manager File menu, then type **REGEDT32**. The Registry Editor appears as shown in Figure 14-6.

Note

> The Registry Editor holds all the configuration information for Windows NT. It takes the place of the SYSTEM.INI and WIN.INI files used in Windows 3.1.

The Registry Editor contains several document windows. Click the one titled "HKEY_USERS on Local Machine." Next, double-click the DEFAULT folder, then double-click the Control Panel folder, and finally double-click the Desktop folder. You then see a list of desktop settings to which you can make changes as described next.

Note

> You must restart Windows NT after making the following changes in the Registry Editor.

Icon Font

To change the font of the icon, double-click the entry called IconTitleFaceName. The following dialog box appears:

The default font is Helvetica (shown as Helv), but you can specify a different font name. Courier, Arial, and Times are just a few of the fonts available.

If you're not sure which font you want, open the Fonts utility in the Control Panel to view the fonts installed on your system. After typing the new font name, click the OK button.

Icon Font Size

To change the size of the font, double-click the IconTitleSize option. The default value is 9, but you can specify a slightly larger value. Take care not to increase this value more than 1 or 2 points or text will overlap. However, you can increase icon spacing as discussed previously to prevent some overlap.

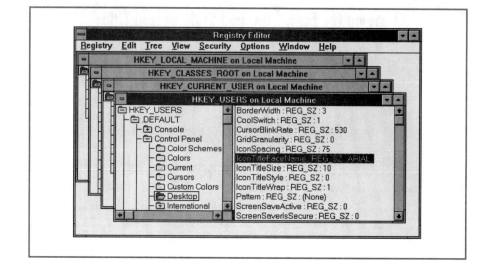

FIGURE 14-6

The Registry Editor

Icon Font Style

Set the style of the icon font to bold by double-clicking the IconTitleStyle option and changing its value to 1. The default value (0) is for a normal style. Bold and normal are the only two styles possible.

SCREEN SAVERS

A *screen saver* blanks your screen after a specified period of time and displays moving objects or messages. This prevents *screen burn*—faint ghost images that become part of your monitor and never go away—which occurs when an image is left on the screen too long. When the screen saver image is present, simply moving the mouse or pressing a key on the keyboard restores your screen. You also can require a password to restore the screen, which allows you to leave tasks running on your system while you step away from your desk and still maintain security on the system.

Use the Screen Saver options on the Desktop dialog box to specify the type of screen saver and the time interval of nonactivity that must pass before a screen saver takes over the screen. To install a screen saver, open the Desktop dialog box to see the Screen Saver field shown here:

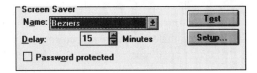

Click the down arrow button in the Name box, then highlight a screen saver, such as Starfield Simulation. Once you've selected a screen saver image, you can test it by clicking the Test button. To stop the test, move the mouse or press any key on the keyboard.

Select other screen savers and click the Test button to see how they look. The Marquee screen saver has unique features that are covered separately later in this chapter. To install a screen saver, set the desired delay time in the Delay box, then click the OK button on the Desktop dialog box.

Customizing a Screen Saver

You can change the parameters of a screen saver by selecting it, and then clicking the Setup button. For example, select the Starfield Simulation screen saver in the Name field of the Screen Saver box, then click Setup. The Starfield Simulation Setup dialog box shown in Figure 14-7 appears.

You can adjust the following settings in the Starfield Simulation Setup dialog box. (For a more complete description, click the Help button.)

☑ Adjust the Warp Speed slider to change the speed of the moving starfield.

☑ Change the value in the Starfield Density box to increase or decrease the number of stars.

FIGURE 14-7

The Starfield Simulation
Setup dialog box

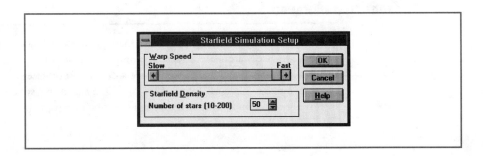

Click OK, then click the Test button to see the changes. You also can make changes to the settings of the Mystify and Marquee options. Click the Help button after opening the Setup dialog box for each screen saver to get additional information. The options for Marquee are discussed later in this chapter.

Setting a Password

Screen saver passwords prevent others from accessing your system. However, if you use a password for a screen saver and the delay time is short, it can be a nuisance to type a password to recover your screen. Increase the delay time in this case.

To add or change a password, follow these steps:

1. Choose a screen saver from the Screen Saver Name box, then click the Setup button.

2. Click the Password Protected check box to make the Set Password button available, and then click the Set Password button.

3. When the Change Password dialog box appears, type a password in the New Password field, then retype it in the Retype New Password field and click OK or press ENTER.

> **Note**   If a previous password was set, you need to type that password in the Old Password field before you can change it.

If you forget the password for a screen saver, you'll need to restart your system to get back into Windows NT. The logon security of Windows NT then takes over to prevent intruders from accessing your system.

Creating a Marquee

Use the Marquee screen saver to create a message that scrolls across the screen. The most useful way to use Marquee is as a screen prompt for a demonstration package. For example, the message might say "Press a key to see a demo." Another example might display the opposite message, such as "Hands Off!" or "Don't turn this system off! " if your system is working on an important task that shouldn't be interrupted.

To create a marquee, select Marquee from the Name drop-down list box in the Screen Saver field. The Marquee Setup dialog box appears as shown in Figure 14-8. From the Marquee Setup dialog box, you can set these features:

☑ Select a font and size by clicking the Format Text button.

☑ Select a text and background color in the Background Color box.

☑ In the Position box, choose where you want the text to scroll—either across the center or randomly on the screen.

☑ Select a speed for the scrolling marquee in the Speed box.

☑ Type the text you want to display in the Text box.

Click OK or press ENTER to save the changes and return to the Desktop dialog box. Set a delay if necessary in the Delay box. To test the marquee, click the Test button, then press any key to return to the Desktop dialog box. Once the marquee looks the way you want it to, click the OK button or press ENTER to close the Desktop dialog box and execute the changes.

SOUNDS

You use the Sound utility to assign sounds to system events, such as when Windows starts or an error occurs. To hear the sounds listed in the Sound utility, you'll need a sound board installed in your system with a connection to a set of speakers.

FIGURE 14-8

Setting up the Marquee screen saver

Figure 14-9 shows the Sound dialog box. Click one of the events in the Events box on the left, then click the sound that you want to assign to that event from the Files box on the right. Click the Test button to hear the sound. When all events have the sounds you want, click the OK button.

THE KEYBOARD SETTINGS

Use the Keyboard utility to adjust the settings of the keyboard. You can adjust the *delay*, which is how long a key is held down before it starts repeating, and the *repeat rate*, which is how fast the key repeats as you hold it down. To change the delay and repeat rate, double-click the Keyboard icon in the Control Panel to display the Keyboard dialog box shown in Figure 14-10, and follow the instructions given next.

Delay Drag the Delay Before First Repeat slider button left to increase the time before a key starts repeating when held down. Drag it right to decrease the delay.

Repeat Rate Drag the Repeat Rate slider button left to decrease the speed at which the key repeats when held down. Slide it right to increase the speed. Test the new settings by clicking the Test box and holding down a key.

SETTING THE DATE AND TIME

To set a new date and time, double-click or select the Date/Time icon on the Control Panel. The dialog box in Figure 14-11 appears.

FIGURE 14-9

Assigning sounds to events

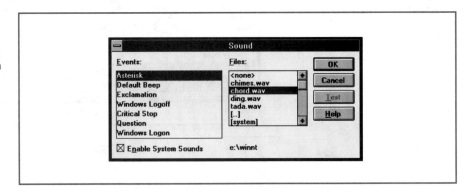

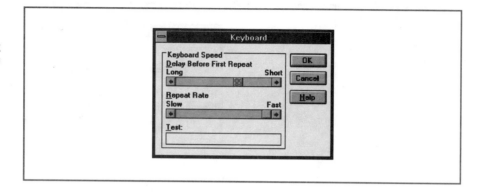

FIGURE 14-10

The Keyboard dialog box

Double-click on the portion of the date or time you want to change, then type a new value. Alternatively, click the up arrow or down arrow button to change the values. In the Time Zone field, choose a time zone in the drop-down list box.

THE MOUSE

To change the functions of the mouse, double-click the Mouse utility on the Control Panel. The Mouse dialog box shown in Figure 14-12 appears.

Mouse Tracking Speed   Drag the Mouse Tracking Speed slider button left or right to adjust the speed at which the mouse pointer moves across the screen in relation to the movement of the mouse. After adjusting the speed, drag the mouse to see how the new setting affects the tracking speed. Adjust the slider button further, if necessary. Try a slow tracking speed if you are a new mouse user, or if you're working on precise graphic images.

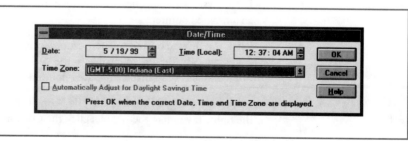

FIGURE 14-11

The Date/Time dialog box

FIGURE 14-12

Changing mouse settings

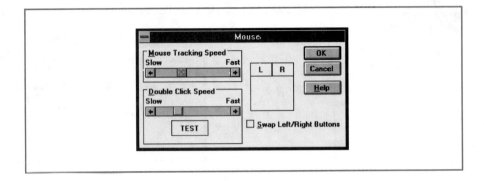

Double-Click Speed   Drag the Double Click Speed slider button left or right to adjust when Windows registers a double-click of the mouse button. After adjusting the slider button, double-click in the Test box to check the new setting. The box turns black when it registers a double-click.

Swap Left/Right Buttons   If you are left-handed, you can swap the functions of the left and right mouse buttons by clicking the Swap Left/Right Buttons check box. The right button then becomes the button used for the majority of tasks, such as selecting items and executing commands.

CUSTOMIZING THE MOUSE POINTER

In Windows NT, the mouse pointer is animated—literally. You can switch from the old standard pointing arrow to animated pointers that include peeling bananas, flipping coins, beating drums, running horses, grabbing hands, and even an arrow with a "wagging tail."

To change the cursor, double-click the Cursors icon in the Control Panel. You see the dialog box shown in Figure 14-13.

1. In the System Cursors field, select the pointer type that you want to change to an animated pointer.

2. Click the Browse button to choose a new pointer. The dialog box in Figure 14-14 appears. Be sure to change to the \WINNT\SYSTEM32 directory so you can see the list of available animated pointers.

3. Click any of the ANI files in the File Name list. A sample appears in the box on the right. If you like the sample, click the OK button.

FIGURE 14-13

Adding animated pointers

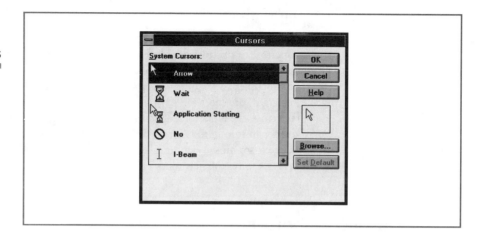

Assign COUNTER.ANI to the Wait and Application Starting pointers so you can time Windows NT events and compare system speeds.

MISCELLANEOUS FEATURES

The following features provide ways to further customize Windows NT.

FIGURE 14-14

Choosing an animated pointer type

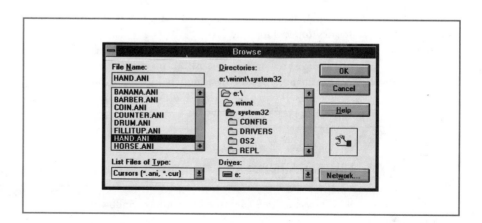

Insertion Point Blink Rate

You can increase or decrease the blink rate of the insertion point (cursor) so it is easier to locate. Don't confuse the insertion point with the mouse pointer. The insertion point appears in document text, or in dialog box fields. You can move it with the arrow keys on the keyboard, or reposition it by clicking with the mouse pointer.

To change the blink rate, open the Desktop dialog box in the Control Panel, then drag the slider button in the Cursor Blink Rate box. As you adjust the blink rate, watch the blinking cursor on the right until it blinks at the rate you want. Click the OK button or press ENTER to set the new blink rate.

Windows Border Width

You can adjust the width of window borders to make it easier to differentiate between windows on the desktop. To adjust the width, open the Desktop utility and change the value in the Border Width box. The default setting is three pixels. If you have a high-resolution display, or are having trouble clicking on borders to resize a window, increase the border width by a few pixels.

Granularity (Sizing Grid)

The *granularity* of the desktop determines the density of an invisible grid on the desktop that windows snap to when moved or resized. The granularity is initially 0, but you can set it from 1 to 49, with each increment representing 8 pixels. To get an idea of pixel size, note that the default border width is 3 (or 24 pixels). Generally, setting a granularity of 1 is useful because it makes windows align more evenly and keeps your desktop looking tidy.

To set granularity, open the Desktop dialog box in the Control Panel, then click the up arrow or down arrow button to change the value. Click the OK button to save the changes. At the desktop, try moving windows around with the new granularity settings. If you have a high-resolution display, it may be useful to set a granularity value of 5 or greater.

Switching Methods

There are three ways to switch among windows:

▨　Press CTRL-ESC to open the Task List.

▨   Press ALT-ESC to switch to each window, one after another.

▨   Press ALT-TAB repeatedly to view the titles of open applications. Stop when the title you want to use appears.

You can change the switch method of the ALT-TAB key by opening the Desktop utility and removing the check mark from the Fast "Alt+Tab" Switching option. This saves time because when you then switch with ALT-TAB, the title bar appears for each window, but the entire window is not painted on the screen. Set this option if you need to see part of the window during switching.

Inside

- Changing Startup Options
- Environmental Variables
- Configuring Virtual Memory
- Multitasking Options
- The Windows NT Setup Utility
- The Drivers Utility
- Managing Windows NT Services
- Starting and Stopping Devices
- Configuring Serial Communications
- Configuring Multimedia Equipment

& Out

CHAPTER 15

Configuring System Settings

This chapter covers topics related to system hardware setup and configuration, and is written for more advanced users who need to change the default settings of Windows NT. The utilities located in the Control Panel that were not discussed in Chapter 14 are covered here. In addition, this chapter looks at the Windows NT Setup utility, which is listed in Table 15-1.

TABLE 15-1	
Windows NT Setup Utility	

Icon	Utility	Description
	System	Sets features of the operating system, such as virtual memory or environment variables.
	Ports	Sets features of serial ports.
	Drivers	Installs special drivers for multimedia equipment and other add-ons.
	MIDI Mapper	Configures MIDI (musical instrument device interface) devices.
	Services	Starts or stops operating system services.
	Devices	Starts or stops operating system services.

CHANGING STARTUP OPTIONS

If other operating systems besides Windows NT are installed on your computer, a boot load sequence asks which operating system you want to boot when the computer starts. Normally, after a timeout period, one of the operating systems boots automatically. If Windows NT was the last operating system you installed, it is the operating system that loads by default after the timeout period.

You can change the timeout period and default operating system settings with the System utility in the Control Panel. Open the Control Panel and double-click the System icon. The dialog box in Figure 15-1 appears.

The Startup drop-down list shows each of the operating systems installed on your system (except those that Windows NT setup was unable to identify). Choose which operating system you want Windows NT to load by default after the timeout period.

In the Show list for field, click how long (in seconds) you want the list of alternate operating systems to appear when the system boots. If you normally boot into the selected default operating system, you might want to reduce this value to a few seconds, just long enough to choose an alternate if necessary.

FIGURE 15-1

Changing system startup options

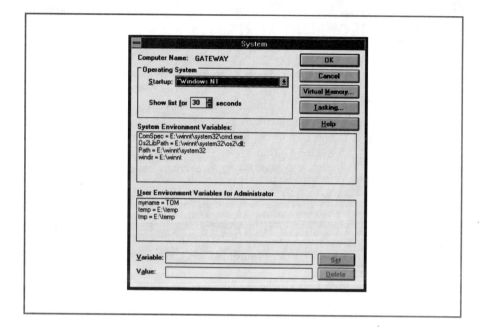

Click OK when finished. The next time you start your system, the new settings take effect.

If You Add Another Operating System

On Intel-based systems, information about other operating systems is stored in a file called BOOT.INI in the root directory of your computer's primary hard disk. On RISC-based systems, the information is stored in non-volatile RAM.

If you install another operating system on Intel-based computers after you've installed Windows NT, you'll need to add the path to that operating system in the BOOT.INI file under the [operating systems] title. The Windows NT and MS-DOS operating systems are referred to this way in the file:

```
d:\winnt="Windows NT 3.1"
c:\dos="MS-DOS"
```

Use a similar strategy to name a new operating system. You can place any string between the quotes to identify the operating system. This text appears in the Startup field of the System dialog box shown in Figure 15-1 (however, you must specify a valid drive before the string).

ENVIRONMENT VARIABLES

Environment variables control the Windows NT operating system and MS-DOS subsystem environments. In most cases, environment variables are set by the operating system, or added when you install a new program, so you don't need to be too concerned with them. However, you can use environment variables to enhance batch files and other commands you might run in the Command Prompt, as described after this brief introduction.

There are two types of environment variables:

✔ *System* environment variables are set by the operating system and cannot be changed.

✔ *User* environment variables are manageable by the user and may include variables automatically added by the operating system.

The system path setting is the most common environment variable. It specifies a search path to program directories so you can run the programs in those directories while you're working in other directories, such as data directories. Windows NT sets a path to the \WINNT\SYSTEM32 directory on the drive where its files are located. If your system also has DOS FAT partitions, the Windows NT path is appended to the DOS path. In this way, you can run Windows NT and any DOS program from any other directory.

Another common environment variable is COMSPEC. It specifies the command processor for the currently running operating system. In DOS, the COMSPEC variable is usually equal to C:\DOS\COMMAND.COM. In Windows NT, the COMSPEC variable is equal to C:\WINNT\SYSTEM32\CMD.EXE. However, the drive letter will differ from system to system.

Still another common environment variable is PROMPT, which sets the type of prompt you see on the command line in the Command Prompt window. The PROMPT variable is typically PROMPT=pg, which displays the name of the current directory.

To view the current environment variables on your system, start the Command Prompt and type **SET**. Figure 15-2 shows a typical SET listing.

Some of the settings in this list are for the MS-DOS environment and were automatically set when Windows NT was installed. When Windows NT boots, it also looks in the AUTOEXEC.BAT file on your DOS partition and adds any set variable in that file to the environment. Environment variables that you are likely to find of use when creating batch files are described here:

USERDOMAIN	The name of the computer workgroup or domain for the current user
USERNAME	The name of the currently logged on user
PROCESSOR	The type of the computer the user has

FIGURE 15-2

Viewing the current
environment variables on
the system

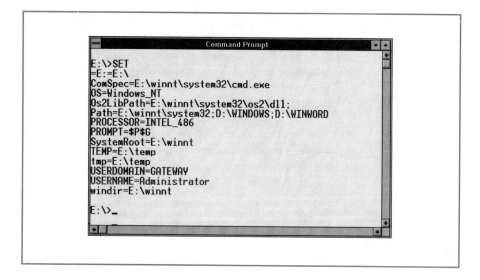

```
E:\>SET
=E:=E:\
ComSpec=E:\winnt\system32\cmd.exe
OS=Windows_NT
Os2LibPath=E:\winnt\system32\os2\dll;
Path=E:\winnt\system32;D:\WINDOWS;D:\WINWORD
PROCESSOR=INTEL_486
PROMPT=$P$G
SystemRoot=E:\winnt
TEMP=E:\temp
tmp=E:\temp
USERDOMAIN=GATEWAY
USERNAME=Administrator
windir=E:\winnt

E:\>_
```

Adding User Environment Variables

You can add your own environment variables in batch files or when working in the Command Prompt. Open the System utility by double-clicking the System icon in the Control Panel. The dialog box shown previously in Figure 15-1 appears. The unchangeable system variables appear in the System Environment Variables field. The user variables you can change or add to are listed in the User Environment Variables field.

To add a variable, type its name in the Variable field, then type its value in the Value field, and finally click the Set button. Variables are set immediately. You don't have to reboot the system. For example, if you start a Command Prompt and type **SET**, you see the new variables.

You can set environment variables at the Command Prompt using the SET command, but keep in mind that the variables are only valid for the current Command Prompt session. For example, you could type a command similar to the following to add your name to an environment variable called MYNAME:

SET MYNAME=Tom Sheldon

If you later want to clear this variable, type **SET MYNAME=** without specifying a value. Refer to the SET command in the Command Reference for more information.

Note

To create variables for every Command Prompt session, specify the variables in the System dialog box as outlined earlier in this chapter.

Using Environment Variables

You can use environment variables in batch files that users run when working in the Command Prompt. The variable name must be between percent signs and is replaced with the current value of the variable when the batch files run. Note that because variables can change for each user that logs on, the commands in batch files that use variables execute differently for each user, depending on the current value of the variables.

For example, if you are an administrator, you could create a batch file that switches users to a personal data directory, then starts a program. A batch file command that uses the USERNAME variable ensures that each user is switched to their own directory. Here are the commands:

```
CD \DATA\%USERNAME
WORD
```

The first command places the user in his or her personal data directory. So if JWALKER is logged on and executes the batch file, the first command switches him to the \DATA\JWALKER directory. If ASmith logs on and runs the batch file, she is placed in the \DATA\ASMITH directory.

CONFIGURING VIRTUAL MEMORY

When a computer doesn't have enough RAM memory, you are limited in the number of programs you can run simultaneously, or the size of files you can open. Virtual memory provides a way to simulate more memory than your system has physically available. Information in memory is swapped to a special *swap* or *page* file to free up memory for other tasks. The information in the swap file remains in a ready state so it can be swapped back to RAM memory when needed. Swapping occurs in the background, although you might see an occasional flickering of the hard disk light. Obviously, disk swapping doesn't provide the same performance as RAM memory, but it does add the ability to run more programs than the physical RAM in your system normally allows.

The Windows NT installation program creates a virtual memory swap file automatically. This section describes how to change the size of the virtual memory paging file or create additional paging files on other local hard drives. You might need to increase the virtual memory size if you are working with large graphic images that requires a lot of memory, or if you open many programs at the same time. If you ever get an "out-of-memory" error, you need to increase the size of the paging file.

Note the following about virtual memory:

☑   Only members of the Administrator group can make changes to the virtual memory configuration.

☑ Because virtual memory simulates real memory, make sure paging files are put on the faster hard drive in your system to get the best performance.

☑ Windows NT recommends a paging file that is equivalent to the RAM in your system, plus 12 MB. In many cases, this is too much virtual memory and you should reduce it if you are running short on disk space.

☑ There must be an upper limit on the paging file if disk space is limited.

☑ If you have multiple hard drives, create small swap files on each rather than one large swap file on one drive. This distributes the read and write tasks among the drives.

☑ The virtual memory paging file is called PAGEFILE.SYS. It cannot be deleted while running Windows NT.

Using the Virtual Memory Dialog Box

To open the Virtual Memory dialog box, double-click the System icon on the Control Panel. The System dialog box appears as shown previously in Figure 15-1. Click the Virtual Memory button to display the dialog box shown in Figure 15-3.

In the Drive field, you can click each drive listed to view its current space and page file settings in the middle field. The current page file settings, if a page file exists, are listed in the Initial Size and Maximum Size fields.

The Total Paging File Size for All Drives box lists the total paging file size, including files that are located on other drives.

FIGURE 15-3

Changing virtual
memory settings

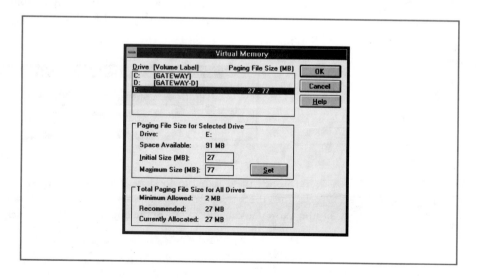

To change the page file size, or add a new page file on another drive, follow these steps:

1. Choose from the Drive field the drive you want to edit or add a page file to.

2. In the Initial Size box, type the minimum size for the page file. This is the amount of space on the disk that will always be reserved for the file.

3. In the Maximum Size field, type a size that the page file should never exceed. This value might be quite high by default. You may want to reduce it to a more reasonable amount if you are short on disk space.

4. Click the Set button if you want to edit or add page files on other drives, or click the OK button to save your changes and exit.

MULTITASKING OPTIONS

When you run several applications at once, the application that runs in the active window gets more of the system's attention than applications running in background windows. This is normally how it should be, but you might want to change this configuration in some cases. For example, assume you need to sort or index a large accounting database, but you also need to have a customer database open to reference in case one of your clients calls. You make the customer database the active window, and push the accounting database sort routine into the background, but this reduces the amount of processing time the sort routine gets. To even up processing time, open the Tasking dialog box shown here and choose the option that gives both active and background applications the same amount of processing time, Foreground and Background Applications Equally Responsive.

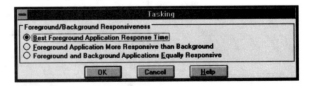

To open the Tasking dialog box, double-click the System icon on the Control Panel. When the System dialog box appears (it's shown in Figure 15-1), click the Tasking button. Now you can choose one of the options, as described next.

Best Foreground Application Response Time Choose this option if you want the active application in the foreground to get most of the processor's attention.

Foreground Application More Responsive Than Background This option gives a little more processing time to background applications than the previous option, but the foreground application is still the primary focus.

Foreground and Background Applications Equally Responsive This option gives all applications, whether foreground or background, an equal amount of processing time.

THE WINDOWS NT SETUP UTILITY

The Windows NT Setup utility lets you change or update system hardware drivers and settings or the software configuration. The following describes the tasks you can perform with the Setup utility. (Unless another chapter is noted, you will learn how to do all of these things in this chapter.)

- ☑ Change the display, mouse, and keyboard drivers.

- ☑ Add or remove SCSI (Small Computer System Interface) adapters that support CD-ROM drives, hard disks, and tape drives.

- ☑ Add or remove tape controllers.

- ☑ Add or remove software components of the Windows NT system, such as games files, screen savers, wallpaper files, and others.

- ☑ Create startup icons for applications (primarily DOS applications). This procedure was covered in Chapter 12.

- ☑ Delete User Profiles, as covered in Chapter 16.

Any changes you make in the Windows NT Setup utility require that you restart Windows NT before they take effect. If the new devices or drivers are not working correctly and Windows NT cannot start with the new settings, they are disabled and Windows NT starts with the settings that were in effect before you loaded the new devices or drivers.

Double-click the Windows NT Setup icon now in the Main group of the Program Manager to display a dialog box similar to what you see in Figure 15-4.

FIGURE 15-4

The Windows NT Setup
utility main screen

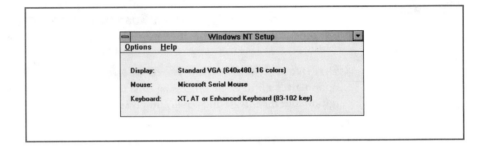

Changing Display, Mouse, and Keyboard Drivers

The initial Windows NT Setup screen displays the current display, mouse, and keyboard settings. To change these settings, open the Options menu and choose Change System Settings. The following dialog box appears:

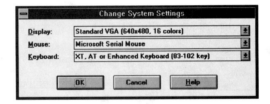

Click the down arrow button in each field to select from a list of available drivers. Type the first letter of the driver you are searching for to quickly jump to or near the driver. If you can't find the driver you need to load in the list, choose Other at the end of the list, then insert the disk containing the driver in the floppy drive.

After you specify new devices, click the OK button. Windows NT Setup asks you to specify the location of the drivers with a dialog box similar to the following:

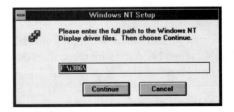

Once you click OK, Windows NT Setup copies the driver from the disk or CD-ROM to your Windows NT directory. You then need to restart the system for the changes to take effect.

Adding or Removing SCSI and Tape Adapters

If you add an SCSI (Small Computer System Interface) adapter to your system, choose the Add/Remove SCSI Adapter option from the Windows NT Setup Options menu to install the driver for the device. A dialog box similar to the following appears:

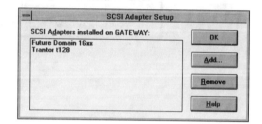

Existing drivers are listed in the box. Click Add to install other drivers or Remove to delete an existing driver from the list. When you click Add, a dialog box appears so you can select from a list of available drivers. Click the Install button after selecting a driver. If the driver for your SCSI adapter is not on the list, choose Other at the end of the list. Windows NT Setup then asks you to insert a disk for the driver in the floppy drive.

Note

Follow the same procedure to add a tape drive adapter, except choose Add/Remove Tape Devices from the Options menu.

After installing or removing an adapter driver, you must shut down Windows NT and restart your system. Always choose the Shutdown option on the Program Manager File menu before turning your system off.

Adding or Removing Software Components

The Windows NT Setup utility lets you remove software components, or add those that weren't installed or that were previously removed.

You can remove some of the components of the Windows NT system if you are short on disk space, or you know you'll never use them. For example, you could remove all the games and gain 343KB of disk space. You also might choose to remove components just to prevent other users from using them.

FIGURE 15-5

Adding or removing
Windows NT components

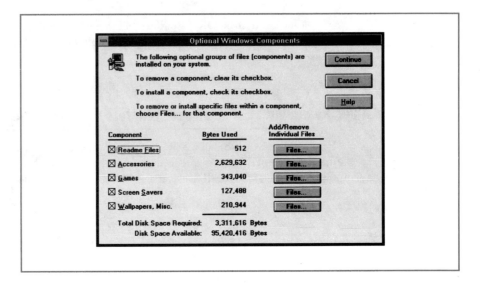

To remove or install components, choose the Add/Remove Windows Components option from the Options menu. The Optional Windows Components dialog box appears as shown in Figure 15-5.

Groups of components are listed on the left, for example, Accessories or Games. Those currently installed are marked with an X. The total size of the group is listed in the Bytes Used column.

To remove the entire group, click its check box. If the group is already removed and you want to add it, click it to mark the check box. To add or remove individual files within a group, click the Files button for that group and refer to the next section "Customizing Files." As you add and remove components, the total disk space required and available disk space values at the bottom of the dialog box change.

When finished selecting components to add or install, click the Continue button. Windows NT Setup may ask you to place a disk in the floppy drives, or the Windows NT CD-ROM in its drive. If you're removing components, the disk space used by the components is made available for other uses.

Customizing Files

When you click the Files button for a group, a dialog box similar to the one shown in Figure 15-6 appears. The files listed on the left are files that are currently installed. Files listed on the right are files that were never installed, or that were removed.

FIGURE 15-6

Adding or removing
individual files

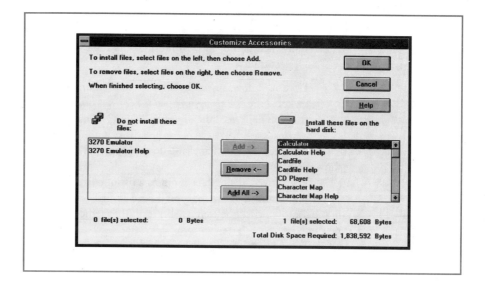

To install components, click one or more files on the left, then click the Add button. To remove components, click one or more files on the right, then click the Remove button. To add all the components on the left, click the Add All button.

THE DRIVERS UTILITY

All hardware devices added to your system require software drivers to work with Windows NT. A driver provides Windows NT with all the details it needs to use the device and communicate with it. Windows NT comes with a set of drivers for the most popular devices, and it will install those drivers during the installation process if it detects a device. In some cases, Windows NT will not properly detect a device and you'll need to install the driver manually using the Drivers utility. Additionally, you use the Drivers utility to install new drivers, upgrade existing drivers, or remove drivers.

Note

Most Windows 3.1 drivers are not compatible with Windows NT. You can try the Windows 3.1 driver, but if it's not compatible, you'll need to obtain new drivers for your devices from the manufacturer.

Before installing any hardware devices in your system, resolve interrupt and I/O conflicts with other boards and devices. Refer to Appendix A for a discussion of interrupts, I/O ports, and conflict resolution.

Keep these points in mind when dealing with drivers:

- Only members of the Administrator group can install device drivers using the Drivers utility.

- Do not remove any of the drivers installed during Windows NT installation. You see these the first time you open the Drivers dialog box. Although it may appear that you don't need the driver, Windows NT may reference it for other tasks.

Open the Control Panel and double-click Drivers to display the Drivers dialog box shown in Figure 15-7.

The Drivers dialog box contains a list of currently installed drivers. To upgrade a driver that is already installed, you'll need to first remove the old driver. Click its name in the list, then click the Remove button. After removing the old driver, you can add the new one.

To add new drivers, click the Add button to display the Add dialog box shown in Figure 15-8.

Note
Microsoft provides a Windows NT Driver Library disk that contains drivers for many popular devices. You can obtain this disk from Microsoft.

To install new drivers, highlight a driver in the Add dialog box list, or choose "Unlisted or Updated Driver." Place the disk containing the driver in the floppy drive and click OK. Another dialog box appears that lists the drivers on the disk. There may only be one. Highlight the driver you want to install and click the OK button. Once the driver installs, you'll need to shut down Windows NT and reboot the system to activate the new driver. Windows NT asks if you want to continue operation or shut down. You can continue operating to wrap up other tasks before shutting down, but the device won't be accessible until you restart.

Note
In cases where you've removed a previously installed driver, you'll see a message that the driver already exists on your system. Click Current to use that driver, or choose to install a new driver from disk.

FIGURE 15-7

The Drivers dialog box

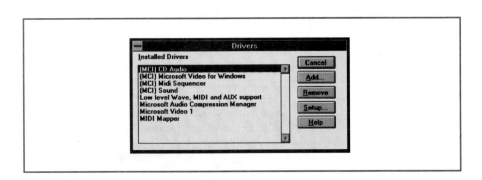

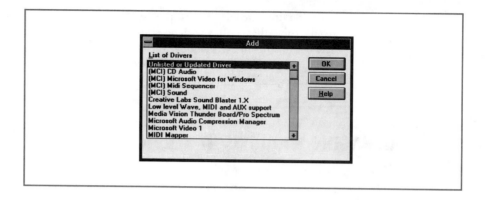

FIGURE 15-8

The Add dialog box

Setup Options

Some drivers require setup information, such as the interrupt and the I/O port used by the board. A Setup dialog box appears to request the values for these settings. Some Setup dialog boxes also provide control panels where you can set some default settings for the device. For example, the MCI Waveform driver has this Setup dialog box:

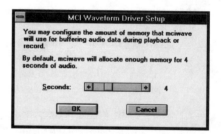

and the Microsoft Video for Windows driver has these setup options:

If a driver requires interrupt and I/O port settings, it is very important that you avoid settings that conflict with other boards or components in your system. If a conflict does occur, you'll need to remove the board and try a different setting as outlined in the board manual. You then restart Windows NT and specify the new settings in its driver setup dialog box.

MANAGING WINDOWS NT SERVICES

You can control the types of services that are installed when Windows NT boots, and you can stop or start those services at any time with the Services utility in the Control Panel.

You might want to disable a service to free system memory and resources when that service is not required. Alternatively, if a service fails to start when Windows NT starts, you can try restarting after taking corrective action

Note that if you are a member of the Administrator group, you can use the Services dialog box to assign the startup of specific services to specific users on the computer. The services then start when the user logs on.

Double-click the Services icon in the Control Panel to open the Services dialog box shown in Figure 15-9.

The Services column in this dialog box lists available services. The Status column lists whether the services are currently started or stopped. (If services are not started, the Status field is blank next to the service.) The Startup column indicates whether the service automatically starts when Windows NT is started, or whether you need to start the service manually.

Here's a description of the basic services:

- *Alerter* Notifies selected users when an administrative alert occurs. The Messenger service must also be running.

- *Computer Browser* Keeps a list of computers on the network. The list appears whenever users are browsing for computers to connect to.

- *Directory Replicator* Provides a way to replicate directory information between computers on a network.

- *Event Log* Provides a way to track and log systems, applications, and security events for auditing purposes.

- *Messenger* Provides the ability for message transfer by administrators or the Alerter service.

- *Net Logon* Provides authentication services when users log on.

- *Schedule* Supports the Command Prompt AT command, which is used to schedule the time and date that commands or programs execute.

FIGURE 15-9

Controlling services

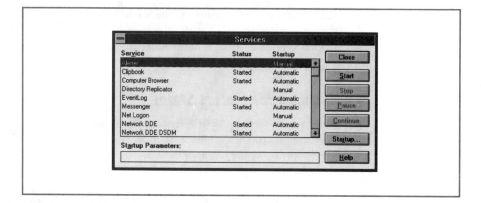

- [x] *Server* The main network service, Server provides remote procedure calls (RPC) so users can share files, printers, and messages.

- [x] *UPS* Provides communications with an uninterruptable power supply.

- [x] *Workstation* Allows a workstation to act as a client and connect with computers acting as servers. The Workstation service provides network communications.

Starting and Stopping Services

To start a service, click its name in the Services dialog box, and then click the Start button. To stop a service, click its name and then click the Stop button. While you can stop a service during your current session, it will still restart in the next session if the Startup field indicates Automatic. You can change the startup status of any service (as you'll see in this section).

Caution

Be careful when stopping the Server service. Other users connected with your system will be disconnected and may lose files. Use the Chat utility to warn users that you are stopping network service. Chapter 17 describes how to determine who is currently using your system.

If the service is already started, click the Stop or Pause button to remove the service for the current session. You can restart the service later, or if it is marked Automatic in the Startup column, it will restart the next time you start Windows NT.

If the service is stopped, click the Start button to start if for the current session only. If you want the service to start in every session, refer to the next section, "Changing the Startup Status."

Note that some services accept startup parameters, which are settings you can use to customize the way the service starts. You can type these parameters in the Startup

Parameters field at the bottom of the Services dialog box, then click the Start button. The default services provided with Windows NT do not require startup parameters, but services you obtain from other vendors might, so refer to the services documentation.

Changing the Startup Status

If you want a service to start every time Windows NT starts, or if you want to disable the automatic startup of a service, first click the service name, then click the Startup button. The following dialog box appears:

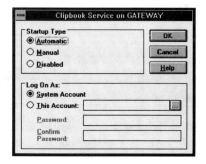

In the Startup Type field, choose between Automatic, Manual, or Disabled.

Automatic   The service starts automatically every time Windows NT starts.

Manual   The user must start the service by opening the Services dialog box.

Disabled   This option prevents the service from being started, either by a user or other service.

In order for a service to start, it must log on with one of two accounts. The System account is always started as part of the Windows NT operating system and is owned by the system. Services that log on with the System account are basically default services that are required for all users. Other types of services can log on when a user logs on by logging on with the user's account. Note that the default services provided with Windows NT log on with the System account, except for the Directory Replicator service and Schedule service, which can start with other accounts.

In the Log On As field, click one of the following options to specify whether a service starts for every Windows NT logon session, or whether it starts for a particular user.

System Account   The service starts with the system account.

This Account   Click the This Account button to display a list of user accounts for this system. You can then specify which user the service will start with. You must type the password for the user in the Password and Confirm Password fields to verify the service startup options.

STARTING AND STOPPING DEVICES

You can control the startup and configuration of device drivers on your system by opening the Devices dialog box. Double-click Devices in the Control Panel to display the dialog box shown in Figure 15-10.

The Device column lists the names of device drivers available in Windows NT. Many of these devices are vendor-specific and will have no relevance on your system. The Status column indicates whether the device is started. (A blank field indicates the device is not loaded.) The Startup Column indicates how and when the device starts, as described in a moment.

You should leave most devices that have started as they are. The operating system may not run properly if you disable them. If you remove a physical device from your computer, either permanently or for service, you might want to disable the device driver. For example, if you installed a CD-ROM drive so you could run the Windows NT setup program, then removed the CD-ROM drive, you might want to disable the adapter drivers for the CD-ROM.

To start or stop a device during the current session, highlight its name and click the Start or Stop button. The device will restart in the next session if it is designated to do so unless you change the Startup option as discussed next.

Changing the Startup Option

To change how a device starts when Windows NT starts, click the device name, then click the Startup button. A dialog box similar to the following appears:

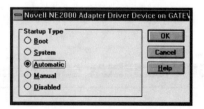

FIGURE 15-10

Controlling device
configurations

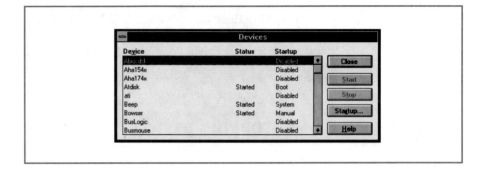

You can choose one of the following options, depending on how you want to start the device.

Boot   When the Boot option is enabled, the device starts when the computer starts and before any other devices start. Some devices must start before others, because the others are dependent on them.

System   Devices with the System setting start when the system starts but after devices that have the Boot startup setting.

Automatic   Devices with the Automatic setting start after devices with the Boot or System startup setting. Use this setting when a device is not critical to system operation. A network card driver is an example of such a device since the rest of the operating system can start up without it.

Manual   Set the Manual option if you want a user of a dependent system service to start the device.

Disabled   The Disabled option prevents the device from being started by any user or system service.

Avoid changing the startup type for the devices installed during Windows NT installation. Windows NT may fail to boot if you change the device.

CONFIGURING SERIAL COMMUNICATIONS

To configure the COM ports in Windows NT, double-click the Ports icon in the Control Panel to display the Ports dialog box shown here:

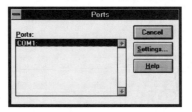

A list of available COM ports on your computer appears in the Ports field. To change a port's settings, double-click its name, or highlight it and click the Settings button. A dialog box similar to the one shown here appears:

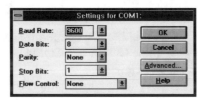

Usually, you only need to change these settings when configuring a serial printer. If you are communicating with another computer over COM ports and modems, configure the COM ports in the communications software package that you are using. The settings of these options will depend on the device you are connecting to (refer to its user's manual for more information). Click the down arrow button on each field to see a list of options. In the Flow Control field, select Xon/Xoff in most cases, unless the printer or other device specifically controls the flow of data. Refer to the printer's manual for details.

The Advanced Settings

The advanced settings are important if you have more than two serial ports in your system. The original IBM PC supported COM1 and COM2 and provided standard I/O port addresses and interrupts for them. COM3 and COM4 were added later, but they were assigned interrupts that can conflict with COM1 and COM2 as shown in Table 15-2.

Notice that COM1 uses the same interrupt as COM3, and COM2 uses the same interrupt as COM4. This is only a problem when you install the extra ports and then attempt to run multiple applications in Windows NT that use the ports, or when you have a mouse connected to one of the ports. For example, a device on COM1 such as a modem would conflict with a mouse on COM3. This interrupt conflict was allowed because early PCs had a shortage of interrupts, and usually only ran one application at a time anyway, so conflicts were rare except in the case of the mouse.

TABLE 15-2

Common I/O Port Addresses and Interrupts

Port	Address	IRQ
COM1	03F8h	4
COM2	02F8h	3
COM3	03E8h	4
COM4	02E8h	3

Note

IBM PS/2 Micro Channel systems and EISA bus systems allow interrupt sharing and do not have a problem with interrupt conflicts.

To avoid conflicts on ISA (not MCA or EISA systems), change the jumper or dip switch of the COM3 and COM4 ports and use the Ports utility to tell Windows NT about the new setting.

Click the Advanced button on the Settings dialog box and specify the new base I/O port address and interrupt for the selected port.

Tip

Microsoft recommends that you always use the lower-numbered ports before using the higher-numbered ports. Place the devices that need the best performance on the port that has the lowest interrupt number (COM2 or COM4 if using the defaults) to gain better service from the CPU.

CONFIGURING MULTIMEDIA EQUIPMENT

Multimedia integrates sound and graphics into an interactive medium for learning and entertainment on computers. This interaction is not only exciting but useful. Multimedia makes computer information easier to access and understand.

A computer that has a specific set of hardware devices and software drivers to support multimedia is called a Multimedia PC, or MPC, for short. The specification for an MPC is defined by Microsoft and the Multimedia Marketing Council.

You'll need each of the components listed on the left in Table 15-3 to *play* multimedia titles and record and play back sounds. The components of a full-blown system—everything you'll need to *author* multimedia titles—are listed on the right.

The playback system listed in Table 15-3 is the minimum system that you can use. A Musical Instrument Digital Interface (MIDI) synthesizer or sound module is useful if you need professional sound quality when playing MIDI files. You can even try authoring your own multimedia presentations using prerecorded sounds or sounds you capture with a microphone. The remaining discussion focuses on waveform audio and MIDI components.

Playback System	Authoring System
CPU	CPU
Color display	Color display
CD-ROM drive (optional)	CD-ROM drive
Sound board	Sound board
Speakers or headset	Speakers or headset
	Microphone
	Electronic synthesizer
	Video camera
	Capture board
	Video disc player
	Scanner

Waveform Audio   Waveform audio is a digital representation of sound waves. You can record and play back sounds using a compatible sound board. The Sound Recorder accessory records and plays back wave audio and you can assign sounds you've recorded to system events using the Sound utility in the Control Panel.

MIDI Audio   Musical Instrument Digital Interface (MIDI) files contain music event commands, not a digital representation of sounds. Thus, they require less storage space and suffer no loss in quality during recording and playback. A MIDI command might instruct a music keyboard synthesizer to play a note for a period of time. The synthesizer generates the sound.

Windows NT does not provide tools for creating MIDI files, but allows you to play them on externally attached synthesizers or on a sound board. MIDI allows you to hook up electronic musical instruments to your system with a connection usually provided by a sound board, or a dedicated MIDI interface adapter. Most sound boards play MIDI files directly using their own sound sources, or let you attach MIDI devices to extend the range of sounds.

Installing Multimedia Products

To install multimedia sound and video cards, start the Drivers utility in the Control Panel. Some multimedia components are already installed, but if you click the Add button, you'll see drivers for sound and video boards like the following:

Creative Labs Sound Blaster
Media Vision Thunder and Pro Audio Spectrum

Microsoft Sound System
MIDI Synthesizer

If you don't see a driver listed for your hardware, choose Unlisted or Updated Driver from the top of the list and click the OK button. You are asked to insert the disk that comes with the board.

After installing a sound or video board, you can use accessories like Sound Recorder and Media Player immediately. If you are attaching MIDI-compatible devices, refer to the next section, "MIDI," for more details.

MIDI

MIDI is a specification developed in the early 1980s that defines how electronic musical instruments can interface and communicate with one another. The interface defines the physical connection (cables and connectors) among instruments, and the protocols for communications. MIDI also defines the type of information transmitted over the cables and how that information is stored in memory or on disk. MIDI information consists of messages, rather than the actual wave forms of sound. A message might instruct a synthesizer to play (turn on) middle C, then another message might turn it off. These on/off messages and other instructions provide a much more efficient way of storing musical information, when compared to saving digital waveforms, but it requires that you have a device that understands MIDI messages.

The need for MIDI arose because musicians often had several keyboards at their disposal, but only two hands with which to play them. By connecting keyboards with a MIDI cable as shown in Figure 15-11, musicians (and non-musicians) can "play" the attached keyboard "remotely." Any key played on the main keyboard also plays on the remote unit. This doubling up of sounds helps to produce "fatter" notes. The notes played on the remote keyboard might be moved an octave up or down, or assigned a different sound altogether. You can combine a piano sound on the main keyboard with a string sound on the remote keyboard, for example.

A computer can be added to this setup to provide enhanced control of the MIDI system. MIDI connections form a daisy-chain arrangement in which a large number of MIDI devices are connected together. The keyboard can send its information to the computer, which means you can record the notes played at the keyboard using a computer program called a *sequencer*. A sequencer records a series of notes and system event commands and saves them for future playback. A sequencer is also like a multi-track tape recorder—you can record a piano sound on one track, then go back and add a flute sound on another track while listening to your piano recording.

MIDI information is directed to synthesizers over numbered *channels*. For example, you might send a flute sound out over Channel 1 to play on a specific synthesizer set up to receive Channel 1. When you set a synthesizer to a MIDI channel, it plays only the

FIGURE 15-11

A main MIDI keyboard can control another MIDI keyboard

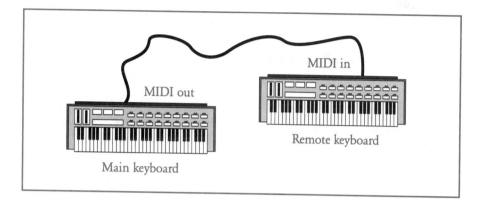

MIDI in

MIDI out

Remote keyboard

Main keyboard

notes designated for that channel in the sequencer program. In this way, you can easily move equipment around, change sounds, and switch devices to customize playback.

Sequences recorded with a computer are saved as MIDI files with the extension .MID. Windows NT comes with one sample MID file and you can obtain others from bulletin boards, MIDI equipment vendors, and other sources. Of course, if you have a sequencing package, you can create your own. The following information will help you understand the use of the MIDI Mapper.

Base-Level and Extended-Level Synthesizers

The Multimedia specification classifies synthesizers and sound boards into two levels: base-level synthesizers and extended-level synthesizers. This classification is based on the number of instruments and notes the synthesizer can play, not on the quality or the cost of the synthesizer. The following table shows the minimum capabilities of base-level and extended-level synthesizers:

Synthesizer	Melodic Instruments		Percussive Instruments	
	Number	*Polyphony*	*Number*	*Polyphony*
Base-level	3 instruments	6 notes	3 instruments	3 notes
Extended-level	9 instruments	16 notes	8 instruments	16 notes

Polyphony is the number of notes the synthesizer can play simultaneously. The polyphony expressed above applies to each group of instruments, both melodic and percussive. For example, an extended-level synthesizer can play 16 notes distributed among nine melodic instrument sounds and 16 notes distributed among eight percussive sounds. MIDI channels are normally arranged as follows, depending on the level of the synthesizer:

☑ *Base-level synthesizers*   MIDI channels 13 through 16 are used for melodic instruments, with channel 16 reserved for key-based percussion instruments.

☑ *Extended-level synthesizers*   MIDI channels 1 through 10 are used for melodic instruments with channel 10 reserved for key-based percussion instruments.

Note the differentiation between melodic and percussive instruments. You can assign melodic instruments to different MIDI channels, and then assign a specific *sound patch* (flute, piano, bass, etc.) to that channel.

Percussive instruments are all on a single MIDI channel and *key-based*, which means that each key or note on the keyboard plays a different percussion instrument. For example, the middle C key is usually a high bongo, the D key in the same octave is a mute high conga, the E key is a low conga, and so on.

General MIDI

The MIDI Manufacturers Association (MMA) has a General MIDI specification that defines what percussive instrument each key on the keyboard plays, and what instrument is assigned to each patch number. The general MIDI specification is important because it helps standardize the way MIDI files will sound on any system. It defines the sounds for each patch number and the percussion sounds for keys on the keyboard. In this way, multimedia authors and MIDI musicians can create MIDI scores that can be played back on other systems with the assurance that those other systems will play the intended instruments.

In other words, General MIDI ensures that a honky-tonk piano plays back the honky-tonk piano sound on another synthesizer. If a non-general MIDI keyboard is used that has a violin assigned to patch 3 instead, then the honky-tonk piano track (channel) will play with a violin sound. You use the MIDI Mapper utility in the Control Panel to correct these situations (the next section discusses this). The MIDI Mapper rearranges the patch and percussion key mappings so MIDI files play correctly on keyboards that don't conform to the general MIDI specification.

The MIDI Mapper

Double-click the MIDI Mapper icon in the Control Panel to display the MIDI Mapper dialog box shown in Figure 15-12. You use this to change the channel, patch, and key mappings if a synthesizer is attached that does not conform to the General MIDI specifications. Some older keyboards do not. Also note that if you're working with a sequencer and creating your own MIDI files, channel mappings and patch assignments are controlled within the sequencer software. The MIDI Mapper is mostly designed for users who play back MIDI files on non-standard equipment.

FIGURE 15-12

The MIDI Mapper dialog box

In the Show field, you click either Setups to change channel mappings, Patch Maps to change the configuration of a patch, or Key Maps to change the assignment of percussion sounds on synthesizer keyboards. You can edit an existing channel, patch, or key map by choosing it in the Name field and clicking the Edit button. Click New to create a new map, after first selecting setups, patch maps, or key maps in the Show field.

Note

In most cases, about the only thing you need to do in the MIDI Mapper is specify the port for your synthesizer in the Port Name field of the MIDI Setup dialog box, as discussed next.

Click the Setups button in the Show field, then choose a setup in the Name field that matches your synthesizer and click the Edit button to access the channel map. You'll see a MIDI Setup dialog box similar to the one shown in Figure 15-13.

FIGURE 15-13

Changing channel mappings and patch assignments on the MIDI Setup dialog box

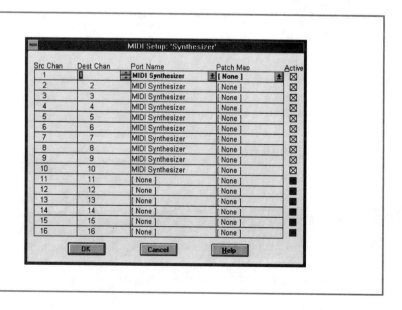

In the Dest Chan column, you can optionally assign a different channel on the destination device for each source channel. Click in each cell to change its contents.

In the Port Name column, specify the device that will play the channel, either an internal or external MIDI device. Some systems have both internal and external synthesizers. For example, a Creative Labs Sound Blaster is an internal adapter with a synthesizer that also has a MIDI port for external synthesizer connection.

In the Patch Map column, specify a different patch map if your synthesizer doesn't conform to general MIDI.

If you want to turn off a channel, disable its Active check box.

There are several ways you might use the channel mapping feature. Assume your system has a sound board and all the channels are assigned to a port name that matches the sound board. Now assume you have temporary use of a MIDI synthesizer. You could create a new channel map that directs all the channels to the MIDI port, while keeping your old settings in another channel map so you can revert back to just the sound board when the MIDI synthesizer is gone.

If your channel map has mixed port assignments in which some channels are directed to an internal sound board and others are directed to the MIDI port, you may need to change the patch maps for either the sound card or the MIDI port. Most sound cards conform to general MIDI specifications, so you can usually specify None in the Patch Map Name column settings.

Note that changing a patch map, even if a sound board or synthesizer doesn't need a change, can produce interesting results. Basically, the instruments in the MIDI score are changed to the instrument numbers in the new patch. Keep in mind that the results may not sound the way the composer intended.

Note

For information on the remaining MIDI Mapper options, refer to the Help system.

Inside

- Creating User Accounts

- Creating Local Groups

& Out

CHAPTER 16

Managing User Accounts

Users who access the Windows NT system locally—that is, by working at the computer itself rather than from another computer over the network—must have a user account. You create new users with the User Manager utility in the Administrative Tools group. Users at remote network computers gain access to shared directories via the Network user group and do not need a special user account on remotely accessed servers. However, server administrators can set permissions on shared directories to control the type of access network users have.

Recall from Chapter 3 that three default local user accounts are created during the NT installation process:

- Administrator
- Guest
- Initial User (with an account name the installer supplies)

The Administrator account is usually reserved for emergency access or high-level system configuration tasks while the Initial User account typically belongs to the person who installed NT on the system. Other users can log on using the Guest account, but it usually provides limited access. To provide a user with access beyond that provided by the Guest account, you'll need to create accounts for the users with the User Manager utility. Once a user account is created, you add it to a group. Membership in a group provides the users with the appropriate rights they need to access the system. For a discussion of these rights and a description of the NT built-in groups, refer to Chapter 3.

The Administrator can perform all the functions provided in the User Manager utility. Members of the Power User group can create new users and groups in the User Manager.

Options for installing the NT auditing system are located in the User Manager utility. You specify which events you want to track, then view the log of events in the Event Viewer. Auditing is discussed further in Chapter 21.

The User Manager is shown in Figure 16-1. You use it to perform the following tasks:

- Create new accounts for local users
- Change the parameters of existing accounts
- Create new groups

FIGURE 16-1

The User Manager window

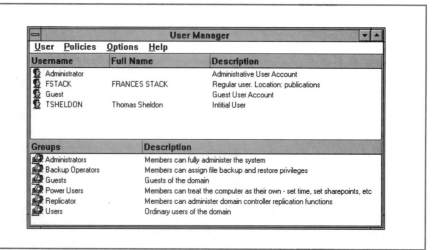

▨   Add members to groups

▨   Change the settings of groups

CREATING USER ACCOUNTS

Administrators control user logon to the system through user accounts. You can set various properties for accounts, as listed here:

▨   *Password options*   Forces the users to change their passwords or prevent them from ever changing their passwords. You can also set default password options that apply to all accounts on the workstation.

▨   *Disable the account*   Temporarily or permanently prevents access to the system with the account.

▨   *Logon script*   Specifies the name of a logon script that runs when a user logs onto the account. The logon script is a text file created with Notepad or a DOS command line editor such as EDIT or EDLIN or an executable program with the .EXE extension.

▨   *Home Directory*   Specifies the path to a directory where the account user can store personal files.

▨   *Group membership*   Makes the user account a member of a group.

Once a user account is created, it appears in the top pane of the User Manager window. You can double-click on the account name to make changes to any of these options. You also can add the user account to a group listed in the lower pane, or create a new group and add the user account to it.

Creating New User Accounts

Choose the New User option on the User menu to create a new user account. The New User dialog box appears, as shown in Figure 16-2. You need to supply the following parameters in this dialog box:

Username field   Type an abbreviated form of the user's name. Since user names appear in lists that you select from and search on, devise a consistent naming scheme. For example, you could adopt a policy of using the last name and first initial as in SHELDONT for Tom Sheldon. Listings then show users in the order of their last names. If

FIGURE 16-2

Creating a new user
account

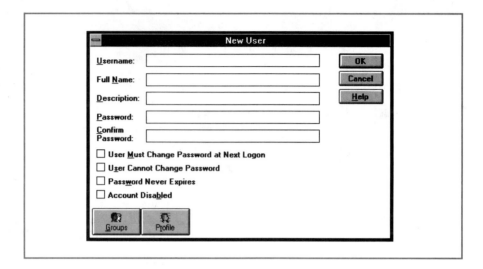

your network is small, you can use the first name and last initial as in TOMS, or first initial, last name as in TSHELDON.

Full Name field   Type the full name of the user for accurate identification.

Description field   In this field, type any important information about the user, such as his or her location, department, phone number, or responsibilities on the system.

Password options   Type a password for the account in the Password and Confirm Password fields. Mark one of the lower check boxes depending on how you want passwords handled for the user. Refer to help or the section called "More About Password Settings" later in this section for more information.

Account Disabled   Click the Account Disabled check box to prevent a user from accessing an account or to create an inaccessible template that you can use to create other accounts.

Groups   Click the Groups button to make the new user account a member of a group. Alternatively, you can make a user a member of a group later, using group options.

More About Password Settings

When you create a new user account, the "User Must Change Password at Next Logon" option is initially enabled. The first time the user logs on, they must type the password given to them by the administrator. Windows NT then asks them to specify a new password. If the user retypes the same password, they are asked for a new password the next time they log on. If they type a new password, the option is cleared. Here are some other password anomalies:

☑   If the "User Must Change Password at Next Logon" option is set, do not enable the "User Cannot Change Password" option.

☑   The "User Must Change Password" is usually applied to the Guest account or a temporary account.

☑   The "Password Never Expires" option overrides the "User Must Change Password at Next Logon" option.

You can apply default password settings to all user accounts by opening the Account Policy dialog box as shown in Figure 16-3. Choose Account from the Policies menu.

In the Account Policy dialog box that results, you can set the number of days before the user is asked for a new password in the "Maximum Password Age" field or set the number of days that users must retain their current password in the "Minimum Password Age" field.

To ensure unique passwords, specify a length of up to 14 characters in the "Minimum Password Length" field. Another way to ensure password uniqueness is to prevent users from using a password they recently used. In the "Password Uniqueness" field, you can prevent a user from using up to eight recently used passwords.

Creating User Profiles

Click the Profile button on the New User dialog box to specify a logon script and home directory for the user account. The User Environment Profile dialog box appears as shown in Figure 16-4. Its features are described in the following sections.

FIGURE 16-3

Setting default password options for all accounts

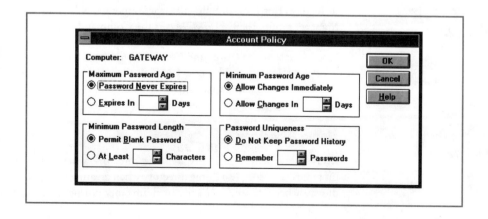

FIGURE 16-4

Changing user profiles

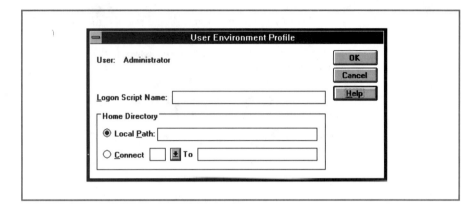

Logon Script

User accounts can include a logon script that runs after the user successfully logs onto the Windows NT system. User account logon scripts are similar to DOS batch files and contain DOS commands or batch file commands that set up a special environment for the user. You can create a logon script by following these steps:

1. Place the logon script in the \WINNT directory.

2. When creating a new user (or modifying an existing account), click the Profile button on the New User dialog box to specify a logon script. The User Environment Profile dialog box appears as shown in Figure 16-4.

3. Type the name of the logon script in the Logon Script Name field of the User Environment Profile dialog box. Do not type a path. The operating system looks in the \WINNT directory automatically.

As mentioned, logon scripts are similar to DOS batch files. You should create a logon script with the same criteria you would create an AUTOEXEC.BAT file on a DOS system. For a description of the commands and batch file parameters that you can include in logon script files, double-click the Windows NT Help icon in the Main Program Manager group, then choose "Access the Command Reference Help."

Note

When starting the Command Prompt in Windows NT to run DOS or other programs, Windows NT runs its own startup file called AUTOEXEC.NT and CONFIG.NT. Chapter 11 covers this in more detail.

Home Directory

Every user account can have a home directory where users place personal files and programs. You specify a home directory when creating or modifying a user account. That directory becomes the user's personal directory during their logon session.

You can locate the home directory on the local workstation or another server. Note the Home Directory options in Figure 16-4. Local Path is the path of a directory on the workstation where the user account is located. Use the Connect option to specify the path to another workstation on the network that has a shared drive.

When the User Manager creates a home directory for a user, it grants the user full access to the directory. If the directory already exists, the User Manager does not grant rights—you must do so by using the Permissions option in the File Manager.

The %USERNAME% variable substitutes the user account name in the path field. For example, if you type

C:\USER\%USERNAME%

in the Local Path field while creating a user account called TBONES, the User Manager creates a directory called C:\USER\TBONES.

Other User Account Options

There are a number of other user account administrative tasks. You can duplicate existing accounts to speed up the job of creating multiple accounts, and you can assign properties to multiple accounts at the same time. Choose the Rename option on the User menu to change the user name of a selected account.

You can use the Delete option to remove an account, but it's preferable to simply disable it for a while before actually deleting it.

Account Mass Production

If faced with the task of creating a number of user accounts, you can speed up the process by copying an existing account. First select the account that has the properties you want to copy, then choose Copy from the User menu. You then see a user account properties dialog box with the settings of the account you selected.

You need to supply a new user account name, description, and password. Note that if you used the %USERNAME% variable, a new directory is created with the new user name appended to the existing path. If you used a name in the original account instead of the %USERNAME% variable, the new user name is substituted. If you specified a directory name that does not match the user's account name, the same directory is used for the new account. For example, if you specified \PROGRAMS\DATA as the original home directory, this is also used for the new account since it doesn't include the user's name at the end.

Modifying Multiple Accounts

To change properties of multiple accounts at the same time, drag through the accounts with the mouse, or hold the CTRL key while clicking on selected accounts. Press ENTER or choose Properties from the User menu. The User Properties dialog box that appears should look similar to Figure 16-5.

Changes you make to any field are applied to all selected accounts, and the Description box is blank if each selected account has a different description. A check box option appears dark if the value differs among the selected accounts. Changing a darkened option changes all accounts in the same way.

If you want to keep the individual values for each account, don't change the fields when editing multiple accounts.

CREATING LOCAL GROUPS

This section describes how to create new groups and modify existing groups. For more information about group concepts, refer to Chapter 3. After creating user accounts, you add them to existing groups or custom groups. User then get the rights assigned to the groups. New user accounts are automatically added to the Everyone and User groups. The Administrator and Guest groups are built-in groups that can't be removed. You can perform the following in the User Manager with regard to groups:

☑ Create a new group by choosing the New Local Group option on the User menu

☑ Make a new group by copying an existing group, thus duplicating many of the original group settings

☑ Delete a group

☑ Change the properties of existing groups

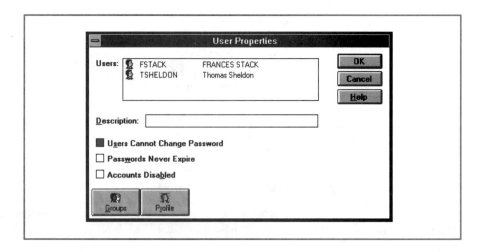

Note	To change the properties of any group, simply double-click the group, or highlight it and choose Properties from the User menu.

Creating New Groups

You choose New Local Group from the User menu in the User Manager to create a new group. Before choosing the option, you can select one or more user accounts that you want to add as members of the group. Hold the CTRL key and click each user account with the mouse. When you choose New Local Group, a dialog box similar to that shown in Figure 16-6 appears.

The users you selected before opening the dialog box appear in the Members list. You can perform any or all of these options in the dialog box:

☑ Type a descriptive name for the group in the Group Name field.

☑ Type a description of the group in the Description field. This description appears in list boxes, so make sure it accurately describes what the group is.

☑ Click the Show Full Names button to show the full name of user accounts in the Members field.

☑ To remove a member, click the name, then click the Remove button.

To add additional user accounts or group accounts, click the Add button. The dialog box shown in Figure 16-7 appears.

On the Add Users and Groups dialog box, you can select user and group accounts on the local system. If you are connected with a Windows NT Advanced Server, you can list users and groups in other domains by choosing a domain in the List Names From list box. You can also click the Search button to search for user account names on the local system or in domains.

FIGURE 16-6

Creating new groups

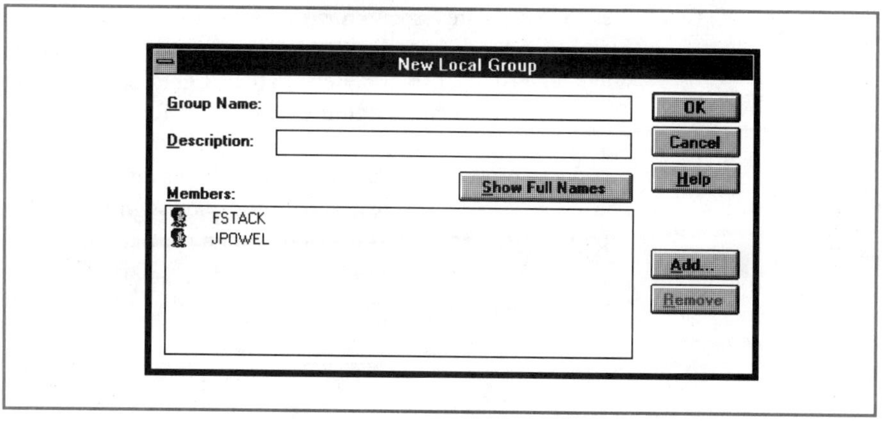

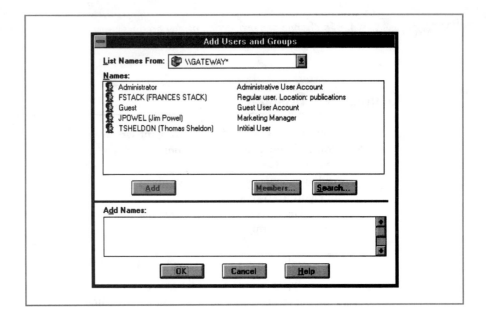

FIGURE 16-7

Adding new members
to groups

When you've filled out the New Local Group dialog box, click its OK button. Now you can assign access rights to the group as described in the next section.

Note

You can copy an existing group along with its member list and access rights by first highlighting the group, then choosing Copy on the User menu. You need to specify a new group name and description.

Assigning Access Rights

You assign access rights to groups to control the capabilities its members have on the system. Rights are associated with system access, rather than directory, file, and printer access, which are controlled by permissions. Rights on Windows NT systems are listed and described in Chapter 3. Refer to the "Rights" section in that chapter for more details.

To assign rights to a group, choose User Rights. A dialog box similar to Figure 16-8 appears.

The procedure for using the User Rights Policy dialog box is a little different than you might expect. You first select a right to assign in the Right list box, then choose a group (or user) account you want to assign the right to.

FIGURE 16-8

Assigning rights to groups

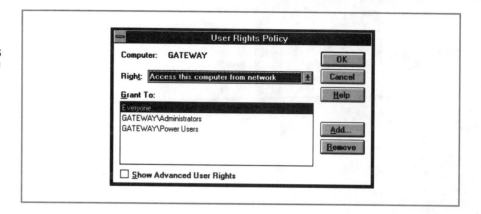

To revoke the selected right for a user or group, click the user or group in the Grant
To field, then click the Remove button.

To add a new group or user account, first select a right, then click the Add button.
The Add Users and Groups dialog box appears as shown in Figure 16-9. Click a group,
then click the Add button to add it to the lower list. You also can click the Show Users
button to list and select a user account in the Names list, and you can click the Search
button to search for account names on the local system or in domains.

FIGURE 16-9

Choosing a group or user
account to assign rights to

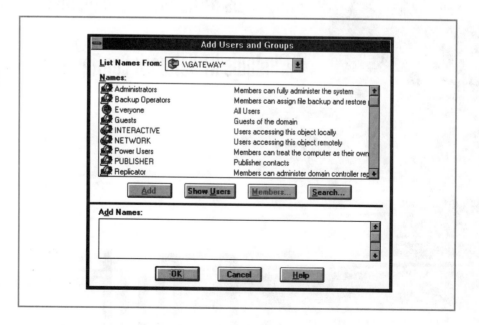

Inside

- Managing the Server

- Windows NT Network Communications

- Windows NT Network Configuration

& Out

CHAPTER 17

Server and Network Management

The Windows NT operating system has integrated network support that provides peer-to-peer networking capabilities. That means any Windows NT workstation can act as a server and/or a client. (You'll remember from Chapter 3 that a server shares its resources with other users and a client is a computer that accesses shared resources on other systems.) In a peer-to-peer arrangement, all machines are somewhat equal in capabilities, but access to resources is restricted at the user account level. In other words, some users have more access to resources on a server than others, based on permissions and rights.

Windows NT provides these networking features:

☑   Directory and file-sharing capabilities, and the ability to connect with shared directories and files on remote computers.

☑   Sharing of a local printer and connection to shared printers on remote systems.

☑   Messaging and electronic mail capabilities among users in workgroups and domains.

☑   An expandable system. Windows NT supports a variety of network interface cards and network communications protocols. This chapter explains how to add and configure network hardware and software. Currently, Ethernet and Token Ring are supported.

☑   Industry-standard methods for establishing network connections and session management. The use of these standards ensures the quick development of software that runs on Windows NT.

☑   Remote Procedure Call (RPC). With RPC, a local workstation can run utilities and functions on remote workstations.

This chapter begins with a description of user and session management for system administrators. You'll see how to view and manage users who are accessing a Windows NT server, and how to view and manage shared resources on that server. Following that is a discussion of network communications methods and management techniques for network hardware and software components.

When a computer running Windows NT shares its resources with other network users, it becomes a server. The administrator of that system must manage the use of resources and the network users who access them, as follows:

☑   The User Manager provides a way to create and manage accounts for local users who share resources on the system.

☑   The File Manager provides a way to share files with other network users and manage the permissions network users have to the system.

☑   The Server utility in the Control Panel provides a way to view and manage the shared resources and users of a server system.

☑   The Network utility in the Control Panel provides a way to view and manage network hardware, software, and connection settings.

MANAGING THE SERVER

This section describes how to use the Control Panel Server utility to view and manage users, sessions, and shared resources. Double-click the Server icon in the Control Panel to display the dialog box shown in Figure 17-1.

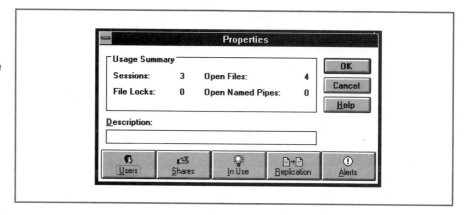

FIGURE 17-1

The Properties dialog box appears when you start the Server utility

The Usage Summary field provides the following information about current network user connections (sessions) and file usage:

Sessions   This field lists the number of users currently accessing the server, including the local logged on user.

Open Files   This field lists the number of files that remote users have accessed and currently have open in the memory of their system.

File Locks   Files that are shared over a network must have locks to prevent multiple users from accessing the file simultaneously and overwriting changes made by other users. Some files are locked completely when one user accesses them. Database files typically allow multi-user access, but lock individual records or groups of records so only one user can access them at once.

Open Named Pipes   A *pipe* is like a communications channel between applications or processes running in the same computer, or on separate network computers. Requests, instructions, and data pass between computers connected by the pipe. A database program running on a server might use named pipes to receive read and write requests from client workstations. When a workstation connects with a shared printer, a pipe is created to handle internetwork printing processes.

At the bottom of the dialog box are buttons you press to obtain detailed information about user connections, directory and file shares, and files in use. You open these boxes to view user connections or resource usage and disconnect users if necessary. You also can configure the replication of server information on other network servers, and set up alerts that send messages to other network users when the server has problems or needs servicing. Each button is described in the following sections.

The dialog boxes that appear when using the Network utility provide several ways to disconnect users who are accessing shared resources on a Windows NT system. There are several reasons why you might want to disconnect users:

- A user may have gone to lunch or home for the evening and inadvertently left their machine on and connected to your system. You need to close files left open by a user and make them available to another user.

- A user might have left his or her system unattended and you want to close the files for security reasons.

- You want to disconnect a user who has gained unauthorized access to your system.

- A system crashed and you need to free up files or resources it was accessing.

- You need to disconnect all users so you can back up the file system, or because your system needs service.

Always remember to inform users that you intend to disconnect them. You can use the Chat utility.

Managing User Connections

You can see which users are connected to your system, then disconnect any of those users if necessary. Click the Users button on the Properties dialog box shown in Figure 17-1 to display the User Sessions dialog box shown in Figure 17-2. You use this dialog box to see session information about each user accessing the computer.

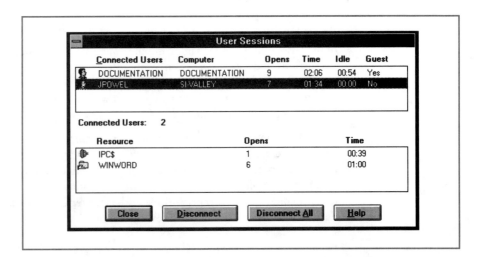

The top field of the dialog box lists current users. Click any user in this field to view information in the lower box about resources the user is accessing. The top box includes the fields described in the following section.

Connected Users This column lists each user that is currently accessing or using resources on the computer.

Computer This column shows the name of the computer from which the connected user is accessing resources.

Opens This column tells the number of resources the user is accessing.

Time This column tells the amount of time that has elapsed since the last access.

Idle This column tells the amount of time that has elapsed in hours and minutes since the connected user actually used the shared resource. If this time is excessive, the user may have forgotten to end their session. You can follow the procedures described later for disconnecting the user.

Guest This column displays Yes if the user is logged on as a Guest, giving you an idea of the type of connection they have.

The lower box displays information for individual users (more about this information shortly). Click a user name in the upper box to display the resources that person is using.

Resource This column gives the shared resources being accessed by the selected user.

Opens This column tells the number of files, printers, or pipes open.

Time This column gives the time since the resource was first accessed.

> **Note**
>
> The User Sessions dialog box does not show individual file usage, only shared directories, printers, and named pipes. To view individual file information, refer to "Managing Shared Resources" later in this chapter.

Disconnecting a User

You can disconnect a user by opening the User Sessions dialog box shown in Figure 17-2 and selecting the user you want to disconnect, then clicking the Disconnect button. You see the following warning message:

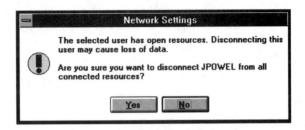

If you're sure you want to disconnect the user, click the Yes button.

Always use Chat or the telephone to warn a user that you plan to disconnect them. They might have information in open files that would be lost.

To disconnect all users, click the Disconnect All button.

Managing Shared Resources

You can view the resources that are shared on your system and the network users who are accessing those shared resources, then disconnect the users if necessary. Click the Shares button on the Properties dialog box shown in Figure 17-1 to display the Shared Resources dialog box shown in Figure 17-3. You use this dialog box to view the current shared resources and to disconnect a user that is using a resource.

Choosing Disconnect breaks all the user's connections to the system, not just the connection to the selected resource.

In Figure 17-3, the shared directory called POWERPNT is highlighted and users currently accessing this directory are listed in the lower box. The following explains the columns in the Sharename box:

Sharename   This column gives the name of the shared resource on the local computer.

Uses   This column gives the number of remote users who are accessing the shared resource.

Path   This column tells the directory path or other resource name.

User names appear in the Connected Users box when you highlight a resource in the Sharename box that is being used. The next section defines the columns in the Connected Users box.

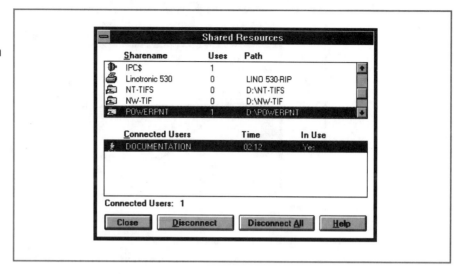

FIGURE 17-3

Viewing shared resources on
the current system

Connected Users   This column lists the names of remote users accessing the
resource.

Time   This column tells the amount of time in hours and minutes since the user first
connected with the resource.

In Use   This columns tells whether the user currently has a file open in the selected
directory.

Disconnecting a User

To disconnect a user, click a user name in the Connected Users column, then click the
Disconnect button. A warning message appears. Use caution since this action completely
disconnects the user from the system, not just the selected resource.
    To disconnect all users, click the Disconnect All button.

Closing Individual Resource Connections

You can see network users' access to individual resources, and disconnect users from the
resource if necessary by clicking the In Use button on the Properties dialog box shown in
Figure 17-1. The Open Resources dialog box appears as shown in Figure 17-4. The dialog
box lists each individual file, pipe, or printer connection. If you need to stop the use of a
resource, click the resource, then click the Close Resource or Close All Resources button.

FIGURE 17-4

Working with individual
resources

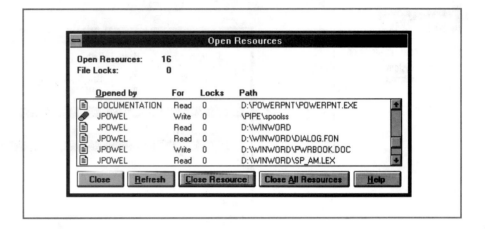

The Open Resources dialog box displays an icon for the type of resource (file, pipe, printer, or other) and the name of the user accessing the resource in the Opened by column. The other fields are covered next.

For   This column tells what permissions the user has to the resource, such as Read, Write, Execute, and others.

Locks   This column tells the number of locks on the resource.

Path   This column tells the drive and directory where the resource exists.

You click the Close Resource button to stop a user's connection to that resource. If you need to disconnect all resources, click the Close All Resources button.

Click the Refresh button to make sure the most current resource information is listed. If the box has been open for a while, its information probably needs refreshing.

Tip

Warn users before disconnecting any resource. They may not have saved their changes.

A user might leave files open when they go to lunch or leave for the evening. If you need to make these files available to other users, you can close the current connection, but use caution. The user might have forgotten to save changes. Alternatively, the connection might be sorting a database. If possible, go to the user's workstation to check the current activity.

Viewing and Closing Shared Files in the File Manager

You can view a list of users accessing a shared file in the File Manager, and if necessary close the user connection. In the File Manager, follow these steps to view or close a shared file:

1. Click the file you want to view or close.

2. Choose Properties from the File menu, then click the Open By button on the Properties dialog box.

The Network Properties dialog box opens for the file, like the one shown in Figure 17-5. It displays the filename and information about the total number of shared files for the computer. The names of users accessing the selected file are listed in the Open by column.

To disconnect a user from the file, click the user's name, then click the Close Selected button. To disconnect all the listed users, click the Close All button.

Directory Replication

Directory replication is a feature of the Windows NT Advanced Server that Windows NT workstations "passively" support. NT Advanced Servers can export copies of directories and files to other servers, or to Windows NT workstations. A Windows NT workstation can import these directories and files for storage, but cannot export directories and files of its own.

Because directory replication is a complex procedure requiring special permissions, it is only briefly mentioned here. Refer to the Windows NT Advanced Server manual for more details.

FIGURE 17-5

Closing shared files in the File Manager

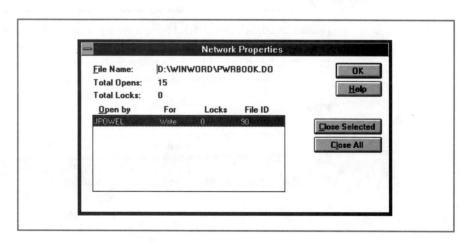

FIGURE 17-6

Replicating directories

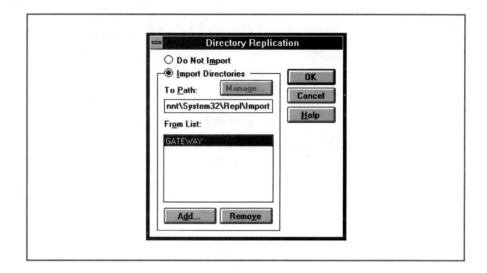

Click the Replication button on the Properties dialog box shown in Figure 17-1 to display the Directory Replication dialog box shown in Figure 17-6.

To allow an NT Advanced Servers to export its directories and files to the local computer, click the Import Directories button. You then specify the location for the imported files in the To Path field. Next, you click the Add button to specify the domain or computer that is allowed to import files.

You can view a list of subdirectories that have been imported to the computer by clicking the Manage button. Refer to Windows NT help for a complete description of the options and fields on the Manage dialog box.

Setting Up Alerts

You can specify which users and computers are notified when administrative alerts occur on the local system by clicking the Alerts button on the Properties dialog box. The Alerts dialog box shown in Figure 17-7 appears.

The following are typical alert events:

- Intruder problems

- User access problems

- Users having trouble with a session

- Power problems when the UPS service is attached

- Printer problems

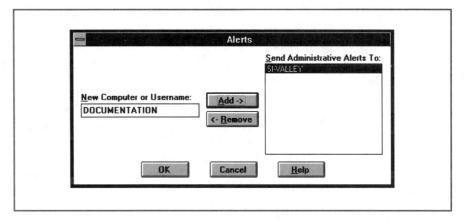

FIGURE 17-7

Specifying an alert list

In the New Computer or Username field, type the name of the user account or computer you want to alert. Click the Add button to add your selection to the list on the right. You can remove a name from the list on the right by selecting it, then clicking the Remove button.

WINDOWS NT NETWORK COMMUNICATIONS

This section discusses the basics of network communications, as well as hardware and software components. The utilities for configuring network interface cards and installing software modules to support network communications are covered, along with background information.

Network Concepts

A computer network includes hardware (network interface cards), media (the cable), and communications software. Each is described here:

- ☑ *Hardware* The type of network interface card used determines the layout or topology of the network (ring, linear segment, and so on), the type of media used, and the data transmission methods and transfer rates.

- ☑ *Media* The media is typically cable, but might also be radio or infrared signals. Cable types include coaxial copper cable, twisted-pair cable, and fiber optic cable.

- ☑ *Software* The network software is based on communications protocols that define how information is prepared, packaged, and transferred across the media.

A protocol is a model with built-in layers that programmers and system designers use to build hardware and software for network communications. Protocols define how information flows between systems, starting with the user's application and moving down through the operating system, network software, and a network card.

An understanding of network communications protocol is important when configuring the various software drivers provided with Windows NT. While Windows NT uses standardized protocols to communicate with other Windows NT and Windows for Workgroup computers, you might need to install additional modules such as TCP/IP to support communications with computers that run other operating systems, like Novell NetWare or UNIX.

Communications Protocols

When describing network protocols, it is most common to reference the International Standards Organization's definition of network protocols, known as Open Systems Interconnection (OSI), and shown in Figure 17-8. It defines network communication in layers, starting at the bottom with the physical hardware and working up to a top layer that defines how applications use networks. A communications protocol is defined

FIGURE 17-8

The Open Systems Interconnection protocol model

Application Layer
Provides the interface between user applications and network support software.

Presentation Layer
Establishes initial data exchange methods between two systems and provides translation between applications if necessary. Network security is handled in this layer.

Session Layer
Establishes and maintains a communication "session" between two systems.

Transport Layer
Provides initial organization and packaging of data. Ensures reliable delivery.

Network Layer
Provides Addressing and routing information. Repackages large packages into small packets if necessary. Handles data transfer problems.

Data Link
Packages data at the bit level and interfaces with the physical layer. Provides error detection.

Physical Layer
Defines the media and signal transfer methods on physical adapters and cables.

primarily for hardware and software architects who design networking products. By following a recognized protocol standard, they can design products that work on a variety of systems using a variety of operating systems, and that communicate with other systems using the protocol.

A protocol defines the flow of information between systems, as shown in Figure 17-9. An overnight package delivery service provides a useful analogy for explaining network protocols. The Quick delivery service ships packages from sender to receiver while a computer network sends packets of data from one computer to another with the same steps:

1.   At the Quick delivery service, an agent takes your call for a package pickup and schedules the delivery. This is analogous to the application computer users work

The flow of information
between network computers

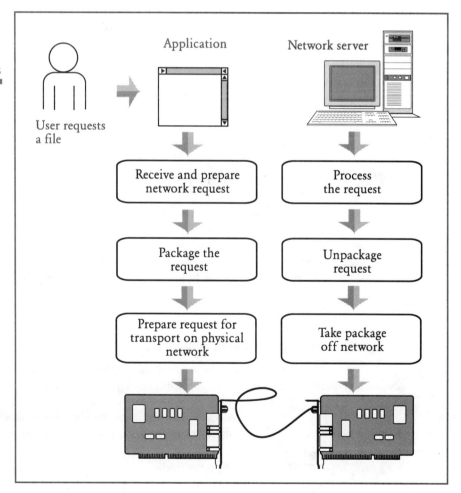

with, in which they make requests for network service. For example, a user working with an electronic mail package makes requests to send mail to another network user. The mail package then uses underlying network communications software to handle the network requests.

2.   When the Quick delivery server driver picks up your package, it is placed in an envelope with a shipping invoice that describes where the package is going and how it must be handled. Likewise, network operating system software takes service requests or data from upper-level applications and places them in "data packages" for transport across the network.

3.   After the Quick delivery service schedules and prepares your package, it is sent by plane, train, or truck to a destination. Likewise, a computer network sends a "data package" over the physical network media to a destination computer. Of course, packages of data must be prepared for placement on the network media, and each type of network (Ethernet, Token Ring, and so on) has its own way of defining how data is sent over the media it uses.

Each layer of communications is handled by software modules or device drivers. Some modules are interchangeable, depending on the type of hardware installed or the systems you need to communicate with. This modular design adds flexibility so you can communicate with a wide variety of systems. The remainder of this section describes the software modules that provide network communications at the various protocol layers.

Windows NT Network Support

The networking architecture of Windows NT and how it fits into the OSI protocol model is shown in Figure 17-10. When Windows NT boots, these modules are loaded to provide network support. On the left is the OSI model and on the right are the Windows NT modules at the location where they fit into the model. Each module interfaces with the one above and below it to provide a way to pass information from one computer to another.

Network Adapter Support

The physical layer in the protocol stack defines network adapter card topologies, media types, and transmission methods. This layer interfaces with the Data Link layer and its network card drivers.

With Windows NT, you can install more than one network interface card in a computer. For example, a system might have an Ethernet card to connect with a network segment in the accounting department, and a Token Ring card to connect with the engineering department's network.

FIGURE 17-10

Windows NT network architecture compared to the OSI model

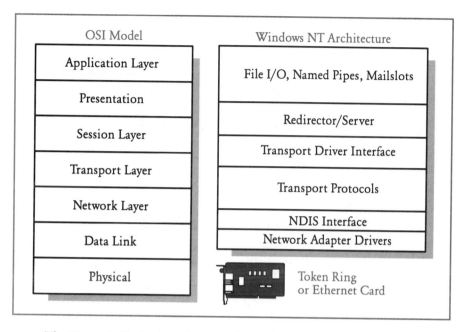

The Network Device Interface Specification (NDIS) manages the flow of data among network interface cards if more than one card is installed. It acts as a traffic director, sending packets to appropriate network cards. Likewise, when packets arrive on network interface cards, the NDIS interface directs the packets to appropriate upper-level protocols.

The advantage of NDIS is that vendors of network interface cards can write drivers to the single NDIS standard. In this way, you can purchase any NDIS-compatible network interface card with the assurance that it will work with Windows NT. Additionally, the NDIS layer can connect with several different upper-level transport protocols and route packets through the appropriate protocol stack, as discussed next.

Transport Protocols

A transport protocol defines the rules for communications between computers on a network. Windows NT provides three protocol standards, one of which is built-in.

◢ *NBF* When Windows NT systems communicate with other Windows NT systems, a built-in transport protocol called NBF is used. NBF is derived from the earlier NetBEUI (NetBIOS Extended User Interface) standard used by LAN Manager, LAN Server, and MS-Net products.

◢ *TCP/IP* TCP/IP is a set of protocols designed to interconnect dissimilar systems and networks. TCP/IP is used by almost all universities and government organizations. You can optionally install the TCP/IP protocol stack if you need to interconnect with UNIX systems or configure diverse internetworks. See Appendix C.

- *DLC* This is a special low-level interface used to directly attach network devices such as printers with built-in Ethernet interface cards. DLC is also used in Windows NT for communications with IBM SNA services.

It is important to note that NBF is not a routable protocol and does not provide efficient internetwork support. The TCP/IP protocol is provided for this purpose, and provides a way to send NetBIOS requests over internetwork connections. See Appendix C for details.

Transport Driver Interface

While NDIS provides an interface for multiple network cards and communications protocols, the Transport Driver Interface (TDI) provides a connection point for protocol stacks to the Redirector layer above.

Redirector/Server

The function of this layer depends on whether a Windows NT system is a server or client. A client system makes requests to a server and any request for network service is sent to the redirector layer, which routes the requests to an appropriate protocol stack for packaging and network transport. At the server, the redirector receives packets from protocol stacks and directs them to higher-level server components.

For example, assume a workstation uses NBF to communicate with other Windows NT workstations and has the optional TCP/IP protocol installed to communicate with UNIX workstations. The user could run Terminal in one window to communicate with the UNIX system, and at the same time, could access files on another Windows NT workstation using the File Manager.

You can see this in Figure 17-11. A computer with one network interface card communicates with a UNIX workstation and another Windows NT workstation on the same network cable. The destination station only picks up the packets that are addressed to it, so it's possible to send multiple-packet types over a single network cable. You could also install two or more network interface cards in a computer to connect with multiple network segments. The NDIS layer routes packets to the appropriate cards.

Application Layer Interface

The application layer provides an interface that programmers can use to create network-aware applications. The interface provides network file-sharing services, print sharing, server browsing, and the ability for applications to set up sessions with similar applications

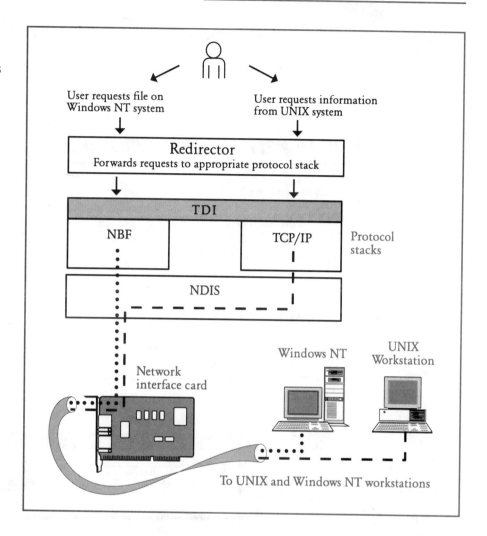

FIGURE 17-11

NBF and TCP/IP requests
over single adapter

on other computers (the Chat utility is a good example). Windows NT uses the following
mechanisms to support network applications.

- *Remote Procedure Call (RPC)* RPC provides a way to split an application into
  client and server components. Part of the procedure runs at a workstation and
  part runs at a server. Because data and other resources are typically centralized at
  servers, it is more appropriate to execute some functions there, rather than at
  the client workstation. The workstation then handles the user interface and data
  presentation functions.

- *Named Pipes and Mailslots* Names pipes, as mentioned earlier, provide a way to
  set up a connection between processes on separate network computers. Mailslots
  provide functions for identifying other computers or services on network.

✔ *NetBIOS and Windows Sockets* These are network interfaces developed in the 1980s. They are included with Windows NT to provide compatibility for applications that require them. Both are used for client/server and peer-to-peer networking by applications.

WINDOWS NT NETWORK CONFIGURATION

This section describes the Windows NT utility you access to change the network hardware configuration, or the protocol modules used to provide network communications. All the options discussed here are found on the Networks utility shown in Figure 17-12, which you can open by double-clicking the Networks icon on the Control Panel. The major options you can set using this dialog box are covered in the following sections.

Changing the Computer Name

All Windows NT workstations that participate in a network must have a name assignment. You usually specify the computer name during installation. To change the name, click the Change button that follows the Computer Name field. The following dialog box appears:

Type the new name and click OK.

The computer name primarily appears in Browse dialog boxes that other users see when searching for shared directories or printers. You might want to change the name to more accurately describe the services or resources provided by your system.

If your computer participates in a Windows NT Advanced Server domain, an account must exist in the domain for the name you specify in the Computer Name field. Coordinate any name changes with the network administrator to ensure proper domain logon.

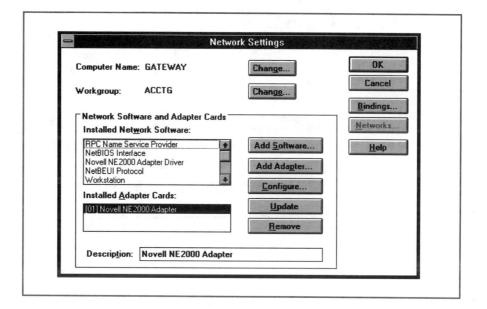

FIGURE 17-12

The Networks utility

Changing Workgroup or Domain Settings

The primary purpose of workgroups is to group computers in a way that simplifies browsing. When you need to connect with a computer that has a shared directory or drive, you see a dialog box that lists workgroups. You then double-click the workgroup for which you are searching to display a list of computers in that workgroup. You can collapse one workgroup list and expand another if you need to search further.

A domain is a Windows NT Advanced Server computer group that provides browsing capabilities and also provides user account management from a centralized location.

To change a workgroup or domain name, or join a new workgroup or domain, click the Change button in the Workgroup field. The dialog box in Figure 17-13 appears.

To change a workgroup name, click the Workgroup option, then type a new workgroup name in the field. To change a domain name, click the Domain option, then type a new domain name.

If an account doesn't exist for the computer on a domain, you can create it if you are an administrator on the domain by filling in the lower field. Click Create Computer Account in Domain, then fill in the user name and password fields to verify your administrator status. An account is then created with the computer name.

Network Adapter Setup

The Network Settings dialog box has buttons for adding and configuring a network adapter driver. If you're adding a new driver, click the Add Adapter button, then select a driver from the following dialog box.

After selecting a driver, click the Continue button to configure the driver. A dialog box similar to the one in Figure 17-14 appears, but the options on the dialog box depend on the adapter driver you've selected. Change the settings on this dialog box to match the dip switch and jumper settings on the network adapter card.

Note

You must ensure that interrupts and addresses don't conflict with other settings in your system. Refer to Appendix A for a discussion of this topic.

FIGURE 17-13

The Domain/Workgroup Settings dialog box

Domain/Workgroup Settings

Computer Name: GATEWAY

Member of:
- ◉ Workgroup: ACCTG
- ○ Domain:

OK
Cancel
Help

☐ Create Computer Account in Domain

Domain Administrator User Name:

Domain Administrator Password:

This option will create a computer account on the domain for this computer. It is for use by domain administrators only.

FIGURE 17-14

The Network Properties
dialog box

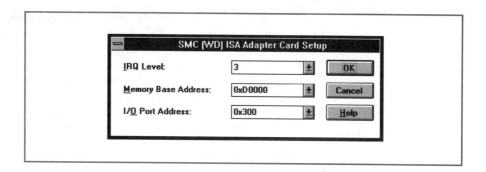

Configuring an Existing Driver

To configure a driver that is already installed, first select the driver name in the Installed
Adapter Cards field of the Network Settings dialog box. The setup dialog box for the
selected adapter then appears (it's similar to the dialog box just shown).

If you change any settings, you must shut down Windows NT and change the
settings on the network adapter as well.

Updating a Driver

If you receive an updated network adapter driver from a vendor or from Microsoft, click
the Update button on the Network Settings dialog box, then insert the disk with the new
driver. The new driver is copied over and the existing settings are retained.

Network Communications Software Setup

Network software provides the protocols necessary to communicate with other computers
on a network. The Network Settings dialog box lists the currently installed software in
the Installed Network Software field. To install additional protocols, click the Add
software button. You see a dialog box similar to this one:

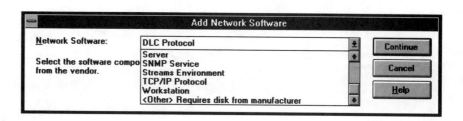

Choose a new software component from the drop-down list, but keep in mind that some of the items are already installed. You might want to add Streams and TCP/IP if you are connecting with UNIX systems or an internetwork. Install TCP/IP, as discussed in Appendix C, if you need to set up wide area networking.

If asked to configure the software, click the Help option to obtain information about the specific component you selected.

Software Configuration

If you need to change the configuration for a software component that is already installed, select the component in the Installed Network Software list, then click the Configure button. A dialog box with specific configuration options for the component appears. Click the Help button to obtain additional information about the options which are specific to the software component.

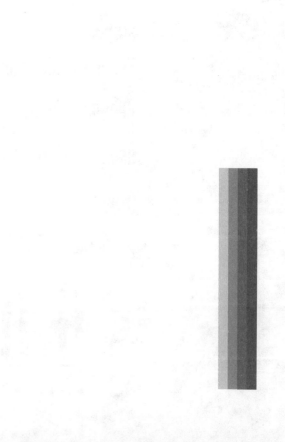

Inside

& Out

CHAPTER 18

Managing Printers and Fonts

The Print Manager is your primary tool for installing and configuring printers, as well as establishing printer connections over the network. A typical Print Manager window looks like Figure 18-1. This window shows the following printers:

▨ *Laser in Acctg* This printer appears as an icon at the bottom of the window. It is a shared printer, as indicated by the hand.

▨ *Laser in Acctg #2* The document window is open for this printer and one print job is visible.

▨ *Epson Dot Matrix* This is a local dot matrix printer. It is not shared.

▨ *DOCUMENTATION HP* This is a network printer to which a connection has been made. The name of the computer is DOCUMENTATION and the name of the printer is HP.

You can double-click on any printer to open its document window and view the status of print jobs sent to it. If you are the Administrator or the owner of a print job, you can pause the job, resume it, rearrange its order in the queue, and delete it as covered in Chapter 8.

THE WINDOWS NT PRINTING ENVIRONMENT

In Windows NT, there is a difference between a "printer" and a physical printing device. A printer is best considered a *logical device* to which you can send print jobs. Think of a printer as the icon you see in the Print Manager, rather than the physical device attached to a computer or the network. The reason for this distinction is described next and illustrated in Figure 18-2.

▨ You can create more than one logical printer to handle print jobs for the same physical device.

FIGURE 18-1

The Print Manager window

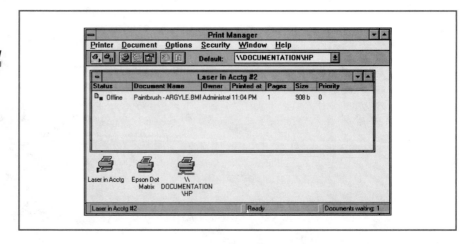

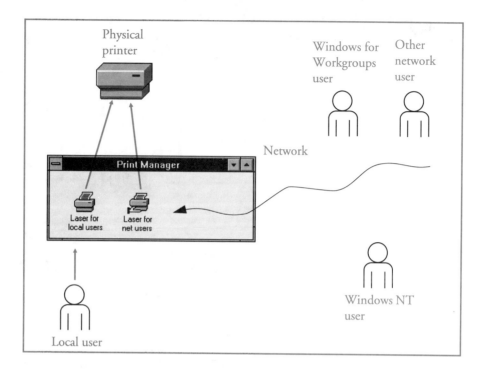

FIGURE 18-2

Windows NT printing
environment

☑ Logical printers that send their print jobs to the same printer can have different properties. For example, one might print late at night while another might print immediately. When printing, you choose which logical printer you want to handle the print job, not a physical printer.

☑ You could create a logical printer for local users and another for network users, then give the local users higher priority than the network users.

☑ You can set different permissions levels on each logical printer, then assign the printers to different groups. For example, you could assign a printer to a Clerks group that has Print permissions only.

☑ You can create a logical printer that always prints to a file rather than a physical device.

☑ If a physical printer is local, it attaches to the LPT and COM ports of the local computer. If it is remote, then it is attached to other network computers (or in the case of some Hewlett-Packard and Compaq printers, directly to the network). Figure 18-3 illustrates the various physical printer connection methods.

You choose the Create Printer option on the Print Manager Printer menu to create logical printer definitions. Quick steps for creating logical printers are covered in the next section, followed by detailed steps for defining special parameters. About the only time

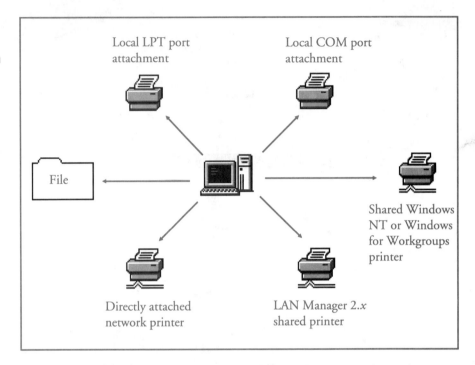

you need to be concerned with the physical printer is when you need to pick up your print jobs. Otherwise, the logical printer should define everything you need to know about the printer. Here are some of the logical printer definitions you can set during installation or when printing:

☑ Print job priority

☑ If you share the printer, its share name

☑ Permission settings for shared printers

☑ The type of form installed in each paper tray

☑ The amount of memory in the printer

☑ The font cartridge installed in the printer

☑ The default job configuration, which includes the form name, orientation (portrait or landscape), number of copies, and other options.

☑ The hours of operation

☑ The contents of a page that separates print jobs

☑ A "pool" of printers that service jobs from many users

☑ Audit options so you can track a printer's usage

Note	From here on, a logical printer is referred to simply as a "printer."

....

QUICK STEPS FOR CREATING A PRINTER

To create a new printer, you must start the Print Manager and open the Create Printer dialog box. You can define all the parameters for a printer when you install it, or you can change a printer's properties at any time by first selecting the printer, then choosing Properties on the Printer menu. The dialog boxes and options are the same whether you are just creating the printer or changing its properties at a later time. Follow these steps to create a printer:

1. Choose Create Printer to define a new printer. The dialog box in Figure 18-4 appears.

2. Specify the printer's name, driver, description, port, and whether you want to share it.

3. Click the Setup button to set specific options for the printer you installed, such as the forms in each paper tray, the amount of memory it has, and the font cartridges installed, as shown in Figure 18-5. These options depend on the printer.

4. Click the Details button on the Printer Properties dialog box to display the Printer Details dialog box shown in Figure 18-6. Set details for the printer, such as its time of operation, separator page, printing priorities, and so on.

5. Click the Job Defaults button on the Printer Details dialog box to specify the default print job. The dialog box in Figure 18-7 appears. A print job defines the form installed, its orientation, halftone options, and other options.

FIGURE 18-4

The Printer Properties
dialog box

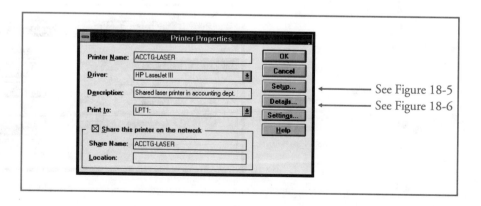

FIGURE 18-5

Defining specific printer
properties

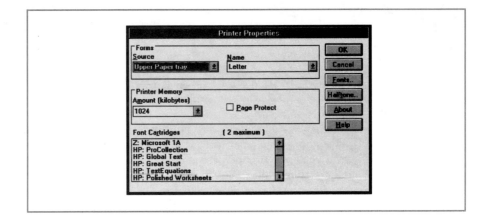

FIGURE 18-6

Setting operating parameters
for the printer

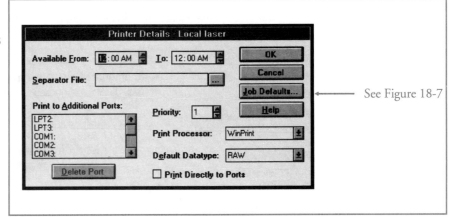

See Figure 18-7

FIGURE 18-7

Setting default print job
properties

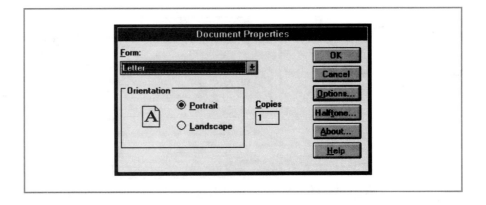

There are of course, a few other minor details you need to set when installing a printer. These are covered in the following sections but the steps just given provide enough detail to let you configure a printer in a hurry.

....

DETAILS FOR CREATING NEW PRINTERS OR CHANGING PROPERTIES

You simply choose the Create Printer option on the Printer menu to define a new printer. To change the properties of an existing printer, first highlight the printer, then choose Properties from the Printer menu.

| Note | A dialog box with the same options appears for either choice; however, the title bar name reflects the name of the menu choice you picked. |

The rest of this section provides details and descriptions of the fields and options on the dialog boxes used to install new printers or change the properties of existing printers.

Defining a Printer's Properties

When you choose Create Printer or choose Properties from the Printer menu, a dialog box similar to the one shown in Figure 18-4 appears. Each of the options on this dialog box is described next.

Printer Name   Type a name of up to 32 characters. This is what appears in a printer's document window or under its icon in the Print Manager. Note that network users see the name in the Share Name field when accessing the printer, not the name in this field. You can use the same name, however.

Driver   Choose a driver for the printer in this field. (The "Installing Drivers" section a bit later in this chapter gives more information.)

Description   Type a useful description of the printer in this field, such as a description of the printer, the type of forms loaded, the priority given to network users, and other information.

Print to   Specify the port where the printer is installed (refer back to Figure 18-4). (The "Printer Port Types" section gives more information.)

Share this printer on the network   Click this check box to access the options in the field.

Share Name   This is the name network users see when browsing for the network printers.

Location   Type a description of the location for this printer so users know where they can pick up their documents. The location information appears in the user's list of available printers once the printer is connected.

Installing Drivers

The Windows NT disks, or CD-ROM, contain a set of the most popular printer drivers. In addition, if a driver is not available for your printer, you might be able to use a compatible driver. For example, HP-compatible laser printers can use the HP LaserJet drivers included with Windows NT.

Tip   *When selecting a driver, type the first letter of the driver name to quickly jump to that part of the list.*

If you can't find an appropriate driver for your printer in the list, choose Other at the end of the list to install a driver on disk that you obtained from the printer's manufacturer or another source. A dialog box appears in which you can specify a floppy disk drive letter where the disk is located.

When network users access a shared network printer, they don't need to have a driver for that printer installed on their local computer. Instead, Windows NT will search for a driver on the computer where the printer is connected. However, if you attempt to connect to a printer on a Windows for Workgroups workstation, you'll need to install a driver on your own system since Windows NT can't use the Windows for Workgroups driver. You'll be asked if you want to install the driver when you attempt to connect with the printer.

RISC systems use different drivers than Intel-based systems. If a RISC system will access a shared printer on an Intel-based system, the RISC drivers can be on the local RISC system, or on the Intel-based system. Some companies will prefer to dedicate a computer as a print server. This computer then holds all the printer drivers required for printing, even RISC printer drivers. In this way, any system can access the printers, and managing and updating the printer driver files is much easier since they are located in one place.

Printer Port Types

As shown in Figure 18-3, Windows NT workstations can send print jobs to printers that are attached in a number of different ways. You choose a port type in the Print to dialog box (see Figure 18-4). The port types are described next.

- *Local ports*   Choose either LPT1, LPT2, COM1, COM2, COM3, or COM4, depending on which ports are physically present on your system. Most Intel-based desktop systems include LPT1 and COM1.

- *Network printers*   Choose Network Printer to define special ports. The following Print Destinations dialog box appears. If you choose Local Port, you can type a new port device name, such as COM5. This port might be supported by a special adapter card. If you choose LAN Manager Print share, a dialog box appears so you can make a network connection to a shared LAN Manager printer.

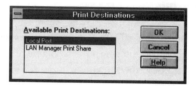

- *Network attached printers*   A new breed of printers from Hewlett-Packard, Compaq, and other vendors include their own network interface card so they can attach directly to the printer. Choose Network Printer in the Print to list, then choose the appropriate printer in the Print Destinations dialog box. Note that you may need to install special link protocols in the Networks option of the Control Panel before the printer's options become available.

Printer Setup Options

To set up options for the specified printer, click the Setup button on the Printer Properties or Create Printer dialog box. The dialog box in Figure 18-5 appears. You can set the following options on this dialog box.

- *Forms*   The Source drop-down list box in the Forms field lists the paper trays or feed mechanisms available on the selected printer. You click a tray in this list, then pick a default form for it in the Name drop-down list box. The "Defining Print Jobs and Forms" section later in this chapter gives more details.

▰   *Printer Memory* Specify the amount of memory installed in the printer in this field. Select the Page Protection option on Hewlett-Packard laser printers with more than one megabyte of memory. It ensures that an image of each page is created in printer memory before it is printed on paper and helps prevent certain types of errors from occurring.

▰   *Font Cartridge* Specify the cartridges installed in the printer.

On some printers, a Fonts button is available. You click this button to install soft fonts from disk into the memory of your printer. Click the halftone button to specify how color images are converted to black-and-white on the printer. Halftoning is a process of converting colors to gray scales, as discussed in Chapter 8.

Once you've modified the setup options, click OK to return to the main Printer Properties dialog box, shown in Figure 18-4. You now can set printer details, discussed next.

Printer Details

The Printer Details dialog box lets you set administrative options for the printer, such as the time the printer is available and priorities. The dialog box is shown in Figure 18-6 and described next.

Available From and To

In the Available From and To fields, you can specify when the printer is available for use. Initially, the time is not limited. Note the following:

▰   Users can send jobs at any time, but they only print during the time specified.

▰   You can create several logical printer definitions for a physical printer, each with different print times to control who prints and when printing occurs.

▰   Set nighttime printing hours for users who print large documents that don't have priority requirements.

Separator File

A separator file is a page that prints before your document to separate it from any other documents that may be in the output tray of a printer. Separator pages are vital on busy printers. Windows NT includes the four types of separator pages described next. To use one of the pages, simply type its name in the Separator File field.

- ▰ *DEFAULT.SEP* Works with PCL-compatible printers (Hewlett-Packard) and prints a page before each print job. You cannot modify this file.

- ▰ *PSLANMAN.SEP* This PostScript-compatible separator page prints a page before each print job. This page can be edited with a PostScript-compatible editor.

- ▰ *PCL.SEP* This editable version of DEFAULT.SEP switches printers to PCL printing.

- ▰ *PSCRIPT.SEP* This editable version of PSLANMAN.SEP switches to PostScript printing.

Print to Additional Ports

Use this option to specify other physical printers that can print jobs for the printer you are defining. This is known as printer *pooling*. All the physical printers in a pool must be the same type so the printer can divert jobs from one to the other and ensure that all jobs are printed the same way.

To create a pool, attach physical printers to the LPT or COM ports on the back of the computer, then select the ports in the Print to Additional Ports field of the Printer Details dialog box.

You also can make network printers part of the pool. Refer to the "Printer Port Types" section earlier in this chapter for information on configuring network ports.

Priority

Printers with higher priority get to send their documents to the physical printer before printers with lower priority. When you create two or more printers that are serviced by one physical printer, you can control which printer gets higher priority by setting values in the Priority field. Typically, you might give the printer you use for local printing a higher priority than the printer used by network users.

A priority of 1 is the lowest priority and a priority of 99 is the highest priority. If you have two printers, setting one to a priority of 2 is sufficient to give it priority over a printer set to 1.

Print Processor

Change this option only if requested to do so by a specific application.

Default Datatype

Change this option only if requested to do so by a specific application.

Print Directly to Ports

Selecting this option disables the spooler function for the printer. When a document is *spooled*, it is first stored on disk, then sent to the printer. This allows you to resume work almost immediately. To print directly to the printer, disable this option.

Setting the Timeout Option

You can specify the amount of time the Print Manager continues to retry access to a printer that is not responding by clicking the Settings button on the Printer Properties dialog box pictured in Figure 18-4. The following dialog box appears:

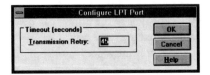

If is often necessary to increase the Transmission Retry option when printing large documents, graphics, or PostScript files that fill the printer's buffer and prevent Windows NT from sending more information. Windows NT continues to retry sending to the printer, but if the buffer depletes slowly, Windows NT assumes the printer is stalled and displays an error message. You can continue printing in a few seconds by responding to the error message, but to prevent the error message from appearing in the first place, increase the transmissions retry setting.

DEFINING PRINT JOBS AND FORMS

Print jobs are settings that you assign to a printer to control the following:

- ☑ The form to use
- ☑ Orientation (either portrait or landscape)
- ☑ Number of copies
- ☑ The graphics resolution
- ☑ Halftone settings for color to black-and-white conversions

Defining Print Job Settings

To define print job information, click the Job Defaults button on the Printer Details dialog box shown in Figure 18-6. The Document Properties dialog box appears as shown in Figure 18-7.

Choose one of the forms in the Form drop-down list box. You can create your own form by following the instructions in the next section, "Defining Forms." Choose the orientation and number of copies to print.

Click the Options button to define Advanced settings such as the graphics resolution and optimization methods. Click the Help button for information on these options. Click the Halftone button to specify the halftone settings for color to black-and-white conversion. Click the Help button here also to get more information.

Defining Forms

Windows NT comes with a set of default forms, but you can create your own by choosing the Forms option on the Printer menu. The Forms dialog box appears as shown in Figure 18-8.

From this dialog box, you can choose a form in the top list box to view its settings in the Form Description field.

Every form has a name and a paper size. Margin settings are optional. To create a new form, highlight a form that closely matches its settings, then change the name and optionally change the paper size and margins. Click Add to create the new form and add it to the list.

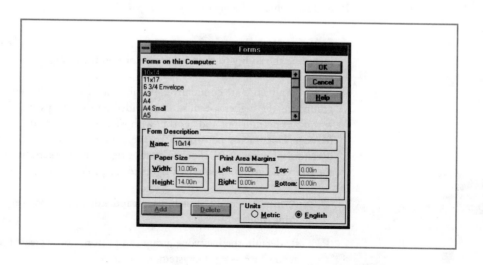

| Note | You can only delete forms you create. |

Once you've defined forms, you can select them when creating new printers or changing the properties of existing printers. Notice the Forms options for printer setup in Figure 18-5 and for job configuration in Figure 18-7.

PRINTER SECURITY OPTIONS

Security permissions provide a way to control who gets to use printers, who manages print jobs, and who controls permissions of printers. Permissions are typically assigned by the Administrator or a user with the Full Control permission. The printer permissions you can assign in the Print Manager are described next. You assign these permissions by choosing Permissions on the Print Manager Security menu.

No Access Permission   Blocks all access to the printer, except to members of the Administrator group.

Print Permission   This permission lets users send print jobs to the printer. Users can control—pause, resume, restart, and delete—their own print jobs but not the print jobs of other users. These permissions are referred to as the *Creator Owner* permissions.

Manage Documents Permission   This permission allows users to control the settings of documents, as well as to pause, resume, restart, delete, and rearrange the order of documents in the queue.

Full Control Permission   This permission gives users full control over the printer, including the ability to change permissions on the printer.

Permissions are cumulative, meaning that a user with membership in two or more groups has the highest permission provided by the groups. So if you belong to a group with Print permissions and another with Manage Documents permissions, you have the Manage Documents permission to the printer. However, the No Access permission overrides all other permissions. To grant rights to only specific users or groups, remove the Everyone group, then assign rights to the groups you want. Also note the following:

- Permissions apply to each printer individually, not to every printer listed in the Print Manager.

- By default, the Everyone group can print to newly created printers. That means anyone accessing the system, either locally or over the network, can print.

- Users can control the documents they send to a printer, but not the documents of other users unless they have the Manage Documents or Full Control permission.

- The Full Control permission is required to change permissions on a printer.

Managing Permissions

You change the permissions of a printer by first selecting the printer, then choosing the Permissions option on the Security menu. The dialog box in Figure 18-9 appears.

The name of the selected printer appears at the top along with the name of the person who created it (the owner). The Name field lists the current groups that have permissions to the printer. By default, the groups listed in Figure 18-9 are granted permissions to printers. You can remove the Everyone group to prevent all users from accessing the printer. The Creator Owner is any user who sends a document to the printer. The permissions are listed to the right of each group name.

You can change the permission of any user or group listed in the Name field by clicking the name, then selecting a new permission in the Type of Access field. To remove a user or group from the list, click its name, then click the Remove button. To add a new group, click the Add button and refer to the next section.

Adding a New User or Group

Click the Add button on the Printer Permissions dialog box to add a new user or group. The dialog box in Figure 18-10 appears.

FIGURE 18-9

Managing printer permissions

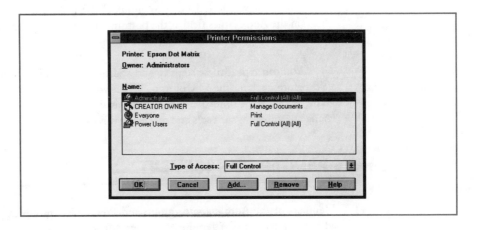

FIGURE 18-10

Adding a new user or group

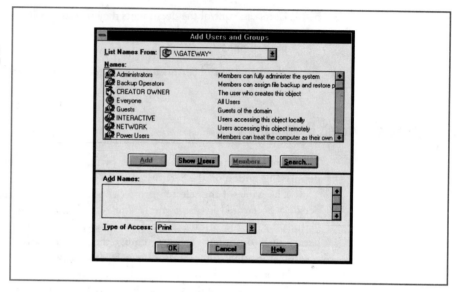

From this dialog box, you can do the following:

- Choose a different domain in the List Names From field if you are connected to a Windows NT Advanced Server network.

- Click the Search button to search for a user or group in a domain.

- Choose a user or group to add in the Names field. Click the Show Users button to display users.

- Highlight a group and click Members to see the users who belong to the group.

- Once you've selected a user or group, click the Add button. The name appears in the Add Names field at the bottom. You can then change the permission in the Type of Access field.

You can repeat these steps to add additional users and groups to the Add Names field before clicking the OK button. When you click OK the names are added to the Name list on the Printer Permissions box as shown in Figure 18-9. Note that you can change permissions for users and groups in this dialog box as well.

REMOTE PRINTER MANAGEMENT

Members of the Administrator group and Power User group can install, remove, and administer printers on remote Windows NT servers. Anyone with the Full Control permission on the remote printer also can perform these management tasks.

Choose the Server View option on the Printer menu to select the computer where the physical printers you want to manage are attached. A dialog box similar to the one in Figure 18-11 appears.

When you select a computer and click the OK button, a new window appears in the Print Manager as shown in Figure 18-12.

From this window, you can perform many of the management functions discussed in previous parts of this chapter, such as choosing Create Printer to install a new printer, choosing Remove Printer to remove a selected printer, and choosing Properties to change the properties of the selected printer.

AUDITING PRINTERS

You audit printers to track events and usage. The information is stored in a log that you can view using the Event Editor as discussed in Chapter 21. You must also enable auditing in the User Manager as discussed in Chapter 21. The events you can audit are described here:

- Document printing
- Changes made to the settings of documents
- Pausing, restarting, deleting, and arranging documents
- Sharing printers
- Changing printer properties and permissions
- Deleting a printer

To set up auditing, choose Auditing from the Security menu in the Print Manager. The dialog box in Figure 18-13 appears.

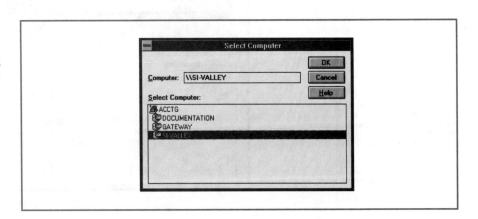

FIGURE 18-11

Managing remote printers

FIGURE 18-12

A print server management window

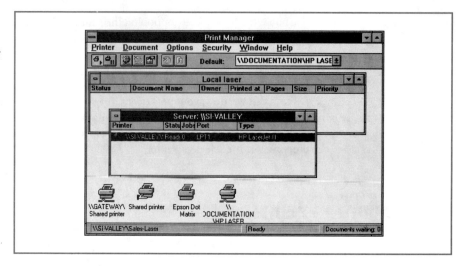

You choose the name of a user or group to audit in the Name field, then choose the type of auditing to perform in the Events to Audit field. To add users or groups to the Name field, click the Add button. You'll see a dialog box similar to the one in Figure 18-10. Refer to the "Adding a New User or Group" section earlier in this chapter for instructions on how to use the Add Users and Groups dialog box.

Print events are recorded as either a completion or failure to print a document. You can record the success or failure of an event by clicking the appropriate check box next to the event.

FIGURE 18-13

Setting up printer auditing

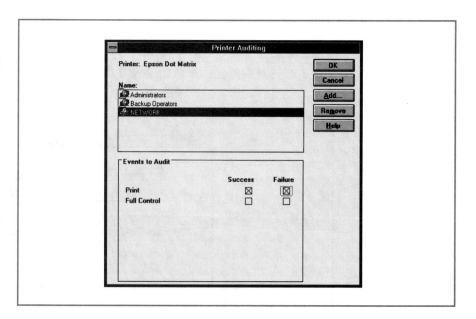

Full Control events are all the management functions described above except printing documents.

USING POSTSCRIPT PRINTERS AND DRIVERS

The graphical nature of Windows NT provides an ideal environment for graphical applications and documents. It's easy to create graphics in drawing, painting, spreadsheet, and other applications, then insert them into documents for in-house or commercial publication. To get the highest quality printout, you must have access to a laser printer, preferably one that supports PostScript. While Windows NT provides TrueType fonts that print with excellent results on non-PostScript printers, PostScript is still a requirement for high-quality graphics. This section discusses the installation and use of PostScript printers and drivers.

Note that you can install and use a PostScript driver even if you don't have a PostScript printer. The reason for this is important. Many organizations that need high-quality (1200 dots-per-inch or better) output rely on service bureaus to produce this output. By installing a PostScript driver on your system, you can produce "print files" that service bureaus can use to print your documents on their high-resolution PostScript printers. You can still use a low-quality (300 dots-per-inch) laser printer for in-house use and rough drafts, but when you're ready to print the files, you switch to the PostScript driver and produce the PostScript print files that the service bureau can use.

Many desktop computers now have sophisticated video display equipment that supports thousands or millions of colors at extremely high resolution. Drawing and painting applications are available that use this equipment and provide a way to work with lifelike, full-color images. If these images are destined for full-color brochures, magazines, or other production jobs, you'll need special equipment to separate colors and produce output. Once again, the service bureau provides the equipment you need, but you'll need to install PostScript drivers in most cases to create and store the images destined for the service bureau. Many graphics applications now produce color separations of their own, but for high-resolution output, you'll still need to produce print files that you can take to service bureaus.

PostScript

PostScript is a command language created by Adobe Systems that provides a way to describe how graphics and text are printed on a PostScript-compatible printer (or displayed on a PostScript-compatible display device). When using PostScript illustration packages such as Adobe Illustrator, CorelDRAW, or Micrografx Designer, you draw images on the screen in the normal way. While those images are displayed using the pixels of your screen, in the background the application creates a PostScript text file that contains a series of commands that let you print the file at any time, on any PostScript-compatible printer, and at the highest resolution of that printer. This last point, *resolution independence*, is an important feature of PostScript.

As mentioned, you can create PostScript files even if you don't have a PostScript printer. You install the PostScript driver for the output device you plan to use (call your service bureau for the exact specifications). You then print the image to a file and take that file to the service bureau.

PostScript defines fonts on a page and any graphics that go with those fonts, such as boxes that surround text, underlines, or bold blocks in headers and footers. You could call this type of PostScript file *normal* because it does not contain special Encapsulated PostScript (discussed in a moment) graphics that might be imported from another application. Printing a PostScript file on a PostScript printer is not much different from printing any other file. You don't need to be concerned with the PostScript commands since the printer handles everything in the background.

A PostScript print file can be listed like any text file when you want to view the commands within. The file starts off with a *header* that provides information about what is in the file and the application used to create it. The header also contains the file's creation date, the fonts used, and any fonts needed, as well as the paper size and number of pages. Header information sets up the printer for the print job and is necessary if you're sending files to a shared network printer that may be in another print mode from a previous job. Following the header is the actual imaging information. PostScript experts may want to change this information to make fine adjustments in a PostScript file, but in most cases, if you need to make changes it's best to go back to the original application to edit and reproduce the file.

Encapsulated PostScript Files

An *Encapsulated* PostScript (EPS) file is a special version of a PostScript file that supports graphics. It was developed by Altsys, a company that developed an illustration program called Freehand for Aldus. The EPS file format is unique in that it contains the PostScript commands to print graphics, and a displayable bitmap of the graphic. When the EPS file is pasted into a document, the bitmap displays the image, but the PostScript information is used to print it. On PCs, the bitmapped image is usually in the TIFF format and is embedded in the EPS file.

The EPS format is supported by most illustration packages such as CorelDRAW, Micrografx Designer, and others. You create an EPS file by *exporting* it to a separate file with the .EPS extension. For example, the Export command in Micrografx Designer is a file conversion utility that lets you save images in a number of formats. Besides PCX, TIFF, and several others, there are two EPS formats, one with the TIFF preview image and one without. Page layout programs such as Aldus PageMaker and Ventura Publisher have *importing* options used to paste EPS files into documents. Note that export and import provide the same functionality as copy and paste, but are quite different since a separate file is created during an export.

The TIFF preview bitmap is optional, but recommended if you are pasting a number of graphics into a document. As you scroll through the document, you'll be able to see what the image looks like and visually scale and crop it if necessary. In addition, the TIFF format displays the graphic image quickly. The alternative is that the image simply displays as a gray block that approximates the size of the image.

Note

Some high-resolution output devices don't handle EPS files well. Graphic images are rotated and may be too long to fit on the output film. In this case, save your documents to a print file.

As always, if you plan to send your files to an outside service, check with them to determine the compatibility of your PostScript files. It's best to create some test files in advance and send them to the service bureau before starting full production on your documents and graphics.

Installing a PostScript Driver

Windows NT supports a wide range of PostScript printers. You can view the list by starting the Print Manager and choosing Create Printer from the Printer menu. Click the down arrow in the Driver field. The installation of the Linotronic Imagesetter 530-RIP driver is discussed in the following section.

During the installation of a PostScript printer driver, you click the Details button to change PostScript features. If the driver is already installed, select the printer, then choose Properties from the Printer menu to display the Printer Properties dialog box.

Note

If you plan to print to a file so you can take the output to a service bureau, choose File in the Print to field of the Printer Properties dialog box shown in Figure 18-4.

Next, click the Details button and when the Printer Details dialog box appears, click the Job Defaults button to display the Document Properties dialog box. Finally, click the Options button to display the Advanced Document Properties dialog box shown in Figure 18-14.

Set the specifications for the PostScript output on this dialog box. You might want to go through this information with a representative from your service bureau.

Print To

Choose Printer if your system is directly connected to the physical printer or you plan to print to a print file. Choose Encapsulated PostScript File to create an EPS file that you

FIGURE 18-14

The Advanced Document
Properties dialog box

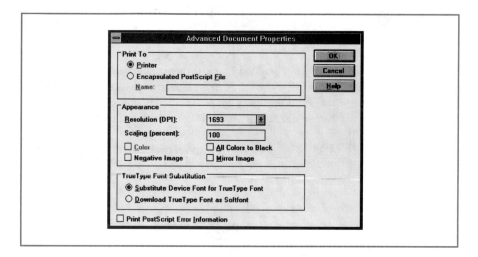

can insert in another document or take to a service bureau. Type the name for the EPS file in the Name field.

Appearance

There are several options in the Appearance box. Each is explained next.

Resolution   Choose the resolution in dots per inch for the printer. In most cases, there is only one choice because it is automatically set by the PostScript device.

Scaling   Type in the percentage you want to scale (shrink or grow) the document.

Color   If the printer supports color, the Color option will be available. Enable it to print the image in color.

All Color to Black   Choose All Colors to Black only in rare cases where you don't mind losing gray-scales or when outputting black-and-white images.

Negative Image   Choose Negative Image to reverse the output. Blacks print white and whites print black.

Mirror Image   Choose Mirror Image to flip the output horizontally.

TrueType Fonts

If your document has TrueType fonts, you can specify whether the PostScript device substitutes its own fonts for TrueType fonts, or whether TrueType font information is downloaded with the document. If you have a specific TrueType font and you don't want it substituted, select the Download TrueType Font as Softfont option. Make sure the output device support this feature, however.

Print PostScript Error Information

Enable this check box to debug printer problems. Errors are then printed as part of the document to help you determine the source of problems.

FONTS

Windows contains an assortment of fonts for the screen and for printers that are designed to provide *WYSIWYG* (What You See Is What You Get) output. Ideally, the text you see on your screen should look as close as possible to the way it appears when printed. This section describes how to install new fonts or remove fonts from memory using the Fonts utility in the Control Panel. You remove fonts you don't need to free up memory or disk space. This section of the chapter also discusses TrueType fonts.

All displays and most printers produce characters and images using a pattern of tiny dots. How characters are formed depends upon the font technology in use, as described next.

Screen Fonts

Screen fonts—often called *raster fonts*—are bitmapped fonts. The font file contains a bitmapped image of each character in each size provided by the file. Bitmapped files display characters quickly on the screen because the characters are already formed; the disadvantage to this is that font files can be relatively large in size. Because including every font size possible would mean font files of impossible length, manufacturers make a limited number of font sizes available. The Windows screen fonts include the point sizes 8, 10, 12, 14, 18, and 24.

Choosing a size outside the normal range of a screen font can result in poor quality. The Windows NT screen fonts can only be sized in even multiples, and the larger the font size, the more jagged characters become. Only the original font sizes in the font file are designed with precision. Bold and italic are usually not designed into the screen font set. Instead, bits are simply added to the font to give it the appearance of bold or italic.

There are six sets of raster fonts in Windows NT as listed here:

- *Courier* A monospaced (fixed-width) font sized from 8 to 15 points for EGA resolution and from 10 to 15 points for other resolutions.

- *MS Serif* A proportionally spaced font with serifs similar to Times Roman. A serif is a short line or ornament added to the top or bottom of a character.

- *MS Sans Serif* A proportionally spaced font without serifs, similar to Helvetica.

- *Symbol* A symbol font.

- *Small* A small font used to display page previews or other small text.

- *Special EGA Fonts* Two special raster fonts, Arial and Times, are included for EGA displays. The fonts are both 8 and 10 points in size.

Each typeface includes a set of files to match the resolution of most displays. Double-click the Fonts utility in the Control Panel to see a list of these fonts. The font names include the range of sizes available for the font.

Printer Fonts

A *printer font* is a bitmapped font that has been hard-coded into a printer. Most printers include a built-in set of bitmapped fonts. Windows displays the names of these fonts in the Fonts dialog box when the correct printer driver is installed. It then uses a closely matching screen font to depict the printer font on the screen. Some printers come with a set of screen fonts you copy to your computer to display when working with the printer fonts. They more accurately depict the font than do the screen fonts that Windows uses. These are installed using the Fonts utility.

Printer fonts are displayed in font lists next to a printer icon. When assigning fonts to characters in an application such as Write, you can often produce excellent printouts by choosing these printer fonts; however, they are often limited in scalability.

Not all printer fonts are hard-wired into the printer. Some are available on optional plug-in *cartridges* or by downloading a font definition file from your computer into the printer's memory.

Outline Fonts

Outline fonts are drawn by the computer or the printer itself, based on a mathematical description of each character. Such fonts are referred to as *scalable* fonts, because you can scale them to any size without loss of resolution. Outline font files take up much less memory and disk space than bitmapped font files because they do not contain a representation of every character in every size. The only drawback is that each character must be drawn on the spot, which can slow performance. TrueType is one brand of outline font language; others include PostScript fonts and those from third-party suppliers, such as Bitstream's FaceLift.

Many users will be happy with the TrueType fonts supplied with Windows, but if you do page layout or production work for other people, PostScript is often a better choice. As mentioned, you can install a PostScript printer driver even if you don't have a PostScript printer to gain access to on-screen PostScript fonts, then create PostScript print files and send those files to service bureaus that have PostScript printers.

The WingDing font, shown in Figure 18-15, is a set of special symbols and characters. Use the Character Map utility to access these characters and paste them into your documents.

USING THE CONTROL PANEL FONTS UTILITY

Use the Fonts utility to view currently installed fonts, and to add or remove fonts. Windows installs all TrueType fonts and plotter fonts during setup. It installs only the bitmapped fonts appropriate for your screen resolution. As new TrueType fonts become available, you can use the Fonts utility to install them into your system. You also can install other bitmapped fonts just to have them available for use, although with TrueType, there is little need to do so.

When Windows NT uses a font, it takes up memory. You can use the Fonts utility to remove a font you don't need.

Viewing Fonts

You can use the Fonts utility to browse through fonts. Open the Control Panel and double-click the Fonts icon. When the Fonts dialog box opens, it appears as shown in Figure 18-16.

The Installed Fonts field displays a list of fonts currently in use by Windows. Click on any font to display it in the window. Also notice that the size of the font file on disk is displayed at the bottom of the dialog box.

Installing Fonts

To add fonts, click the Add button to open the Add Fonts dialog box shown in Figure 18-17. Initially, the dialog box may not list any files to add. You first select the floppy disk or hard

FIGURE 18-15

The WingDing font

CRC

drive directory where the font files are located. To install new fonts from a floppy disk, select drive A or B in the Drives list box. To install fonts already on disk, choose a drive, and then choose a directory in the Directories list box. The Fonts utility scans the disk for available font files, and then displays them in the List of Fonts field.

Note | Look in the \WINNT\SYSTEM32 directory for additional font files.

Click one or more font files that you wish to install. Hold the CTRL key and click to select multiple font files, or click the Select All button to select all the fonts.

FIGURE 18-16

The Fonts utility

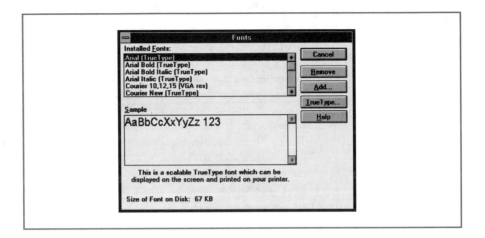

The Copy Fonts to Windows Directory is an important option. If the fonts are already on your hard drive in another directory, you should disable this option, otherwise a duplicate copy of the font is made in the Windows NT directory. If you disable the option, Windows NT will find the fonts in their original directory. If the files are on a floppy disk, make sure this option is enabled. Click OK to install the fonts.

TrueType Settings

From the Fonts dialog box, click the TrueType button, then mark the Show Only TrueType Fonts in Applications option if you only use TrueType fonts, and no other fonts. Usually this is a good idea since it reduces the list of fonts in dialog boxes and frees

FIGURE 18-17

Installing new fonts

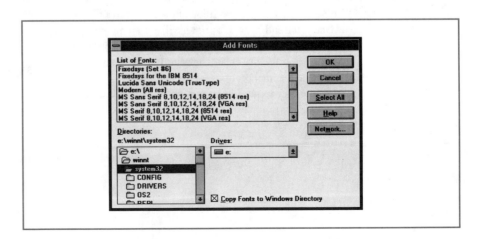

memory. Don't enable this option if you've installed special bitmapped character sets or are using PostScript fonts.

TrueType provides every user with scalable WYSIWYG fonts and *document compatibility*. Users can now interchange documents, knowing the fonts they use will work on another user's system and printer.

In TrueType, every straight line and curve is mathematically defined. TrueType then resizes the characters over a wide range with little loss of resolution. It then rasterizes the characters for display on the bitmapped display. *Rasterizing* is the process of converting the outline to a bitmapped image. Fonts are also rasterized when sent to a printer. The TrueType rasterizer adds additional instructions, called *hints*, which improve the screen or printed image by removing jagged edges and smoothing curves. It is this process that makes TrueType superior to other outline fonts. The result is true WYSIWYG because TrueType creates a good match between the fonts it creates onscreen and those it sends to the printer. If the printer is a laser printer or high-resolution typesetter, the printout will be improved even further. The TrueType rasterizer is built directly into the Windows NT interface, making the whole display and print process more efficient. Fonts are cached in memory.

The print driver provides TrueType with the specifications for rasterizing, based on the graphics resolution of the printer. Unlike PostScript, which rasterizes at the printer, TrueType rasterizing takes place in your computer. A bitmapped image is then sent to the printer. Therefore, any bitmapped printer (and almost all printers are) can print TrueType images.

If you send files to service bureaus, use TrueType fonts with caution. First determine whether the service bureau supports TrueType, and whether you can mix TrueType fonts and PostScript data. For best results, you should probably disable TrueType and use only PostScript when creating these files.

Note

Keep in mind that TrueType defines fonts only. PostScript defines both fonts and vector graphics, so PostScript is superior if you are working with mixed documents.

When TrueType is output to a PostScript device, it rasterizes fonts into bitmapped types that match the resolution of the printer. If a file contains both TrueType and PostScript data, you'll end up with a print file that has a mixture of bitmapped data created by TrueType and outline font and graphics commands for PostScript. Such a file may not print correctly if the driver used to create the print file (set at say 300 dpi) is different than the printer used to create the final printout (say 1200 dpi). The TrueType fonts may appear incorrectly sized because they've already been rasterized for 300 dpi. The PostScript data will size correctly because it is rasterized at the printer, based on that printer's resolution.

Inside

- Using the Disk Administrator

- Deleting Volumes and Volume Sets

& Out

CHAPTER 19

Disk Management

When you first install Windows NT, you can reconfigure the disks in your system or use the existing disk configuration. For example, you could reformat a system's entire disk drive to use the Windows NT native file system (NTFS). Alternatively, you could keep an existing DOS partition and install Windows NT on another partition or even on the same partition as DOS. If multiple operating systems are installed, a screen appears when the system boots that lets you select the operating system you want to start.

After Windows NT installation, you can expand the disk storage system in several ways at any time. Typically, you'll add a new hard drive. At that time, you start the Windows NT Disk Administrator utility and use it to prepare the new drive. Figure 19-1 shows a typical Disk Administrator window. Directly under the menu bar is a graphical illustration of the drives and how they are configured. The blocks to the right of the drive label illustrate its partition layout, as discussed in a moment.

FIGURE 19-1

The Disk Administrator
window

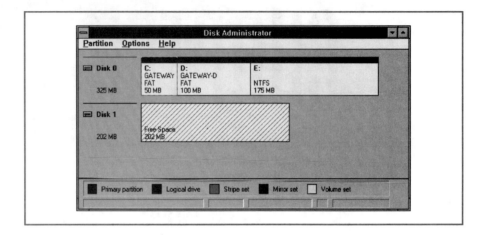

In Figure 19-1, Disk 0 was the original system drive on which DOS (FAT) was already installed on drives C and D. Drive E was created during the Windows NT installation process. Disk 1 is a new 202MB drive that has just been added to the system. This chapter will illustrate the partitioning and formatting steps for this new drive.

Before you get started, familiarize yourself with some disk terminology.

Disk   A disk is a physical storage device that you can partition and format into drives. Don't confuse physical disks with drives. Drives are partitions of a disk that are assigned letters such as C, D, E, and so on. The first disk in the system is disk 0. Other disks are numbered sequentially. The Disk Administrator shows disks as follows:

Disk 0

Free Space   Free space is any unused disk space that you can partition and format into drives. It appears in the Disk Administrator, as shown here:

When you install a new disk and restart Windows NT, the disk appears as free space in the Disk Administrator until you partition and format it.

Partition   Before you can format and store files on a disk, you must partition and assign drive letters to the disk. Partitions can encompass the entire disk space, or you can create multiple partitions on a single disk. Each partition can hold a different operating system if necessary. In the following illustration, a 325MB disk is divided into three partitions, which are assigned the drive letters C, D, and E. Drives C and D are formatted to the DOS FAT file system and drive E is formatted to the Windows NT file system (NTFS).

Primary and Extended Partitions Disks can have a maximum of four partitions, one of which can be an extended partition. Partitions other than the extended partition are called primary partitions. An extended partition can be subdivided into logical drives. In the following illustration, drive G is a primary partition and drives H, I, and J are subdivisions of an extended partition.

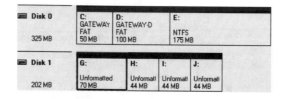

Note In this example, the drive letter F was previously assigned to a CD-ROM drive before the new hard disk was installed and partitioned, so the drive letter does not appear in the Disk Administrator.

System Partition A system partition is a primary partition that is marked as the *active* startup partition.

Boot Partition A boot partition holds the Windows NT operating system files. The boot partition and system partition can be the same. In addition, the boot partition can be formatted for the NTFS, FAT, or HPFS file system.

Volumes A volume is a disk storage area composed of one or more partitions and referred to with a drive letter. There can be 24 hard disk volumes labeled C through Z. Drive letters A and B are reserved for floppy disk drives.

Volume Sets Volumes can span multiple partitions. When they do, they are called *volume sets*. You typically create volume sets to expand the size of an existing volume, or to improve performance in some cases by distributing reads and writes among drives. In the rare case that you run out of drive letters, the only way to add new disk storage is to make it part of an existing volume set. In the following illustration, the entire space on Disk 1 is added to the existing G volume. Drive G expands from its original size of 75MB to 277MB.

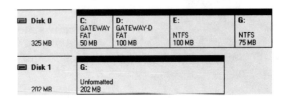

A typical reason for creating volume sets on some operating systems is to store large database files. However, doing so on a Windows NT system is not advised because you can't mirror or duplex the spanned volumes under. If one partition in the volume set fails, the entire database would be unusable, assuming it is spread over several drives. To store large databases, use Windows NT Advanced Server, which provides disk mirroring, duplexing, and RAID level 5.

When you install a new disk, all of its disk space is free. You then partition the disk and format it to either FAT, HPFS, or NTFS. Here are some additional things to note about disks under Windows NT:

☑ Windows NT and MS-DOS can share the same partition, but the partition must be formatted as a File Allocation Table (FAT) drive.

☑ The first active partition is drive 0. Windows NT starts from this drive.

☑ After partitioning disks in the Disk Administrator, you need to restart Windows NT, then format the partitions by starting the Command Prompt and using the FORMAT command.

About RISC-Based Computers

Partitions on RISC-based computers are set up using the configuration programs supplied by the manufacturer:

☑ They are not marked active.

☑ The system partition must be formatted for the FAT file system.

☑ The system partition can never be part of a stripe set or volume set.

USING THE DISK ADMINISTRATOR

You start the Disk Administrator by double-clicking its icon in the Administrative Tools group of the Program Manager. You can also type **START WINDISK** in a Command Prompt window. Part of the disk configuration procedure is to format newly created partitions using the FORMAT command in a Command Prompt window, so you might prefer to start the procedure in the Command Prompt.

You can make any changes you want in the Disk Administrator, but those changes do not take effect until you attempt to exit the Disk Administrator. You are then asked to confirm the changes. At that point, Windows NT shuts down and restarts. Upon restarting, you format the new partitions. You can choose to exit the Disk Administrator without making any of the changes you specified.

Caution | Use care when changing existing partitions. Changing a partition's size or deleting a partition results in irreversible loss of data.

Customizing the Interface

Before you get started, you might want to customize the interface. You can do all of these things with options on the Options menu:

  Choose Status Bar to toggle the status bar on or off.

Choose Legend to toggle the color legend at the bottom of the screen on or off.

Choose Colors and Patterns to change the colors and patterns that designate each partition in a drive. The procedure is simple. Pick an element that you want to change from the drop-down list box of the dialog box that appears, then pick a new color and pattern.

Choose Region Display to change the relative sizes used in drive bars to display partitions. You first choose the disk you want to change from the For Disk field. In the Region Size field, choose either to display relative sizes, equal sizes, or Disk Administrator defaults.

Note | Leave the Status Bar on. As you work with the Disk Administrator, it displays important information about disks and partitions.

Creating New Primary Partitions

After installing a new drive and restarting Windows NT, you start the Disk Administrator to partition the disk. A message appears to inform you that the Disk Administrator has detected a new drive. When the Disk Administrator screen opens, you see the disk listed as free space, similar to Disk 1 in Figure 19-1.

If Windows NT is the only operating system you plan to run, keep things simple by creating one partition per drive and format the partitions for NTFS to get the best performance. To install other operating systems, partition disks to create space for those operating systems. It's also possible to format a partition with the MS-DOS FAT file system and store Windows NT files on that partition. However, this arrangement is typically used only when a FAT partition already exists.

To create a new partition on a disk with free space, follow these steps:

1. Click the free space area with the mouse pointer. The free space is outlined with a bold line.

2. Choose the Create option on the Partition menu. The following dialog box appears.

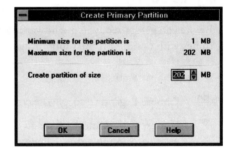

The maximum amount of free space is listed in the scaling box. If you click OK, the entire free space is used for a partition. You can further divide the free space into subpartitions by reducing this number. Any space you don't select is left as available free space that you can assign to other partitions.

3. Change the partition size or accept the default and click the OK button.

The new partition appears as an unformatted drive with a color coding that indicates it is a primary drive.

Drive Letters

The new partition is given the next available drive letter but you can change that drive letter by clicking the partition and choosing Drive Letter on the Partition menu. The following dialog box appears:

You can choose a higher drive letter. Lower drive letters are not accessible unless you reassign the letter on a lower drive to a higher letter. Drive letters A and B are reserved for floppy drives. If you run out of drive letters, you'll need to make any new disk space part of an existing volume.

Caution

Don't change the letter of a drive referenced by programs and batch files unless you also change those references. For example, if your backup program is set to back up drive E and you change the letter of drive E to F, the backup won't work. Also, program startup icons in the Program Manager refer to specific drives. Those icons won't start programs if you change drive letters for the programs they start.

Before you start the Disk Administrator for the first time, drive letters are assigned using the MS-DOS naming rules. The first primary partition on the first drive is assigned the letter C. The next primary partition is assigned the letter D, and so on. After all the primary partitions are assigned, logical drives in extended partitions are assigned. This presents an interesting arrangement on multiple drive systems, as shown here:

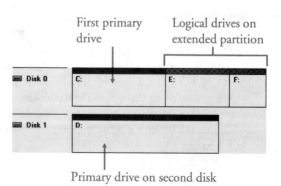

Note that letter C is assigned to the first primary partition on Disk 0 and letter D is assigned to the first primary partition on Disk 1. Letter E is then assigned to the first logical drive, back on Disk 0. Once you start the Disk Administrator for the first time, the arrangement of drives can be changed and made permanent. In other words, the MS-DOS rules are no longer used when you add new drives. Any drive assignments you make become static once you've run the Disk Administrator.

Creating Extended Partitions

Every disk can have one extended partition, which you can subdivide into multiple logical drivers. For example, you might have primary partitions with drive letters C, D, and E. A fourth extended partition could then be subdivided into drives F, G, H, and so on.

To create an extended partition, follow these steps:

1. Select a block of free disk space, then choose Create Extended from the Partition menu. The Create Extended Partition dialog box appears with the minimum and maximum partition sizes listed.

2. In the scaling box, type or set the size of the extended partition, then choose OK.

3. Subdivide the partition into logical drives. First select the extended partition, then choose Create from the Partition menu.

    The Create Logical Drive dialog box appears. On this box, you can specify a size for each logical drive within the extended partition.

4. In the scaling box, type or set the size you want for the first logical drive and click OK.

5. Repeat step 4 for each logical drive.

Formatting Partitions

Once you've created primary partitions and logical drives, you need to format those partitions. To do so, you'll need to exit the Disk Administrator, then close down and restart Windows NT. When you exit the Disk Administrator, a message box appears asking if you're sure you want to make the changes you've made. Choose Yes if you're sure.

Once Windows NT restarts, double-click the Command Prompt icon. When the Command Prompt window appears, you can execute the FORMAT command. Note the following:

☑ Type **FORMAT /?** to view help information for the FORMAT command (most options are used when formatting floppy disks).

◪   Type **FORMAT** followed by the drive letter of the partition you want to format. For example, to format drive G, you would type the following:

FORMAT G:

◪   Specify the type of file system you want to format the partition to as shown here:

FORMAT G: /FS:*filesystem*

Replace *filesystem* with either FAT, HPFS, or NTFS.

Once the volume is formatted, you can type **EXIT** to return to Windows NT and view the status of the newly formatted disk in the Disk Administrator.

Expanding Volumes

When you add a new drive, you can partition it and add the space in the partition to an existing drive. The partition appears with the same drive letter as the volume it was added to. Note the following:

◪   Only volumes formatted for NTFS can be extended.

◪   You cannot extend the partition containing Windows NT system files.

◪   When files are stored on volume sets, the first partition in the volume is filled up, then the second, and so on.

◪   A volume set can contain a maximum of 32 disks.

◪   You can free up drive letters by deleting existing partitions and making the space part of a volume set.

◪   There is some improvement in performance as disk reads and writes are spread out over multiple disks and controllers. This is most visible on SCSI systems since disks can perform most disk activities on their own without assistance from the system's processor.

In the following illustration, drive F on Disk 0 is expanded by adding the total disk space on Disk 1 to it:

Disk 0	C:	D:	F:
	GATEWAY		DB-VOLUME
	FAT	NTFS	NTFS
325 MB	50 MB	100 MB	175 MB

Disk 1	F:
	DB-VOLUME
	NTFS
202 MB	202 MB

Note that both partitions get the same drive letter and volume label. The color code above each partition also indicates that it is part of a volume set.

To create a volume set, follow these steps:

1. Select the partitions for the volume set. Hold down the CTRL key and click each partition. A dark line appears around each partition you select.

2. Choose Create Volume Set from the Partition menu. A dialog box similar to this one appears:

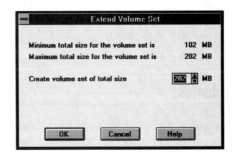

It displays the minimum and maximum sizes for the volume set. Note that the minimum size is 1MB greater than the original volume size.

If disks are selected and you choose to use less than the maximum size, the Disk Administrator allocates partition space equally over the selected drives.

3. Choose the OK button to create the volume sets.

DELETING VOLUMES AND VOLUME SETS

You can delete most partitions and volume sets by first selecting the partition you want to delete, and then choosing Delete from the Partition menu. Note the following:

☑   You cannot delete the partition containing Windows NT system files.

☑   Back up all data before deleting a partition. Data is permanently removed from deleted partitions.

☑   Clicking any partition in a volume set selects the entire volume set. You can only delete an entire volume set; you cannot delete individual partitions in it.

☑   Use caution when deleting on RISC-based computers. It's possible to delete the system partition that holds the Windows NT load files.

☑   For extended partitions, first delete all the logical drives in the partition, then delete the extended partition.

Inside

& Out

CHAPTER 20

Protecting the System

Windows NT provides a wide variety of methods for protecting your systems from data loss, power failures, and electrical line problems. Two of these methods, tape backup and fault tolerance, target the data stored on your hard drive. The other method uses a UPS (uninterruptable power supply) to protect the entire system. Of course, none of these methods will help much if you don't use them on a consistent basis. While the UPS and fault tolerance are fairly automatic, it does take time and patience to get them up and running. The tape backup system is a lot easier to use, but requires a daily effort on the part of the Administrator. This chapter describes and shows you how to use all three of these very important protection techniques for your computer system.

UPS INSTALLATION

Installing a UPS on your computer is a fairly simple task. The first step is to install the UPS hardware according to the instructions provided by the vendor. Make sure you get a UPS that supports some type of monitoring using the serial ports and that the detection scheme matches the one used by Windows NT. Otherwise, Windows NT will not detect a loss in power and the dwindling resources of the UPS. If Windows NT doesn't detect power loss, it will not shut the system down, which partially defeats the purpose of buying a UPS in the first place. (Of course, a UPS is always a good investment; monitoring just maximizes that investment.)

Once you do get the UPS installed, start Windows NT as the system administrator. You will need a copy of the UPS documentation for the setup. Windows NT needs to know how to interact with the UPS and what capabilities the UPS possesses. Double-click the UPS icon found in the Control Panel. You should see the UPS dialog box shown in Figure 20-1.

The first option that you must select is the "Uninterruptable Power Supply is installed on:" box. Select the correct serial port as well. You may choose among COM1, COM2, COM3, and COM4. Windows NT does not support a UPS that uses the mouse port for communication purposes.

Once you select a connection, you must tell Windows NT how to interact with your UPS. There are three different techniques you can use: power failure signal, low battery signal, and remote UPS shutdown. You may select any or all of the options, as described next.

FIGURE 20-1

The UPS installation log

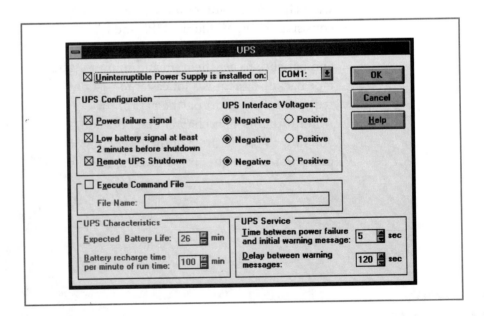

- *Power failure signal* The power failure signal appears at the clear to send (CTS) connection of the serial port. (The CTS signal appears on pin 5 of a DB25 connector or pin 8 of a DB9 connector.) It tells Windows NT that UPS shutdown is imminent. This means that Windows NT will not receive any warning about the power failure. A UPS that supports the low battery signal provides more advance notice to Windows NT. It provides a two-minute warning that Windows NT can use to warn users to get off the network.

- *Low battery signal* The low battery signal uses the data carrier detect (DCD) connection of the serial port. (The DCD signal appears at pin 8 of a DB25 connector or pin 1 of a DB9 connector.) The only connection from Windows NT to the UPS is the remote UPS shutdown. This allows Windows NT to tell the UPS to shut itself down, effectively turning the power switch of the computer off.

- *Remote UPS shutdown* The remote UPS shutdown signal appears on the data terminal ready (DTR) connection of the serial port. (The DTR signal appears at pin 20 of a DB25 connector or pin 4 of a DB9 connector.)

The UPS configuration section also asks you to provide an interface selection voltage for each of the UPS signals. Normally you check the UPS documentation for this information. It usually gets buried somewhere in the back of the manual. Providing Windows NT with this information might prove a little more difficult if your UPS vendor decided not to document the level of the voltages (or even what voltages the UPS supports). Calling technical support is the first step in this case. However, you may find that technical support isn't very helpful.

If you can't find the voltage in the manual or from technical support, there are a few ways you can test for the appropriate signals. The best method is to buy an RS-232 breakout box from a vendor such as Black Box Corporation (412-746-5530). These devices range in price from $39 to $250. They allow you to monitor all the signals between the UPS and Windows NT without interfering with the signal. Simply unplug your UPS, check which signal lines show activity, then mark the appropriate option in the dialog box. You can use this same method to check the remote UPS shutdown signal. Simply wait for Windows NT to send the signal over the DTR line of the RS-232 port and watch the reaction of the UPS.

Refer to the vendor manual to fill out the rest of the UPS dialog box. However, you may want to perform an actual test to provide a value for the Expected Battery Life field. Even though the vendor may provide you with an average battery life value, knowing the precise battery life for your UPS is much better. Provide the UPS with a full charge, then attach the load you expect to back up (computer, monitor, printer) and wait for it to run down. Make sure you enter a value at least two minutes less than the tested time. That way you'll have some battery life left when the UPS shuts down.

After you fill out the entire dialog box, click OK. Windows NT will ask if you want to start the UPS service. Click the Yes button. You will notice a delay as Windows NT checks for signals on the serial port. If you provided all the right answers, the UPS service will start and you will have power protection for your system.

UPS Maintenance and Troubleshooting

The UPS vendor should provide you with specific instructions for UPS maintenance. Unfortunately, these instructions often fall short of actually testing the UPS. In addition, they won't test the signal interchange between Windows NT and the UPS.

You will require a RS-232 breakout box to test your UPS. This allows you to monitor the signals between the computer and the UPS. If you don't check these signals, you can't make sure that the UPS actually works. While the UPS signal may sound and it will appear that everything works, there is no way you can know how well the UPS will perform. The following procedure shows you how to perform a complete test of the UPS:

1. Connect the breakout box between the end of the UPS serial port connector and the computer.

2. Start Windows NT. Make certain that the UPS service starts and that Windows NT is properly set up to monitor the UPS. Don't open any applications or data files. Choose a time when there are no users connected to the system.

3. Perform any vendor-specific UPS tests. This usually includes pressing a test button somewhere on the UPS. Vendor-specific routines check the UPS internal circuitry.

4. Unplug the UPS from the wall and start a timer. You should hear a change in frequency or some other audible cue as the UPS power runs down. (Most vendors supply some type of audio signal for their UPS.)

5. Monitor the RS-232 breakout box lights for the appropriate signals between the computer and the UPS. You should see some type of activity on the DTR if the UPS supports the remote UPS shutdown signal. The CTS line should light if the UPS supports the power failure signal. Check the DCD light if the UPS supports the low battery signal.

6. Windows NT should display warning messages telling you to shut down the computer as the UPS power runs down.

7. Make sure that Windows NT performs an automatic shutdown before the UPS stops working. If your UPS supports the remote power shutdown signal, it should automatically shut the system down after Windows NT shuts itself down. If not, the computer will continue to run until the UPS is out of power. Check the time interval between the Windows NT shutdown and UPS failure. You should see an interval of at least two minutes.

As you can see, the UPS test is very easy to perform. You don't have to perform this check very often; semiannually is more than sufficient to ensure that the UPS will continue to provide you with good service.

POWER SUPPLY PROBLEMS

Electrical power is rarely supplied as a smooth wave of energy. You can see this when lights flicker as a load is placed somewhere on the power line. Electrical connections are polluted with surges and spikes (transient energy). You can think of these surges and spikes as shotgun blasts of energy to the delicate components in your computer. Electronic equipment handles transient energy in unpredictable ways. Here are three likely scenarios:

- *Data corruption* Electrical disturbances can cause RAM memory to change states or can disturb signals traversing a network cable. This type of disturbance causes memory errors or system lockups that are often mistaken for software bugs.

- *Equipment failure* High levels of transient energy can cause permanent damage to equipment. While surge suppressors can protect attached equipment from this type of energy, they often divert the energy back into the electrical system where it can affect other equipment, as discussed in a moment.

- *Slow death* Repeated exposure to low-energy surges and noise can cause equipment to fail over time. Delicate chip circuits break down and the equipment fails for no apparent reason. Noise often "sneaks" through inadequate surge and noise suppressors.

Any service technician can tell you a number of stories about customers who bring equipment in for repair, only to find it works fine in the shop. Once the customer returns to the office, the problems resurface. Most likely, the supply of electrical power at the customer site is unstable. Technicians can test your electrical environment for these problems. In addition, adequate surge suppressors and line filters are also important. Some UPS devices completely separate computer equipment from the commercial power supply by providing clean and steady power from the battery supply at all times.

Grounding Problems

In recent years, engineers and technicians have pointed out a number of problems and misconceptions about power grounding methods and equipment design. Buildings have ground connections to earth that protect people from electric shock. If equipment is not properly grounded, a charge will follow the path of least resistance, possibly through a person, to earth.

This problem escalates when networks are installed. Consider that devices on networks are usually connected to different sources of power, which are isolated and separately grounded. When networks are attached, ground loops can form because the network cable can bridge the formerly isolated power sources together. Basically, each electrical system transformer has its own characteristics and grounding that should be isolated from other transformers. When separate transformers are joined by a network connection, transient energy seeks equilibrium by flowing from ground to ground, and consequently through computer systems attached to the cables.

To solve such problems, it is important to keep equipment on one power source isolated from equipment on another power source. On large networks, this can be a problem. Networks often link distant power sources, any of which can introduce electrical problems into the network.

One solution is to connect the entire network to one central power supply, but this is usually impractical on large networks. To get around the problem, you can set up surge suppression equipment at the feed to the electrical panel to catch all surges before they get into the building. Additionally, you can place power conditioning equipment and UPS devices at workstations to provide a steady source of power.

When installing large networks in which equipment is attached to different power sources, you can avoid ground loops by using nonconducting fiber optic cable to interconnect network segments attached to different power supplies. This keeps each network segment isolated to its own power source and lets you more easily control grounding and noise problems. If fiber optic links are prohibitive, then you should install adequate transient protection equipment between the network links.

| Note |

The most important point is to use surge suppression equipment that can absorb surges, rather than divert those surges to ground.

TAPE BACKUP METHODS

Creating a backup of the data on your drive is the most important way you can protect it. It surpasses anything else you can do to ensure the data you created today will still be available tomorrow, especially if you take those backups off-site to protect them against fire and theft.

Tape Drive Installation

The first step in creating a backup is to get the backup software installed and configured. To install the software, open the Windows NT Setup utility in the Main folder. You should see a dialog box containing the current video adapter, mouse, and keyboard selections. Select the Add/Remove Tape Devices option on the Options menu. The following dialog box appears:

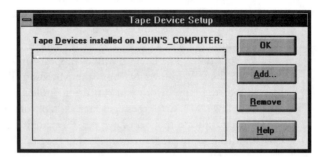

The four buttons are fairly self-explanatory. Press the Remove button to discontinue using a tape device. The OK button accepts any changes you make while the Help button provides information about tape drive installation. Pressing the Add button displays the dialog box shown here:

This screen has the drop-down box displayed to show the drives you can select directly. Most of the drives are SCSI compatible. The one non-SCSI drive selection allows you to use floppy-based QIC 80 drives. (The QIC 117 designation refers to the interface, not the more familiar tape format.) Simply select the tape drive type that you want to use and press the Install button. Windows NT will ask you for the location of your tape drive system files if you don't have access to a CD-ROM drive or if the drive does not contain the proper CD.

Note

Not every tape drive will work with the drivers supplied with Windows NT even if it appears that the driver will support the drive interface. Different vendors use different command sets for their tape drives, making it difficult at best to support them all. This is especially true of the QIC 117 interface drivers. If you find that your drive does not work with the default driver, get a Windows NT-specific driver from the vendor. Use the Other option during installation and Windows NT will ask you to supply the vendor-specific driver.

Creating a Backup

To use the tape drive installed on your system, simply start the Windows NT Backup program. This is a full-featured backup program that works with the tape drives shown in the previous section. (If you don't see a tape drive specifically supported by the Windows NT software, make sure the tape drive vendor supplies an appropriate driver for your unit.) The Backup window appears in Figure 20-2.

Since Windows NT uses the Microsoft Tape Format version 1.0, you need to format the tape before you can use it (unless you get tapes specifically formatted for Windows NT). Error messages such as "tape format not recognized" or "drive not ready" usually indicate that you have not formatted the tape. If you want to use a tape that another backup program created, select the Erase Tape option from the Operations menu. (As an alternative, you can click the eraser displayed on the Toolbar.) Click the Quick Erase option, then press the Continue button. After a few warning messages, Windows NT will modify the tape for use. You can verify successful completion by looking for "The tape in the drive is blank" in the Current Tape field of the Backup Information dialog box.

The first step in starting your backup is to select the drives you want to back up. In the Drives window, you can either choose a complete drive by marking its check box, or you can double-click the icon for the drive to display a list of directories and files on that drive. You then mark the check boxes of the specific directories and files you want to back up. In most cases you will want to select the entire drive. Figure 20-3 shows both methods of selecting the files you want to back up.

FIGURE 20-2

The backup program
provided with Windows NT

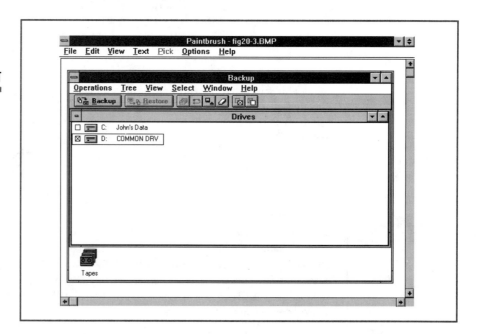

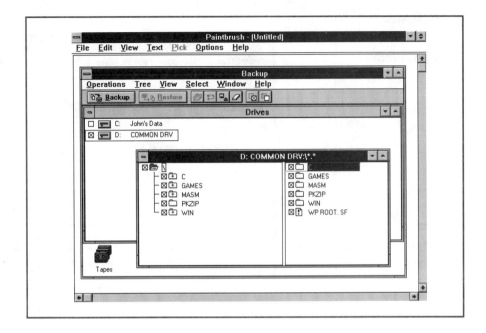

FIGURE 20-3

Selecting drives and files for backup

Once you select the files you want to back up, click the Backup icon on the Toolbar. The backup program will display the dialog box shown in Figure 20-4, where you specify what type of backup you want to perform.

The backup program automatically fills in the Current Tape, Creation Date, and Owner fields. The Tape Name field allows you to provide a specific name for your tape. Whenever you put the tape into the drive, you can identify it by its name. By default, Windows NT uses the creation date for a tape name. You can choose either the replace or append operation—the replace operation overwrites all data on the tape, while the append operation adds the new tape data to the end of the current data.

One of the more important fields is Verify After Backup. You should always check this field to ensure the data on the tape matches the data on your drive. Of course, this means that the backup will take approximately twice as long to perform.

The Backup Local Registry option allows you to protect your configuration data by placing it on tape.

The Restrict Access to Owner or Administrator field helps you protect the data from others who may want to see the contents of your hard drive.

The Backup Set Information tells you about the drives that the backup program copied to tape. There is one backup set for each drive. Click the scroll bar to move between backup sets. The description field allows you to describe the backup conditions for the drive. The Backup Type field allows you to select the backup method for the drive. You have five methods from which to choose:

FIGURE 20-4

The Backup Information dialog box

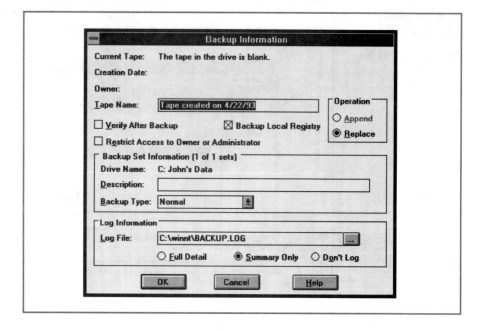

Normal Use this option to create a full backup of your entire drive. This is the option you use to create a base backup of your drive to support differential or incremental backups later. As Windows NT copies your files to tape, it removes the Archive attribute from the directory entry. The next time you modify the file, the application marks the Archive attribute. This allows the backup program to find the files you modified since the last full backup. Incremental and differential backups save time since they allow you to add only changed files to the tape.

Copy This option works much like the Normal selection; however, it doesn't modify the Archive bit. Use this option if you don't plan to create incremental or differential backups of your system.

Incremental The incremental option allows you to add any files that changed since the last normal or incremental backup to the tape. It resets the Archive attribute of each file it copies to tape. This is the fastest method of backing up your system. Unfortunately, you trade some of that time during a restore. You must begin by restoring the full backup, then proceed to restore each incremental backup until you finish with the most current incremental backup.

Differential This option works much like the incremental option except that it does not reset the Archive attribute of the file. Using the differential option usually represents a middle-of-the-road approach to tape backup. It saves time by reducing the number of files you need to copy to tape after a full backup. However, it also reduces restore time. Instead of restoring every backup you made since the last full backup, the differential backup requires that you restore only the full backup and the last differential backup.

☑   *Daily Copy* Use this backup option to make a copy of the files that changed today. It essentially ignores the Archive attribute of the files and uses date as the backup criteria. This option does not change the Archive attribute. You could use it to back up today's work to tape, then restore it on your home machine.

The Log Information section of the dialog box allows you to maintain a record of the backup. In most cases the summary selection is fine; it provides you with a list of major operations performed on the tape along with a list of any errors the backup program found. However, the Full Detail selection provides you with a log of all the filenames as well.

Once you complete the configuration dialog box you can start the backup. The Windows NT Backup program displays the dialog box shown in Figure 20-5, which gives you the backup status. This screen contains the number of directories, files, and bytes copied to tape in the upper-left corner of the dialog box. The upper-right corner tells you about any file errors that the backup program may find. (Some "errors" found may not be errors at all. For example, a skipped file is not necessarily an error, but it does tell you that your backup may not be complete.) The middle of the display provides a drive, directory, and file indicator showing what the backup program is sending to disk. The Summary section of the dialog box tells you about the overall tape operation and any hardware-related errors that the backup program may find.

FIGURE 20-5

The Backup Status
dialog box

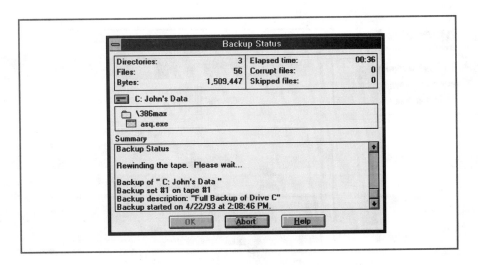

Restoring a Backup

Getting the data back off your tape is fairly easy with the Windows NT Backup program. Start the application and double-click the Tapes icon at the bottom of the display. The dialog box shown in Figure 20-6 appears.

Backup maintains a history of the tapes you back up and the files they contain. Each entry contains the drive name, backup set and tape, backup method, the date and time you created the backup, and the description you provided prior to creating the backup. If you want to fully restore a backup, simply select the backup you want to restore by checking the appropriate box. Double-clicking the folder icon allows you to choose individual files and directories.

Once you decide what you want to restore, press the Restore button on the Toolbar. The Windows NT Backup program displays the dialog box shown in Figure 20-7.

Most of the entries are self-explanatory or automatically filled in by Windows NT from the tape header or log files. The Restore to Drive field allows you to restore the data to a different drive than the one you originally used for backup.

The Alternate Path field allows you to restore the data to a different directory than the original directory. (Windows NT assumes that you want to use the root directory of the drive you select as the starting point for restoration.)

The Verify After Restore is an important option if you want to make sure that the data you copy from tape is an accurate representation of the data. This is especially important for the large files used by database management systems where a single bit error can make the difference between good and unusable data.

Never select the Restore Local Registry or Restore File Permissions options unless you experience a total hard disk failure or need to back the entries up to an earlier state. Restoring these entries on a fully functional system could have unintended results. You

FIGURE 20-6

The Tapes window, which displays information about the backup tapes

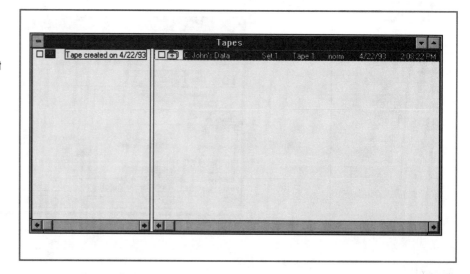

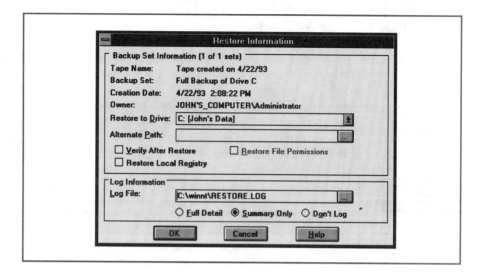

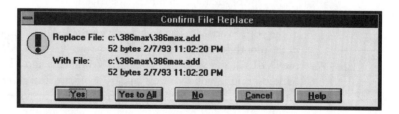

should always log your restoration session. A full detail log is a good precaution against damage in this case. The log allows you to detect problem areas before they become disasters.

Once you complete the Restore Information dialog box, start the restoration process by clicking OK. Windows NT Backup will display a dialog box similar to the one provided with the backup part of the program. While you can allow the backup part of the program to proceed unattended, you should monitor the restoration process. Whenever Windows NT Backup finds that a file you want to restore on disk has the same name as one you want to restore from tape, it asks your permission to restore it.

You can restore the file, restore all files whether or not they have the same name as files on the disk, choose not to restore the file, or cancel the entire restoration process. The Help button allows you to ask for help as needed. Using the Yes to All button is fairly dangerous if you are not absolutely certain that you want to restore all the files from tape. You may find that you accidentally overwrote some important piece of data if you use this option. If you select the Cancel button, Windows NT Backup will ask if you want to abort the restoration. Clicking Yes takes you back to the main backup dialog box; clicking on No returns you to the previous dialog box.

Tape Rotation Methods

Some people maintain a single tape throughout the existence of their system and wonder why their data gets lost when they need it most. You need to maintain more than one tape for your system to get the full benefits of a tape backup strategy. Storing some of those tapes at an off-site location, preferably in an insured tape storage facility, reduces the chance that a fire, flood, or other disaster will destroy all your chances of creating a tape backup of your system. It is typical to create a new job description for a person that rotates backup tapes to the off-site location.

Note

A hidden virus attack can quickly destroy a single-tape backup strategy. Assume you make a successful backup on Tuesday, and a virus attacks your system on Wednesday. Not knowing about the virus, you back up your system Wednesday night, in the process overwriting Tuesday's good backup with Wednesday's virus-infected data. If you back up with three or four different tapes, one for each day, you'll have a better chance of full recovery in the event of a disaster. The more tapes you use, the better.

There are a number of tape backup strategies that vendors advocate. Some are very complex; others are very simple. Just about every tape and operating system vendor provides you with at least a few ideas on how to rotate your tapes. The least complex tape rotation scheme uses three tapes: the current backup, the previous backup, and backup from two weeks ago. Each tape contains one week's worth of information. You start with a full backup on Monday, then create an incremental backup each day until Friday. The following Monday you insert a new tape and start the process over again. The current backup stays with the machine, you store the previous backup in a nearby vault, and store the two-week-old tape in an off-site location.

One of the most common tape backup rotations is the "Grandfather" method. It uses 22 tapes. You label 5 tapes DAILY, 5 tapes WEEKLY, and 12 tapes with the months of the year. Every Monday you start with the DAILY tape that corresponds to the week of the month (the first Monday of the month you use DAILY1, the second Monday you use DAILY2, and so forth). Tuesday, Wednesday, and Thursday you make incremental backups. Friday, you retrieve a tape from off-site storage, create another full backup and send it to off-site storage. Always use the tape that corresponds to the current week of the month. At the end of every month you make another backup and place it in off-site storage. This strategy allows you to retrieve data from a year ago if necessary and ensures that you will never lose more than one week's worth of data. Keeping the daily backups nearby allows you to retrieve up to a month's worth of data without waiting for a tape to be retrieved from off-site storage.

Whatever tape rotation strategy you use, make sure it allows for both on-site and off-site storage. You need to keep more than one tape near your machine in case your current tape breaks or fails in some other way. Ideally, you should have backups in both places, because waiting for someone to retrieve a tape from off-site storage is inconvenient—but losing your data to fire is devastating.

You also need to consider replacement of the actual tape. There are two schools of thought in this area. The first method replaces a tape after a certain date. This method compensates for the environmental factors that break down the tape media. (If you place an unused tape in storage long enough, the glue used to hold the oxide to the tape will break down.) Most technicians agree that a tape is good for at most five years with correct on-site storage. High humidity and/or heat reduce the lifespan of your tapes, so you need to adjust replacement dates accordingly. If you use the tape on a regular basis, consider replacing it within two years of first use. The combination of tape wear and environmental factors breaks down the media even faster than if you only use the tape occasionally. The other tape replacement technique is to replace the tape after a certain number of uses. This method uses as its determining factor the amount of wear that a tape receives during use. Most technicians that use this method replace the tape after a maximum of 40 uses.

FAULT TOLERANCE

Note

The following discussion applies to Windows NT Advanced Servers only.

Fault tolerance is essential for a file server and makes sense on critical engineering workstations. One of the most vulnerable components of a computer is the drive system. This is about the only mechanical part that can fail besides the fans used to cool the system. Mechanical parts usually have higher failure rates than solid-state devices such as the motherboard and expansion boards. As a result, you can greatly reduce the chance of total system failure by protecting the hard drives in your system.

There are two levels of non-RAID (redundant array of inexpensive disks) fault tolerance provided by Windows NT Advanced Server. You'll remember from Chapter 2 that disk mirroring is the process of running two drives from the same controller. Each drive contains the same information (a mirror) as the other drive. This method protects your system from a hard disk failure. The other method is disk duplexing. As shown in Chapter 2, this method uses two controllers and two drives to provide an even higher level of protection. Both drive paths are fully redundant, making it very unlikely that you'll experience a failure. When a failure does occur with one drive, the other drive is still usable for those who need to access critical data. You can take the machine off-line to replace the redundant drive during non-peak hours. While some may balk at using valuable disk space to duplicate data, consider the value of your data and what it would cost your company to not be able to access that data. Also consider the cost of reentering the data, if that's even possible.

Another level of fault tolerance, called RAID level 5, is provided in the Windows NT Advanced Server. Essentially, data is written to a set of disks as if they were one disk using a technique called striping (covered in Chapter 2). Data bits are distributed among the drives. This increases throughput and the apparent speed of your system. One drive stores a parity bit that is used in case any other drive in the array should fail. The parity bit helps reconstruct the data from the missing drive. This protection scheme doesn't work if two drives should fail because the parity drive can only supply information for one missing drive. However, a dual drive failure is highly unlikely.

Note

A Windows NT workstation (not an Advanced Server) supports RAID level 0, but this is not a fault-tolerant system because it does not provide a parity drive. Its only benefit is a potential increase in performance, but there is also a greater potential of data loss should one of the drives in the stripe set fail. There is not a parity drive to recover data from the failed drive and you can't mirror or duplex the drives to provide an alternate level of back-up. Data striping on Windows NT is not recommended.

While RAID allows you to make better use of your drive capacity, it does extract a higher initial cost than simply disk mirroring or duplexing. To get the most from RAID, buy systems that are designed specifically to support RAID, rather than building up a system yourself. Many RAID systems allow you to replace a drive without bringing the system down. This means that you could replace a failed drive during normal working hours and no one would even notice.

Inside

- Performance Monitor

- Event Viewer

& Out

CHAPTER 21

Monitoring the System

Windows NT provides two monitoring tools
that can help you track several aspects of your
computer performance or the performance and
activities of network computers. Both tools
appear in the Administrative Tools group.

◪   *Performance Monitor*   You can use the Performance Monitor to tune your machine to meet your work needs or to monitor the workload placed on various components in case you are evaluating upgrades or system add-ons.

◪   *Event Viewer*   The Event Viewer displays monitored events, such as system startup problems, errors, and security events like logons and access to resources.

The following sections show you how to use both tools to get the maximum output from your machine using the least amount of resources. The Performance Monitor is covered first.

PERFORMANCE MONITOR

Performance Monitor is a tool for charting and reporting on the performance and usage of your local system, or a remote computer on the network. Use Performance Monitor to determine the cause of performance loss and to monitor overall throughput of the system. You can set counters to monitor the use of disks, queues, and other system resources by local or remote network users. You can also set alerts to warn of performance problems, overuse of resources, and other events. Here's a partial list of what Performance Monitor can do:

◪   Create charts that monitor system activities

◪   Export data from charts to spreadsheets

◪   Create alerts that warn you or other users when an event threshold is met

◪   Perform automatic activities when certain values go over or under a predefined level

◪   Create log files that hold information about computers and their activities

◪   Save charts, logs, and reports for later use

Monitored Resources

Every computer has a set of components or processes that Performance Monitor can track. These components and processes are called *objects*. Tracking these objects will be of most interest to system administrators, programmers, and system designers. The major objects are listed here:

◪   cache

◪   logical disk

- memory
- objects (software objects in this case)
- paging file
- physical disk
- process
- processor
- redirector
- server
- system
- thread

Each object provides one or more *counters*. Think of a counter as a way to keep track of an object and gauge whether it is over or under values you specify when tracking the object. Each one of these counters would tell you about a different aspect of the object.

An object also provides *instances*. There is one instance of an object for each physical device in your machine. For example, if you have two physical hard drives, then there are two instances of all the objects that relate to that hard drive.

Report Types

Performance Monitor provides four ways to view data gathered in the process of monitoring resources, in either text or graphic form.

- *Chart* displays system information using graphs.

- *Alert* monitors the system for specific events and keeps a record of when they occur.

- *Log* maintains a permanent record of system events. You can monitor several systems at once using this option. The Log display doesn't show any recorded data. Use the other three displays to show the contents of the log file you create using this option.

- *Report* allows you to create a written report of when specific events occur.

Choose one of these views by clicking a button on the Toolbar or by choosing an option from the View menu. You can save each type of view for future use, and if you set up several different views, you can save them collectively as a "workspace" using options on the File menu.

Using Performance Monitor

Before you get started with Performance Monitor, you need to execute the DISKPERF (Disk Performance) command in the Command Prompt window. Start the command prompt, then type **DISKPERF**. This will tell you whether DISKPERF is already started or not. If not, type **DISKPERF -Y** at the command line, then exit the Command Prompt and choose Shutdown from the Program Manager File menu to restart your computer.

| Note |

You can start DISKPERF on a remote network computer by typing the computer's name. Type DISKPERF /? in the Command Prompt for more information.

All four Performance Monitor modules (Chart, Alert, Log, and Report) use the same Toolbar and other Performance Monitor window features. Select the view you want to see by choosing Chart, Alert, Log, or Report from the View menu, or by clicking the appropriate Toolbar button.

We'll look at the Graph module now, and discuss later how the other modules differ from the Graph module. Figure 21-1 shows a typical Graph display. The legend at the bottom of the screen indicates that three disk events are being monitored. An actual screen displays lines or bars in different colors. The vertical bar in the graph window scans from left to right, updating the graph at intervals that you specify. The default interval is every second.

FIGURE 21-1

A typical Performance Monitor window

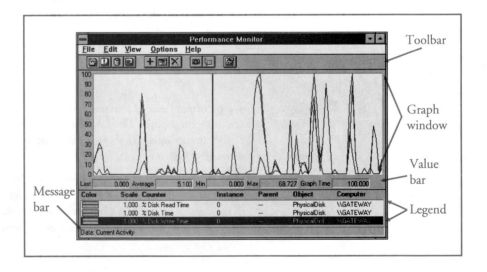

There are ten buttons on the Toolbar for quickly executing options or switching between the Chart, Alert, Log, or Report windows. The button options duplicate some of the options available on pull-down menus and are listed in Table 21-1.

The File menu has important options for saving and reusing the settings you specify for graphs and other monitoring features. The operation of the File commands may be little different from what you are used to. The names of the options change, depending

Icon	Application	Description
	Chart button	Click this button to move from any other module to the graph module.
	Alert button	Click this button to jump to the Alert module.
	Log button	Click this button to jump to the Log module.
	Report button	Click this button to jump to the Report module.
	Add button	Click this button to add new items to graphs or reports. A list of objects that you can add appears.
	Edit Line button	Click this button to change the contents of a graph or report. You don't have to start all over again when you make a mistake in selecting elements to add.
	Delete From button	Click this button to remove counters from your graph or report. Simply highlight the counter entry you want to remove and click the Delete button.
	Update Now button	Click this button to take a picture of the current counter contents. Normally you set an interval for automatically detecting these events. The Snapshot feature allows you to take a manual sample.
	Bookmark button	Click this button to add notes to your data. This is an especially important feature for logs where you may not remember specific events later. This feature also allows you to find specific areas that you may want to use for reports or graphs.
	Options button	Click this button to change the methods used to create a graph or report. This usually includes the method of presentation and the time interval used to prepare the graph or report.

on the type of window (Chart, Alert, Log, and Report) that is open. Here's the File menu as it appears when Chart is selected:

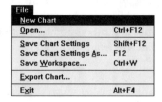

Generally, the options perform similar tasks. The New option opens a new Chart, Alert, Log, or Report settings file, and the Open option opens an existing Chart, Alert, Log, or Report settings file. The settings files have the following extensions:

.PMW   A workspace file that contains a group of Chart, Alert, Log, or Report settings files created in a previous session

.PMC   A Chart settings file

.PMA   An Alert settings file

.PML   A Log settings file

.PMR   A Report settings file

Note that file listings in the Open dialog box depend on the current setting of the View menu.

Use the Save options to save the current view, or use the Save Workspace option to save all views together in a single file that you can restore at any time. Use the Export option to send settings files to a file that you can import into a word processor, database, or spreadsheet.

The Export As dialog box is shown in Figure 21-2. You can save data with comma or tab separators, depending on the application in which you plan to use the data. Most

FIGURE 21-2

The Export As dialog box

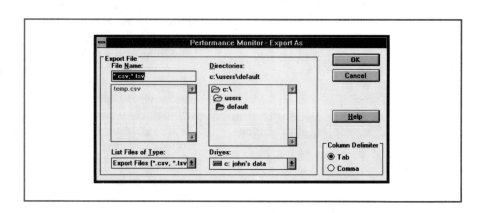

word processors use tabs, while most database managers use commas. When saving the export file, use a file extension that matches the one that your word processor, database manager, or spreadsheet expects.

Chart Options

The procedure for setting up a chart is to first specify the objects and counters you want to track. Choose Chart from the View menu, then choose the Add to Chart option from the Edit menu to display the dialog box shown in Figure 21-3.

Before setting options on this dialog box, click the Explain button to see an explanation of counter types. Also, you can select multiple items in some lists by holding the CTRL key while clicking items.

- ☑ In the Computer field, choose either the local computer, or a remote network computer.

- ☑ In the Object field, choose the type of process you want to track.

- ☑ In the Counter field, choose the event or process that you want to count for the selected object. A definition appears in the Counter Definition field if you clicked the Explain button.

- ☑ In the Instance field, choose one or more instances of the object. For example, if your system has two disks, they are listed as instances 0 and 1.

- ☑ You can select a color, scale, width, and style in the lower boxes, although the defaults are usually sufficient. The color changes automatically as you add objects to the chart.

| Note |

For more information on objects, counters, and instances, refer to *Inside Windows NT*, by Helen Custer (Microsoft Press, 1993).

FIGURE 21-3

The Add to Chart
dialog box

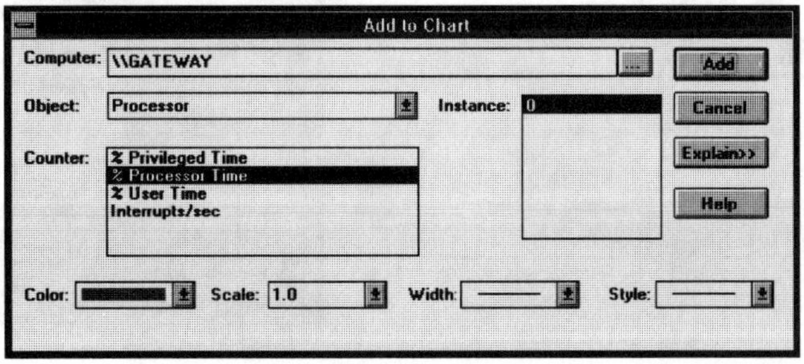

Click the Add button to add the selected object and continue adding more items as necessary. Click Done when you've added enough items. To change the features of a chart line, click its legend at the bottom of the chart, then choose Edit Chart Line from the Edit menu. If you decide to remove a chart line, click its legend and choose the Delete from Chart option on the Edit menu.

Once you've set up a chart, you can change other options by choosing Chart from the Options menu. The dialog box in Figure 21-4 appears.

Legend   This option, which is set to on by default, displays a legend for each line or bar. You might want to turn it off if you're tracking a lot of events and the legend takes up too much of the window.

Value Bar   Choose this option to turn the value bar on or off. It shows maximum levels reached by entries and provides the average level of all the entries. If all the entries refer to the same type of information (a percentage of activity, for example), then the value bar can provide you with very useful information at a glance.

Gallery Field   Choose Line Graph to show the value of each entry over time. Choose Histogram to show the current value of the data in moving-bar form. Histogram provides a good comparison of current object values, but it does not provide the historical reference information that is useful for monitoring peaks or lulls in performance.

Update Time Field   Choose Manual Update if you want to update the chart information on your own. Click the Snapshot button or choose Update Now from the Options menu to update a chart when Manual Update is set. Choose Periodic Update to update the chart at an interval you specify in the Interval field. Selecting a small interval gives you a more accurate view of the performance data. Selecting a large period lets you monitor the data over a longer interval without overwriting the old data.

FIGURE 21-4

The Chart Options
dialog box

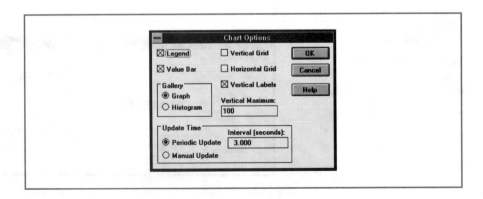

Grid options   Choose Vertical Grid to add vertical lines to the chart. Choose Horizontal Grid to add Horizontal lines to the chart. Choose Vertical Labels to add or remove the labels corresponding to the horizontal grid. In the Vertical Maximum field, type a value that provides enough room for the maximum data value you expect, yet displays the average data around the middle of the graph. Of course, it isn't always possible to follow this rule. If you don't need to know absolute maximums, you can usually get a better idea of your machine's status by placing the average data value at the middle of the graph.

Once you've set up a chart, you can save it by choosing the Save Chart Settings As option on the File menu. Optionally, you can create other settings as described next and save them together as a workspace.

Alert Options

To set up Alerts, first choose Alerts in the View menu, then choose Add to Alert from the Edit menu. The dialog box shown in Figure 21-5 appears, on which you can choose the Computer, Object, Counter, and Instance, similar to the way you set up Charts as discussed in the previous section. Be sure to click the Explain button to get a description of counters.

There are two additional options. In the Alert If field, choose the minimum or maximum threshold for the alert. The counter description can help you with this setting. In the Run Program on Alert field, type the name of a program to run if the alert criterion is met.

After setting alerts, you can customize the Alert view by choosing Alert from the Options menu. The Alert Options dialog box pictured in Figure 21-6 allows you to control three vital areas of the Alert module. Unlike the other modules, the Alert module is designed to help you locate critical machine or network events. The Alert Options dialog box reflects the role of the Alert module.

FIGURE 21-5

The Add to Alert dialog box

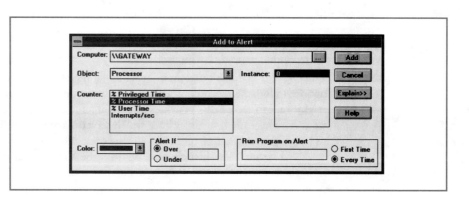

FIGURE 21-6

The Alert Options dialog box

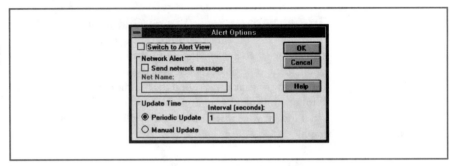

Switch to Alert View   Check this box to automatically switch your display to the Alert module of Performance Monitor whenever the machine or network exceeds the predefined values. This is where the "alarm" nature of the Alert module resides. This service is exceptionally important for a network administrator. Setting these alarms can help you react to an emergency before it becomes critical. It also acts as a means for documenting the need for additional network hardware and software. On a stand-alone machine, you could use these alarms to help you revise your work habits. Are you trying to perform multiple disk intensive tasks at once? Why not change your work habits to intermix those tasks with CPU intensive tasks? This allows you to balance the load on your machine and could prevent unacceptable work delays.

Network Alert Field   Click this option to have Performance Monitor send a message to the specified network name whenever an alert occurs.

Update Time Field   Change options in this field to set how often the Alert module updates the display. Choose too short of an interval and you'll waste CPU cycles (not to mention the number of messages you'll receive every time an alert occurs). The default value of five seconds seems to work in most situations. You may want to increase this value to ten seconds in a network environment. Selecting a value exceeding fifteen seconds could allow critical events to pass unnoticed.

Log Options

The Log option doesn't present information; it merely records it for later use. You set up options to log, then record information about the objects for later use. For example, you might want to record disk activities on several remote servers over a period of time, then view these logs at a later time to see which servers have more activity. Perhaps you need to justify the purchase of additional storage or of additional servers.

To set up a log, first choose Log from the View menu, then choose Add to Log from the Edit menu. The following dialog box appears:

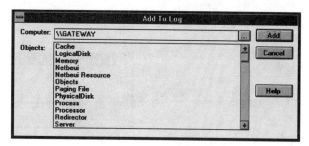

Choose the objects you want to log, holding down the CTRL key if you want to select multiple items. Click Add to add the items and Done when you're through selecting.

To change logging options, choose Log from the Options menu. The Log Options dialog box presents two simple selections, as shown in Figure 21-7. First, you need to choose which file you want to use to store the data. The second option allows you to choose a recording interval. If you record too often, the data file could get large very quickly. In most cases using an interval of 3 to 10 seconds seems to work best for the Log module. Choosing a longer interval means that you usually won't get enough data resolution to make reasonable decisions about the data you collect. A shorter interval usually results in massive files that consume an inordinate amount of disk space.

Interpreting Logged Data

So how do you use the data you collect with the Log module? You first open the data file in which you collected the information, then open any of the chart, report, or workspace settings files you created to view the data you want to interpret.

FIGURE 21-7

Setting log options

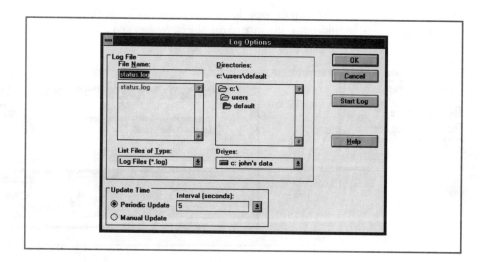

First, select the Data From option on the Options menu to display the following dialog box:

It contains three entries. Choose Current Activity or Log File as a data source. When you choose Log File, you also need to supply the name of a log file created with the Log module.

Once you select the data you want to look at and the format you want to see it in, it's time to look at specific areas of the log file. Choose the Time Window option of the Edit menu to display the Input Log File Timeframe dialog box as shown In Figure 21-8.

On this dialog box, you can select the period of time you wish to examine using either of two methods. The first method is simply to move one of the two thumbs along the time line. The thumb on the left shows the starting time of the data you wish to view; the thumb on the right shows the ending time. The two ends of the time line show the file's beginning and ending times. All you need to do is drag the thumbs to the starting and ending points.

You can jump to bookmarks you added to the data by highlighting the bookmark you want to use and pressing either the Set as Start or Set as Stop buttons. Performance Monitor automatically selects the right time on the time line.

Report Options

The Report view lets you monitor object information in columnar form for each individual instance of the object. System and disk performance are monitored as shown

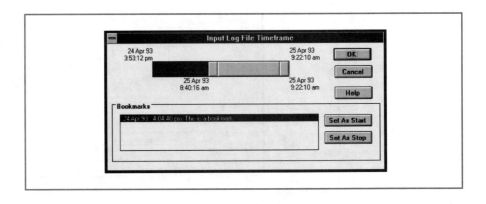

in Figure 21-9. Notice that information is displayed in real time—there is no historical information.

To set up reporting, first choose Report from the View menu, then choose Add to Report from the Edit menu. The dialog box that appears has features in common with those discussed for the other view options. You select an object, counter, and instance, then click the Add button. Hold the CTRL key to select multiple counters and click Done when you've finished.

Next, you can choose Report from the Options menu to display the Report Options dialog box:

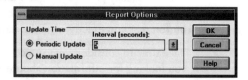

On this dialog box, choose between periodic or manual mode. In most cases you'll want to use manual mode for a report so you can get stable data for input. If you do choose periodic input, make sure you don't select an interval that makes it difficult to read the information. The default selection of five seconds works fine in most cases.

Creating Useful Data

There is a problem with using Performance Monitor that you might not notice immediately. How do you tune your system using the information you receive from this valuable tool? One look at any of the displays shows a confusing array of objects that you can monitor. In addition, you can monitor specific counters for each of the objects. The number of permutations is mind boggling. Clearly you need a plan when using Perfor-

Monitoring system and disk performance

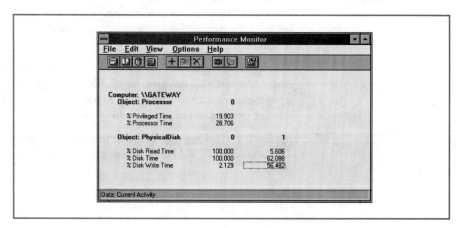

mance Monitor. While there are no cut and dry rules for using this tool, there are some things you should consider.

- Look at your applications and decide what types of tasks you perform with them. For example, if you're using a database manager, then you will want to focus on the disk-specific counters of Performance Monitor. A high powered spreadsheet may warrant looking at the processor or memory. This first step allows you to start cutting the number of objects you look at.

- Once you choose a set of objects, you need to choose which events to monitor. You can usually get a pretty good idea of what a statistic tells you by its name. However, make sure you click the Explain button when adding objects. This button tells you exactly what the statistic offers as information.

- Take time to consider what subject this graph or report is trying to display. Are you looking for information about the efficiency of a particular spreadsheet? Make sure you keep the graph focused, or you will end up with a lot of seemingly useless information.

- You might also want to monitor how network users are accessing your system and how it reacts under the load of many users.

EVENT VIEWER

The Event Viewer is much more than just a simple method of maintaining a log of major system events. You can use it for a variety of purposes, including monitoring your work habits. Event View can maintain three different logs:

- *System*   Records system component events. This log can provide extremely useful information about components that fail to load, such as network cards that are having interrupt conflicts with other devices in the system. It also records information about new components and drivers that were added to the system.

- *Security*   This log tracks events related to system security. When auditing is enabled, events such as logon, logoff, file access, system restart, and system shutdown are tracked, as well as management functions like user and group account creation or changes in security policy.

- *Application*   This log records events produced by applications, such as errors. The Windows NT Backup program records failures to back up specific files in this log.

To enable security tracking, choose Audit on the Policies menu in the User Manager, then click the Audit These Events button on the Audit Policy dialog box. Choose the events you want to audit. Any occurrences of these events are listed in the security log of the Event Viewer.

Since you can set Windows NT to log user-specific events like opening and closing files, the security log can also act as a means of monitoring your work habits. You can actually detect work patterns by checking the files you open and close. Using the security log this way provides the input you need to "tune" your work habits and optimize the way you use your computer.

The Event Viewer presents a list of events for the selected log as shown in Figure 21-10. You see the date, time, and source of the event. For detailed information, double-click an event. The Event Details dialog box (pictured and described later in this chapter) provides additional information about the event.

You switch between logs by choosing their names on the Log menu.

Setting Event View Options

There are a number of options for changing the way events are displayed and what events are displayed.

- Choose the Save As and Open options to keep a record of important logs and view them later.

- If you want to clear a log, choose the Clear All Events option on the Log menu.

- To log information on another computer, choose Select Computer from the Log menu.

FIGURE 21-10

A typical Event Viewer window

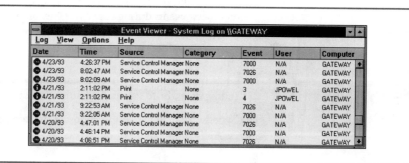

◪   If you need to stop event logging, do so in the Control Panel Services utility.

The Clear All Events option of the Log menu allows you to remove old events manually.

Another way to clear events is to have Event Viewer do it automatically. Choose the Log Settings option of the Log menu to display the following dialog box:

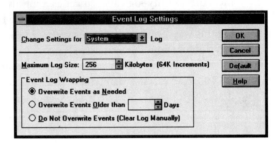

First choose the event log to change in the drop-down list box at the top, then set a maximum size for the file so it doesn't get too large. In the Event Log Wrapping field you can set how you want to handle old events when the file reaches its maximum size or when a specified number of days have passed.

The View menu, as shown below, provides options for changing the appearance of the Event Viewer entries:

For example, you can choose between looking at the oldest or the newest events first.

Choose the All Events option to see every event in the log. Of course, if the log gets too large you could find the amount of data difficult to sift through. Choose the Filter Events option to view events during a specific time, or to view specific types of events like warnings, errors, and the success or failure of audit events. The Filter dialog box, shown in Figure 21-11, has the following features:

◪   The View From and View Through entries allow you to select specific starting and ending dates, or to use the beginning and end of the log.

◪   The Types section allows you to choose from Information, Warning, Error, Success Audit, and Failure Audit events.

FIGURE 21-11

The Filter dialog box

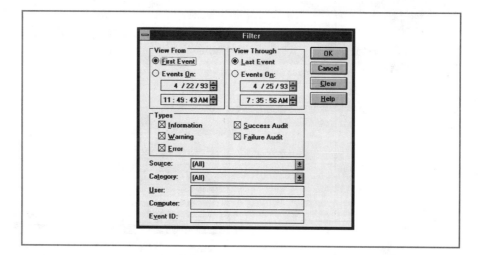

The Source drop-down box allows you to choose a particular device or other object to look at. You can further refine this selection by entering a value in the Category field.

The User and Computer entries help you refine your selection on a network.

The Event ID selection allows you to look at specific events based on identification numbers.

Click the Find option of the View menu (or press F3) to search for a particular entry in the event log. The Find dialog box provides essentially the same entries as the Filter dialog box.

Viewing Event Details

Every event listed in a log window has specific identification information and descriptions that help you identify what the event was. This information is extremely useful when debugging system startup or system problems. A Details dialog box, as shown in Figure 21-12, appears when you double-click an event, or choose Details from the View menu.

The dialog box includes the date, time, user, computer, event ID, source, type, and category of the entry. All these items are pretty self-explanatory. The Description section provides you with a plain language description of what happened to make the event occur. Of course, the clarity of this message depends on the process that created the entry. The Data section is primarily meant for programmers and system debugging.

You can use the Refresh option of the View menu to update the data on the display if you've kept the Event Viewer open for a while. Windows NT continues to record data in the log even after you open it with the Event Viewer. However, it does not automatically update the display, so you can maintain a static environment in which to view the logs.

FIGURE 21-12

The Event Detail dialog box

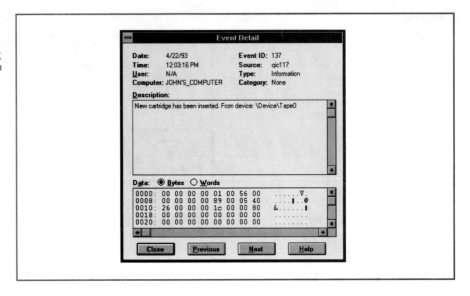

PART FOUR

Network Applications

Inside

- Postoffice Components
- Using Mail
- Composing and Sending Messages
- Reading Messages You've Received
- Folders
- Archiving and Deleting Messages
- Message Templates
- Message Finder
- Working Offline
- Administrative Tasks

& Out

CHAPTER 22

Microsoft Mail

Microsoft Mail provides electronic mail services to Windows for Workgroups users. You can write memos and send them to other users or groups of users in your workgroup. You can also forward messages you've received to other users. In addition, you can attach files to memos, which greatly simplifies the transfer of information between co-workers. Just about any type of information can be attached to a mail message, such as pictures, spreadsheet data, voice-annotated sound files, and even video clips.

A *postoffice* is set up and used as a clearinghouse for user mail. One system on the network serves as the postoffice and one user serves as the postoffice manager. To send a memo with Mail, simply compose the memo, select the recipients, and click a button to distribute the memos. The steps of printing, copying, and hand delivering memos are eliminated. You can also keep a personal address book of users and groups to whom you send mail on a regular basis.

Microsoft Mail is a "store and forward" application. That means messages from users are stored in a central postoffice location where they are forwarded to the recipient. The important point is that recipients can "pick up" mail at their convenience and that senders don't need to contact recipients to alert them that they have mail. Each user has a mailbox in the postoffice to hold messages, and they access those messages when they log on to Mail.

The Mail postoffice is efficient in that it stores only one copy of each mail message, even if that message is addressed to multiple recipients. When messages are retrieved, they are removed from the postoffice. However, recipients can choose to store messages on their own computers.

Mail includes its own editor, so users can create messages within Mail, but one of the best features is that it allows users to attach files created in other applications to Mail messages. For example, you can attach a monthly report that contains graphics, spreadsheet information, and text to a mail message and send it to one or more people. You can also embed objects such as pictures and spreadsheets directly into a message you are creating with the Mail message editor. Cut and paste is supported, so you can work on multiple messages at once and transfer information among them.

Mail uses the folder metaphor as a way to help users organize the messages they receive. While many messages can be discarded immediately, others need to be saved for future reference (or for legal reasons). You can create a folder to store business messages, another to store personal messages, and still another to store messages you need to archive (back up to a disk and remove from your hard drive). You can search for messages in folders using keywords, such as the sender's name, dates, or other descriptions.

POSTOFFICE COMPONENTS

Before you can use Mail, you'll need to create a postoffice. An *administrator* (postoffice manager) creates, manages, and maintains the postoffice. The administrator sets up a shared directory on one of the computers in the workgroup and creates a postoffice in that directory. The administrator then sets up an *account* for each person who wishes to access the postoffice.

Each Mail user is assigned a private *message file* or *mailbox* that is used to store messages. The message file is located on the user's own computer, and the postoffice is located in a shared directory on a central system set up by the administrator. Each mailbox is protected by a *password*. This restricts users other than the owner of the mailbox from accessing the mailbox. The owner is the only person who can change the password (except, of course, the postoffice manager).

When you sign in to Mail, you are presented with an *Inbox* window similar to the one shown in Figure 22-1. The Inbox window contains information about messages you have received from other postoffice users, including who sent the message, the subject of the message, and the date and time the message was placed in your mailbox.

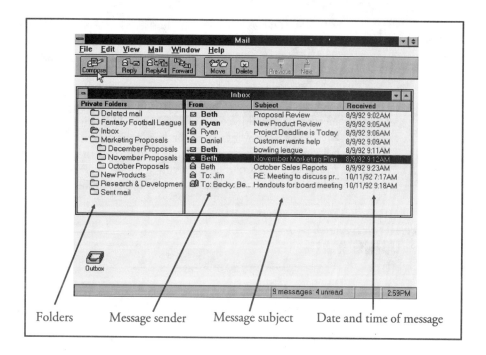

FIGURE 22-1

Startup screen

Folders   Message sender   Message subject   Date and time of message

Messages contain icons as shown here:

⊠ Unopened mail

◿ Opened mail

❗◿ High-priority indicator

↓⊠ Low-priority indicator

◿◖ Mail with attached file

If the message is high priority, you see an exclamation point, and if it is low priority, you see a down arrow. An open envelope indicates the message has already been read, and a closed envelope indicates unread messages. An envelope with an attached paper clip indicates messages with attached files, such as text documents, spreadsheet data, graphic images, or even voice messages created with a sound utility.

To create a message, click the Compose button, type your message, address it, and finally click the Send button. You address messages by selecting names from *address lists*. The *Postoffice Address List* contains the names of users in the postoffice. You can also maintain a *Personal Address List* to track a list of users that you correspond with frequently or a *Personal group* list for groups of people you correspond with frequently. When you address a message with a group name, the message is sent to all the individuals included in the group.

The *Outbox* provides a handy place to drop your mail for delivery. You simply drag messages from your Inbox or any other folder to the Outbox, where they are automatically forwarded to the recipients. Messages that you compose and send are stored immediately in your *Sent Mail* folder.

Folders provide a way to organize your mail messages. For example, you could create a folder called "Board Presentation" and use it to store messages related to an upcoming meeting. You could also create a folder called "Archive" and use it to store messages you've already read, but want to keep on hand for future reference. A folder can be exported to a floppy disk to free space on your hard disk, then imported back to Mail in the event you want to read one of the archived messages. It's possible to share folders to make messages in them accessible to other members of the workgroup.

USING MAIL

Before anyone can use Mail, the Mail administrator must create the postoffice. The procedures for doing so are covered later in this chapter under "Administrative Tasks." This section describes how nonadministrative users log on to Mail for the first time and get started. Double-click the Mail icon in the Program Manager Main group. If your account is already set up, you see the Mail Sign In dialog box shown here:

Type your mailbox name and password to gain entry to Mail. If you can't get past the logon screen, check to make sure you are using the correct mailbox name and password. If Windows is unable to find a postoffice, the following dialog box appears:

You have the option of creating a new workgroup postoffice or connecting to an existing postoffice. Read through the next section if a postoffice has already been created, or refer to "Administrative Tasks" later in this chapter if you need to create a new postoffice.

Connect to an Existing Postoffice

Click this option to connect to an existing workgroup postoffice. The Network Disk Resources dialog box comes up. You use this box to browse for the postoffice directory in the same way you use other network browse boxes to connect with shared directories.

Enter the network path if you know it or click the shared directory where the postoffice is located. The Network Path field is automatically filled in. Click the OK button to create the postoffice connection. Consult the Postoffice Administrator for the information you need to type in this box.

Mail Startup Trick

You can alter the Mail startup icon in Program Manager so it automatically enters your mailbox name when you start the program. You can also include your password, but that is not recommended since other users could gain access to your mail by simply double-clicking your Mail icon. To add your mailbox name, do the following:

1. Highlight the Mail icon in Program Manager and choose Properties from the Files menu.

2. Change the Command Line to include your mailbox name, as shown here:

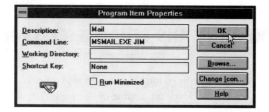

3. Click OK when done.

If other people use your system, they can use this technique as well, since the Program Manager saves each user's logon session information.

Changing Your Password

Changing your password periodically is a good idea if you are concerned about security in your work environment. Follow these steps to change your password:

1. Select Change Password from the Mail menu.

2. Enter your old password.

3. Enter your new password.

4. Verify your new password.

5. Click OK when done.

The OK button will be grayed out until you successfully enter your current password and then enter and verify a new password. On the screen you will see asterisks instead of the characters you type so that other people are unable to read your password as you enter it. Mail will notify you when the operation has been completed successfully. Be sure to make a mental note of your new password.

Exiting Mail

When you're done with Mail, you can choose from two exit options on the File menu. Choosing Exit ends your Mail session but leaves your mailbox open for other applications such as Schedule+ to use. Choosing Exit and Sign Out ends your Mail session and closes your mailbox.

COMPOSING AND SENDING MESSAGES

Once you've logged on to Mail, you're ready to compose notes and send them to other users. Here's an outline of the procedure for creating a message:

1. Click the Compose button.

2. Select the Mail users you want to send the message to as outlined in the following section.

3. Address the message as described in the following sections.

4. Type the subject of the message and your message text.

5. Click the Send button to send the message to the recipients.

Address the Message

To address the message, type the account names or click the Address button to access the Postoffice address list. Click the personal address book icon to display your personal address list. In this example, notes are addressed to Ryan and Daniel and a courtesy copy is sent to Becky, as shown in Figure 22-2.

1. Click the Address button.

2. Click Ryan's name.

3. Click the To button.

4. Click Daniel's name.

5. Click the To button.

6. Click Becky's name.

7. Click the Cc button.

Typing a letter will allow you to zero in on names in the address list. For example, typing J will position the scroll bar at the first name beginning with J.

The names are placed in the appropriate To and Cc fields at the bottom of the dialog box. When you click OK, you can type the subject and text of the note in the dialog box shown in Figure 22-3.

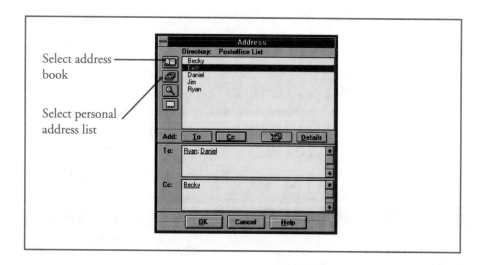

FIGURE 22-2

Address dialog box

Select address book

Select personal address list

FIGURE 22-3

An addressed Send
Note form

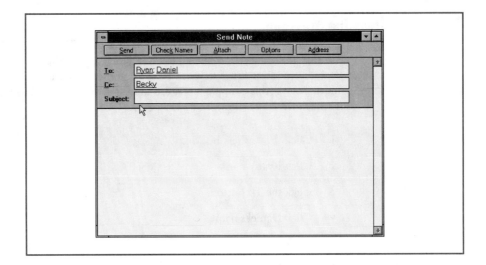

Using Groups to Address Messages

You can create groups of users that you need to send mail to on a regular basis, such as the people in your department. It's easier to send mail to a group than it is to address mail messages to individual users. To create a group, follow these steps:

1. Choose Personal Groups from the Mail menu to create the new group in your personal address book.

2. Click the New button.

3. Type the name of the new group (for example, "Board Presentation").

4. Click a user's name in the list, then click the Add button.

5. Continue choosing new group members and clicking the Add button until you have added everyone to the group.

6. Click the OK button. The new group name appears in your Personal Address Book, similar to what you see in Figure 22-4.

    To address a message to a group, click the personal address list icon. When the list appears, click the group, then click the To button. The To portion of your Send Note form is filled in with the group name as shown in Figure 22-5.

FIGURE 22-4

The new group name appears in your Personal Address Book

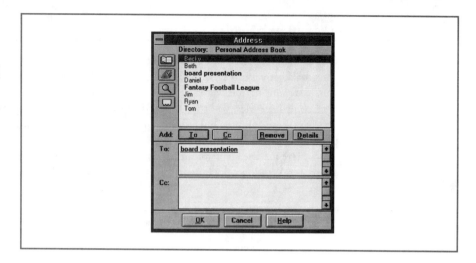

Type the Subject and Message

In the Subject field, type a short description of the message. This field appears as part of the message header information in the Inbox of the recipient. Make sure this field is as descriptive as possible.

In the lower part of the dialog box, type the text of your message. Many standard word processing features such as word wrap are available. The lines of text scroll as you fill up the page.

FIGURE 22-5

The To portion of your Send Note form is filled in with the group name

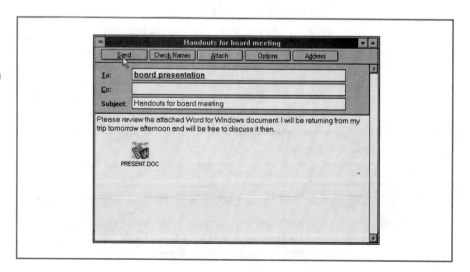

Attaching Files to Messages

One of the best features of Mail is that you can attach files of any kind to your messages. This makes it easy to send documents to other people. You could share a directory on your system using File Manager, then give other users access to the directory. After users have copied the files, you then stop sharing the directory. Mail provides a better way to do this. You simply attach the file to a mail message and send it to the recipient, who then picks up the file at their convenience.

Here are the steps for attaching a file to a message. In this example, a Microsoft Word for Windows document for an upcoming board presentation is attached to a message. It is assumed that you have a Compose window open.

1. Click the Attach button or press ALT-A.

2. Locate and click the file you want to attach using normal Browse procedures.

3. Click the Attach button.

An embedded icon is added to your message text. Figure 22-5 shows a message with a Word for Windows icon embedded in the text. The recipient of the message can double-click the icon and the document is automatically loaded into Word for Windows. You can also attach voice annotations created with Sound Recorder or pictures created with programs like Paintbrush.

> **Note**   If the File Manager window is placed next to the Mail window, you can drag and drop file icons from File Manager to your mail messages.

Mailing Packaged Objects

Recall from Chapter 10 that Object Packager is used to create a packaged object with OLE links. You can add a packaged object to a mail message that includes a pointer to a file located on another network computer's shared directory. This is useful if you want to send a message to another user that includes a reference to a file on your system. Since the package points to the file on your system, you don't need to embed it in the message itself. When the recipient reads the message, they double-click the packaged object icon to view its contents. One advantage to this technique is that you can change the object at any time.

Here are the steps for creating a packaged object:

1. Start Mail and prepare a message to send to another user.

2. To create the package, choose Insert Object from the Edit menu and choose Package from its Insert Object list.

3. When Object Packager opens, choose Command Line from the Edit menu and type the document name in the field. For example, to include the document REPORTS.WK1 in the EXCEL directory on your computer (which is called THEBOSS for this example), you would type the following:

    \\THEBOSS\EXCEL\REPORTS.WK1

4. Click the Insert Icon button and select an appropriate icon.

5. Choose Label from the Edit menu and type the name you want to appear under the icon.

6. Choose Exit from the Edit menu, then choose Yes when asked if you want to update the package.

The packaged object now appears in the message text area. You can finish creating the message and send it to the recipient.

Send the Message

When you are done creating the message, you can click the Send button to send it to the recipient, or you can specify additional options by clicking the Options button, which brings up the Options dialog box shown here. Set options on the dialog box as described in the following paragraphs.

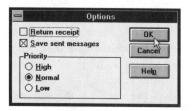

Return Receipt   Check the Return Receipt option if you want to receive notification that recipients have received and read your message.

Setting Priority   Click the appropriate button indicating the priority of the message. The default is Normal. Click the top button to change the priority to High. Click the bottom button to change the priority to Low.

Save Sent Messages   Check this option to save messages in a folder called Sent Mail. The default is to save messages.

READING MESSAGES YOU'VE RECEIVED

To read messages, first scan through the list of received messages that appear in your Inbox. Use the mouse or arrow keys to highlight the messages you want to read. Recall that a closed envelope icon indicates an unread message. Double-click the message you want to read, or highlight it and press ENTER. A form similar to the following appears:

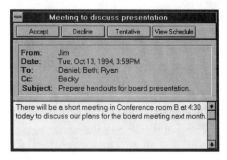

The header displays who the message is from, the date and time it was placed in your mailbox, any other people who received the same message, and the subject of the message.

Replying to Messages You've Received

Once you have opened and read a message, you can reply to it by clicking the Reply button on the main Mail window. Mail presents a reply form similar to the one shown in Figure 22-6. The message is automatically addressed to the person who sent the original message. Type your reply, then click the Send button on the reply dialog box. The original message is placed in the new message area.

FIGURE 22-6

Reply note form

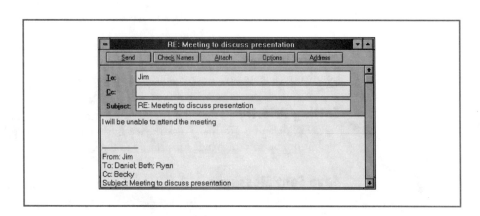

Forwarding Messages You've Received

You can forward messages you've received to other people who need to review them. Choose Forward on the Mail menu, or simply drag the envelope icon to your Outbox. Mail will present a forwarding dialog box that looks similar to Figure 22-6. Address the message as you would any other message and click the Send button. The options you consider when you send your own messages—Return receipt, Save sent messages, and Priority settings—are also available for messages you forward.

FOLDERS

Mail does not force you to perform message housekeeping chores. You could simply leave all the messages that you receive in your Inbox. However, it won't be long before your Inbox starts looking like a kitchen drawer with too much in it. Locating messages becomes increasingly hard. You could use the Message Finder described later in this chapter, but it's better to organize messages into folders.

Once you've read a message, you can move it to a folder by dragging and dropping its icon. For example, you could create a top-level folder called Board Presentation and create a subfolder for each of the topics to be presented at the meeting. The subfolder could be called Monthly Sales Figures and contain documents related to monthly sales.

Creating a New Folder

To create a new folder, choose New Folder from the File menu. The New Folder dialog box appears as shown here:

This dialog box contains fields for the folder's Name and Type. Clicking the Options button brings up the New Folder dialog box, shown in Figure 22-7 and described in the following sections.

FIGURE 22-7

New Folder dialog box

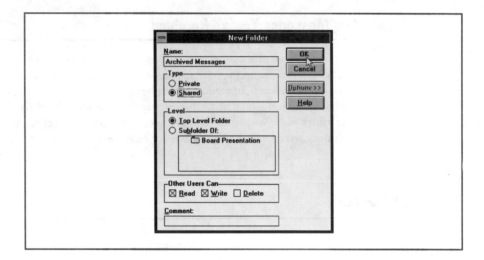

Name   Enter a descriptive name for the new folder.

Type   Click either the Shared or Private button. Shared folders reside at the location of the workstation postoffice. Private folders reside on your own machine. If you select Shared, you can set whether other users will have the ability to Read, Write, or Delete the message in the folder.

Make folders shared if you have limited disk space on your own machine.

Level   In this box, choose whether the folder will be a Top Level Folder or a Subfolder. For example, you could have a top-level folder called "Meetings" and a sublevel folder for each month.

Other Users Can   In this box, choose the access rights other users will have to the new folder. Click any combination of the three options, which are Read, Write, and Delete. Remove the check mark on all three to prevent other users from accessing your shared folder.

Comment   In this field, type any comments about the folder, such as a detailed explanation of the folder contents.

Moving Messages into Folders

After your folders have been created, you can copy messages into them by dragging and dropping the message envelopes into the new folder icons. Drag a message by following these steps:

1. Click the message you want to drag.

2. Hold the mouse button down as you move the envelope to the desired folder.

3. Release the mouse button.

ARCHIVING AND DELETING MESSAGES

Since each message in your mailbox takes up disk space on your hard disk, you will want to go through your folders occasionally and delete messages that are no longer needed. This is done by dragging messages to your Deleted mail folder. Note that the messages aren't actually deleted until you exit Mail.

You'll often have messages you want to keep a copy of for future reference, but that you don't want cluttering up your existing Mail screen. You can copy these messages to an archive folder and export the folder to a floppy disk or to another hard drive before deleting the messages. You would continue to use your Deleted mail folder for messages that you want to remove permanently, and to use your archive folder for those messages you wish to save.

When the archive folder is full or when you're ready to archive it, choose Export Folder from the File menu. The Export Folders dialog box appears, in which you can type the name of the export folder. Type a name such as A:EXPORT.MMF. When you click the OK button, you are asked to select the folders you want to export, as the example in Figure 22-8 shows.

Click the folder you want to export, or to export all folders (for backup reasons), click the All Folders option. Note the Move and Copy buttons. Move places the files in the folder into the export file, then empties the folder you selected. Copy keeps the files in the folder you selected. In either case, the folder's contents are saved to the export file. You can retrieve the contents of the export file at any time by selecting Import Folder from the File menu.

FIGURE 22-8

Export Folders dialog box

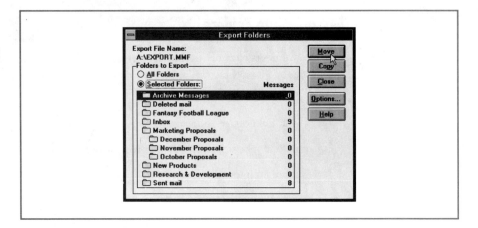

MESSAGE TEMPLATES

Use message templates when you frequently send messages that follow the same general format. For example, you could compose a message to use when sending weekly bowling results to members of your company bowling league. To save a message on a template, simply write it, then close it without sending the message. It is placed in your Inbox for future use.

The next time you need to send out your weekly bowling results, drag the message to your Outbox or type ALT-M-F to Forward the message as discussed earlier in this chapter. You then get a chance to add your bowling results or make any other changes to the message before clicking the Send button.

MESSAGE FINDER

Even if you do a good job organizing your messages using folders, there are times when you want to search through your messages for a text string. For example, you may remember receiving a message describing a new product having to do with laser printers. You could search for messages using the keyword "laser." To start a search, choose Message Finder from the File menu and type the search criteria in the Message Finder dialog box as shown here:

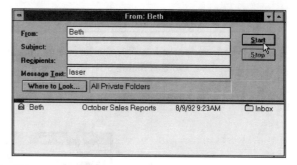

Select the Where to Look button to choose the folder you want to search through. The Where to Look dialog box appears, as shown here:

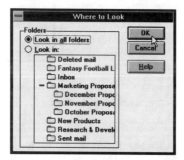

Click the Look in All Folders button to search through all the messages in all folders, or click a folder in the listing to search through just that folder. Click the Start button to begin the search. Any messages that contain the text are listed in the Message Finder dialog box. To view the contents of any message, double-click it with the mouse.

WORKING OFFLINE

You can compose messages in Mail even if you are not connected to the postoffice. The messages are saved and sent the next time you connect with the postoffice. This is useful for traveling salespeople, or when the postoffice system is not up and running.

ADMINISTRATIVE TASKS

The administrator of a workgroup creates the postoffice and is responsible for maintaining the postoffice accounts. Some of the tasks of a postoffice administrator are discussed in this section.

Creating the Postoffice

When you enter Mail for the first time, you are presented with the Welcome to Mail dialog box. On this dialog box, you can choose to connect with an existing postoffice or create a new one. If you choose to create a new postoffice, Mail displays the Create Workgroup Postoffice dialog box shown here:

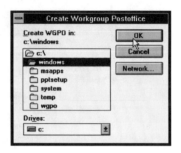

The computer used as the postoffice must be left on at all times so users can access mail.

In the directory listing, choose the directory for the postoffice or just click OK to create it in the default directory. Click the Network button if you want to choose a directory on another computer for the postoffice. Once you click the OK button, you are prompted with the Administrator Account Details dialog box as shown here:

Fill out the dialog box with the postoffice administrator's information. The Name, Mailbox, and Password fields are required. The remaining fields are optional.

Name   Enter your first and last name. Other users will specify this name when addressing messages. The maximum length of the account name is 30 characters.

Mailbox   Enter the name of your mailbox. Typically, this is the first letter of the first name, then the last name, such as JDoe. The maximum length of the mailbox name is 10 characters. Note that the space between the first initial and the last name is usually left out, but you should check to see what your company's policy is on this. Everyone should use the same format to avoid confusion.

Password   Enter the password you will use to gain access to Mail. Choose a password that is easy for you to remember but not easy for intruders to figure out. The maximum length of the password is 8 characters and the default is PASSWORD.

Phone #1   Enter your primary telephone number. The maximum length of the telephone number is 32 characters.

Phone #2   Enter an alternate telephone, fax, or modem number. The maximum length is 32 characters.

Office   Enter your office number or name. The maximum length is 32 characters.

Department   Enter your department name. The maximum length is 32 characters.

Notes   Enter notes or comments about your account in this field, such as your normal office hours or emergency information. The maximum length is 128 characters. The text will scroll as you fill up the visible area.

Click OK when the fields are filled out the way you want. You are now ready to use Mail. The next time you start Mail, you will be presented with the Mail Sign In dialog box. Simply type your mailbox name and password to gain access to Mail.

Once you click the OK button, Mail reminds you that you need to share the directory in which the postoffice resides. Follow these steps to share the directory:

1.   In the File Manager, locate the WGPO directory.

2.   Click the WGPO subdirectory.

3.   Click the Share button, or choose Share As from the disk menu.

     Mail displays the New Share dialog box.

4.   Accept the default settings, making sure that Unlimited is checked in the User Limit field.

5.   Click OK when done.

Postoffice Manager Duties

If you are the postoffice manager, you can access the Postoffice Manager dialog box, as shown in the following illustration, and make changes to postoffice mailboxes and users. Choose Postoffice Manager from the Mail menu, then refer to the following sections for instructions on using the dialog box features.

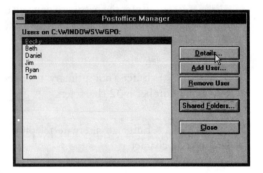

Viewing and Modifying Existing Accounts

To view or change an account, click the account name in the list and then click the Details button. A dialog box appears with information about the account that you can change if necessary.

Adding Users

Click the Add User button to add a new account. An Add User dialog screen appears. All of the fields are empty with the exception of the password field. The password is defaulted to PASSWORD. You must enter the Name and Mailbox fields. All of the other fields are optional.

Removing Users

To delete an account, first click the account name on the Postoffice Manager dialog box, then click the Remove User button. You are then asked to verify the deletion.

Checking and Compressing Folders

As the manager, you will need to monitor and manage the disk space on the computer where the postoffice resides. To check the status of a folder, select Postoffice Manager from the Mail menu, then click the Shared Folders button to display the Shared Folders dialog box shown here:

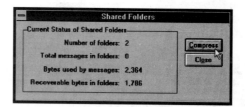

Be sure to note the number of recoverable bytes in folders. The bytes are unused because messages in the folders have been deleted. Click the Compress button to free up the recoverable space.

Inside

- Appointment Book

- Task List

- Planner

- Setting Display Defaults

- General Options

- More About Schedule+

& Out

CHAPTER 23

Microsoft Schedule+

The Schedule+ accessory helps keep you and your workgroup on track. This personal and group scheduling tool registers upcoming meetings and appointments. It also notifies you of upcoming important events, such as birthdays and anniversaries. When you use Schedule+ in a workgroup, you can view other users' schedules and coordinate meetings with them. Schedule+ automatically scans the appointments of members in your workgroup and helps you schedule meetings during times that everyone is available.

Before using Schedule+ for the first time, you or someone else in your workgroup must create a Mail postoffice, as discussed in the previous chapter. Anyone who has a postoffice mailbox will show up in your scheduling system. Schedule+ contains an Appointment Book, Task List, and a Planner. It also has a message window that contains a list of meetings you've requested and the responses from other workgroup members as to whether they can attend the meeting or not.

APPOINTMENT BOOK

The basic Schedule+ window is shown in Figure 23-1. You use the Appointment Book to create all kinds of appointments—definite, tentative, recurring, and private—as described in the following list:

☑   *Normal appointment*   A normal appointment is definite, not tentative. Normal appointments appear as white blocks of text in the Schedule+ window.

☑   *Tentative appointment*   A tentative appointment may be cancelled or changed. You create tentative appointments to set aside a block of time when you think you might be busy or when you are trying to arrange meetings with other users. Tentative appointments appear as gray blocks of text in the Schedule+ window.

☑   *Recurring appointment*   You set recurring appointments for meetings that occur every week or every month, or for regular activities that are important to remember, like paying the mortgage.

☑   *Private appointment*   Normally, other Schedule+ users can view your appointments so they can schedule an appointment with you when you are not busy. You can designate some appointments as private so other users cannot see those activities, but can see that you are busy.

FIGURE 23-1

Basic Schedule+ window

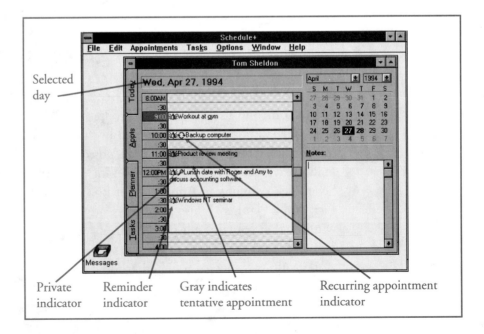

Schedule+ also provides a Daily Note section located in the lower-right corner of its window. Use this section to enter general notes about the day.

Viewing Your Appointments

To change the dates you can view other appointments, click day, month, or year buttons. When you first start Schedule+, the calendar is positioned at the current day, month, and year as shown here:

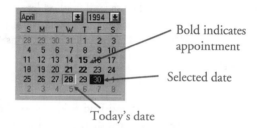

Days that have scheduled appointments are displayed in boldface text. To change to a different day, click the numeral of the day you want to view. The new day is displayed, but note that the current day appears indented.

To change the month, click the down arrow button in the month field and choose a different month from the drop-down list box. To change the year, click the down arrow button in the year field and choose a different year from the list.

Click the Today button located in the upper-left portion of the schedule window to return to the current day.

Go To Date

Instead of selecting a new date from the drop-down menus, you can use the Go To Date dialog box by pressing CTRL-G or by selecting Go To Date from the Edit menu. You can manually type in the date you want or click the up and down arrow buttons to change the date. Use this option to jump to dates that don't appear on the calendar.

Adding a One-Time Appointment

After you've selected a day, you're ready to enter appointments. The left portion of the schedule window is divided into time slots in half hour increments, as you can see in Figure 23-1. Click the time slot where you want to make an appointment or press the

DOWN ARROW and UP ARROW keys to change time slots. You can also click and drag through several time slots if an appointment lasts longer than a half hour.

You can use either of the following methods to create an appointment:

☑   Simply type the text for the appointment in the time slot. It scrolls to the left as you type. If you drag through several time slots, they all convert to text fields when you start typing.

☑   Double-click the time slot (or press CTRL-N), then fill out the Appointment dialog box as shown in Figure 23-2.

The second method lets you specify additional information for the appointment, such as whether it is tentative or private. The fields of the Appointment dialog box are described in the following sections. Once you've filled out the fields, click the OK button.

Entering Times and Dates   Type the starting and ending time and date for the appointment or change the time or date by clicking the up and down arrow buttons in the Start and End fields. If you dragged through several time slots before opening the Appointment dialog box, the time field reflects the time slots you selected.

Making the Appointment Tentative   Check the Tentative box to make the appointment tentative. As mentioned previously, use this option to reserve a block of time when arranging meetings with other users. A tentative appointment appears gray instead of white in the main schedule window and in the Planner, discussed later in this chapter.

Entering an Appointment Description   Type information about the appointment in the Description field, but keep in mind that not all of this text will appear in the time slot for the appointment on the Schedule+ window. Be sure to type information that uniquely identifies the appointment. For example, instead of typing just "lunch," you could type "lunch date with Rodger and Amy to discuss accounting

FIGURE 23-2

Appointment window

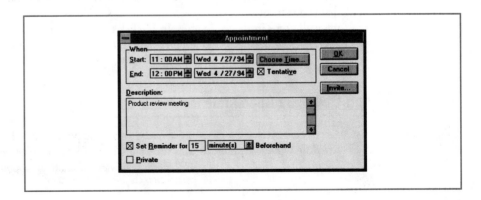

software." Adding more information helps you easily search for and identify the appointment. In some cases, you might need to locate a previous appointment. It's much easier to search for keywords like "Rodger," "Amy," or "accounting," rather than scan through all the appointments described as "lunch."

Set Reminder   Enable the Set Reminder box to set a reminder for an appointment. Click the down arrow button in the Beforehand field, then choose either minute(s), hour(s), day(s), week(s), or month(s). In the field preceding it, type in the quantity, such as "2 minutes," "2 hours," and so on. A bell icon appears next to appointments that have reminders. When the reminder is activated, Schedule+ displays a reminder message similar to the one shown here:

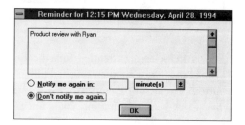

You then read the text of the appointment or click the "Notify me again in" button if you want another reminder. You can make reminders appear when you first start Windows NT by copying the file MSREMIND.EXE into the Program Manager Startup Group.

> **Note**   You can disable all reminders by selecting Turn Off Reminders from the File menu. To re-enable reminders, choose Turn On Reminders from the File menu.

Making Appointments Private   Click the Private box to make an appointment private. A key icon appears next to private appointments on the main Schedule+ window. The text of private appointments can't be read by other Schedule+ users who connect with your schedule over the network.

Inviting Meeting Attendees

Click the Invite button on the Appointment dialog box to display a list of other possible meeting attendees from your workgroup, as shown in Figure 23-3. The list displays all users with Mail mailboxes in your workgroup. Click the icon labeled "Other lists" in Figure 23-3 to display a list of other address books you can search through, or click the Personal address book icon to display your personal address list. To select attendees, click their names in the top list, then click the Add button. Their name then appears in the lower list. Alternately, you could choose a *group* of preselected names. For example, you might select a group called "board presentation" that you had previously set up in Mail.

FIGURE 23-3

Select Attendees dialog box

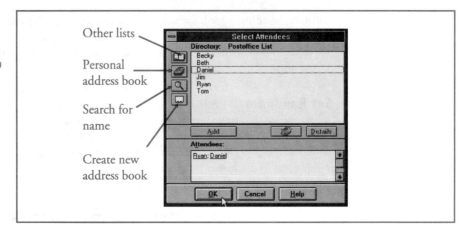

After selecting attendees for a meeting, click the OK button on the Select Attendees dialog box. If you are then finished filling out the Appointment dialog box, click its OK button. The Send Request window then appears as shown in Figure 23-4. Fill out this dialog box with information you want to send to other users about the meeting. The information will appear in their Mail Inbox and in their Schedule+ Message window. You can make changes to the Subject box and type additional information about the meeting in the lower text box. Enable the Ask for Responses box to request a reply.

When everything is filled out, click the Send button. Schedule+ sends the messages and displays a handshake icon in the appointment slot.

Note

If attendees haven't responded to your meeting request, you can pester them by choosing the Re-Send Mail option from the Appointments menu.

FIGURE 23-4

Send Request dialog box

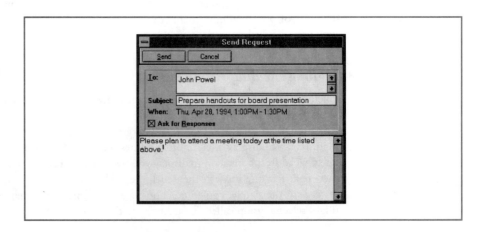

Replying to Appointment Requests

If someone requests your presence at a meeting, the request appears in the Schedule+ Message window. Double-click the message to pull up a Meeting Request dialog box, as shown in Figure 23-5. To respond, check the Send Response box, then click one of the following buttons:

- ▱ Click View Schedule to see if the meeting can be arranged within your schedule.

- ▱ Click Accept to notify the sender that you will attend the meeting.

- ▱ Click Decline to notify the sender that you will not attend the meeting.

- ▱ Click Tentative to notify the sender that you are unsure of your attendance.

If you click Accept, Decline, or Tentative, the Send Response dialog box, shown in Figure 23-6, appears. Fill in the message area if you wish and click the send button.

Request Receipts

Once attendees have responded to a meeting request, their responses appear in the meeting organizer's Message window. Figure 23-7 shows the various message headers and icons that indicate responses to meeting requests. Double-click any message header to view the request receipts.

You can also double-click the appointment in the Schedule+ window to view similar information on the Appointment dialog box, as shown in Figure 23-8. A closed envelope next to the addressee indicates that a person has not responded or that there is an incomplete response from a group.

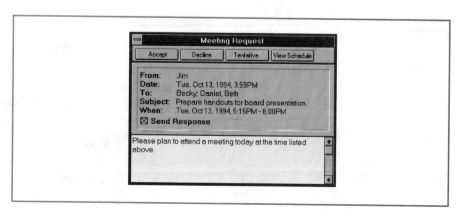

FIGURE 23-6

Send Response form

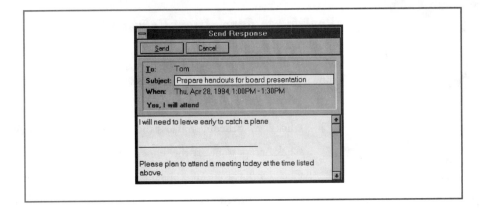

FIGURE 23-7

Messages window

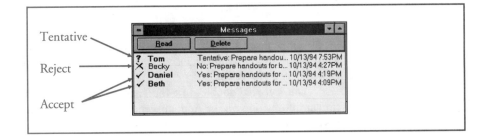

FIGURE 23-8

Appointment window

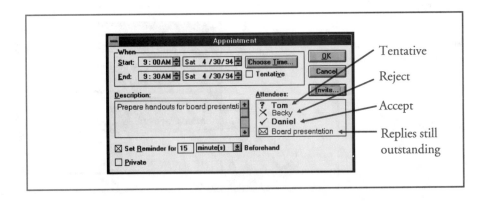

Recurring Appointments

You can set recurring appointments for events or meetings that occur on a regular basis. Schedule+ automatically adds the appointments to your schedule at the appropriate times and dates.

The first step to creating a recurring appointment is to select the time and date of the first appointment. Next select New Recurring Appointment from the Appointments menu. Schedule+ presents the Recurring Appointment window shown in Figure 23-9. Each section of the dialog box is described in the following sections. Once you have created a recurring appointment, a circular-arrow icon indicating recurring appointments appears next to the appointment description on the main schedule window.

Recurring Details

Click the Change button to open the Change Recurrence dialog box shown in Figure 23-10. Fill out the box as discussed in the following sections.

Time Increment   Enable Daily, Weekly, Bi-Weekly, Monthly, or Yearly in the This Occurs field. The box on the right changes depending on the option you selected.

- *Daily*   When you click Daily, you can choose Every Day or Every Weekday on the right.

- *Weekly*   When you click Weekly, you can choose the day of the week on the right.

- *Bi-Weekly*   When you click Bi-Weekly, you can choose the day of the week on the right.

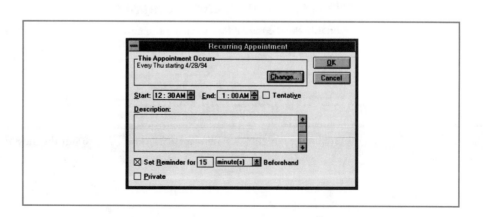

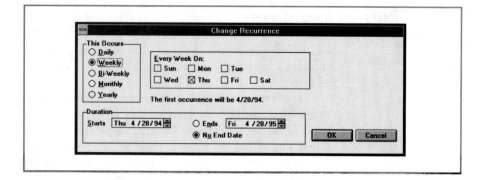

- ▰ *Monthly*   When you click Monthly, you can select either the number of days into the month or the actual day of the month.

- ▰ *Yearly*   When you click Yearly, you can set a specific date or select the day, month, or number of days, weekdays, or weekend days that the appointment should occur.

Duration   Select the time period for the recurring appointments in this field. Either click Ends and enter an End date or click the No End Date button.

Once you've filled out the Change Recurrence dialog box, click the OK button to return to the Recurring Appointment dialog box.

Starting and Ending Times

In the Start and End fields, enter the starting and ending times. Click the up and down arrow buttons to adjust the Start and End times in 15-minute intervals.

Making the Appointment Tentative

Enable the Tentative box to make the appointment tentative. Tentative appointments appear in gray rather than white in the main schedule window and Planner.

Entering Appointment Descriptions

Enter a brief description of the recurring appointment such as "sales meeting—monthly" or "bowling night" or "Windows NT class." Try to put the most descriptive word first.

Here is an example that shows what happens when more than one appointment is scheduled for the same time slot:

Here is the same schedule entry with the keyword entered first:

You can see that placing keywords first helps you quickly identify an appointment. Also notice that an entry doesn't necessarily need to be an appointment. You can also type reminders, so there will be instances when you have multiple entries at the same time slot.

Reminder

Check the reminder box and set the time interval for the reminder message. For example, you could set Schedule+ to remind you two days before an anniversary or birthday.

Making Appointments Private

As with regular appointments, you can make an appointment private by checking the Private box. A key icon next to the appointment description on the main schedule window indicates a private appointment. Other users cannot see details of your private appointments.

Editing Recurring Appointments

Select Edit Recurring Appointments from the Appointments menu to edit recurring appointments. A window containing your existing recurring appointments appears, similar to this:

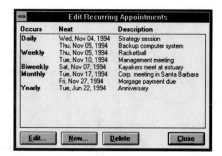

Use a mouse or the DOWN ARROW or UP ARROW keys to select an existing recurring appointment. Edit the recurring appointment details just as you would when adding a new one.

Changing Appointments to Recurring Appointments

You can change a one-time appointment to a recurring appointment. For example, assume you have an appointment with a research and development group, and the group decides to meet at the same time and date each month. Follow these steps to change a one-time appointment to a recurring appointment:

1. Click the appointment.

2. Select New Recurring Appointment from the Appointments menu or press ALT-M-R.

3. Enter the recurring appointment information.

The boxes in the recurring information window default to the information for a one-time appointment.

Finding Appointments

You can have Schedule+ search for appointments by choosing Find from the Edit menu. For example, let's assume you know you have a lunch date with Sally sometime this week, but you can't remember when. You would type **Sally** in the Search For field of the Find dialog box as shown in the following illustration. Then choose one of three buttons: Forward from today, Backward from today, or Whole schedule. Click OK when you are ready to search.

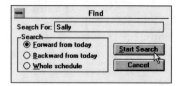

Schedule+ displays the first appointment where it finds the text. The keyword is highlighted in the appointment as shown in Figure 23-11. The Find dialog box remains on the screen so you can continue searching for other appointments. The Start Search button becomes a Find Next button. Click the Cancel button to stop searching or the Find Next button to continue searching. You can also type other text to search for.

If the Initial search or the Find Next search is unsuccessful, you'll see a message box. Click OK and check your spelling of the keyword. Correct your spelling or look for a different keyword. You may have misspelled Sally's name in the appointment itself. Search for a different keyword such as "Sal" or "lunch" in further attempts to find the appointment. Change your search criteria to search the entire schedule just in case you already missed your appointment. If you did miss your appointment, make sure you enable the reminder feature of the appointment next time.

Setting Access Privileges

You can set the access privileges that other users have to your schedule. Choose Set Access Privileges from the Options menu to display the Set Access Privileges dialog box as shown here:

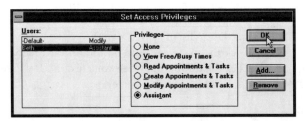

Click one of the Privileges buttons to set access levels for other users. All users are assigned the default privileges unless you add their names to the list of users. Follow these steps to assign access privileges:

1. Click the Add button on the Set Access Privileges window. A list of names appears.

2. Click a name.

3. Click the Add button on the user list screen.

4. Click the OK button.

5. Click a privilege button.

Note

If you have a secretary or other assistant who helps you manage your schedule, give that person the Assistant privilege.

FIGURE 23-11

The Find dialog box

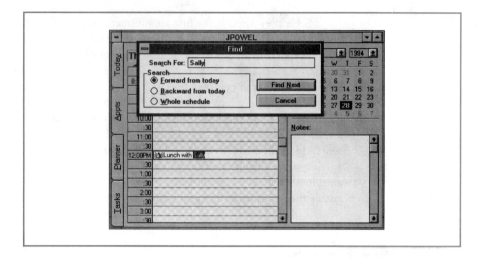

Opening Other Users' Appointment Books

You can open other users' appointment books to schedule joint appointments. Note that you can only open another user's Appointment Book if you have appropriate access privileges. Select Open Other's Appt. Book from the File menu to open someone else's schedule. A list of names or groups appears to choose from, similar to that in Figure 23-12. Click the name and Add button for each name (or group name) you want to include. Click the OK button when you are done. If you selected multiple users, the windows are displayed in cascade formation.

FIGURE 23-12

Open Other's Appt. Book dialog box

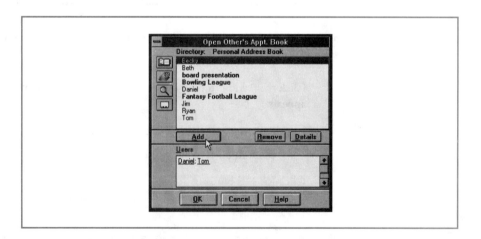

Exporting and Importing Appointments

You can export your Schedule+ data to disk or another computer and later recall its contents back to your own computer. This is useful for backing up or moving a specific range of appointments.

Note	If you need to take a copy of your schedule with you on a trip, you can move the schedule to a floppy disk by choosing the Move Local File command from the File menu. To archive appointments, refer to the following section.

Click Export Appointments from the File menu to bring up the Export Appointments dialog box shown here:

In the File Format field, choose the schedule format to export the entire schedule. If you choose text format, you can enter a date range of appointments in the Schedule Range field. You can also choose Include Daily Notes to copy daily notes to the exported schedule.

The Export Appointments file section dialog box appears when you click the OK button. Enter a filename or choose an existing file from the directory. The filename defaults to the name of your mailbox and a .SCH extension. Click the OK button to export the schedule.

Select Import Appointments from the File menu to import schedules that were previously exported. Schedule+ is also capable of importing schedules from Windows Calendar or WordPerfect Office. Type the name of the file and click the OK button. The Import Format dialog box shown here appears:

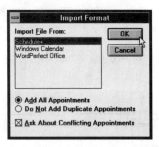

Choose a format and select one of the following options from the Import Format dialog box, then click the OK button.

▨ *Add All Appointments*   Click this button to add all appointments, regardless of whether they already exist in your current schedule.

▨ *Do Not Add Duplicate Appointments*   Click this button to merge the imported appointments with those already in your schedule.

▨ *Ask About Conflicting Appointments*   Click this button if you want Schedule+ to get your OK prior to adding any conflicting appointments.

Archiving Appointments

You can remove appointments from your schedule, but save them for later, by using the archiving option. Select Create Archive from the File menu to create an archive file. You can later open the archive file and view or modify its schedule entries. Select Open Archive from the File menu to open an existing archive file. Follow these steps to restore archived schedule entries back into your primary schedule:

1. Open an Existing Archive.

2. Export the schedule entries in the archive.

3. Select your primary schedule.

4. Import the schedule entries from the exported file.

TASK LIST

Tasks, unlike appointments, are activities to which you assign priorities and desired completion dates. You can use the Schedule+ *Task List* to create tasks, then you can assign priorities and completion dates to each task and group them into *projects* if necessary. You can optionally tell Schedule+ to create appointment entries from your tasks.

Adding a One-Time Task

Select the Task tab button from the schedule window or press CTRL-T to add a new task. The following Task dialog box appears:

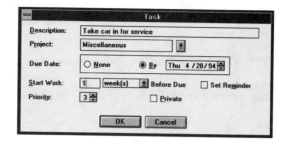

To create a task, fill out the fields on the Task dialog box as described here:

▧ *Description* Type the description of the task.

▧ *Project* Type a project name or select from existing projects if there are any.

▧ *Due Date* Select the date the project is due.

▧ *Start Work* Enter the number of days, weeks, or months prior to the due date that you should begin work.

▧ *Set Reminder* Enable this to be reminded of a start work time.

▧ *Priority* Set the priority level. The tasks are ordered by priority. In addition, you can print reports based on the priority of your tasks.

▧ *Private* Enable this box if you do not want others to see the task details.

Recurring Tasks

You can set tasks to recur on a regular basis. Select New Recurring Task from the Tasks menu and fill in the boxes as you would for a one-time task. In addition, click the Change button to change the recurrence of the task. The Change Recurrence dialog box appears, and you can fill it out as discussed previously in this chapter under "Recurring Appointments."

Viewing Tasks

To view your current tasks, click the Tasks tab button. Schedule+ displays a list of tasks similar to the one shown in Figure 23-13. To edit or view the details of a task, simply double-click it, or use the arrow keys to first highlight a task, then click the Edit button. You can also create a new task from this dialog box by typing a name for it in the New Task field and clicking the Add button.

There are several options for viewing that make it easy to find the item you are looking for or to determine which task you should work on next:

View by Project   Select View by Project from the Tasks menu to sort tasks by projects and project names. Use this in combination with the sort options described next to manipulate the view of your tasks.

Sort by Priority   Select Sort by Priority from the Tasks menu to sort tasks by priority. If you enabled View by Project, then your tasks are sorted by priority within each project. Otherwise, you will see a combined task list sorted by priority.

Sort by Due Date   Select Sort by Due Date from the Tasks menu to sort your task view by due date. If you have enabled View by Project, then your tasks are sorted by due date within each project. Otherwise, you will see a combined task list sorted by due date.

Sort by Descriptions   Select Sort by Descriptions from the Tasks menu to sort tasks by description. Your tasks are sorted by due date within each project if you have enabled View by Project. Otherwise, you will see a combined task list sorted by due date.

Show Active Tasks   Select Show Active Tasks from the Tasks menu to view only tasks that are currently active. Any tasks with a due date prior to the current date are excluded from the display.

FIGURE 23-13

Task list

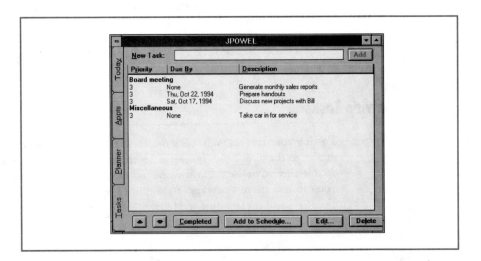

PLANNER

The *Planner* is used to scan your own and other users' appointments in order to set up group meetings. Browse through the days in Planner to view others' and your own availability. The *Auto-Pick* feature automatically selects times in which all parties are available.

The planner window shown in Figure 23-14 appears when you click the Planner tab button or press ALT-P. The blocks are shaded to indicate attendees' availability:

■   *Dark block*   You are busy.

■   *Gray block*   At least one other attendee is busy.

■   *Striped block*   You and at least one other attendee are busy.

Schedule+ displays a checkmark or an X next to the attendees' names to indicate their availability. Look next to the attendees when you click on a time slot. A checkmark indicates the person is available and an X indicates they already have an appointment scheduled.

Select Auto-pick from the Appointments menu to automatically search for the next time slot in which all attendees are available.

Click Request Meeting once you have selected a time for an appointment to pull up a Send Request form similar to Figure 23-4. The To box is filled in with the attendees

FIGURE 23-14

Planner window

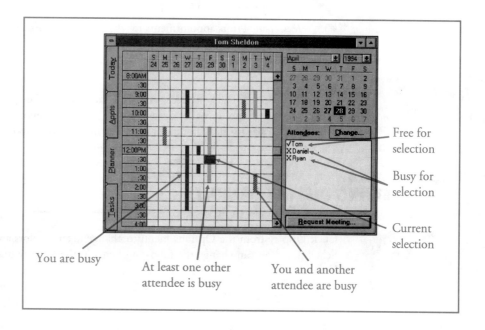

you had selected in the planner window. Enter a subject, check the Ask for Responses box, fill in a short memo, and click the Send button. You are notified that the meeting is booked successfully.

Printing Appointments and Tasks

Select Print from the File menu or press CTRL-P to print a copy of your appointments and tasks. Select the criteria for the report from the dialog box shown here:

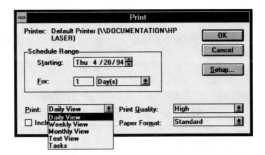

You have the option of printing your schedule or tasks in the following formats:

☑ *Daily View*   Prints the appointments for a single day.

☑ *Weekly View*   Prints the appointments for a single week.

☑ *Monthly View*   Prints the appointments for a month in calendar format.

☑ *Text View*   Prints appointments for the day in text format. Unlike Daily View, it does not include time slots.

☑ *Tasks*   Prints a complete list of active tasks.

Click Print Quality to select either High, Medium, Low, or draft quality. Click Paper Format to choose either Standard (8.5"x11.5"), Junior (5.5"x8.5"), or Pocket (3.75"x6.75") size for the printout. These sizes match most appointment books.

SETTING DISPLAY DEFAULTS

Click Display from the Options menu to change default colors and font sizes used by Schedule+. You can change the following items in the Display dialog screen as shown here:

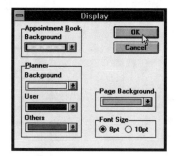

■ *Appointment Book Background* Color used for time slots that have not been filled.

■ *Planner Background* Color used for time slots that are available for all attendees.

■ *Planner User* Color used in Planner to indicate that you are busy.

■ *Planner Others* Color used in Planner to indicate that others are not available.

■ *Page Background* Background color used on Appointment Book, Planner, and Task List.

■ *Font Size* The size of the characters on the screen. Choose either the 8-point or 10-point size.

GENERAL OPTIONS

Click General Options from the Options menu to change many of the default settings in Schedule+ as shown in Figure 23-15.

Enable the Startup Offline option if you want Schedule+ to start in the offline mode rather than attempting to connect with the network. Select one or more of the options in the Reminders box to set how you want reminders to operate. Set the remaining fields according to how you want Schedule+ to display your schedule.

MORE ABOUT SCHEDULE+

Schedule+ is an application that uses Microsoft Mail for many of its functions, such as logging on, and sending and receiving messages. It also uses the address books created in Mail. User account information is automatically translated from Mail to Schedule+.

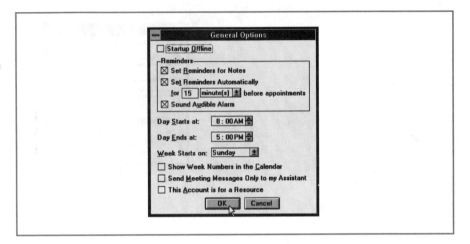

FIGURE 23-15

General Options dialog box

If you need to change the time and date display format, choose the International icon in the Control Panel. If you want to change the reminder sounds (assuming you have a sound board), choose the Sound option in the Control Panel.

The following sections present additional information about Schedule+.

Offline and Online Modes

You can use Schedule+ in offline or online modes. When working in the offline mode, Schedule+ operates as a stand-alone application and maintains a local calendar file on your hard disk. In online mode, Schedule+ uses a calendar file in the WGPO\CAL directory of the workgroup postoffice. You can use the offline file when the Schedule+ server is unavailable. Both online and offline files are kept synchronized as described here:

☑ The offline file is updated to match the online file every time you start and quit Schedule+ or connect and disconnect from the server.

☑ Appointments in the offline file are added to the online file.

☑ Deleted appointments in the offline file are removed from the online file.

☑ Changes made to the offline file take precedence over changes made to the online file.

Viewing Reminders at Windows NT Startup

Normally, you won't see any appointment reminders until you actually start Schedule+ and log on. If you want to see appointment reminders as soon as Windows NT itself starts, you'll need to create a startup icon for the file MSREMIND.EXE in the Program Manager Startup group. The following steps explain how to do this:

1. Highlight the Startup Group in the Program Manager by clicking it once.

2. Choose New from the Program Manager File menu.

3. Choose Program Item when the New Program Object dialog box appears.

4. On the Program Item Properties dialog box, click the Browse button, then select the file MSREMIND.EXE in the Windows NT directory and click OK.

5. When you return to the Program Item Properties dialog box, click OK to create the icon in the group.

The next time you start Windows NT, the Mail logon dialog box appears. Enter your logon name as usual. If there are any appointment reminders to display, a reminder dialog box appears for each one.

Creating Resource Accounts

Although Schedule+ helps people organize their time, it can also be used to schedule the use of high-resolution printers, conference rooms, and other company resources that many people need to share. The network provides an excellent way for many users to view the schedule of the resource and book it for future use. To create a resource, follow these steps:

1. Create an account for the resource using Mail in the same way you would create an account for a regular user. You must assign your password to each new resource account so you can log onto them from your workstation and perform step 2.

2. Start Schedule+ and log on using the new resource account name. Since you used your existing password for each resource, Schedule+ lets you sign into a different account during the same session.

3. Choose General Options from the Options menu, then enable the check box labelled "This Account is for a Resource".

Enabling this option changes the access privilege for the resource account to the "create appointments and tasks" option so that other people can access and reserve the resource. For example, if the resource is a conference room, a user organizing a meeting can select the conference room at the same time they choose attendees for the meeting. If the resource is a printer or other equipment, they can reserve it for future use by choosing the Open Other's Appt Book option on the File menu. They can then specify a time to use the resource in the same way they would create an appointment.

PART FIVE

Appendixes

Inside

- Preparing the Hardware

- Installing Windows NT

- Troubleshooting

& Out

APPENDIX A

Network Hardware Settings

This appendix covers installation steps for Windows NT systems and the Windows NT operating system. It is not meant to be a detailed explanation, only a step-by-step guide for those planning the installation or experienced users. Refer to the Windows NT manual for more details.

PREPARING THE HARDWARE

The Windows NT installation program does a good job of detecting what type of equipment you have and many of the component settings. It's a good idea to set up all the hardware before you begin the software installation. The installation process has two modes: Express setup and Custom setup. If you choose Express, default settings for detected hardware are used. If you need to install special drivers or specify special hardware settings, you need to use the Custom setup. Each is discussed in step 2 in the "Installing Windows NT" section later in this chapter.

SCSI Hard Disk and CD-ROM Adapters

If you are installing an SCSI adapter, the first and last device attached to the adapter must have a *terminating resister*. This is a removable pack mounted on the circuit board attached to the drive. Most drives come with the terminator mounted. If a drive is not the last drive in a chain of drives connected by the SCSI cable to the SCSI adapter, you'll need to remove the terminating resister pack. The adapter itself is usually the first device; however, if you attach external drives and also have internal drives, this often places the adapter in the middle, in which case, you'll need to remove the terminator from the adapter and make sure the last internal device and the last external device are terminated.

| Note | Make sure that CD-ROM drives are not set to ID 0 or 1, which are usually reserved for hard drives. If a CD-ROM drive is configured improperly, you may see an additional partition where one doesn't exist. |

Running the Configuration Utility

Most computer systems have a configuration utility you need to run when adding additional memory, disk drives, or other equipment. Be sure to run this utility after installing the memory or adapters and before running the Windows NT installation program.

Video Equipment

Most video adapter cards require special drivers to work with Windows NT. While Windows NT comes with a full set of popular drivers, you might need to copy and configure a special driver or an updated driver before you can start Windows NT.

During installation, Windows NT will substitute a VGA or other standard video driver if it doesn't recognize your video adapter. While these settings are usually sufficient to get you through the installation, you can use the Windows NT Setup utility to install special video drivers either during or after the installation. In some cases, it makes sense to use the basic drivers and make sure Windows NT completely installs, and then set up your custom video drivers using Windows NT Setup. Doing so reduces the investigative work you have to do when Windows NT doesn't work right because if the problem occurs after you set up the video driver, you can isolate the problem to the video driver.

Video drivers often have different resolution settings. You can select higher resolution settings only if your video card has enough on-board memory to support the resolution. If it doesn't, use a lower setting or add more memory to the card.

Installing Adapters

Installing network interface cards and other adapters in your computer is not often a simple matter. You usually need to ensure that settings on the cards don't conflict with the settings of other devices in the computer. These settings are the interrupt (IRQ) and base I/O port address.

To confuse matters, settings that work under DOS don't always work under Windows NT. This can often send you down the wrong path when investigating a problem; you might assume that because a network card worked fine in DOS, it is not the cause of problems in Windows NT. Fortunately, Windows NT comes with the Event Viewer, which creates a log of startup problems that helps you debug situations such as interrupt conflicts.

Interrupts

When a device such as a network interface card needs attention from your computer's CPU, it sends a signal over an interrupt line. The computer must "answer" the interrupt and service the request. No two devices in the computer can use the same interrupt simultaneously. Table A-1 lists the most commonly used settings.

You'll want to install your network card with an interrupt that is not already in use. If you have Windows 3.1 installed, use the Microsoft MSD utility to determine the current interrupt usage for your system. Type **MSD** to start the utility, then type **Q** to select IRQ Status from the Main menu. Use an IRQ number that lists No in the Detected column.

I/O Port Addresses

An I/O port address is a memory location that network cards or other devices use to transfer information to the CPU. No two devices can use the same I/O port address simultaneously. Table A-1 lists common I/O port addresses.

TABLE A-1

Commonly Used
Interrupt Settings

System Component	IRQ	I/O Port Address
EGA/VGA video adapters	2	3C0 to 3CF
EGA/VGA video in color mode	2	3D0 to 3DF
COM1,COM3	4	3F0 to 3FF
COM2,COM4 (if used)	3	2F0 to 2FF
Floppy disk controller	6	3F0 to 3FF
Parallel port LPT1	7	3B0 to 3BF
Parallel port LPT2 (if used)	5	370 to 37F
System clock	8	
Math coprocessor	13	
Hard disk controller	14	320 to 32F
Game port		200 to 20F
Bus mouse		230 to 23F

INSTALLING WINDOWS NT

How you install Windows NT depends on whether you have an existing system or a new system that doesn't have an operating system installed. Have a blank disk ready; during the installation, you'll be asked to insert it so the install program can create an emergency recovery disk.

If Already Set Up for DOS and Windows 3.1

If your system is already set up to run DOS and Windows 3.1, you have several installation options:

▰   Completely reformat the disks for the NTFS file system and install Windows NT. None of the DOS or Windows 3.1 environment is saved or used to configure the Windows NT environment. Back up programs and data, then restore them once Windows NT is installed.

▰   Retain any partitions formatted for DOS or other operating systems. You can install Windows NT on a DOS FAT drive, but you won't get NTFS features such as security and long filenames. However, you can convert to NTFS during installation or at a later time.

▰   If you want to keep any existing file systems, your best option is to make additional disk space available for NTFS. You might want to install an additional disk, or back up and remove an existing DOS or HPFS partition other than the one you want to keep.

Note   The first active internal disk (drive C) holds startup information for Windows NT. It must be formatted to either DOS FAT, HPFS, or NTFS.

Note   If Windows 3.1 is installed on an existing system, the Windows NT installation process uses some of the Windows 3.1 environment settings. It also helps you install any programs that were configured to run under Windows 3.1.

If Multiple Systems Exist

If multiple operating systems exist on the computer, a boot loader utility appears when you first start the computer to let you choose which operating system you want to start.

If Part of a Network

You need to know the following if your Windows NT workstation will become part of a network:

- The settings of the network interface card installed in your computer, as discussed in Table A-1.

- The name of any workgroups or Windows NT Advanced Server domains you plan to join.

- A name for your computer that other users will see when they need to access it.

Step 1: Starting Setup

Windows NT comes on floppy disk and CD-ROM. You can also install Windows NT from another computer on a network.

- *From floppy disk*   To install Windows NT from floppy disk, insert Windows NT Setup Disk #1 and turn on the computer.

- *From CD-ROM*   To install from CD-ROM, insert the Windows NT Setup floppy disk and then start the computer.

- *From a server*   To install Windows NT from a server, connect to the directory where the Windows NT shared files are located, then type **WINNT** and follow the instructions on the screen. Refer to the following section, "Installing Windows NT Master Files on a Server," for more details.

- *From RISC-based systems*   On RISC-based computers, follow the instructions supplied by the manufacturer for installing Windows NT. Each manufacturer has slightly different procedures.

The Microsoft *Windows NT Resource Kit* (available separately) has a Profile Setup utility that is useful when setting up a large number of similarly configured computers. It lets you create setup templates for various hardware configurations, which simplify installing Windows NT on those computers. Contact Microsoft for more details.

Installing Windows NT Master Files on a Server

If you are an Administrator, you can copy all the Windows NT files to a server that other users can connect to and use to install Windows NT on their own system. The necessary files are copied to the users' system from the master directory over the network cable. This eliminates the need to install a CD-ROM at workstations or run the installation using the tedious floppy disk method.

Note

This method works with Intel-based computers that are connected to a server using the most popular networks, such as Novell NetWare, Microsoft LAN Manager 2.1, and Banyan VINES. It does not work on RISC-based computers.

The server must be running Windows NT. Here are the steps for installing the master files:

1. Create a directory on the server for the master files, then make sure users have read access to that directory.

2. Start the Command Prompt and type a command similar to the following:

    SETUP –n –i INITIAL.INF –s *source* –d *destination*

    Replace *source* with the drive and directory where the original files are located. On CD-ROM, this is the \i386 directory, preceded by the letter of the CD-ROM drive. Replace *destination* with the name of the shared network directory.

3. Follow the remaining instructions on the screen to complete the file copy procedure.

Step 2: Choosing Express or Custom Setup

After the installation program starts, you can choose either Express or Custom setup. If you choose Express setup, recommended settings are used and you only are asked to install a printer and verify other settings, such as the network interface card.

If you choose Custom setup, you can set options on your own, overriding default settings. For example, you can specify a different display adapter, change virtual memory settings, and specify which existing applications you want to install.

Note

You can run Express setup, then change any settings afterward using the Setup utility.

Step 3: Deciding What to Do with Existing Systems

If your system has an existing copy of Windows 3.1 or Windows for Workgroups, and thus an existing DOS partition, Windows NT asks if you want to install in the DOS partition. You can install there, but Windows NT will not have security features.

Remember that you can convert to NTFS later. If you have free disk space, choose to partition that space for Windows NT and format it for NTFS.

> **Note**
>
> You also can delete and repartition disks, but this destroys any existing information on those disks, so make sure you have a sufficient backup before proceeding.

Step 4: Specifying Setup Parameters

In this step, you specify several custom parameters, or choose the default settings set by the installation program. You need to configure the following:

- The directory in which you are installing the Windows NT files. The default is \WINNT but you can specify another directory.

- A name for the computer that appears in workgroup listings.

- A language setting.

- Virtual memory settings. The default settings are recommended, but you can increase or decrease the size of the virtual memory paging file, as discussed in Chapter 15.

- Printer configuration. You need to specify drivers for local printers only. It's not necessary to install drivers for remote network printers you plan to use. Refer to Chapter 18 for details.

- Network adapter card settings, as discussed earlier in this chapter and in Chapter 17. Make sure the interrupt number, I/O port address, and other network card settings match the settings of the card itself.

The installation program checks for network adapters and recommends a card, but not all cards are recognizable. If you need to install additional cards or change settings, you can do so during installation or later using the Network utility in the Control Panel.

At this point, files are copied to the specified Windows NT directory over a period of a few minutes.

Step 5: Workgroup, Domain, and Local Account Settings

After files are copied, you need to specify whether the computer is part of a workgroup or Windows NT Advanced Server domain. You can make these settings now or wait until after installation is complete to make the correct settings. To make them later, specify any name for the workgroup now, then change it whenever you want to.

If this is the first computer in a network workgroup, you can create a new workgroup name. If it is joining an existing network, find out what the workgroup name is, or specify it later when you do find out what it is.

To join a Windows NT Advanced Server domain, that domain must already exist with an account for your computer.

At this point, specify a name for the Initial User account. This is an account with Administrator rights that has a name you choose. For example, you might type your first initial and last name. You then type and verify a password for the account.

Step 6: Setting Up Applications

The installation program gives you a chance to set up applications that might already be installed on your system. Basically, the Windows NT Setup utility is started as discussed in Chapter 15. You select drives to search, and a list of the applications on the drives appears. You then choose which applications you want to create startup icons for in the Program Manager.

Step 7: Restarting and Logging On

The final step is to restart Windows NT and log on as the Administrator or the local user. Chapter 4 covers the logon process and how to begin working with Windows NT.

TROUBLESHOOTING

Once Windows NT installs, you might see a message similar to the following that indicates the operating system is having trouble accessing components or the network:

Click OK to bypass the message, then open the Event Viewer located in the Administrative Tools group to see more information about the problems. An Event Viewer window is shown in Figure A-1.

Most of the alerts listed in this window were generated by a failed network interface card. You can view any alert by double-clicking it. You see messages about failed NetBIOS services, and other associated network services. However, the most important message is one that tells you about hardware conflicts, as shown in Figure A-2. In this case, the NE2000 network interface card's interrupt setting of 4 is in conflict with another device. In some cases, you also see information about the device the component is conflicting with.

It's usually best to install the network cards and resolve conflicts before installing Windows NT on the computer, but problems often occur after the installation. If you can't get a computer to operate after installing a network card, or if you can't get Windows NT to recognize other computers on the network, you'll need to do a little investigative work. Write down all the settings for cards in the system and the settings listed in the documentation for your computer. Make sure there are no conflicts.

The following tips may help you resolve network card problems or connection problems:

- If a device such as a mouse fails to work after your system is started, the network card is probably using the same IRQ as the mouse. Try setting a different IRQ for the mouse or the network card.

- If you've installed a sound board, make sure it's not conflicting with interrupt 7, which is typically assigned to a printer.

- If Windows NT starts, but has problems when you attempt to connect with a shared drive, try debugging the IRQ and I/O settings as discussed in the "Installing Adapters" section earlier in this chapter.

- Make sure all the cables are installed properly and that each has a good connection. If you have network problems after installing a new workstation, you probably have a faulty cable segment. Try reattaching the connectors. If

FIGURE A-1

The Event Viewer window

Date	Time	Source	Category	Event	User	Computer
5/1/93	3:01:47 PM	NetDDE	None	204	N/A	GATEWAY
5/1/93	3:01:46 PM	Service Control Manager	None	7000	N/A	GATEWAY
5/1/93	3:01:44 PM	Service Control Manager	None	7002	N/A	GATEWAY
5/1/93	3:01:44 PM	Service Control Manager	None	7002	N/A	GATEWAY
5/1/93	3:01:44 PM	Service Control Manager	None	7000	N/A	GATEWAY
5/1/93	3:01:44 PM	NE2000	None	5004	N/A	GATEWAY
5/1/93	3:01:44 PM	NE2000	None	5018	N/A	GATEWAY
5/1/93	3:01:44 PM	NE2000	None	24	N/A	GATEWAY
5/1/93	3:01:44 PM	NE2000	None	24	N/A	GATEWAY

Event Viewer - System Log on \\GATEWAY

Log   View   Options   Help

FIGURE A-2

The Event Detail screen, showing a hardware conflict

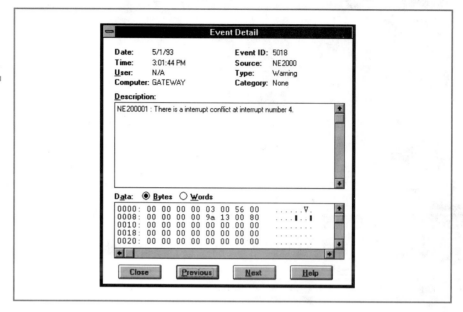

possible, use an ohm meter to check continuity between the center pins at each end. If they test fine, check continuity between the ground wire (the connector casing itself) at each end of the cable.

Most network interface cards come with a diagnostic utility that performs a loopback test on the cable connector. You can use it to check the connector and cable segments. Start by checking the card itself. Attach a T-connector that has a terminator on both ends, then run the test. If everything tests fine, attach a cable segment and move one of the terminators to the end of the cable segment. Run the test again. Continue testing in this way until you find the cable segment that causes the loopback test to fail.

Note

Keep in mind that on large networks, Windows NT may take a few minutes before it recognizes new computers on the network. You might, at first, think you have a connection problem. Just wait a little while and try the connection again. In some cases, you might need to restart the new computer, or all the computers.

Inside

& Out

APPENDIX

B

Command Cross Reference

This cross-reference list is designed to help you locate keywords and command names in the Windows NT Command Reference. Access the Command Reference by double-clicking the Windows NT Help icon in the main group, then clicking the icon labeled "Access the Command Reference Help." When the Command Reference opens, click the button next to the command you referenced in this appendix.

Command help. See HELP.

Command help for network. See NET HELP.

Command history buffer. See DOSKEY.

Command interpreter location, specifying alternate. See SHELL.

Command interpreter, start new. See CMD.

Command prompt change. See PROMPT.

Command Prompt windows title, changing of. See TITLE.

Command scheduler, See AT.

Command startup, scheduling of. See NET START SCHEDULE.

COMP, Compares the contents of two files or sets of files.

Comparison of files. See COMP or FC.

Computer browsing service. See NET START COMPUTER BROWSER.

Computer, adding/deleting in a domain database. See NET COMPUTER.

Conditional processing in batch files. See IF.

Configuration of devices. See MODE.

Configuration of domain database. See NET COMPUTER.

Configuration of keyboard. See KEYB.

Configure server services. See NET CONFIG SERVER.

Configure services. See NET CONFIG.

Configure workstation services. See NET CONFIG WORKSTATION.

Connection status of network. See PING.

Continue suspended services. See NET CONTINUE.

CONVERT, Converts FAT or HPFS volumes to NTFS. You cannot convert
    the current drive.

COPY, Copies one or more files to another location.

Copy disk command. See DISKCOPY.

Copy files between computers. See RCP.

Copy files, File Transfer Protocol. See FTP.

Copy files on local system. See COPY or XCOPY.

Country, specifies the country format to use for dates, money, etc.

Create directory. See MKDIR or MD.

Data file paths, setting up of. See APPEND.

Data stacks, specifying. See STACKS.

Database configuration for domain. See NET COMPUTER.

Date settings. See DATE.

DATE, Displays or sets the date.

DEBUG, Used to view and change MS-DOS executable files.

Deleting files. See DELETE or ERASE.

DEVICE, Loads device drivers.

Device codepage setup. See DEVINFO.

Device configuration. See MODE.

Device driver loading. See DEVICE or DEVICEHIGH.

DEVICEHIGH, Loads device drivers into upper memory.

DEVINFO, Prepares devices to use code pages.

Dynamic Link Library search path, OS/2. See LIBPATH.

DIR, Displays a list of files and subdirectories in a directory.

Directory change command. See CHDIR (or CD).

Directory, return to previous pushed (PUSHD) name. See POPD.

Directory listing command. See DIR.

Directory removal. See RMDIR (RD).

Directory replicator service startup. See NET START DIRECTORY REPLICATOR.

Directory search path for OS/2. See LIBPATH.

Directory, create. See MKDIR or MD.

Directory, move files between. See MOVE.

Directory, store current for later return. See PUSHD.

Directory search paths. See PATH.

Directory structure tree. See TREE.

Disk backup. See BACKUP.

Disk check command. See CHKDSK.

Disk compare. See DISKCOMP.

Disk copy command. See DISKCOPY.

Disk directory listing command. See DIR.

Disk file recovery. See RECOVER.

Disk formatting command. See FORMAT.

Disk performance counter. See DISKPERF.

Disk volume label change. See LABEL.

DISKCOMP, Compares the contents of two floppy disks.

DISKCOPY, Copies the contents of one floppy disk to another.

DISKPERF, Stops and starts the system performance counter.

Display account information for user. See NET ACCOUNTS.

Display configuration. See MODE.

Display connections. See NET USE NOTES.

Display directory tree. See TREE.

Display DOS version table. See SETVER.

Display environment settings. See SET.

Display file contents. See TYPE, MORE, EDIT, or EDLIN.

Display files currently open and shared, See NET FILE.

Display global groups on NT Advanced Server. See NET GROUP.

Display groups. See NET LOCALGROUP.

Display hostname. See HOSTNAME.

Display local groups. See NET LOCALGROUP.

Display messaging names on local station. See NET NAME.

Display network services. See NET CONFIG.

Display print and queue information. See NET PRINT.

Display protocol statistics for NetBIOS/TCP connection. See NBTSTAT.

Display server list and shared resources. See NET VIEW.

Display server service settings. See NET CONFIG SERVER.

Display servers and resource shares. See NET VIEW.

Display services and configure them. See NET CONFIG.

Display services that are started. See NET START.

Display session connections. See NET SESSION.

Display shared resources. See NET SHARE.

Display statistics log for workstation. See NET STATISTICS.

Display system status. See MODE.

Display user accounts on local server. See NET USER.

Display user information on remote system. See FINGER.

Display workstation settings. See NET CONFIG WORKSTATION.

Domain database configuration. See NET COMPUTER.

DOS command, force start. See FORCEDOS.

DOSKEY, Edits command lines, recalls previous commands, and runs keyboard macros.

Drive letter/path association. See SUBST.

Driver loading. See DEVICE or DEVICEHIGH.

ECHO, Displays messages, or turns command echoing on or off.

ECHOCONFIG, Sets message display in CONFIG.NT and AUTOEXEC.NT batch files.

EDIT, A menu-based text editor.

Editing text files. See EDIT or EDLIN.

EDLIN, A text-based line (one-line-at-a-time) editor.

End Command Prompt. See EXIT.

ENDLOCAL, Ends localization of environment changes in a batch file.

Environment variables in batch files. See SETLOCAL and ENDLOCAL.

Environment variables, setting of. See SET.

ERASE, Deletes one or more files. See DELETE or DEL.

Error message help. See NET HELPMSG.

Ethernet translation from IP. See ARP.

Event logging. See NET START EVENTLOG.

Executable file conversion. See EXE2BIN.

Executable search paths. See PATH.

Execution, remote. See REXEC or RSH.

EXIT, Quits the CMD.EXE program (command interpreter).

FAT volume conversion to NTFS. See CONVERT.

FC, Compares two files or sets of files, and displays the differences between them.

File access specifier. See FILES.

File attributes, changing of. See ATTRIB.

File backup, restoring files. See RESTORE.

File backup. See BACKUP.

File comparison. See COMP or FC.

File contents, sorting of. See SORT.

File control block (FCB) specifier. See FCB.

File conversion, executable to binary. See EXE2BIN.

File copy between computers. See RCP.

File copying. See COPY or XCOPY.

File debugging. See DEBUG.

File delete. See DELETE or ERASE.

File, displaying contents of. See TYPE or MORE.

File editor. See EDIT or EDLIN.

File, listing of in directories. See DIR.

File locks, See NET FILE.

File, moving. See MOVE.

File output redirection. See MORE.

File paths, configuring. Use APPEND.

File printing. See PRINT.

File recovery. See RECOVER.

File renaming. See RENAME (REN).

File replacement between directories. See REPLACE.

File, search for text in. See FIND or FINDSTR.

File system conversion from FAT or HPFS to NTFS. See CONVERT.

File system conversion from OS/2 LAN Manager to NTFS, use ACLCONV.

File Transfer Protocol, Trivial. See TFTP.

File transfer to/from FTP server. See FTP.

FILES, Sets the number of files MS-DOS can access.

Files, open and shared. See NET FILE.

FIND, Searches for keywords in a file or files.

FINDSTR, Searches for strings of text in files.

FINGER, Displays information about a user on a specified system.

Floppy disk comparison. See DISKCOMP.

Floppy disk copy command. See DISKCOPY.

FOR, A batch file command that runs a specified command for each file in a
set of files.

FORCEDOS, Runs MS-DOS programs not recognized by Windows NT.

FORMAT, Formats a disk for use with Windows NT.

Formatting command for disks. See FORMAT.

FTP, Transfers files to and from a node running an FTP server program.

GOTO, Directs Windows NT to a labeled line in a batch program.

GRAFTABL, Enables Windows NT to display an extended character set in
graphics mode.

GRAPHICS, A utility for printing color screens on various printers.

Graphics mode extended character set. See GRAFTABL.

Graphics printing. See GRAPHICS.

Groups, configure on Advanced Server. See NET GROUP.

Groups, configuration of. See NET LOCALGROUP.

Hard disk initialization. See FORMAT.

Help for error messages. See NET HELPMSG.

Help for network commands. See NET HELP.

HELP, Provides help information for Windows NT commands.
High memory area for DOS. See DOS.
History buffer for commands. See DOSKEY.
HOSTNAME, Displays the current host name.
HPFS volume conversion to NTFS. See CONVERT.
IF, Performs conditional processing in batch programs.
Information, viewing NT and network status. See Display entries in this appendix.
Initialization command for disks. See FORMAT.
INSTALL, Loads a memory resident program.
Installing programs. See INSTALL.
International settings. See COUNTRY.
Internet file transfer. See TFTP.
IP-to-Ethernet/Token Ring address translation. See ARP.
KEYB, Configures a keyboard for a specific language.
Keyboard configuration. See KEYB or MODE.
Keyboard conversion command. See SWITCHES.
Keyboard macro utility. See DOSKEY.
LABEL, Creates, changes, or deletes the volume label of a disk.
Label, changing on disks. See LABEL.
LAN Manager (OS/2) conversion to NTFS, use ACLCONV.
LIBPATH, Specifies directories MS-OS/2 searches for dynamic link libraries.
Load program command. See LOADFIX.
Load program in upper memory. See LOADHIGH.
LOADFIX, Loads a program above first 64K of conventional memory and runs it.
LOADHIGH, Loads programs into upper memory.
Local group configuration. See NET LOCALGROUP.
Locator service (RPC). See NET START LOCATOR.
Locks on files. See NET FILE.
Log, statistics. See NET STATISTICS.
Logging of events. See NET START EVENTLOG.
Logon service startup. See NET START NETLOGON.
LPT port configuration. See MODE.
Macro, keyboard. See DOSKEY.
Make directory command. See MKDIR or MD.
Management services. See NET START SNMP.
MD, Creates a directory.
MEM, Displays memory statistics.
Memory statistics. See MEM.
Memory, load DOS high. See DOS.
Memory, Load programs high. See LOADHIGH.
Message help for errors. See NET HELPMSG.
Message send. See NET SEND.
Message system startup. See NET START MESSENGER.
Messaging name for computer. See NET NAME.

MKDIR, Creates a directory.

MODE, Configures a system device.

Monitor disk performance. See DISKPERF.

MORE, Displays output one screen at a time.

MOVE, Moves one or more files from one directory to another directory on
the same drive.

MS-DOS version number, setting. See SETVER.

Name, messaging. See NET NAME.

NBTSTAT, Displays information about NetBIOS over TCP/IP connection.

NETSTAT, Displays protocol statistics and the state of the current
TCP/IP network connection.

NET ACCOUNTS, Updates the user accounts database.

NET COMPUTER, Adds or deletes computers in a domain database.

NET CONFIG, Displays and configures services.

NET CONFIG SERVER, Displays and changes server services.

NET CONFIG WORKSTATION, Displays and changes workstation services.

NET CONTINUE, Reactivates suspended services.

NET FILE, Displays the names of open shared files on a server and locks on files.

NET GROUP, Adds, displays, or modifies global groups on Windows NT
Advanced Servers.

NET HELP, Displays help for network commands.

NET HELPMSG, Provides error message help.

NET LOCALGROUP, Adds, displays, or modifies local groups.

NET NAME, Adds or deletes messaging name (alias).

NET PAUSE, Pauses running service.

NET PRINT, Displays or controls print jobs and printer queues.

NET SEND, Sends messages on network.

NET SESSION, Lists or disconnects sessions between server and workstation.

NET SHARE, Configures shared resources.

NET START, Starts and displays network services.

NET START ALERTER, Starts the network alerter service.

NET START COMPUTER BROWSER, Starts the service that provides browsing
of computers on the network.

NET START DIRECTORY REPLICATOR, Starts the directory replicator
service.

NET START EVENTLOG, Starts event logging on the local computer.

NET START LOCATOR, Starts the Remote Procedure Call (RPC)
Locator service.

NET START MESSENGER, Starts the Messenger service so the workstation can
receive messages.

NET START NETLOGON, Starts the net logon service, which
authenticates users.

NET START SCHEDULE, Starts the Schedule service, which enables computers
to start programs at times specified by the AT command.

NET START SERVER, Starts the Server service, which enables computers to share resources.

NET START SNMP, Starts the simple network management protocol (SNMP) so a server can report its status.

NET START TCPIP NETBIOS PROTOCOL, Starts the NetBIOS over TCP (NBT) service.

NET START TCPIP, Starts the TCP/IP services.

NET START TELNET, Starts the Telnet client service to provide terminal emulation of TCP/IP in Windows Terminal.

NET START WORKSTATION, Starts the workstation service.

NET STATISTICS, Displays the statistics log for the local workstation or server.

NET STOP, Stops the Windows NT network service.

NET TIME, Synchronizes the local computer's clock with a server or domain.

NET USE, Connects or disconnects from a shared network resource.

NET USER, Adds or modifies user accounts or view user account information.

NET VIEW, Displays server lists or shared resources on a server.

NetBIOS service on TCP. See NET START TCP/IP NETBIOS PROTOCOL.

NetBIOS statistics. See NBTSTAT.

NETSTAT, Displays information about TCP/IP network connections.

Network command help. See NET HELP.

Network computer browsing service. See NET START COMPUTER BROWSER.

Network connection status. See PING.

Network information. See Display entries in this appendix.

Network management services. See NET START SNMP.

Network resource sharing. See NET USE.

Network routing table manipulation. See ROUTE.

Network services, Advanced Server domain update. See NET COMPUTER.

Network services, Advanced Server group configuration. See NET GROUP.

Network services, alerter startup. See NET START ALERTER.

Network services, browser startup. See NET START COMPUTER BROWSER.

Network services, command scheduling. See NET START SCHEDULE.

Network services, continue suspended services. See NET CONTINUE.

Network services, directory replicator. See NET START DIRECTORY REPLICATOR.

Network services, disconnect from workstation. See NET SESSION.

Network services, display and change for server. See NET CONFIG SERVER.

Network services, display and configure workstation. See NET CONFIG.

Network services, event logging. See NET START EVENTLOG.

Network services, file shares. See NET FILE.

Network services, group configure. See NET LOCALGROUP.

Network services, Locator. See NET START LOCATOR.

Network services, logon service startup. See NET START NETLOGON.

Network services, messaging name for computer. See NET NAME.

Program load command. See LOADFIX.

Program load in upper memory. See LOADHIGH.

Program loading. See INSTALL.

Program scheduler. See AT.

Program startup command. See FORCEDOS.

Program startup in separate window. See START.

Program startup, scheduled. See NET START SCHEDULE.

PROMPT, Changes the Windows NT command prompt.

Prompt, changing. See PROMPT.

Protocol statistics of TCP/IP. See NBTSTAT.

PUSHD, Saves the current directory then changes it.

Queue control. See NET PRINT.

Quit a command interpreter environment. See EXIT.

RCP, Copies files between computers on the network.

RD, Removes a directory.

RECOVER, Recovers readable information from a bad or defective disk.

Redirection of output. See MORE.

REM, Records comments (remarks) in batch files or CONFIG.SYS.

Remote execution. See REXEC or RSH.

Remote Procedure Call Locator service. See NET START LOCATOR.

Remote user information. See FINGER.

REN, Renames a file or files.

RENAME, Renames a file or files.

REPLACE, Replaces files.

Replicator service startup. See NET START DIRECTORY REPLICATOR.

Resource sharing, See NET SHARE, NET START SERVER, NET USE.

Resources, viewing shared. See NET VIEW.

RESTORE, Restores files that were backed up by using the BACKUP command.

REXEC, Executes files at remote systems.

RMDIR, Removes a directory.

ROUTE, Lets users manually manipulate network routing tables.

Routing table manipulation. See ROUTE.

RSH, (Remote Shell) connects to a specified host and executes commands.

Scheduling command startup. See NET START SCHEDULE.

Scheduling commands, See AT.

Screen output control. See MORE.

Search for string in file. See FIND or FINDSTR.

Search paths. See PATH.

Send messages. See NET SEND.

Serial port configuration and status. See MODE.

Server service startup. See NET START SERVER.

Server services, display and change. See NET CONFIG SERVER.

Server statistics, viewing. See NET STATISTICS.

SETLOCAL, Begins localization of environment changes in a batch file.

SETVER, Sets the MS-DOS version the MS-DOS subsystem reports to a program.

Shared files. See NET FILE.

Shared resources, viewing. See NET VIEW.

Sharing of resources. See NET START SERVER or NET SHARE.

SHELL, Specifies an alternate MS-DOS command interpreter.

SHIFT, Shifts the position of replaceable parameters in batch files.

SNMP services. See NET START SNMP.

SORT, Sorts input.

Sorting command. See SORT.

Start alerter service. See NET START ALERTER.

Start network services. See NET START.

Start suspended services. See NET CONTINUE.

Start workstation services. See NET START WORKSTATION.

START, Starts a separate window to run a specified program or command.

Startup of program in separate window. See START.

Statistics about users. See FINGER.

Statistics log, viewing. See NET STATISTICS.

Statistics of TCP/IP connection. See NBTSTAT.

Statistics of TCP/IP network. See NETSTAT.

Statistics, memory. See MEM.

Status of network connection. See PING.

SUBST, Associates a path with a drive letter.

Synchronization of time. See NET TIME.

Table manipulation, routing. See ROUTE.

TCP, NetBIOS service on. See NET START TCP/IP NETBIOS PROTOCOL.

TCP/IP command. See NBTSTAT.

TCP/IP network statistics. See NETSTAT.

TCP/IP server status reporting. See NET START SNMP.

TCP/IP services, See NET START TCPIP.

TCP/IP terminal emulation. See TELNET.

TCP/IP utilities, See TCP/IP in Command Reference for list.

Telnet service. See NET START TELNET.

TELNET, Starts a terminal emulator on TCP/IP networks.

Terminal emulation and TCP/IP. See NET START TELNET or TELNET.

Text file editor. See EDIT or EDLIN.

Text file printing. See PRINT.

Text search in files. See FIND or FINDSTR.

TFTP, Provides Internet Trivial File Transfer Protocols.

Time synchronization. See NET TIME.

TIME, Displays or sets the system time.

TITLE, Sets the window title for a CMD.EXE session.

Token Ring translation from IP. See ARP.

TREE, Graphically displays the directory structure of a drive or path.

Trivial File Transfer Protocol. See TFTP.

TYPE, Displays the contents of a text file.

Update of user accounts. See NET ACCOUNTS.

Upper memory area for DOS. See DOS.

User account update. See NET ACCOUNTS.

User accounts configuration. See NET USER.

User group configuration. See NET LOCALGROUP.

User information. See FINGER.

Variables in batch files. See SETLOCAL and ENDLOCAL.

Variables, environment. See SET.

Viewing information. See Display entries in this appendix.

VER, Displays the Windows NT version.

VERIFY, Tells Windows NT whether to verify that your files are written
    correctly to a disk.

Version number, setting in MS-DOS. See SETVER.

Version numbers for MS-DOS. See VER.

VOL, Displays a disk volume label and serial number.

Volume conversion to NTFS. See CONVERT.

Volume information. See VOL.

Volume label change. See LABEL.

Window title for command prompt, changing. See TITLE.

Windows NT Advanced Server domain update. See NET COMPUTER.

Windows NT Advanced Server, Adds, displays, modifies groups. See NET GROUP.

Workstation service startup. See NET START WORKSTATION.

Workstation services, display and change. See NET CONFIG WORKSTATION.

Workstation session disconnect. See NET SESSION.

Workstation statistics, viewing. See NET STATISTICS.

XCOPY, Copies files and directory trees.

Inside

- What is TCP/IP?

- Installing TCP/IP

- TCP/IP Related Commands

& Out

APPENDIX C

Internetwork Connections with TCP/IP

TCP/IP (Transmission Control Protocol/Internet Protocol) is a protocol suite designed with internetworking in mind. In the early '80s, there was a need to interconnect dissimilar computers on a global scale. TCP/IP grew out of research done by DARPA (Defense Advanced Research Projects Agency) and an internetwork called *ARPAnet* was formed, which later evolved into the *Internet*.

The purpose of TCP/IP is to provide the protocols for transmission of information independent of the network or hardware. Because the protocol is so flexible and well established, it has moved out of the realm of the Internet and into organizations that need to connect diverse LANs.

This appendix provides a brief introduction to TCP/IP for people who need to communicate with computers attached to other networks as well as those who need to communicate with UNIX systems.

The NBF protocol that provides network communication in Windows NT networks is based on the older NetBEUI (NetBIOS Extended User Interface) protocol. However, NetBEUI is not a routable protocol because its original designers assumed that gateways would be used to establish internetwork connections. *Gateways* are systems that provide a connection point for two computers and run special software that translates and transfers packets between the networks.

To circumvent NetBEUI's being unroutable, Microsoft supplies the TCP/IP protocol suite with Windows NT and a protocol module called NetBIOS over TCP/IP (NBT) that provides a way for NetBIOS applications to communicate across internetworks using TCP/IP. A system that operates as a gateway under Windows NT consists of two network interface cards. Each card connects to separate LANs that are each assigned a specific Internet Protocol (IP) address as shown in Figure C-1. (IP addressing is discussed in a moment.)

This appendix introduces the basic concepts of TCP/IP and how you use it to set up internetwork communications.

WHAT IS TCP/IP?

The TCP/IP protocol suite defines a packet-switched network, which simply means that information transferred between computers is divided into small packets that contain a

FIGURE C-1

An internetwork consists of LANs connected by gateways

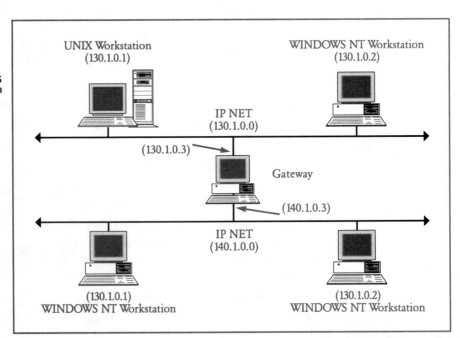

"payload" of data and header information such as the destination address, and error-correction codes. While some commands and requests only require one packet, lengthy file transmissions are divided into multiple packets that include sequence numbers so they can be reassembled at the destination.

One of the TCP/IP protocol's most important features is its network addressing scheme. It provides a way to address different networks and the nodes on those networks. The addressing scheme is extensive, providing for millions of potential addresses on a global scale. In fact, Internet addresses are registered and assigned by the following organization to prevent address conflicts (although it's not essential to register addresses if you're simply building your own in-house internetwork):

DDN Network Information Center
SRI International
333 Ravenswood Avenue, Room EJ291
Menlo Park, CA 94025

TCP/IP is actually composed of several separate and distinct protocols. Each falls into a layering scheme that is often compared to the Open Systems Interconnection (OSI) model as described in Chapter 17 and illustrated in Figure 17-8. The following describes each protocol.

TCP (Transmission Control Protocol)   The TCP protocol corresponds to the Session and Transport layer in the OSI model. TCP receives information from applications that operate at higher levels in the protocol stack and is responsible for packaging and sequencing network transmissions. TCP passes packets to IP.

IP (Internet Protocol)   The IP protocol corresponds to the Network layer in the OSI model. It creates packets of information and is responsible for adding the all-important source and destination IP addresses.

One thing IP doesn't do is provide a guarantee that packets will arrive at their destination and in their proper order. Instead, TCP adds information to the packets it creates to provide these services. If IP loses a packet, TCP is responsible for determining which packet was lost and resending that packet.

About IP Addresses

The Internet Protocol address (IP address) for a node is a logical address that is independent of the physical address assigned to a network interface board by its vendor. The IP address is also independent of the network configuration. IP addresses have the same form, no matter what network type is used. This form is a 4-byte (32-bit) numeric value that identifies both a network and a local host or node on the network. Each IP address must be unique and consist of four decimal numbers separated by dots. For example, in Figure C-1, the UNIX workstation is at address 130.1.0.1.

As mentioned, IP addresses are not dependent on any type of network. That means packets can traverse network types. On each network type, the TCP/IP protocol maps the IP address to a physical node address for delivery. Packets contain the sender's IP address so a receiving station can reply if necessary. The IP address identifies the network and the node on the network where the sender is located.

One way to set IP addresses is to join the DARPA Internet community by contacting the DDN Network Information Center, as mentioned earlier. If you don't care to officially register your network, you can choose an arbitrary number that follows the IP addressing scheme (four decimal numbers separated by periods). However, it is recommended that you use the DARPA Internet scheme in case you need to connect to the Internet at some point in the future.

The 4-byte IP address is divided into a network portion that identifies the network and a host portion that identifies the computer (node). The network portion must be the same for every node on the network, while the host portion must be unique for every node on the network. There are several different schemes for mapping these numbers:

▨   *Class A addressing scheme*   The first byte is the network address, and the last three bytes are the node address. The range of the first byte is 1 through 126, which allows 126 networks with 16 million nodes per network.

▨   *Class B addressing scheme*   The first two bytes are the network address, and the last two bytes are the node address. The range of the first byte is 128 through 191 and the second byte further identifies a network. This allows 16,000 networks and 65,000 nodes. In Figure C-1, the number of the top network is 130.1.0.0 and the number of the bottom network is 140.1.0.0.

▨   *Class C addressing scheme*   The first three bytes are the network address, and the last byte is the node address, which allows 2 million networks with 254 nodes each.

Some addresses are reserved, and the highest order bit in each address requires a special identifier number.

You can split a single network into a number of subnetworks so you can use multiple media types, or to reduce congestion by reducing the number of workstations on a network. When subnetworks exist, the IP address consists of a network address, a subnetwork address, and the host address. The host address portion of the IP address is split to include the subnetwork address and the host address. To outside remote networks, your network still appears as a single network with a single network address.

For more information on IP addressing, refer to your Microsoft NT manuals, or contact the DDN Network Information Center.

NetBIOS Over TCP/IP (NBT)

One important distinction between NetBIOS and other network protocols is that NetBIOS establishes connections with other computers using names. The computer name you give to a Windows NT workstation during configuration is used by other computers to locate and establish a communications session with your computer. When TCP/IP support is installed, your computer is also assigned a unique IP address.

In order for a Windows NT workstation on one network to communicate with a Windows NT workstation on another network, it must acquire its IP address. Initially, a special query procedure takes place to discover the names of computers and their associated IP addresses. Once addresses have been established, all communications between the computers use the IP address.

INSTALLING TCP/IP

It is relatively easy to install TCP/IP support on a Windows NT workstation, assuming that you know and understand the IP addressing scheme. This section merely provides an overview. Refer to the online help for specific configuration information. You'll also need the IP address for the computer from your network administrator.

The first step is to start the Network utility in the Control Panel. When the Network Setting dialog box appears, click the Add Software button. The Add Network Software dialog box appears as shown in Figure C-2. Select the TCP/IP Protocol option on the drop-down menu and click Continue.

Once the software installs, you can configure the address of the node and the address of the gateway that it communicates through to other networks. The dialog box in Figure C-3 appears when you click the Configure button. If you don't see it, try closing the Network Settings dialog box.

FIGURE C-2

Selecting the TCP/IP protocol for installation

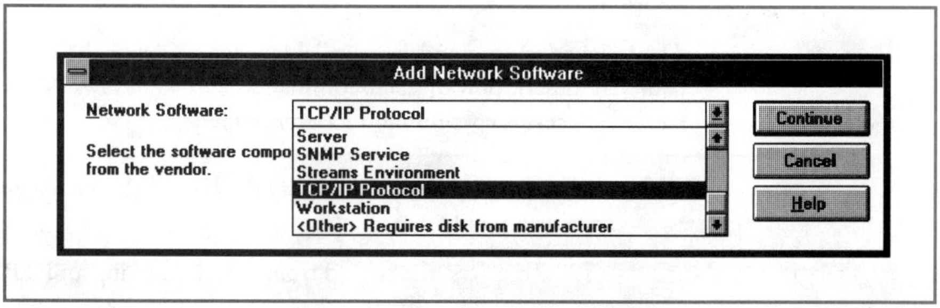

From the TCP\IP Configuration dialog box, you can configure the local IP address of the workstation in the IP Address field. If there are multiple adapters in the workstation, you first choose which adapter will use TCP/IP in the Adapter drop-down list box. Click the Connectivity button to specify remote TCP/IP nodes by their host names, rather than their IP address and to set up Domain Name Service (DNS) hierarchical naming. Click the Help button to get additional information.

TCP/IP RELATED COMMANDS

The following commands are available when you start the Command Prompt. To get a complete description of each command, start Windows NT Help and click the icon labeled "Access the Command Reference Help."

- *ARP* Lets you view and modify the IP-to-Ethernet or Token Ring address translation table.
- *FTP* Transfers files to and from a node running an FTP server program.
- *HOSTNAME* Displays the current host name.
- *NBSTAT* Displays information about NetBIOS over TCP/IP connection.

- *NET STATISTICS* Displays the statistics log for the local workstation or server.

- *PING* Displays information about network connections.

- *RCP* Copies files between computers on the network.

- *REXEC* Executes files at remote systems.

- *ROUTE* Lets you manually manipulate network routing tables.

- *RSH* (Remote Shell) connects to a specified host and executes commands.

- *TFTP* Provides Internet Trivial File Transfer Protocols.

Index